Pressure from Without
in early Victorian England

Pressure from Without

in early Victorian England

edited by
Patricia Hollis

Edward Arnold

First published 1974 by
Edward Arnold (Publishers) Ltd
25 Hill Street, London W1X 8LL

ISBN: 0 7131 5730 5

Printed in Great Britain by
Richard Clay (The Chaucer Press) Ltd
Bungay, Suffolk

Contents

Abbreviations

ARA	Administrative Reform Association
BPU	Birmingham Political Union
BAPCK	British Association for the Promotion of Cooperative Knowledge
COS	Charity Organization Society
CSU	Complete Suffrage Union
LTRA	Land Tenure Reform Association
LWMA	London Working Men's Association
LDOS	Lord's Day Observance Society
MPU	Metropolitan Political Union
NPU	National Political Union
NUWC	National Union of Working Classes
PFRA	Parliamentary and Financial Reform Association
RRA	Radical Reform Association
UKA	United Kingdom Alliance

Preface

Pressure groups come in two bundles: those that speak for an interest, whose bond comes from their common economic base, the blind, the British Medical Association, the Automobile Association, the National Union of Students; and those which crusade for a cause, whose bond comes from their common goal, CND, anti-vivisection, family planning, National Council of Civil Liberties. The Victorian equivalents might have been the ship-owners lobby, the railway or West Indian interest on the one hand, and the Health of Towns Association or the Lords Day Observance Society on the other. Certain pressure groups then as now were intentionally hybrid, the Anti-Corn Law League then, the National Council of Women now.[1] I suspect we regard the crusade as morally more legitimate than the lobby. For the Victorians, the reverse would have been true; just because the lobby was protective of its economic interest, just because it was rooted in property, it could claim to be consulted within the political community. The status of the crusading pressure group, however, remained morally ambiguous though politically more and more powerful.

Pressure from Without is a collection of original essays on the nature and functioning of certain nineteenth century pressure groups, of the crusading style, in the years between the two Reform Acts. Before 1832, such groups were thought to be illegitimate, as they disturbed the deliberative role of parliament, and unnecessary as they spoke for no recognizable corporate or community interest. After 1867, such groups were increasingly redundant, displaced by national party political machines which were providing both ideology and organization for the

[1] Since the middle 1960s, it is possible that we have seen the emergence of a third sort of pressure group, the altruistic campaign for the underprivileged, Shelter for the homeless, Age Concern, Mind for the mentally ill or defective, Disablement Income Group, Child Poverty Action Group. In the nineteenth century they would have been conceived as charities; but with the emergence of a positive concept of state welfare, with all its gaps but with all its resources and all its promises, such charities have entered politics to become pressure groups, to fight for government intervention rather than to organize voluntary remedial effort.

parliamentary parties. Between these two Reform Acts, parliament became increasingly responsive to public opinion, and increasingly tolerant in its definition of it. Pressure from without, then, is used here in the sense that contemporaries used it, to refer to those more or less radical and mainly middle class pressure groups, pursuing specified goals and working for legislative change by putting pressure on parliament and on government; possessing a sophisticated organization over a defined period of time; and invoking a moral language, by claiming to speak for the People, the Nation or the Country. Such a definition is meant to exclude the working class protest movement as such, Chartism or the Anti-Poor Law Movement,[2] as being too diffuse; to exclude the protectionist or self-interested lobby as being too limited and too defensive; and to exclude the round of petitions, say on the Marriage to the Wife's Sister Bill in the 1850s, as being too transient. All definitions can provoke counter-examples and boundary disputes; but the early Victorians would surely have considered the Anti-Corn Law League as the archetypal model of pressure from without; and the Catholic Association, the political unions and the Anti-Slavery Society before it, and the Health of Towns Association, the Freehold Land Society, the National Public Schools Association, the Liberation Society, the Reform League and the Reform Union, after it, as being of the same species. And it is with that species only that this book is concerned.

The first essay is hopefully synthetic, deliberately speculative and necessarily tentative: we need what we don't have, a host of specialized monographs before any firm conclusions can be confidently advanced. The essay seeks to examine the propriety and ideology of pressure from without, its machinery, and some assessment of its impact; as well as to point towards some of the following studies. These are of two main styles, though I have not grouped them separately. The first are studies of pressure groups, individual societies such as the Liberation Society or the Administrative Reform Association, or a network of pressure groups around a continuing concern: land reform, the suffrage, moral reform, anti-slavery. The second type are studies of four professionals in the field: the philosophic radicals as a group and Shaftesbury as an individual operating pressure within the House of Commons, Edward Baines, a prominent provincial Whig, operating it from outside, and by contrast William Lovett, doubly excluded, both from the House and from the franchise but co-opted almost despite himself into the ideology of traditional pressure from without. The piece on Urquhart and the foreign affairs committees spans both approaches. In choosing these subjects, I have tried to avoid too much overlap between them on the one hand—the Liberation Society therefore precludes a separate study

[2] See J. T. Ward (ed.), *Popular Movements c. 1830–1850* (1970), for other examples.

on Edward Miall, Edward Baines is represented rather than an educational pressure group; while seeking some sort of balance between the concerns of Victorian political life on the other, between fundamental land reform and organic parliamentary reform, between administrative and moral reform, between domestic and foreign policy concerns.

Certain questions appear and reappear in these essays. What *was* public opinion in these years, and how was it related both to formal and to informal politics? How did pressure groups operate and how effective were they? What were their class, religious, and regional roots? What were the wider implications of pressure from without for the political community? Can it be said to have radicalized politics, contained class conflict, made more pluralist the political structure? Some men, such as Samuel Morley or Joseph Sturge, passed through many pressure groups. How did they see these as relating to each other? What indeed happened when, as with Baines, they patently did not?

Certain questions we think are posed, and certain conclusions seem to emerge. Nineteenth century pressure from without did have some effect on legislation; had a marked effect on class harmony and social tranquillity; and both enlarged the realm of government and the breadth of base of government. Much of this is due to the characteristics of Victorian politics, to the limited franchise in which only one adult male in five had the vote, to the limited concept of government, to the lack of ideologically powerful political parties. Yet certain aspects of pressure group politics transcend the years between the two reform acts. Then as now, pressure group politics seem to entail a sense of political pluralism; a belief that politics and political life are highly significant; that existing channels of political activity, the lobby, the party, the town hall, are inadequate, and that alternative modes of political expression must be found, if political health is to be preserved. Within central and local government, then as now, there is the same unease at the unauthorized nature of pressure from without, at its critical stance and its populist claims. Finally, pressure groups, then as now, seem to be a continuing source of ideological change, forcing flexibility into existing political organizations, casting political parties as umbrellas over a bundle of more or less minority and more or less welcome concerns.

I

Pressure from Without: an introduction

Patricia Hollis

Thomas Attwood, leader of the Birmingham Political Union, told a meeting on 7 May 1832:

> The enemies of the people have told their Lordships that the country is indifferent to this great cause. If we hold no meetings, they say we are indifferent; if we hold small meetings, they say that we are insignificant; and if we hold large meetings, they say we are rebellious and wish to intimidate them. (laughter.) Do what we will, we cannot do right it seems.[1]

Attwood's difficulties were rather larger than he imagined. Whatever the size of his meetings, on a traditionalist account of the House of Commons, they could never be legitimate.

For the Conservative version of parliament rested on certain inter-locking premises which pressure groups offended. Parliament was the deliberative assembly of the nation; and unruly constituencies, such as Yorkshire in 1830, or unruly unions, such as the Birmingham Political Union in 1832, were thought to pre-empt or intimidate its deliberative role. By extension, so also did pledges, a platform and a crusading press. Parliament embodied and weighed those legitimate interests which were rooted in property or community. To quote Canning, a year after Peterloo:

> The law prescribes a corporate character. . . . To bring together the inhabitants of a particular division, or men sharing a common franchise, is to bring together an assembly, of which the component parts act with some respect and awe of each other. Ancient habits, preconceived attachments, that mutual respect which makes the eye of a neighbour a security for each man's good conduct—all these things make men difficult to be moved, on the sudden, to any extravagant and violent enterprise. But brings together a multitude of

[1] C. Wakefield, *Life of Thomas Attwood* (1885), p. 201.

individuals having no permanent relation to each other, no common tie but what arises from their concurrence as members of that meeting, a tie dissolved as soon as the meeting is at an end—in such an aggregation of individuals there is no such mutual respect, no such check upon the proceedings of each man from the awe of his neighbour's disapprobation; and if ever such a multitudinous assembly can be wrought up to purposes of mischief, it will be an assembly so composed. . . .[2]

Lord Liverpool took the argument a step further. 'We ought not then,' he said, 'to begin first by considering who ought to be the electors, and then who ought to be the elected; but we ought to begin by considering who ought to be the elected, and then constitute such persons electors as would be likely to produce the best elected.'[3] This was an extreme because it was an older version; but it was a repeated theme that the people were entitled to good government, not to self-government—Russell on Hume's Little Charter in 1848, Lowe in 1867[4]—and therefore what mattered was the quality of the House and not the quantity of its voters, the balance of its composition and not the fitness of its citizens. It was accordingly no part of Parliament's task to consider the wishes of the populace, only their well being, of which the people themselves were not fit judges.

Conservatives added two further arguments. One was that the so-called voice of the people was often falsely stimulated by travelling demagogues who created the unrest for which they spoke, whose activity was a self-fulfilling prophecy, and who sharpened social antagonism and undermined good order—a charge variously levelled in 1842 by Peel against the League lecturers, by the League against O'Connor, and by the Whigs against both. Even where it was authentic, the voice of the country was often unsure, uncertain, temporary and transient. A healthy sluggishness on the part of Parliament was a fair test of its significance and staying power. So, in the reform debates of 1831, a Conservative backbencher, North, was as ready as any man 'to obey any

---

[2] Quoted in H. Jephson, *The Platform* (1892), volume I, pp. 508–10. Joshua Toulmin Smith was still arguing in 1851 that pressure from without was 'generally artificial, always suspicious, never healthy'. Local self government, by contrast, 'gives the constant opportunity for the lawful and peaceful uttering of true and soundly formed Public Opinion on every question that arises' (*Local self-government and Centralization* (1851), p. 43).

[3] Jephson, *op. cit.*, volume I, p. 207.

[4] 'The end we ought to have in view is not the class which receives the franchise, not the district which obtains the power of sending members to parliament, but that parliament itself. . . . To consider the franchise as an end in itself . . . to suppose that we should confer it on any one class of persons because we think them deserving . . . is . . . to mistake the means for the end.' R. Lowe, Hansard, 13 March 1866.

steady and deliberate call of the people of England; but he was not to be told that every transient emotion of their minds, every flash and outbreak of their fiery tempers, every partial flowing and ebbing of the popular opinion, was to be considered as its deep and irresistible current.'[5]

In any case, much of a positive nature demanded by the popular voice was beyond the power of government to effect. Macaulay complained in 1832 and again on the presentation of the second Chartist petition in 1842, that 'there has been a systematic attempt for years to represent the Government as being able to do and bound to attempt, that which no Government ever attempted.' The work of the League, its publicist Cooke Taylor claimed in 1842, showed 'that the importance of government is enormously overrated, that it does not deserve all this stir, that there are vastly more effectual means of human happiness.'[6] The price of government intervention was to undermine voluntary and local effort, a point made by Urquhart against the Public Health Bill of 1848, by Edward Baines in his Crosby Hall Lectures against State intervention in education in the same year. 'Our duties are the discipline ordained by Heaven for our moral improvement . . . to relieve men of their duties is to deprive them of their virtues.'[7]

Attwood, therefore, was faced by a closed circle. If parliament already represented all properly constituted interests, then external pressure was the artificial voice of a rootless mob; and if in any case parliament already cared for the people's interests, but not at all for their views, then such pressure was not only illegitimate but unnecessary as well. The excluded could never enroll themselves, pressure from without could never establish its claim to speak for the country. Attwood had no way in. Radicals would have to construct an alternative account of the political community.

Naturally, then, radicals denied that they were a mob encroaching on the proper role of parliament. Following the lead of the philosophic radicals,[8] they spoke for the People, for the *common* interest as against the exclusive class interest of the ruling aristocracy. The People were not Canning's aggregate bundle of atomized individuals, fickle and rootless; they were bound, not by property, granted, but by the morality of 'a national mind', in Matthew Davenport Hill's phrase:[9] 'stable, reflective, self-disciplined, and self-educating'. Behind the radicals' claim lay their rationalist assumption that all men of good will,

[5] North, Hansard, March 1831 (column 154–5).
[6] Macaulay, Hansard, 3 May 1842; W. Cooke Taylor, *Notes of a Tour* (1842), p. 270.
[7] E. Baines, *Crosby Hall Lectures*, p. 6.
[8] See W. Thomas, 'The Philosophic Radicals', chapter 3, below.
[9] M. D. Hill, 'Post office reform', *Edinburgh Review*, 1840.

undeflected by sordid self-interest, would come to common conclusions on the common good. 'Discussion,' said the radical MP Roebuck, 'will soon establish what is true and expose what is erroneous.'[10]

This was accompanied by a somewhat forlorn quest for respectability. As political lecturers, like political agents, were disreputably occupied, it was thought daring of the Anti-Slavery Society to employ them; and the League searched hard for men with more respectable backgrounds than the oft-imprisoned James Acland and the Chartist Henry Vincent: it acquired an ineffective Edinburgh solicitor, Sydney Smith, to raise their tone. Francis Place, not usually afraid of knockabout politics, tried to tame his turbulent working class colleagues, busy flouting the law with unstamped newspapers, by taking them into a demure Society for the Promotion of the Repeal of the Stamp Duties in 1835. MPs sympathetic to administrative reform in the 1850s would have no part in the agitational side of the Administrative Reform Association, and when Samuel Morley, the stocking millionaire, displaced Layard as its spokesman, mass meetings, mass lobbying and mass publications were dropped.[11] High subscriptions were designed to have the same effect. When C. D. Collett, organizing a second round of agitation against the remaining taxes on knowledge at the ends of the 1840s, sought Cobden's advice, he was good-naturedly told:

You are sometimes a little too plain spoken for your clients—I mean for those in whose name you speak—and it arises probably from your not always bearing in mind that the 'Association' does not always consist of the millions who will benefit by the repeal of the taxes on knowledge, but of a few men who, having themselves the advantage of seeing a daily newspaper, would wish every man in the kingdom to enjoy the same privilege. If you had for your client the 'fierce democracy' . . . you might then fling saucy phrases at the head of a Chancellor of the Exchequer with consistency. But cast your eye over the subscription list of the 'Association' and you will see how exclusively almost we comprise steady, sober, middle class reformers —free trade, temperance, education, peace advocates—who will stand by you from year to year and gather about them an increasing moral power, provided you handle them judiciously, and do not place them in a position in which they think they are committed to a *tone* of agitation which does not represent their feelings. . . .[12]

[10] Roebuck's Penny *Pamphlets for the People*, no. 7, 1835.
[11] See O. Anderson, 'The Administrative Reform Association', chapter 11, below.
[12] C. D. Collet, *History of the Taxes on Knowledge* (1933 edn.), pp. 112–13.

It meant, on the working class side, the willingness of Lovett to plead that moral reform must accompany political reform, that a new move must precede a New Moral World.[13] And so the titled were sought as presidents, gentlemen as corresponding secretaries, magistrates and local councillors as branch chairmen, and clergy to give their moral authority to the whole.

If the first accusation against pressure groups was that they were mere mobs, the second was that they pre-empted or intimidated parliament.

The version which radicals much preferred was that pressure from without had achieved what there was of social and political progress—catholic emancipation, the 1832 reform act, the end of slavery, the repeal of the corn laws. These 'agencies out of doors,' argued Gladstone in the House of Commons in 1867, formed and matured public opinion, and were therefore 'the legitimate expressions of the people, by which bad legislation is to be corrected.'[14] As government was invariably languid, it was only by pressure from without that the Health of Towns Association thought anything useful could be accomplished: petitions must be procured 'to awaken the Legislature from the torpor to which it is *properly* addicted'.[15] They added that they had no more wish than their critics for a centralist state with an extended bureaucracy which would merely offer more patronage for an aristocratic clique. Viscount Morpeth defended his Public Health Bill in 1848, not altogether convincingly, from the charge of centralization by asserting that as he proposed to work through local agencies, he was in fact revitalizing the powers of local corporations and not superseding them.[16] Advocates of national education in the 1850s, among them Cobden and Lovett, wanted their schools locally controlled and rate-financed. John Stuart Mill, writing on centralization in the *Edinburgh Review* in 1862, expected government to provide lighthouses, but thought that lifeboats could safely, properly and desirably be left to voluntary effort. Even those apparently least embarrassed by government intervention, the prohibitionists and sabbatarians, were pressing, on closer view,[17] for a legal code to embody the moral order, rather than for humdrum powers of prosecution. The withering away of the State was one of the more common clichés.

When pushed, radicals agreed that pressure from without could appear intimidating, but that was just because parliament was improperly constituted. Finsbury, it was argued in 1831, should have two

[13] See D. Large, 'William Lovett', chapter 5, below.
[14] Hansard, 17 May 1867.
[15] Health of Towns Association, 11 December 1844.
[16] Hansard, 10 February 1848.
[17] See B. H. Harrison, 'State intervention and moral reform', chapter 12, below.

MPs and not one, to give it 'a safety valve by which the opinions of an immense part of the population would reach the House in a constitutional way'.[18] Cobden developed the theme.

> You glorify yourselves that you have abolished the slave trade and slavery. . . . Whatever you have done to break down any abomination or barbarism in this country has been done by associations and leagues out of this House; and why? Because, since Manchester cannot have its fair representation in this House, it was obliged to organize a League, that it might raise an agitation through the length and breadth of the land, and in this indirect manner might make itself felt in this House. Well, do you want to get rid of this system of agitation? Do you want to prevent those leagues and associations out of doors? Then you must bring this House into harmony with the opinions of the people. Give the means to the people of making themselves felt in this House. . . . For is this not a most cumbrous machine?—a House of Commons, by a fiction said to be representative of the people, meeting here and professing to do the people's work, while the people out of doors are obliged to work?[19]

By 1867, the very argument that trades unions were dangerous was used to ensure their admission into the political community. 'If the idea of the integrity of the representation requires that the House of Commons should be the centre of all political life, the sole arena of serious social contest, the mirror of the public mind,' then, said Lord Houghton, 'they dare not be excluded.'

Radicals willing to employ such arguments were usually willing to sally into parliamentary reform to correct the House of Commons if it should prove refractory. But certain other reformers by-passed this de-

---

[18] John Smith, Hansard, July 1831, column 764.

[19] See also John Warden's defence in *Northern Star*, 11 April 1840 (reprinted P. Hollis (ed.), *Class and conflict in 19th Century England* (1973), p. 239). 'Do the rich manufacturers desire a repeal of the Corn Laws? They appeal to the people. Is a reform in the corporations considered desirable? The people are appealed to. Does one great body advocate church extension? Lecturers are sent out, and the people are appealed to. . . .' Warden was charged with riot in Bolton. Croker replied in the *Quarterly*, 1849: 'One of the advantages promised by the advocates of the Reform bill, was that it would put an end to the illegal associations and other popular demonstrations which it was alleged only arose out of it, and were irregular compensation for, the injustice of the old system of representation; and that, when Manchester and Birmingham had legitimate organs in the legislature, the voice of seditious agitation would no longer be heard. Has such been the result? Have not, on the contrary, the excitement on public questions, the demonstrations in populous districts, the riots, the disturbance, the whole system of agitation—that is, *intimidation*, become much more constant and audacious and especially in the very districts to which the pretended panaceas of representation had been applied. . . .' ('Democracy', p. 219.)

bate altogether. They claimed an anterior and higher moral law than that of mere constitutional convention. A friend wrote to Joseph Sturge, the Quaker corn-merchant, about anti-slavery in 1833: 'Sin will lie at our door if we do not agitate, agitate, agitate.' And Sturge himself argued in 1830 when he tried to persuade the Anti-Slavery Society to adopt 'total and immediate emancipation':

> When the Christian is convinced that the principle upon which he acts is correct, I believe it does not become him to examine too closely his probability of success, but rather to act in the assurance that if he faithfully does his part, as much success will attend his efforts as is consistent with the will of that Divine leader under whose banner he is enlisted. . . .[20]

Anti-slavery, the work of Shaftesbury, the repeal of the Corn Laws, Urquhart's foreign affairs committees, the taxes on knowledge, Josephine Butler's campaign to remove the Contagious Diseases Act, all invoked the language of sin, of the identity of public and private morality, of a distaste for expediency and mere party consideration. All required that their crusade be given special status and special treatment. Ministers and especially dissenting ministers of religion, were in frequent demand to support campaigns and to give them their imprimateur of moral immediacy—the conference of 700 ministers in August 1841 witnessing against the Corn Laws was possibly the most remarkable example. Such reformers were not reluctant to use large language: taxes on windows became a tax on light, taxes on newspapers a tax on knowledge, taxes on soap a tax on cleanliness; the Corn Laws were a bread tax, church rates a tax on religion. Whatever was morally wrong could not of course be politically right.

During these years, and in the subsequent essays, three groups of reformer appear and reappear: the parliamentary reformers, the Manchester free traders, and dissent. From them, other issues emerged—education or game laws—and to them yet other issues were reduced, such as Attwood's currency reform, and the alignments on factory legislation. For as Cobden said to Sturge, 'all good things pull together', and he cited free trade, peace, financial reform, and equitable taxation.[21]

[20] H. Richard, *Memoirs of Joseph Sturge* (1864), p. 89.
[21] *Ibid.*, p. 424. Curiously, the Catholic Association of the 1820s was an oddly insulated experience: it was seldom publicly and almost never privately quoted as a model for action. Instead, Irish radicalism seems to have fed to some degree into the National Union of the Working Classes of the 1830s, and through that into Chartism and a concern with land reform. However, it may also have been mediated through the Birmingham Political Union, of which O'Connell was a member, and on to political unionism.

The parliamentary reformers were led by Joseph Hume and inter-
mittently aided by Roebuck and later by Sir Joshua Walmsley into the
1850s, and from the late 1850s and with significant reservations by
John Bright and Samuel Morley. They derived their intellectual
authority from the philosophic radicals of the 1830s, Grote, Warburton,
Molesworth in parliament, and the Mills outside it, who added a
Benthamite overlay to the common ground of Painite radicalism and
Ricardian political economy. The legislature they argued was
dominated by the aristocracy in their own interest; power must be
given to the People, 'the numerous masses' who by definition had
'no interest in common to them which is not common to the rest of the
country'.[22]

So, although parliamentary reformers favoured a wide ranging attack
on all monopolies—financial, religious and economic—they believed
that organic reform must precede fundamental reform.[23] By extension,
parliamentary reform (household suffrage, the ballot, triennial parliaments) must be accompanied by governmental reform: parish reform
leading to Hobhouse's Vestries Act of 1831, municipal reform in 1835,
administrative reform in 1855, and a concern with colonial affairs which
took the Mills into Indian and Buller into Canadian administration.
Such measures would diminish aristocratic patronage and corruption,
improve efficiency, cut costs. Parliamentary reform also required that
the people exercise their votes wisely and independently and this necessitated popular education, as a form of moral rearmament against the
seductions of aristocratic influence. Roebuck's 1833 motion on national
education was sustained in the 1850s by the National Public Schools
Association; and it spilled over into Brougham's Mechanics Institutes,
Charles Knight's Society for the Diffusion of Useful Knowledge,
Rowland Hill's post office reform, Place's campaign for cheap newspapers, Ewart's for public libraries, Lovett's for rational Sundays,
Collet's work for the removal of the last penny on newspapers.[24]

More than any other group, the parliamentary reformers were
London-based, secular, rationalist, republican, drawing on the artisan

[22] James Mill (1829), quoted J. Hamburger, *Intellectuals in politics* (1965), pp. 46–7.
[23] See W. Thomas, 'The Philosophic Radicals', chapter 3; and A. Wilson, The
Suffrage Movement', chapter 4. C. D. Collet in the 1840s, though a free trader,
refused to attend the League meetings because he insisted that parliamentary reform
had the prior claim. Repeal changed his mind for he saw them 'doing, in spite of us,
by their own method, what we had told them they could accomplish only by accepting
ours'. C. D. Collet, *loc. cit.*, p. 44.
[24] Said Cobden to Collet: 'The only way to bring a sufficient force of moral power
to our aid, and to put the *education-loving* Government in a crucible from which they
can never escape, with the dross of the taxes on knowledge sticking to them, is in
making it an education question.' *Loc. cit.*, p. 111.

and small shopkeeper class. And unlike the free-trader, their concept of
the People entailed the suppression of distinct class language.[25] They
were usually ready to reach out to Lovett in the 1830s and 1840s, to
Ernest Jones in the 1850s, and Morley to the Reform League in the
1860s. When forced to choose between Chartism and the League, they
theoretically favoured Chartism, though they were frozen into im-
mobility by its language of physical force.

One of the difficulties of parliamentary reform was that it required
positive legislation, unlike the more negative dismantling of monopoly
demanded by free-traders. On the other hand, one of its strengths was
that parliamentary reform was the residual beneficiary of most pressure
group activity. Thomas Attwood, baulked on currency reform, turned to
parliamentary reform; so too did the Leeds free-traders, including Samuel
Smiles. The Reverend Edward Miall suspected that parliamentary reform must precede dissenting freedom when in 1841 he founded, with
Sturge, the Complete Suffrage Union; Walmsley, likewise, went beyond
the original Liverpool financial reform association to join with Hume
in 1849 in the Parliamentary and Financial Reform Association; Bright
regularly lobbied Cobden to follow suit. Samuel Morley when he
abandoned the Liberation Society in 1859 for parliamentary reform was
only following in their path.

Less directly, pressure group activity out of doors fed back into parliamentary reform when it focused attention on electoral corruption: a
recurring theme of the Administrative Reform Association was that the
electors, as much as the elected, stood in need of moral reform; and
when, as so many groups did, they turned to the size and state of the
electoral register and to the quality of local government. Joseph Parkes,
a Birmingham solicitor and friend of Place, appears to have trained
a whole generation of electoral agents to service the cause of radical
reform.[26]

The second group of reformers that reoccur time and again were the
Manchester free-traders, led by Cobden and Bright. They attacked a
parasite class, landlords, as well as a specific grievance, the Corn Laws.
They denied the morality, necessity and legitimacy of an idle landed
class living off unearned incomes: a diagnosis that was a by-product of
Ricardian economics in which wages and profits were earned but rents
were not. Parliamentary reform and administrative reform would

[25] Place's National Political Union of 1831 was 'not a Union of the Working
Classes, nor of the Middle Classes, nor of any other Class, but of the Reformers, of
the masses and of the millions. The National Political Union is essentially a Union
of the People and is the first instance on record of the Nation breaking through the
trammels of class, to associate for the Common interest in a Common cause'. (*Place
Papers*, November 1831.)

[26] For Joseph Parkes, see W. Thomas, 'The Philosophic Radicals', pp. 68–70.

merely change the superstructure of aristocratic power; land reform would destroy its very foundation.[27]

The landed interest, they insisted, was buttressed quite immorally by its monopolies, its monopoly through primogeniture, entail and settlement of the holding of land, its monopoly through the Corn Laws of the economic rewards of land. Free trade would not only attack the landed class where they were most vulnerable, but it would also, on Manchester's under-consumptionist account, allow the turbulent working classes to buy the country's way out of the depression of the Hungry Forties, and smooth class relations sharpened by hunger. Additionally in international terms, free trade was 'God's own method of producing an *entente cordiale*'.

The style of the whole is revealed in a letter from Cobden to Peter Taylor in May 1840, when they had agreed to ask W. J. Fox to write a League address for them.

The terms of course must be left to himself. We don't want the question to be argued, but to be taken upon the primitive ground of right and justice. We don't wish it to be treated as a manufacturer's question, not a capitalist's either; but as a *bread tax* that robs all the country for the clumsy expedient of putting a mere fraction of the booty into the pockets of the robbers. The object of the address should be, to stir up the community to active resistance against a law that degrades us as worse than slaves in the eyes of the world.

Then, the religious and moral feelings must be appealed to, and the energies of the Christian world must be drawn forth by the remembrance of the Anti-slavery and other struggles, and by being reminded that the cause of truth and justice must prosper in the end. The people must be told that there is no hope from the present House of Commons which refused to allow corn to be ground in bond—and which also refused to the Irish to import foreign flour at a time when their own flour was breeding typhus fever!

Then the people should be told that the country's salvation must be worked out at the hustings and the polling booths. We may also glance at the despair which is seizing the minds of many and the desperate course to which men are driven. The increase of the armed military and civil forces to restrain the people might be referred to, and the expense and insecurity of such a state of things may be urged as an argument with the middle and wealthy classes for giving content to the people by allowing them to be fed.

[27] See D. Martin, 'Land reform', chapter 6. For land reform after 1855, see H. J. Perkin, 'Land reform and class conflict in Victorian England', in J. Butt and L. F. Clarke (eds.), *The Victorians and Social Protest* (1973).

We don't want a *long* address—but it must be a blister to the aristocracy and the House of Commons. . . .[28]

With the repeal of the Corn Laws in 1846, the Manchester free traders increased their attack on the Game Laws, and on primogeniture, entail and settlement, issues which gained new impetus from the mid 1860s and the foundation in 1870 of John Stuart Mill's Land Tenure Reform Association.

Cobden's letter obviously employed evangelical, if not specifically nonconformist, language: the third 'core' to pressure group reforming activity was dissent.

The dissent of the Protestant Deputies of the 1830s was devoted to the removal of civil disabilities and Church tithes. The State's offer of matching building grants for schools from 1833 was not especially controversial. But when in 1843 Graham's Factory Bill proposed that the new factory schools would be supervised by the Established Church, Edward Baines, the Whig editor of the *Leeds Mercury*, headed a new wave of militant dissent.[29] For, to quote Wilberforce, religion 'makes teaching education'; to quote Kay Shuttleworth, secretary to the Privy Council Committee on Education, 'The school is part of the machinery of a Christian congregation', and to quote Baines himself, 'Civil government is no fit agency for the training of families or of souls.'[30] Education could not, dare not, be left to Anglicans, free thinkers, bureaucrats or secularists.

If Baines provided dissent with its head of steam, its pressure group organization came mainly from the work of the Reverend Edward Miall, a radical Leicester congregational minister, and ally of Joseph Sturge in the Complete Suffrage Movement, who from 1841 was editing his radical *Nonconformist* to urge the disestablishment of the Anglican church.[31] The Anti-State Church Association followed in 1844 to bring 'public opinion to bear . . . upon the composition of the House of Commons, and upon the decisions of the imperial parliament on matters affecting dissent.'[32] On Baines's suggestion it became the Liberation

---

[28] R. Garnett, *The Life of W. J. Fox* (1910), p. 258.

[29] See D. Fraser, 'Edward Baines', chapter 8, below. Baines also favoured municipal reform, free trade and a cautious extension of the suffrage, *loc. cit.* The Bill was 'a declaration of war against all the Dissenters in the kingdom'—quoted J. Ward, 'A lost opportunity in education' (*Researches and Studies*, 20 October 1959).

[30] J. Kay-Shuttleworth, *The School in its Relations to the State, the Church and the Congregation* (1847), p. 74. E. Baines, *Education best promoted by Perfect Freedom not by State Endowments* (1854), p. 30. S. Wilberforce, *Letter to Brougham* (1840).

[31] See D. Thompson, 'The Liberation Society', chapter 9, below.

[32] The *Congregational Magazine* (1844), quickly criticized the promotion of political ends, and the redress of civil grievances: 'We think that our ministers have nobler and better objects to pursue—that few are qualified for successful political agitation, and that all may be more usefully employed. Our Christian societies are formed for mutual

Society in 1853, its battleground the inequity of Church rates. Naturally this took the Society into local government as well as into the Liberal party; and it intervened crucially in the general elections of 1857 and 1865. Where the parliamentary radicals drew their strength from London artisans, and the free-traders from Lancashire, Cheshire and Yorkshire manufacturers, the Liberation Society was strongest in southern and midland small market towns, such as Worcester, Leicester, and Reading. The Society had connections through Samuel Morley with both administrative and parliamentary reform; through Henry Richard, the friend and biographer of Joseph Sturge, with the peace movement; and as John Vincent has shown,[33] the Society did much to make the nonconformist conscience a political as well as a religious burden to its possessors.

Parliamentary reform, free trade, and dissent provided the main 'cores' to early Victorian pressure group activity, but obviously the amount of overspill in men and ideology was substantial. Take Anti-slavery, the first great English pressure group.[34] Through Sturge it had connections with suffrage, peace, and Corn Law movements; through Robert Charleton of Bristol with peace and temperance; through George Thompson, with free trade and a Garrisonian interest in women's rights; the interlocking Quaker philanthropic families took Elizabeth Fry into prison reform and the founding in 1866 of the Howard League, William Allen of Spitalfields into poor law activity in the East End. Edward Baines' support for anti-slavery provided links to later organized dissent.

In much the same way, there were dramatic late nineteenth century links between concerns with poverty (the Charity Organization Society), and with sabbatarianism, women's rights, temperance and the RSPCA.[35] More modestly, in the mid-century, the Financial Reform Association had ties with the Anti-Corn Law League, the Freehold Land Society, Hume's Little Charter, and national education;[36] and the public health movement with evangelical paternalism (Shaftesbury's 'the body is a temple'), with administrative reform (Chadwick), with the social science association (Shaftesbury again and Sir John Simon), with poor law and national education (J. Kay Shuttleworth, formerly

improvement in piety, and for the extension of Christian truth and privileges to all. If they are ever made political associations, so far their Christian character must be obscured, and their Christian usefulness lessened.' Both extracts quoted in D. Thompson, *Nonconformity in the 19th century* (1972), pp. 124–7.

[33] J. Vincent, *The Formation of the Liberal Party* (1966).
[34] See H. Temperley, 'Anti-Slavery', chapter 2, below.
[35] See B. H. Harrison, 'State intervention and moral reform', chapter 12, below.
[36] W. N. Calkins, 'A Victorian Free Trade Lobby', *Economic History Review* (1960–61).

Dr J. Kay), as well as with orthodox free trade (Viscount Morpeth).

The Birmingham Quaker corn merchant, Joseph Sturge, born in 1793, had powerful links with all three 'core' pressure groups. He was prominent in the peace society from its foundation in 1816 through to the 1850s; in parliamentary reform, as a member of Attwood's Birmingham Political Union, and as the sponsor of the Complete Suffrage Union in 1841–2, founded explicitly to 'effect a better understanding and closer union between the middle and working classes'. He was a free trader bringing 'a sort of conscience' (in the words of his biographer) to the League, though he was to be highly embarrassed when his commitment to anti-slavery led him to favour protective sugar duties. Like Baines, he was opposed to government interference in education and with the police, and like Baines he favoured municipal baths, parks, and works. All this to the distress of his quietest friends who feared he was endangering his immortal soul in 'the perilous vortex of politics'.[37] Or Samuel Morley, born in 1809, and bred a liberal nonconformist: prominent in the Liberation Society and the temperance movement; but also one time corresponding secretary for the Administrative Reform Association, and subsequently of financial strength to the Reform League in the mid 1860s.[38] W. J. Fox (born in 1786) was from 1846 the Unitarian MP for Oldham; before then, he had been the colleague of the London philosophic radicals in the 1830s, a writer for the League in the 1840s, and went on to become an advocate of disestablishment in the 1850s. His introduction to the 1849 edition of his *Lectures to the Working Classes* stated that the reunion of middle and working classes would rest on:

> ... the combination of fiscal reform, the revision of taxation, the principles of economy and peace, and the reform of the representation, as objects of the same movement. These are the people's objects—the legitimate claims of the many as opposed to the sinister interests of the few.

Among his other interests were sanitary reform, Irish land reform, and education.

James Acland, a disreputable radical journalist, is perhaps worth a more extended treatment. A strolling player and itinerant teacher turned journalist, he moved to Bristol in 1827 where his Cobbett-style radicalism simultaneously brought him libel actions and some responsibility for the Bristol riots of October 1831. He speedily retreated to Hull, where he organized a political union for household suffrage, the ballot and

[37] H. Richard, *op. cit.*
[38] E. Hodder, *Samuel Morley* (1888), and O. Anderson, 'The Administrative Reform Association', p. 269, below.

triennial parliaments, and challenged the corrupt corporation's monopoly both of the ferry crossing, with his own steamboats, naturally named *Magna Charta* and *Public Opinion*, as well as the Corporation's monopoly of the market stalls by setting up his own. He issued a stream of libellous newspapers, both stamped and unstamped; broke the Anglican grip on the vestry by becoming its first agnostic church warden; and while in prison on one of his six occasions, opposed M. D. Hill as parliamentary candidate for Hull, in the process acquiring a respectable 433 votes, mainly from the butchers and victuallers who wanted an open produce market. He fed Joseph Parkes with material on Hull for municipal corporation reform. 'His trade was agitation . . . he attacked every institution and every individual member of each institution. . . .'[39]

He prudently took the pledge in 1838, but before the temperance movement sought him out, he was recommended by Parkes as a lecturer to the League, where he fought Chartists literally and the gentry effectively on dozens of provincial tours, sometimes to the despair of more decorous members of the League. In 1855 he was writing pamphlets for the Administrative Reform Association, in the 1860s he was working as a Liberal party agent; in 1867 he was electoral adviser to the Reform League. All sorts of things come out in Acland's tempestuous career: the ties of local government radicalism to political unionism, and both to temperance and free trade. And there are strong parallels with the careers of Robert Lowery, Henry Vincent, and Falvey of Liverpool, who lectured impartially for temperance and the League.

How did pressure from without operate? Its first step was usually to seek direct parliamentary power, to persuade from within. The anti-slavery committee, headed by Thomas Fowell Buxton, had its own parliamentary voice, as of course did the philosophic radicals. Others, like Attwood,[40] Urquhart, Miall, and Baines, became members as a way of bringing pressure from without within, though possibly only Cobden managed this successfully.

Shaftesbury[41] was obviously the outstanding 'insider', combining

39 *Sheahan's History of Hull* (1864), p. 159. For Acland's career, see his own newspapers, particularly *The Libel*, *The Dauntless* (both 1834), and his *Hull Portfolio* (1831–2); supplemented by the *Hull Advertizer*, *passim*. F. Adams, *Eyes for the Blind* (Hull, 1832) was one of the more outspoken counter-attacks on him.

40 Attwood's biographer commented sadly that 'a man possessed of so much power *outside* the House should have exercised so little influence within it.' His career crumbled when his syllogism—currency reform entails parliamentary reform entails Chartism—collapsed, because Russell cruelly produced a Chartist placard denouncing paper money. 'All my hopes have been disappointed. I have found it utterly impossible to do any good to my country by honest means, either *within* the walls of Parliament or *without* the walls of Parliament.' (C. Wakefield, *Life of T. Attwood* (1885), pp. 261, 335.)

41 See G. B. A. M. Finlayson, 'Shaftesbury', chapter 7, below.

social standing, undeniable ability and undoubted moral authority with which to embarrass the government's paternalist conscience. He had loyal parliamentary friends, the high Tory Sir Robert Inglis, the Yorkshire protectionist W. B. Ferrand, and Charles Buller, whom he did not need to whip; but for the most part, he relied on public outcry when he could, and bargained with the government when he could not. On mines, for example, 'the government cannot, if they would, refuse the Bill of which I have given notice, to exclude females and children from coal pits—the feeling in my favour has become quite enthusiastic; the Press is working on all sides most vigorously.'[42] His speech moved men to tears, though the government quietly nullified some of his efforts by failing to appoint inspectors with quite the same alacrity they had shown for factories. But when it came to the Twelve Hours debate in 1844, Peel put on the whip, threatened resignation, and Shaftesbury did not have sufficient parliamentary or national support to call Peel's bluff. In 1845 he took on lunacy bills from Graham when he was promised firm government support; and acted as the parliamentary defender of the Board of Health, rather against his better judgment, because 'I have so many things to ask of them [the government] yet; with what face can I do it if I refuse them when they make a reasonable request to me?' And the usual Shaftesbury touch, 'May God give me strength.'[43] Being inside the House, he could obtain enquiries, the debating of which became an exercise in moral education; his friends rallied the press; and speaking *for* the working classes, he was not vulnerable to charges of intimidating parliament or wielding a mob.

Without such a voice, pressure was more oblique. The Anti-Corn Law League at first adhered to Whig theories of the representation of interests. It tried to persuade the Manchester Chamber of Commerce as an 'interest' to put pressure on MPs to speak up in a House that was overweighted with the landed interest; and for MPs in turn to pressure ministers. Only when such tactics patently failed, did the League stumble into pressure from without. Its modest educational tours of 1839 and 1840 gave way to direct political intervention culminating in the Walsall by-election of 1841. The League next took its organization into working class circles in 1841, into more distant provinces in autumn 1842, into hostile rural areas in 1843, only to provoke counter-organization from Richmond's Central Agricultural Protection Society. Even so, the League maintained its parliamentary lobby, headed by Villiers who annually moved for repeal, and who was joined in 1841 by Cobden and Milner Gibson.[44]

[42] E. Hodder, *Life and Times of Earl Shaftesbury* (1892 edn.), p. 224.
[43] *Loc. cit.*, p. 398.
[44] See D. Martin, 'Land Reform', chapter 6, below.

The problem of the parliamentary voice was obtaining adequate debating time, particularly when after 1836 petitions were no longer discussed.[45] Sharman Crawford for the Complete Suffrage Union had to turn in desperation to filibustering on the Question of Supply.[46] The other difficulty was that parliamentary lobbying was usually only fruitful when the Whig/Liberal party was in power and who might be persuaded to see electoral advantage in adopting a pressure group platform. A change of tactics was forced on the League when Peel returned in 1841, and on the Liberation Society in 1857. It was usually with the failure of a parliamentary motion that: 'whatever pressure is to be put upon the House of Commons must come from *without*'.[47]

Classic pressure from without generally developed by two stages. The first of these was primarily educational, the creation of an enlightened public opinion which, without too much scrutiny of ways and means, was supposed to bear on government. Urquhart's foreign affairs committees represent perhaps the most extreme example of such didactic pressure.[48] Essential to enlightened opinion was respectable journalistic outlets: the philosophic radicals *Westminster Review* and on terms the *Examiner*; Cobden's founding of the *Economist* and financing of the *Sun*; Baines's *Leeds Mercury*, Miall's *Nonconformist*, Urquhart's *Free Press*.

The next requirement was evidence of a 'national voice'. Regional coverage came from a network of local branches: political unions, anti-slavery's Quaker cells in Bristol and Norwich, the response of dissenting chapels to Baines. Anti-slavery had at its height some 1200 auxiliaries; and the League, and later the Reform League and Reform Union, could call upon conference delegates from 200 to 300 towns. Branches were linked by corresponding secretaries to a central council, meeting monthly for the most part, and served in its turn by an inner executive committee which met more often.[49] The main tasks of local branches

[45] P. Frazer, 'Public petitioning and parliament before 1832', *History* (1961); C. Leys, 'Petitioning in the 19th and 20th centuries', *Political Studies* (1955).
[46] See A. Wilson, 'The Suffrage Movement', chapter 4, below.
[47] Cobden to Wilson, 24 February 1842 (Wilson MSS, Manchester Ref. Library). I owe this reference to Dr D. Frazer.
[48] See R. Shannon, 'Urquhart and the Foreign Affairs Committees', chapter 10, below. This educational stage runs together two styles of pressure, analytically distinguished by H. Jephson (*The Platform*, 1892): that 'expressive' of public feeling, and the 'deliberative' which offered rationalist remedy. (For a full discussion of this typology, see O. Anderson, 'The Administrative Reform Association', pp. 263–4.) Mass protest movements stopped short with the first; elitist pressure groups devoted their resources to the second. But for most pressure from without, the one entailed the other. Jephson's third style, that of electoral pressure, is discussed below, p. 17.
[49] The complete suffrage movement had ten regional districts each with their corresponding secretary; the League after 1842, fourteen districts each with their own lecturer-agent; the Liberation Society employed district agents paid by central funds. The ARA on the other hand had four corresponding secretaries whose duties were

were to circulate petitions and subscribe funds; in turn they were fed with lecturers, tracts and research material (such as the Health of Towns 'Weekly Sheet of Facts and Figures'), according to the style and state of funds of the pressure group. Lecturers were particularly expensive, and financial liability and much complaint was passed to and fro between locality and the central committee. Occasionally, a headquarters lost touch, and, if it was in London, was charged with contamination by London's immorality. The provinces by contrast were the home of higher moralism, of immediacy over expediency. This lay behind some of the skirmishes between the London parliamentary radicals who were themselves free-traders, and the Manchester League in the 1840s; and was a recurrent theme in the Liberation Society and Josephine Butler's crusade to name but two.

However, 'many persons say they refuse to give, because they see no use in our movement, because there is no power to carry our question'[50]: and such an attitude took the League, like other groups, from educational into electoral pressure, the second stage of pressure from without.

Most simply, this meant extracting pledges from MPs, itself, in Tory eyes, an invasion of personal judgement: electors were coached in their questions by 'Parliamentary text books' produced by the parliamentary radicals. The League sent every elector a bundle of political literature. Non-voters were encouraged to employ exclusive dealing. The Liberation Society went on to whip the MPs thought to be sympathetic on church rates, and their parliamentary subcommittee determined political priorities and the timing of the snap division. Like the ARA, they kept full records of MPs' voting behaviour.

More generally, electoral pressure entailed a care for the state of the electoral register, and the employment of professional party agents:[51] the scale of their activity comes out in the efforts of urban liberals in the West Riding, who pushed the country franchise up from 18,000 in 1834 to 29,000 one year later, to give the Whig-Liberals a theoretical majority in the county and a claim to share the representation by urban and county members.[52] The League worked some 140 boroughs in this way before it turned to country seats; and the Liberation Society intervened highly effectively in 1857 where it worked eleven counties, and in 1865 where it turned to thirty-three marginal boroughs, both placing candidates and securing for them electoral support.

functionally rather than geographically determined: financial, corresponding, statistical and general secretaries.

[50] Quoted in N. McCord, *The Anti-Corn Law League* (1958), p. 82.

[51] J. A. Thomas, 'The system of registration and the development of party organization 1832–1870', *History*, 1950.

[52] F. M. L. Thompson, 'Whigs and Liberals in the West Riding, 1830–1860', *English Historical Review*, 1959.

The coming of good times destroyed some of the League's political leverage in 1844, so it turned its hand to creating rather than merely eliciting sympathetic votes. 'We must fight the enemy by means of the 40s freehold', said Cobden; and something like £250,000 was alleged to have been spent in Lancashire, Yorkshire, and Cheshire to create 5,000 new votes.[53] The most direct method of all was to run one's own candidate, as the League ran J. B. Smith at the Walsall by-election in 1841,[54] and the Complete Suffrage Union its candidates for local councils.

Occasionally, pressure groups toyed with more desperate measures: the Catholic Association's intervention at County Clare, the threat of political unions in 1832 to go for gold, are both well known. The taxes on knowledge were fought in the 1830s by illegal unstamped newspapers, and in 1851 after much searching C. D. Collet produced a paralysed man to edit an illicit *Stoke-on-Trent Narrative*. The government wisely abstained from prosecution. Attwood's national holiday was a defensive withdrawal of labour that had physical force overtones to it; and the League, in despair at the return of the Tories in summer 1841, contemplated closing mills and refusing taxes. The plug plots were unfortunate for its historical reputation.

Those pressure groups which claimed to speak for the People had to broaden their base in social as well as in regional terms. For, said Cobden:

I want, by constitutional and legal means, to place, as far as I can, political power in this country in the hands of the middle and industrious classes; in other words, the people. When I speak of the middle and industrious classes, I regard them, as I ever did, as inseparable in interest. You cannot separate them. I defy any person to draw the line where the one ends and the other begins. . . .[55]

[53] Between £30 and £50 would buy a plot producing a 40s. freehold. One way was to turn a large estate into allotments. Alternatively a manufacturer would sell a row of buildings to a group of working men who promptly leased it back, receiving in return a rent of 40s. By 1850, the Freehold Land Society claimed 20,000 allotments providing votes, and subscriptions of £750,000.

[54] The Tory won by 363 to 336. For details, see D. Martin, 'Land reform', p. 143.

[55] *Speeches of Richard Cobden*, 26 November 1849. But compare a working class socialist comment:

Those who call themselves the liberal statesmen of the present day, must go progressively with the people; but in the word PEOPLE . . . they must, brethren, include us, the productive labourers, for what are the people without us? And yet, brethren, while we work not for ourselves, but for the capitalists and profit-mongers, we can hardly rank with the PEOPLE. The people have a political position, but we have none that we can make any use of with benefit to ourselves . . . ('Senex', *Pioneer*, 28 June 1834.)

So when a working man, Hutchinson, was asked to call a meeting for the League, the *Quarterly Review* sourly noted that he addressed 'The Trades—Workshops—Religious and Benefit Societies—Chartist, Anti-Corn Law and Repeal of the Union Associations—and other bodies of men of Manchester and Salford.'[56] The Chartists, however, unfortunately for Cobden's thesis, were not gentlemen but cheerfully muscled in on every pressure group meeting they could, in order to put motions for the six points: at the League meetings, at Urquhart's foreign affair committees (who in turn adopted the same technique towards ARA meetings), the Administrative Reform Association, as well of course as the traditionally fair game of sabbatarian meetings. Chartists also sabotaged the delicate ground rules for returning both middle and working class delegates to Complete Suffrage conference, by insisting on a disproportionate number of their nominees.

The parliamentary reformers regularly attempted a 'thorough union of the middle and working classes' and formed the National Political Union in 1831, the Leeds Parliamentary Reform Association of Samuel Smiles in 1840, the Complete Suffrage Union in 1842, the People's Charter Union, and the Parliamentary and Financial Reform Association in the late 1840s, the Reform Union in the 1860s. For, as Miall said most revealingly in 1842, 'They required some stronger lever to move the aristocracy than any they had yet worked, and they could only find that lever by extending the suffrage. . . . Neither the middle nor the working classes were sufficiently powerful to carry their point, but by uniting they would break the yoke beneath which they now groaned.'[57] But as the long debate on the propriety of a middle class alliance in the columns of the *Northern Star* shows, Chartists had no intention of being 'assenting inferiors, or mere pressure-from-without machinery; they asked not of the middle classes leadership but alliance; not superiority but co-operation; their motto was a bold and independent one—with you if we may, without you if we must'.[58] The Chartist journalist, Thomas Frost, rather more cynically described the Parliamentary and Financial Reform Association:

What the middle classes most wanted was a diminution of the pressure of taxation . . . and if the object could have been gained without parliamentary reform, they would gladly have refrained from touching the question. But they could not see their way to its accomplishment without an increase of the voting power of the shop-keeping

---

[56] *Quarterly Review*, December 1842.
[57] *Northern Star*, 19 February 1842.
[58] Letter of Collins and O'Neill, *Northern Star*, 20 February 1841; see also O'Brien, *Northern Star*, 24 April 1841; and in general, D. Large, 'William Lovett', p. 118 f.

classes, and that involved the difficulty that always stood in the way of their success. They could not bring pressure from without to bear upon Parliament with sufficient force for the purpose without union with the working classes, and the support of the latter could be obtained on no other terms than the adoption of the principle of manhood suffrage.[59]

When, as often happened, such union broke down, there was the alternative of separate but parallel organizations. The League had its operative associations in Manchester, Sheffield, Nottingham, Birmingham, Carlisle, Leicester, and Huddersfield, though they were often seduced by the CSU in the 1840s.[60] The campaign in the 1830s against the taxes on knowledge was a middle class parliamentary lobby aided and abetted by the extra-parliamentary and working class unstamped.[61] The Health of Towns Association of 1844 had its central committee and provincial auxiliaries, its bishops and its Lords Normanby, Morpeth, and Shaftesbury. Not surprisingly, perhaps, working class enthusiasts formed their own Metropolitan Working Class Association for Improving Public Health in 1845: their chairman was the former NUWC member and Chartist, Richard Moore, who in turn went on to become chairman, though not of course president, of Collet's campaign to repeal the remaining taxes on knowledge in the 1850s.

Increasingly, as the 'Condition-of-England' question faded after 1848, it became easier to co-opt working men into pressure group activity, into temperance, into education, into land reform, and above all into parliamentary reform, without mutual recrimination and to mutual advantage. Former Chartists appeared to agree with Cobden's remarks to Bright in 1851: 'The mass of the people, however enthusiastic in favour of universal suffrage, have not the power of carrying that or any other measure except with the aid of the middle class.'[62]

Is there any way, then, of assessing the impact of pressure from without on early Victorian politics? In the debates on 1832, such pressure was thought to be the intimidating activity of a mob, illegitimate, artificial; by 1867 for the most part pressure from without was seen as the healthy participation of an active citizenry. Harriet Martineau's *History* asserted that the activity of the League.

---

[59] T. Frost, *Forty Years Recollections* (1880), pp. 203–4.
[60] See D. Fraser, 'Birmingham and the Corn Laws', *Trans. of the Birmingham Archeological Society*, 1967, volume 82; and 'Nottingham and the Corn Laws', *Trans. Thoroton Society*, LXX (1966).
[61] P. Hollis, *The Pauper Press* (1970).
[62] Quoted in D. Read, *Cobden and Bright* (1967), p. 158.

approached more nearly to a genuinely national education than any scheme elsewhere at work. By the anti-corn law league the people at large were better trained to thought and its communication, to the re-organization of principles, the obtaining of facts and the application of the same faculties and the same interest to their public as to their private affairs. . . .[63]

Activity, movement as such, was now positively desirable. In Lowery's words, 'there is always some wrong, some sin—thence some suffering; this suffering is a blessing. . . . It is the divine voice that bids us to be up and find a remedy. . . . Agitation in a right spirit seems to be our normal state.'[64]

Contemporaries were also confident that pressure groups had provided the impetus for social progress, and that the very co-operation of men in working together for such reforms, as well as the effects of the reforms themselves, had done much to produce social tranquillity. This comes out in Elihu Barnett's *Walks in the Black Country*:

On that grand march to political right and power, the masses stood shoulder to shoulder with their leaders. It was a great co-partnership and fraternization of the classes. . . . Birmingham erected public opinion into a mighty power and engine for the common good—a power ever ready to be used against any evil that legislation could remove, or the enlightened mind and conscience of the people could abolish by moral action. It was worked to a glorious triumph at home against slavery in the West Indies, and to an illustrious triumph at home against the corn laws. . . . The ends for which the political unions, the anti-slavery society and the anti-corn law league laboured and the triumphs they won, were of immeasurable value in themselves, but the educational means they employed in enlightening the minds of the masses, in teaching them to think, reflect, compare and observe for themselves, produced results of equal importance. . . .[65]

Social progress, social tranquillity, social harmony, social enlightenment: all were claimed for pressure from without. And certainly the careers of Lovett and Lowery, Acland, Vincent, and Cooper on the working class side, and Smiles, Sturge, Collet, W. J. Fox, Morley, and Miall on the middle class side, show how pressure groups became a mechanism for co-opting working men into the main stream of mid-Victorian liberal politics; and for softening what could have been sharp

[63] H. Martineau, *The History of England during the Thirty Years Peace* (1850).
[64] R. Lowery, *Weekly Record*, 26 July 1856.
[65] Quoted in C. M. Wakefield, *Life of Thomas Attwood*, 1885, p. 120 ff.

and severe social tension left behind by both Chartism and the League.

But pressure groups did more than co-opt working men in an indirect way into political activity. As Cobden said to Villiers, 'We shall radicalize the country in the process of carrying the repeal of the corn laws',[66] and the rejection of established leadership, indirect representation and the mechanism of County Meetings, and the injection of direct democracy, all this meant, for good and for ill, the decline of deference politics with its insistence that the poor were as children and could not therefore be trusted with self-government. The *Nonconformist*, edited by Edward Miall, had argued back in 1841, that on all political questions, the middle class already appealed to the industrious classes, organized them into societies, paraded their unanimity, and it was consequently hypocritical to deny them the suffrage when they were already effectively engaged in politics.[67] Now Shaftesbury, in melancholy vein, recalled in 1875, 'Not only am I not wanted, but my interference would be superfluous and an incumbrance. . . . The working classes have become patrons instead of clients, and they both can and do fight their own battles. It was not so forty years ago when I began the struggle.'[68]

There remains the practical problem of effectiveness, the impact on legislation and the legislature. But even putting the question that way indicates a degree of success. In the 1820s, the House of Commons was a deliberative body, sustaining the Administration, preserving property and contract, supervising fiscal, financial and to a certain extent foreign affairs. Actually passing new laws was fairly low down on its list of priorities. By Josephine Butler's time, parliament was the Legislature, and political parties had an increasingly explicit contract with their electorate. Prime ministerial 'stumping' and Unauthorized Programmes on the one hand, and the classic caucus and national party organization on the other hand, were only a few years away.

What did pressure achieve? The Catholic Association succeeded, though at the price of losing its 40s. freehold votes, mainly because, in Wellington's words, 'If I thought that the Irish nobility and gentry would recover their lost influence, the just influence of property, without making these concessions, I would not stir.' The 1832 reform act D. C. Moore has argued was a 'cure' for the untidiness of existing boundaries which swamped legitimate interests and for the grievances of the ultras, rather than any 'concession' to political unionism; though

[66] H. Jordan, 'Richard Cobden and Penny Postage', *Victorian Studies* (1965), p. 360. According to Spencer Walpole, the Penny Postage Bill was forced upon a reluctant ministry by 'the clamour of a nation'. (*A History of England* (1890), IV, p. 191). Quoted *loc. cit.*

[67] *Nonconformist*, 17 November 1841.   [68] Hodder, *op. cit.*, p. 687.

for 1867, Royden Harrison has insisted that in an important way it was a concession to Hyde Park, and that Disraeli wished 'to destroy the present agitation and extinguish Gladstone and company'.[69] Slavery was abolished after fifty years of pressure from humanitarian and dissenting groups (as well as from the East Indian lobby). An incoming reform ministry, sustained by MPs pledged to abolition, had no wish to defy it since the West Indian colonies were increasingly unruly and the West Indian economy increasingly precarious. But it was the Demerara slave revolt of 1823 that convinced Government it had a problem to solve, and the Jamaican slave revolt of December 1831 that the solution was not amelioration but emancipation.[70] The Corn Laws were repealed with Russell's support some time after Peel had been converted to free trade; and Church rates were abolished and the Irish Church disestablished when Gladstone took up the question. Viscount Morpeth introduced his sanitary legislation of 1847 and 1848 under the aegis of the Health of Towns Association, and much of its content, for instance the exclusion of London, was due to them.[71] But it was palatable to the House of Commons at least as much because of the return of cholera. Revealingly, however, no one challenged the propriety of Morpeth citing the Health of Towns Association as evidence for sanitary reform. The reduction of the Newspaper Stamps in 1836 was due to the lobbying of the stamped newspaper proprietors rather than to the pressure of parliamentary radicals, though Charles Knight on behalf of the Society for the Diffusion of Useful Knowledge, had some weight. The removal of the final taxes in the 1850s, however, came according to J. S. Mill when Collet's friends persuaded the Inland Revenue civil servants of their case, they in turn persuaded their Minister and he the government. From the lobbying that made it politically attractive to remove the assessed taxes in the 1830s, to the removal of the contagious diseases act, it was easier to repeal than to introduce legislation. If the pressure group could defy the government as well, as it could with unstamped newspapers, then government was likely to succumb to a war of attrition. But any assessment in these terms is difficult, for pressure from without to be ultimately effective must come from within, must be taken up inside parliament; and that parliamentary spokesman, be he Minister or backbencher, may not himself depend upon the pressure group. Though Urquhart's claims to have prevented a Chartist

[69] G. Machin, *The Catholic Question in English Politics, 1820–1830* (1964) p. 123; D. C. Moore, 'Concession or Cure', *Historical Journal*, 1966; R. Harrison, *Before the Socialists* (1965), p. 112.

[70] See P. Dixon, 'The Politics of Emancipation. The movement for the abolition of slavery in the British West Indies 1807–1833'. Oxford D.Phil. thesis, 1971.

[71] Hansard, 11 May, 18 June, 2 July 1847; 10 February 1848 (speeches of Viscount Morpeth).

revolution and two general European wars, were somewhat excessive, it remains true that the only clear successes that can be claimed by pressure from without, are likely to be negative ones: that they impeded or prevented the imposition of new law. Positive legislation, including parliamentary reform, is likely to have a pedigree of its own, independent of pressure from without.

Any description and analysis of pressure from without in this period must have implications for three larger questions: the concept of the political community, the concept of party, the concept of government. Pressure groups did extend the concept of the political community, of those who, by engaging in practical politics, could claim the vote as of right. The 'mob' shrank into a 'residuum'. They also sustained a high degree of political pluralism: the *Essays on Reform* commented in 1867 that one of the strengths of England was its 'innumerable personal and local centres for political action'.[72]

Pressure from without also has implications for the notion of party. The period between the two Reform Acts was far from being the golden age of the independent MP: modern research has shown that even before, and certainly after, 1832 MPs were party men; there was little cross voting, and few were uncommitted.[73] But they were party men by loyalty and interest at least as much as by belief in a party platform. During these years, however, more and more MPs seem to have added an ideological dimension to their party commitment, to have imported into their parties views and attitudes acquired from exposure to pressure group ideology outside. In other words, not only were MPs party men, but the parties increasingly stood for something distinctive in the eyes of their backbenchers. In the 1870s, the National Liberal Federation was to develop as a mechanism for imposing on London liberalism a body of provincial beliefs and political planks on education, church and land reform. In the 1830s the reverse seems almost to have been true. Party as a vehicle existed in advance of the beliefs and commitments which were to power it with its purpose. Party had always existed to represent interest and to seek place; it increasingly began to offer a platform, an important part of which was provided by pressure from without.

Accordingly, when Russell in 1839 and 1840 was casting around for an issue with which to recoup his waning electoral fortunes, he was looking for a pressure from without that, on the analogy with parliamentary reform in 1832, would bring him electoral prosperity. He rightly chose

[72] A. Rutson, 'Opportunities and Shortcomings of Government in England', in W. Guttsman (ed.), *A Plea for Democracy* (1967 edn.), p. 154.
[73] D. Beales' 'The Independent Member', in R. Robson (ed.), *Ideas and Institutions of Victorian Britain* (1967); D. Close, 'Two Parties', *EHR*, 1969.

free trade,[74] but underestimated Peel's own willingness to contemplate it. When Russell was again in search of an issue on which to re-align party divisions and produce a decisive majority in the early 1850s, his complaint about parliamentary reform was precisely that it did not offer sufficient pressure, sufficient noise 'out of doors', to provide him with the necessary political leverage. Rather self-consciously, and highly inconsistently, the parliamentary reformers replied that it was safer to enlarge the franchise when people did not clamour for it than when they did.

Pressure from without, then, in areas of parliamentary reform, free trade, Church reform, offered a platform with a guaranteed grassroots appeal, which parties could adopt and co-opt as they saw fit. But although parties came to carry more and more 'causes', nonetheless there were wide tracts of social policy, such as intervention in public health, factories and mines, in which party divisions did not operate. Individual MPs voted as they saw fit.[75] Yet it was in such areas of concern that the period saw the most startling extension of government regulation. Once social conditions were deemed 'intolerable', government intervention developed a momentum of its own with the appointment of inspectors who in turn helped to generate further government growth.[76] But only a strongly held and suitably formed public opinion could deem conditions to be 'intolerable', and thus initiate the process of government intervention, and account for its timing: why factories were regulated a decade ahead of the far worse conditions in the mines, why slum clearance preceded council housing by half a century. For much of this, pressure groups, medical officers of health and sanitary engineers, philanthropists and Tory clergymen, petitions and the press, could claim their share of credit.

W. R. Greg writing in the *Edinburgh Review* of 1852 is worth quoting at some length:

Before the reform bill, parliament was the arena where, by the theory of the constitution, and with nominally closed doors, the affairs of the nation were discussed and settled—it was the body to which the

[74] The League argued that the Whigs needed to give the electors 'some *principles* to contend for. . . . The cry of "keep out the Tories" has had its day, and is no longer available. The people are no longer to be brought to the aid of men who will do nothing for them. If, therefore, ministers do not bring forward measures of substantial reform . . . the people will leave them to settle disputes with their opponents as best they may.' (A. Prentice, *History of the Anti-Corn Law League*, 1853, volume 1, p. 183.)

[75] W. O. Aydelotte, 'Voting patterns in the House of Commons in the 1840s', *Comparative Studies in Society and History* (1963). Though Professor Aydelotte does not make the point, his arena of party divisions, the economic issues affecting the welfare of the rich, was in fact the traditional arena of government, the care for property, order, finance and trade.

[76] O. MacDonagh, 'A Revolution in Government', *Historical Journal*, 1958.

people delegated the task of thinking and acting for them in all
political concerns. . . .

But now all this has changed . . . Parliament is no longer the only,
nor the chief arena for political debate. Public meetings and the press
are fast encroaching upon and superseding its original exclusive
functions. Every man has become a politician. . . . The country often
takes precedence of the Legislature, both in the discussion and decision of public affairs. Public opinion is formed out of doors; and is
only revised, ratified and embodied within. Active and able individuals—sometimes men of business, sometimes philanthropists,
sometimes theoretical economists—study some especial branch of
political philosophy or social well-being, form their opinion upon it,
arrange their arguments, collect their facts, promulgate their views,
inform the public, agitate the country, excite and at length get
possession of the press; and, when by these means the community at
large has become sufficiently inocculated with their doctrine, they
bring it before parliament in the form of a specific proposition;—and
parliament examines, discusses, perhaps modifies and retards, but
never finally rejects, unless the popular feeling which has urged the
measure so far forward should prove to be only a partial or transitory
phase of public opinion. The functions of parliament are no longer
initiary. . . . The independent thinker originates; the Country listens,
disputes, sifts, ripens; the Parliament revises and enacts. . . .[77]

The *Quarterly* echoed the *Edinburgh's* sentiments in 1869. Young politicians found it more effective to arouse parliament from outside than
from within. Should anyone bent upon a great social reform or administrative improvement urge it upon the Minister concerned, and
'ten to one the Minister will tell him it is idle to bring it forward
unless "pressure from without" shall have forced it on public attention,
and given Government power to carry it through a torpid or reluctant
House'.[78]

Forty years before, the existence of such pressure was illegitimate,
unnecessary or both; now it was a necessary tool of social reform, a
necessary aid to government, evidence of healthy public concern.
Pressure from without had both stretched the arena of government and
access to government, and in the process had thrown up feminist groups
or the rights of prostitutes, evangelicals on the wrongs of prostitutes,
public health on the diseases of prostitutes, Shaftesbury and Gladstone
on refuges for prostitutes, and sabbatarians for no prostitution on
Sundays. Victorian political life was engagingly pluralist.

[77] W. R. Greg, 'The expected reform bill', *Edinburgh Review*, January 1852.
[78] 'Politics as a profession', *Quarterly Review*, January 1869.

2

Anti-slavery

Howard Temperley

In 1833, the year of the Emancipation Bill, the British anti-slavery movement was exactly fifty years old. Since its organizational beginnings in the 1780s abolitionists had directed their attention first to ending British participation in the slave trade, then to attempting to secure the suppression of the foreign slave trade and, finally, after 1823, to achieving the overthrow of slavery in the West Indies.

One remarkable feature of this movement was how little its institutional structure had changed over the years. At its centre stood a metropolitan committee, responsible for formulating policies and with authority to speak for the movement as a whole. In 1830 this position was held by the Anti-Slavery Committee (1823–39) with offices at 18 Aldermanbury Street, near St Paul's; ten years earlier the same function had been performed by the committee of the African Institution (1807–27) and, before that, by the committee of the Society for the Abolition of the Slave Trade (1787–1807). In each case the committee had constituted a central directorate composed partly of MPs but mainly of laymen, among whom a significantly high proportion were usually Quakers. In theory, members were elected every year by the society's subscribers, but since subscribers were usually prepared to do what the committee asked of them, these central committees were, in practice, self-perpetuating.

Outside the capital, the movement was represented by a network of auxiliary organizations. These bodies performed the dual function of collecting funds on behalf of the central committee and passing on information to their localities. Again, Quaker participation was much in evidence, although after 1787 few of them were entirely Quaker in membership. The scale of these provincial activities fluctuated. During the period that the African Institution held sway activity declined, but after 1823, with the launching of the campaign against West Indian slavery, it revived until by 1830 there were some two hundred auxiliary bodies scattered around the country. Many were little more than groups of sympathetic parishioners, but others, especially in the larger cities, were vigorous and capable of pursuing independent policies. A few provincial abolitionists, such as James Cropper of Liverpool,[1] became influential figures in the movement. But by and large it was the metropolitan committee that determined policy, the provincial abolitionists who sought, as best they could, to assist in its execution.

How far this formal structure was responsible for the effective working of the movement during these years may, of course, be questioned. Most historians have tended to regard the struggles over slavery as essentially parliamentary matters to be measured in terms of speeches and motions rather than of societies and extra-parliamentary lobbying.[2] This view was also shared by some abolitionists.

Perhaps the strongest statement in support of it comes from Sir George Stephen,[3] the leading chronicler of 1829–33 struggles over West Indian slavery. As the son of James Stephen, he had grown up in an anti-slavery household and so was well acquainted with the progress of the movement, at least from 1807 onwards. In his opinion the movement had been, up to the time he himself became actively engaged in it in the late 1820s, basically aristocratic. No anti-slavery public worthy of the name existed. This merely reflected the nature of British politics during those years. So long as the unreformed parliament held sway, political influence remained the prerogative of a tiny segment of the population, jealous of its privileges and antagonistic to form of outside interference. Thus in anti-slavery matters, as in others, it had been a matter of prudence as well as tradition to leave the cause in the hands of a select group of experienced campaigners. 'The duties of the abolitionists were of that character that not only required the influence and talents of acknowledged men in Parliament, but actually forbade all the obtrusive weight of "pressure from without".'[4] To have broadened the appeal

---

[1] James Cropper (1773–1840), Liverpool Quaker and philanthropist. Cropper was a prominent member of the Anti-Slavery Society and an early supporter of the agency system. For details of his anti-slavery career see David Brion Davis, 'James Cropper and the British Anti-Slavery Movement, 1821–1823', *Journal of Negro History*, 45, 1960, pp. 241–58, and 'James Cropper and the British Anti-Slavery Movement, 1823–1833', *ibid.*, 46 (1961), pp. 154–73.

[2] As is the case with the two standard works on the subject, F. J. Klingberg, *The Anti-Slavery Movement in England* (New Haven, 1926), and Sir Reginald Coupland, *The British Anti-Slavery Movement* (London, 1933).

[3] Sir George Stephen (1794–1879) was also the brother of Sir James Stephen who, as Colonial Under-Secretary, drafted the Emancipation Act of 1833. During the late 1820s he was employed as a solicitor by the Anti-Slavery Society and later became the leading spirit behind the Agency campaign of 1831–3. After he retired from anti-slavery work in 1833 he devoted himself to the relief of pauper prisoners, the establishment of a regular police force and the practice of law. He wrote extensively on all these subjects. Following the triumphal tour of Britain in 1853 by the authoress of *Uncle Tom's Cabin* he wrote his *Anti-Slavery Recollections in a Series of Letters Addressed to Mrs. Beecher Stowe* (London, 1854).

[4] *Ibid.*, p. 112.

would not only have been pointless but might well have proved counter-productive.

Stephen, it should be noted, had reasons for stating his case so bluntly. He was writing an open letter to Harriet Beecher Stowe and was anxious to contrast the British situation with the American where the popular voice in government had always been taken more for granted. He was also concerned to play up the 'complete revolution' in anti-slavery tactics, for which he claimed to be partly responsible, and which, in his view, transformed the movement in the early 1830s.

This 'revolution', as he describes it, was the result of a combination of factors: public indignation at the disclosure that the Mauritian planters, in defiance of the Act of 1807, were still importing slaves; the intransigence of the West Indian assemblies; the obvious ineffectualness of the governments' attempts to meliorate the harsher aspects of slavery; and the dawning realization that, despite optimistic forecasts, the abolition of the slave trade had had no perceptible effect on the way plantations were run. But what made these issues matters of *popular* concern was the growing political awareness of those middle class groups which by the late '20s were demanding, and in 1832, achieved, political representation.

According to Stephen, the materials for making such a revolution had been present for some time but had gone largely unrecognized. The more traditional minded abolitionists, content to continue working through Parliament in the usual way, had failed to grasp the power within their reach. It had thus been left to a breakaway group of younger men—the Young England Abolitionists Stephen calls them—operating through a new organization, the Agency Anti-Slavery Society, to undertake the task of mobilizing and directing public opinion. This they did by hiring itinerant lecturers, such as George Thompson,[5] to proselytize the country, and by shaping their message in such a way as to appeal specifically to middle class sensibilities.

These younger abolitionists argued that the traditional anti-slavery case deferred too much to the objections raised by its parliamentary

---

[5] George Thompson (1804–78) made a name for himself as one of the salaried lecturers employed by the Agency committee. His subsequent tour of the United States (1834–5), undertaken at the invitation of William Lloyd Garrison, was something of a fiasco. As a professional agitator he lent his services to the free trade movement, East India reform and the campaign to reinstate the deposed Raja of Sattara, but his main allegiance remained to the anti-slavery movement. In 1847 he was elected MP for Tower Hamlets but a prolonged absence on a second anti-slavery tour of America antagonized his constituents and he was not re-elected. His friendship with Garrison and his leadership of the Garrisonian faction in Britain contributed to the divisions which afflicted the anti-slavery movement in the 1840s and '50s. During the American Civil War he was an active supporter of the Union and in 1864–5 he made a final triumphal tour of the United States.

critics and to this extent was more concerned with matters of expediency than with driving home the message that slavery was wrong.
So long as parliament was the court of appeal this had been inevitable
and perhaps even salutary. But to arouse *popular* sentiment required
quite a different approach. Practical considerations needed to be
stripped away. The public needed to be shown that the debate was not
about this expedient or that but about the essential sinfulness of slavery
itself. The choice to be made was between good and bad, sin and virtue.
'It was self-evident,' he recalled, 'that if the religious world could be
induced to enter upon the subject, severing it from all its political relations, and viewing it simply as a question between God and man, the
battle was won.'[6]

And, according to his account, this was how the struggle over the
Emancipation Act of 1833 *was* won. The Agency Society provided
central direction, the stipendiary lecturers carried the message to the
country; the number of local auxiliaries grew from 200 to over 1,200;
placards were displayed; marches organized; petitions circulated; editors persuaded to insert anti-slavery material in their newspapers;
prominent selectors canvassed; parliamentary candidates induced to
sign pledges; and lists of MPs who had agreed or refused to support
particular items of legislation publicly circulated. Above all, 'respectability'—to use Stephen's term—showed by its active participation in
these activities that opinion was behind the abolitionists. It was this
mass display of popular feeling which, in the end, led the Whig government of 1833 to sponsor the Emancipation Bill, thereby advancing the
cause 'by at least a generation'.

Yet, even on the basis of Stephen's own evidence, it is plain that this
is not the whole story. There was a national anti-slavery structure in
existence long before the Agency committee launched its campaign.
Whether these bodies were, as he claims, largely dormant is hard to
assess. No doubt many of them were. What is plain, however, is that this
had not always been the case. It had not, for example, been the case
with the very earliest anti-slavery societies. Those bodies, offshoots of the
London Meeting for Sufferings,[7] although entirely Quaker in member-

---

[6] Stephen, *op. cit.*, p. 160.

[7] As its name implies, the Meeting for Sufferings, established in 1675, was originally
designed to protect Quakers from persecution. Very soon, however, it became
recognized as the executive arm of the Society of Friends. Thus, it was to the Meeting
for Sufferings that the Philadelphia Quakers in 1782 wrote urging the British to take
a more positive stand against slavery. After obtaining the approval of the Yearly
Meeting in 1783 the Meeting for Sufferings established two anti-slavery committees,
a formal committee of twenty-three members and an informal committee of six.
Minute Books of the Meeting for Sufferings Committee on the Slave Trade, 1783–92,
and Thompson-Clarkson MSS. 2/9. The activities of these bodies are admirably
summarized in Patrick C. Lipscomb III, 'William Pitt and the Abolition of the Slave
Trade' (unpublished Ph.D. dissertation, University of Texas, 1960), pp. 72–127.

ship, are clearly recognizable as the precursors of the anti-slavery societies of later times. And being Quaker, they had necessarily been concerned, from the first, with bringing pressure to bear on parliament
from without. Indeed to give a full account of the organizational genesis
of the British anti-slavery movement would involve going further back
still to the Quaker political organizations of the 1730s. What concerned
Quakers at that time was not slavery but fighting tithe bills and other
legislation injurious to themselves. In the course of those struggles, utiliz-
ing the existing religious structure of quarterly, monthly and local meetings, they had succeeded in creating a political machine of remarkable
strength and sophistication which combined central direction with
constituency action. Long before anyone else, Quakers had become
adept at using a broad range of techniques designed to exert extra-
parliamentary pressure, including mass petitioning, lobbying, drawing
up voting lists, and obtaining pledges.[8]

It was this political machine which was largely responsible for launching the anti-slavery agitation of the early 1780s which led on to the mass
petition campaigns of 1789 and 1792. This was not the first time that
mass petitioning had been used for secular purposes but in terms of
scale (101 petitions in 1789, 510 in 1792) and organization, it eclipsed
all previous efforts. What is most striking however, is the evidence it
provides of mass support. The 1792 petition from Manchester contained
over 20,000 signatures; even more revealing were the petitions from
some smaller towns which contained the signatures of virtually every
literate inhabitant. The broad social basis of the movement is also reflected in the membership of the auxiliary organizations responsible for
circulating and transmitting these petitions. In origin most of these
bodies were Quaker cells which in the course of time had succeeded in
enlisting the support of local non-Quakers, mostly sectarians or evangelicals, in much the same way that the central co-ordinating body, the
Society for the Abolition of the Slave Trade, had itself originated as an
extension of the 1783 Quaker committees. Most of the members of these
bodies were middle class—merchants, doctors, lawyers, and the like—
but there was also a fair sprinkling of people of humbler status such as
shopkeepers and artisans. Compared with other political movements of
this period, such as the Yorkshire Association,[9] the anti-slavery

[8] N. C. Hunt, *Two Early Political Associations: The Quakers and the Dissenting Deputies
in the Age of Sir Robert Walpole* (Oxford, 1961), pp. 1–112.
[9] The largest and most active of the county associations which, in 1779–80, were
campaigning for parliamentary reform. The county gentry, who dominated these
associations, were cautious over whose support they would accept, whereas the
abolitionists were usually prepared to welcome anyone prepared to contribute to
their cause. It is significant that the largest number of signatures on a Yorkshire
Association petition was 9,000.

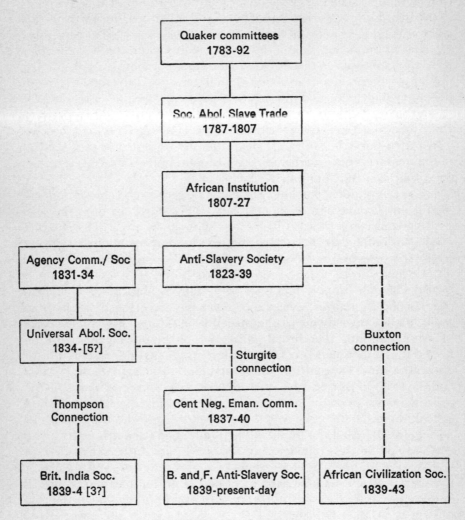

Figure 1 *British anti-slavery organizations, 1783–1840*

movement was unusual to the extent that it was urban based and drew its support from a broad range of social classes.[10]

There are other significant parallels between the 1780s and the 1820s. Up to 1787 the movement was wholly, and from 1787 to 1792 largely, financed by Quakers. During the 1820s the same holds true. In 1826 the anti-slavery subcommittee of the Meeting for Sufferings began making regular grants to the Anti-Slavery Society and in 1832 a similar practice was begun with respect to the Agency Society. In all, the Anti-Slavery Society received £6,000 from this source and the Agency Society £1,800. These sums were in addition to the generous donations of individual Quakers. Since the Anti-Slavery Society's annual budget was normally in the region of £2,500 and the Agency Society's, although undisclosed, was certainly no larger, it would appear that the whole agitation over West Indian slavery was largely paid for by Quakers.[11]

To the extent, then, that it drew on popular support, and sectarian generosity, the 'revolution' of 1829–33 was not a revolution at all but a return to an older practice—a practice which abolitionists had temporarily abandoned because of the discrediting of popular agitation by the French Revolution.[12] Nevertheless it would be a mistake to regard this later agitation as merely a repeat performance of the earlier. The scale of operations was now much greater, a consequence, in part, of the growing size and influence of the urban middle classes from which the movement drew the greater part of its popular support. Less emphasis was now placed on the boycotting of slave produce, a major aim in the 1780s but an impolitic one to embrace in the 1820s and '30s in view of Britain's increasing dependence on American cotton. The practice of publishing anti-slavery journals (the Anti-Slavery Society launched the first of these, the *Anti-Slavery Reporter*, in 1825, and the Agency Society followed suit with the *Tourist*, in 1832) was new. Henceforward no national anti-slavery body would be without its periodical. The practice of hiring salaried lecturers was also an innovation, although it could be argued that Thomas Clarkson had acted in much that capacity in the 1780s.

[10] These matters are analysed in E. M. Hunt, 'The North of England Agitation for the Abolition of The Slave Trade, 1780–1800' (unpublished M.A. dissertation, University of Manchester, 1959), pp. 249–57.

[11] Minute and Account Books of the Standing Committee of the Meeting for Sufferings Appointed to Aid in Promoting the Total Abolition of the Slave Trade and Slavery, 1820–33, MSS. 115–17, Friends House, London; Anti-Slavery Society, *Accounts of Receipts and Disbursements* (London, 1826–31).

[12] Between the abolitionists' 1791 defeat and their partial Commons victory in 1792 they greatly extended their popular appeal; but just as the effect of this agitation was beginning to be felt, events in France obliged them to revert to more conservative methods. For further details see Roger Anstey's forthcoming study of British politics and the slave trade.

But the most striking difference was the new militancy associated with the belief that slavery was a 'sin' and, as such, something to be abolished immediately and without regard to consequence. The seeds of this doctrine may be found in earlier anti-slavery writings. It had been the general assumption of eighteenth century opponents of slavery that the institution was sinful and that slaves possessed a right to their immediate freedom. But it had also been taken for granted that to achieve that freedom would require working through normal political and judicial channels and that abolitionists must construct their programmes accordingly. This did not, as we have seen, rule out the use of extra-parliamentary pressure; in fact the earliest efforts, of necessity, belonged mainly to that category. Nevertheless, a strong preference had been shown for reasoned argument and appeals to economic or national interest. Whatever the rights and wrongs of slavery, it had been assumed that if changes were to be brought about at all they must come gradually, after full discussion and with due regard for the political proprieties.

The abandonment of this doctrine of gradualism in favour of the new doctrine of immediacy, heralded by the appearance of Elizabeth Heyrick's *Immediate, Not Gradual Abolition* (London, 1824), and made explicit in the Agency Society's instructions to its lecturers, may be accounted for in various ways. In part, it was a natural reaction to the peculiar frustrations of the abolitionists in the 1820s in the face of government inaction and planter intransigence. In part, too, it may be seen as a reflection of the religious romanticism of the age as revealed in the increasing popularity, at least among the middle classes, of such notions as immediate conversion, freeing the soul from sin, and asserting the moral primacy of the individual conscience.[13] In the sense that slavery was a crime against God, and thus a concrete manifestation of sin, it deserved no quarter.

The effect of this doctrine was to give a new tone of radicalism to the movement. It was first taken up and popularized by the Young England Abolitionists, but by 1832 had been adopted by the Anti-Slavery Society too, thereby becoming a sort of measure for determining who was and who was not, in the strictest sense, an abolitionist. It also had important political implications.

In the first place, it lifted the campaign against slavery, at least in the estimation of those engaged in it, out of the realm of ordinary politics, by giving it many of the characteristics of a religious crusade. According to Stephen's account, this was partly a deliberate act of policy designed to enlist the sympathies of those who knew little about the intricacies of

[13] David Brion Davis, 'The Emergence of Immediatism in British and American Antislavery Thought', *Mississippi Valley Historical Review*, 49 (1962–3), pp. 209–30.

colonial affairs. 'There never was a case in which *vox populi, vox dei* was more completely verified, though we began by inverting the maxim, and raised the popular cry by the voice of God.' Yet immediatism involved more than a simplification of the traditional arguments for purposes of popular persuasion. Implicit in the argument was the belief that practical considerations were irrelevant and therefore the leaders of the movement need not concern themselves with them either.

In the second place, immediatism gave the slavery issue a special status. It was quite proper that other reformers should continue to work through parliament in the ordinary way, but slavery was an issue of such urgency that its opponents were automatically freed from such restraints. There were those, the Agency Society conceded, who would regard this as an infringement of parliament's prerogatives. Parliament, after all, was a deliberative body and therefore its members ought to be free to approach matters with open minds. In the ordinary way such techniques as demanding signed pledges from candidates would be entirely reprehensible. But this could 'never apply to any matter in which first principles and the immutable laws of God and nature' were involved. Blackstone himself was quite explicit on this very point. Although the term 'higher law' was not used by abolitionists in Britain at this time in the way it later was, in conjunction with similar doctrines, in the United States, the idea is plainly implied in their argument. If parliament would not agree to act voluntarily, then it must be *compelled*.[14]

What effect these notions had on the struggle over West Indian slavery it is hard to say since the government's Emancipation Bill followed so quickly on the launching of the Agency campaign. Whether this was, as Stephen liked to think, a simple case of cause and effect is questionable. Undoubtedly the agitation produced an impressive display of popular feeling, and the effects of the lobbying of MPs both in London and in their constituencies should not be discounted. But the relative decline in the importance of the West Indies to the British economy, the provocative behaviour of the colonial assemblies, the reforming spirit of the 1833 parliament, and the patient work of Buxton and his colleagues over the preceding years were also crucial factors and could, arguably, have produced the same result without the application of any outside pressure.

What is plain, however, is that the developments of these years played an important part in determining the lines along which the movement subsequently developed. It was not entirely a happy experience. Compared with other reformers of the 1830s abolitionists could regard them-

[14] Stephen, *op. cit.*, pp. 164–6, 250. Stephen's account is especially valuable in that it makes use of documents, including private instructions to Agency lecturers, which have since disappeared.

selves as peculiarly fortunate. They had inherited a functioning national organization on which they had enlarged and elaborated and with the assistance of which they had just won a resounding victory. Where others still needed to experiment and build they already had a well tested machine, responsive to their demands, and capable of bringing pressure to bear where and when they wanted. It was thus peculiarly mortifying for them to observe, in the years that followed, this machine shaking itself apart. While other movements grew, theirs waned. By the 1850s little was left but fragments.

It may be argued that the collapse of the anti-slavery movement was a necessary and inevitable corollary of the triumph of 1833. Having got rid of West Indian slavery, abolitionists were left with little to do, or at all events with not enough to do to justify maintaining an organization as elaborate as the one they had built up. Regarded from this standpoint the decline of the movement may be seen as not only inevitable but salutary, reflecting the fact that it had already achieved all or most of what could reasonably be expected of it. One could draw a parallel between the anti-slavery movement in 1833 and the Anti-Corn Law League in 1846 and say that whereas the Leaguers had the good sense to wind up their affairs, the abolitionists lingered on to endure the frustrations, disappointments and internal stresses that are the common lot of movements which outlive their usefulness.

A few abolitionists saw it this way. Sir George Stephen refused to have anything to do with the later movement and even cast doubts on its legitimacy.[15] T. B. Macaulay, who had been an active member of the Anti-Slavery Society, later told the House that any special commitment *he* felt towards the movement had ended with the abolition of slavery in those parts of the globe over which parliament exercised jurisdiction.[16]

Most abolitionists, however, rejected this view. As they saw it, the ending of West Indian slavery was not a final triumph but merely an intermediate success. There was no doubt in their minds that the colonial planters would seek to subvert the Emancipation Act in much the same way that they had got around earlier pieces of legislation. Although slavery had gone, there was every likelihood that unless a watching brief were kept on subsequent developments the West Indian Negroes would end up not as freemen but as serfs. More important was the fact that slavery still flourished on a vast scale in other parts of the world. Quantitatively speaking, the 800,000 slaves freed by the Emancipation Act were only a tiny fraction of those held in servitude. In the United States the slave population amounted to 2,750,000 and in the Americas as a whole to more than 6,000,000. As regards Africa and the East, where most slaves were held by native powers, it was impossible to

---

[15] *Ibid.*, p. 210.   [16] Hansard, 77, 26 February 1845, 1300.

make even a rough estimate, although it was assumed that the numbers were even greater.[17] No less worrying were the continuing activities of slave traders. Since Britain's withdrawal from this traffic in 1807 there had been no sign of its declining and on the basis of available evidence it actually appeared to have grown. Sir Thomas Fowell Buxton put the annual loss to Africa occasioned by the trade at 500,000. Most contemporaries, with justification, regarded this estimate as on the high side, but it was agreed that the numbers ran into hundreds of thousands.[18] Plainly the problems still to be tackled overshadowed anything that had so far been achieved.

Any suggestion, therefore, that the movement lacked issues to justify its continuence was dismissed by anti-slavery activists as utter nonsense. The issues, as they saw it, were as formidable as ever. The principal difficulty was finding ways of getting to grips with them.

This was not an entirely new problem. During the earlier struggles over the slave trade abolitionists had been aware that any final solution would depend on achieving co-ordinated international action. The slave trade, after all, was a form of international commerce in which many countries were involved. It was also true that abolitionists had regarded their role, in part at least, as being broadly educative. By publishing tracts, making speeches and encouraging discussion —which was where the auxiliary societies had had a particular contribution to make—they had sought, with a good deal of success, to bring about a change in national consciousness.

All the same, there were important differences between the situation in which they now stood and those in which they had found themselves in the past. Preaching to the unconverted was one thing; preaching to those who had already proclaimed their conversion, and who could point to specific acts of policy to prove it, was something different. However guilty Britain had been in the past, she had progressed far along the path to redemption. What more could be expected of her? More to the point, was there anything further she *could* do now that those who were guilty of sin, as well as those who were sinned against, were no longer British subjects and so not subject to Britain's authority?

A century later, those Englishmen—comparatively few by that time—

---

[17] British and Foreign Anti-Slavery Society, *Proceedings of the General Anti-Slavery Convention of 1840* (London, 1841), p. 3.

[18] T. F. Buxton, *The African Slave Trade and its Remedy* (2nd edn., London, 1840), pp. 195–202; see also James Bandinel, *Some Account of the Trade in Slaves from Africa* (London, 1842), pp. 285–7, and Hansard, 76 (16 July 1844), 924, 931, 950. The best modern estimate puts the number actually transported annually from Africa to the Americas at this time at around 50,000. Philip Curtin, *The Atlantic Slave Trade: A Census* (Madison, Wisconsin, 1969), pp. 37–49, 266.

who still felt concerned about the existence of human bondage found an appropriate forum for their activities in the League of Nations and, later, in the United Nations.[19] Had such bodies existed in the 1830s and '40s that is undoubtedly where they would have turned. Lacking such a focus for their efforts, they dreamed instead of establishing a world community of abolitionists to which individual national governments would be made morally and, where possible, politically accountable.

In the years after 1833 they laboured to make this dream a reality by sending anti-slavery delegations abroad, summoning international conferences, providing foreign abolitionists with financial subsidies, establishing model settlements in Africa, and by trying to make the West Indies a shining example of what enlightened principles, correctly applied, could achieve. That foreign governments would resent such pressures, had of course, been foreseen. That foreign abolitionists also resented them, on the grounds that they were an embarrassment, proved a disappointment. But the bitterest blow of all came when, for reasons that will be shown presently, the great mass of British liberal, middle class opinion turned against the abolitionists.

Another problem facing the movement at this time was its increasing fragmentation. Up to 1832 it had been remarkable for its institutional cohesion. On one occasion only, and then only briefly, had there been two metropolitan organizations in existence at the same time. That was in 1823–7 when the Anti-Slavery Society had begun its assault on West Indian slavery without waiting for the African Institution to wind up its affairs. But the membership of the two bodies had been largely overlapping and in any case the differences between them related to aims and areas of operation rather than to ideology or method.

The establishment of the Agency Anti-Slavery Society in 1832 thus marks a significant institutional break with the past. During the final stages of the struggle over the Emancipation Bill the two committees had, on the whole, managed to work fairly amicably together, the one concentrating its attention on working through parliament in traditional ways, the other on bringing pressure to bear from without. All the same, it was now an ineluctable fact that there were *two* national anti-slavery organizations with distinctly different views. Both were agreed that the implementation of the Emancipation Act would need careful watching. But in other respects their approaches diverged sharply. The Anti-Slavery Society believed in playing a waiting game. It was still recognizably a pressure group in the sense that it maintained offices, published the *Anti-Slavery Reporter*, and advised Buxton and other spokesmen in Parliament. But it showed little interest in maintaining the national

[19] Sir John Harris, *A Century of Emancipation* (London, 1933), pp. 225–35 and C. W. W. Greenidge, *Slavery* (London, 1958).

anti-slavery network and on one occasion only, and then only half-heartedly, did it appeal to the public for support.[20]

The history of the movement's radical branch is more complicated. Although it had refrained from making public the reasons for its breach with the Anti-Slavery Society there was a good deal of private bitterness over the way Buxton,[21] Suffield[22] and their supporters had handled matters. By agreeing to pay the planters twenty million pounds in compensation and to impose a period of apprenticeship on the freed men they had not only implicated themselves in the sin of slaveholding but had produced a much less effective bill than the radicals had hoped. Their own experience of the 1832–3 campaign had also reinforced their belief in the effectiveness of public agitation as a political weapon and the necessity of using simple moral arguments. Confronting people with the choice between right and wrong, sin and redemption, was a much surer way of getting their co-operation than by repeating parliamentary speeches.

As already noted, this was more than a propaganda device. To a remarkable degree it mirrored the radicals' own way of thinking. Joseph Sturge,[23] William Allen,[24] John Scoble,[25] George Thompson, and James Cropper, to mention the more notable radical leaders of the 1830s, saw

[20] This was during the 1837 elections when it issued a broadsheet calling for agitation against apprenticeship. *Anti-Slavery Society Minute Books*, 13 July 1837, MSS. Rhodes House, Oxford.

[21] Sir Thomas Fowell Buxton (1786–1843) was Chairman of the Anti-Slavery Society. He had begun his anti-slavery career as a member of the committee of the African Institution and, in 1824, took over from Wilberforce the parliamentary leadership of the movement.

[22] Edward Harbord, 3rd Baron Suffield (1781–1835) was leader of the anti-slavery group in the House of Lords.

[23] Joseph Sturge (1793–1859) was a Birmingham Quaker and philanthropist. He was largely responsible for the anti-apprenticeship agitation of the 1830s and in 1839 founded the British and Foreign Anti-Slavery Society. He had earlier been an active member of Thomas Attwood's Birmingham Political Union, in 1841 founded the Complete Suffrage Movement, and throughout his life was a staunch supporter of the Peace Society, of which he was for some years president. At the time of his death he was actively involved in sponsoring adult education, building playgrounds for poor Birmingham children and maintaining out of his own pocket an institution for the reform of delinquent boys. He was an early supporter of the free trade movement, but like many other abolitionists, he broke with it over the sugar issue.

[24] William Allen (1770–1843), London Quaker and founder of the pharmaceutical firm of Allen and Hanburys Ltd. He was a close friend of Wilberforce and Clarkson and served on the committees of the Society for the Abolition of the Slave Trade, the African Institution, and the Anti-Slavery Society. In addition to his anti-slavery work, he campaigned for the abolition of capital punishment and was for a time Robert Owen's partner in running the New Lanark Mills project.

[25] John Scoble (180?–187?) was one of the original salaried lecturers employed by the Agency committee. He was later secretary of the Society for the Universal Abolition of Slavery and the Slave Trade and of the British and Foreign Anti-Slavery Society. In 1852 he became Superintendent of the Dawn Institute, an institution for the settlement of American fugitive slaves in Canada.

the slavery issue—and many other issues besides—in just this light. It is no coincidence that their writings, heavily larded with religious rhetoric and allusions to individual conscience, reveal the workings of minds more at home in the religious than the political sphere. To such minds, politics, like religion, was a matter of first principles.

It was also no coincidence that of the two wings of the movement the radical was the more international-minded, for if morality transcended politics it transcended national boundaries too. In part, of course, internationalism was a necessary condition of the movements continuance. Buxton, although he did not entirely share the radicals' assumptions, also began looking abroad for new fields of action. Nevertheless, the moral impulse of the radicals' beliefs gave the movement a force and direction which it would otherwise have lacked.

The way their minds were turning was revealed in February, 1834, by the transformation of the Agency Society into the British and Foreign Society for the Universal Abolition of Slavery and the Slave Trade (1834–6). The immediate aim of this body was to sponsor anti-slavery missions to foreign countries, beginning with the United States where a national anti-slavery society, modelled on the radicals' own and with a similar commitment to immediatism, had lately been established. William Lloyd Garrison[26] had spent the summer of 1833 in Britain and had extended an invitation to George Thompson, the most successful of the Agency lecturers, to visit America. The Anti-Slavery Society was dubious about this enterprise. But the Edinburgh and Glasgow societies, with which Thompson had maintained close connections, expressed a willingness to put up most of the money needed, and the Universal Abolition Society undertook to provide the rest.

This venture did not work out quite as had been hoped. Americans, it soon became evident, did not take kindly to foreigners who meddled in their affairs, especially on so sensitive an issue as slavery. So stormy was Thompson's reception that his hosts feared for his life and were relieved when finally he departed on a package steamer bound for Nova Scotia.[27]

But the principal check to these international schemes were the tidings from Britain's own West Indian Colonies. Radicals had objected to apprenticeship on the grounds that it was merely slavery under another name; the accounts now reaching them convinced them that it was something much worse. The introduction of treadmills into Jamaica

[26] William Lloyd Garrison (1805–79) editor of *The Liberator* and later to become the leader of the extreme radical wing of the American anti-slavery movement. In 1840 he assumed control of the American Anti-Slavery Society. His 'ultraism' and habit of linking anti-slavery with other issues, such as women's rights, effectively divided the movement on both sides of the Atlantic.

[27] C. Duncan Rice, 'The Anti-Slavery Mission of George Thompson to the United States, 1834–1835', *Journal of American Studies*, 2, 1968, pp. 13–31.

the continuence of corporal punishment, the ineffectualness of the special magistrates sent out from Britain, and, above all, the determination of the planters to extract as much labour as possible before 1840 when the whole system would be swept away, had, so it was claimed, made the lot of the Negroes more wretched than ever. This was something of an exaggeration,[28] although in some respects—the treadmills being a case in point—the new dispensation was harsher than the old. But the reports were enough to convince the radicals, and in particular Joseph Sturge, who now emerged as their leader, that further agitation was needed.

Meanwhile, relations between the two national committees had been deteriorating. Buxton, who was chairman of the Anti-Slavery Society and leader of the abolitionist group in parliament, remained convinced that the best way of proceeding was to continue working from within parliament, lobbying ministers, asking questions, and tabling motions. To the Sturgites this looked like mere time-serving. Parliament had imposed apprenticeship and could hardly be expected to rescind its action unless its hand were forced. Replying to queries from provincial groups, the Universal Abolition Society charged the Buxtonites with timorousness and inertia. Since these groups had been kept in ignorance of the divisions in the anti-slavery leadership, they were surprised and disquieted. In November, 1835, the Sturgites went further by publishing a letter in *The Times*[29] officially dissociating themselves from the policies Buxton had lately been pursuing in the Commons. In a private letter Sturge told Buxton that he felt he could no longer co-operate with one who placed expediency above principle.

What the radicals now wanted was a return to the methods of 1832–3. Apart from a lack of support from the movement's parliamentary leaders, the principal difficulty facing them was the need for precise information about what was going on in the colonies. This problem they solved by sending a group of observers, led by Sturge himself, to the West Indies.[30] It was also clear that to launch a major campaign against apprenticeship would mean putting aside, at least for the time being, their plans for making the anti-slavery movement an international enterprise. Accordingly, a new body, the Central Negro Emancipation Committee (1837–9), was established. The Anti-Slavery Society agreed to send a delegation to its inaugural meeting, held in Exeter Hall in

---

[28] See W. L. Mathieson, *British Slavery and its Abolition, 1823–1838* (London, 1926), and W. L. Burn, *Emancipation and Apprenticeship in the British West Indies* (London, 1937).

[29] *The Times*, 28 November 1835.

[30] Joseph Sturge and Thomas Harvey, *The West Indies in 1837, being the Journal of a Visit to Antigua and Jamaica . . . for the Purpose of Ascertaining the Actual Condition of The Negro Population* (London, 1838).

November, 1837, but on hearing the delegates' report it declined to undertake joint action.[31]

This was no great disappointment for it was evident from the first that the Emancipation committee was well able to stand on its own feet. Its financial resources, were, in fact, greater than those of any of its predecessors, amounting to £4,466 in the first nine months of operation.[32] As always, the most generous donors were Quakers. As in 1789–92 and 1831–3 the agitation was largely paid for by members of the Society of Friends.

The methods, too, were familiar; so also were most of the faces. To a remarkable degree the apprenticeship agitation simply took over where the slavery agitation had left off, the declared object being to achieve, by means of outside pressure, what the anti-slavery group within parliament, because of its pusillanimity and neglect of correct principles, had failed to achieve. And, once again, the government found itself stonewalling in the face of mounting popular indignation as expressed through tracts, newspaper articles, public meetings, placards and a flood of petitions from provincial organizations. The first motion for the ending of apprenticeship was easily defeated, but as the pressure mounted votes began to shift with the result that on 22 May 1838, on a snap division in a thinly attended House, a motion for the ending of apprenticeship was actually passed. This decision was subsequently reversed by government intervention. Whether the government would have continued to take this line is doubtful. In the end, however, it was the West Indian assemblies, mindful of what had been passing in Britain but also weary of the problems of coping with a labour force half slave and half free, that settled the issue by agreeing to end apprenticeship as of 1 August 1838.

It was now evident to abolitionists of all persuasions that if the anti-slavery movement were to continue in any form at all a reassessment of goals would be needed. This brought them back to the problems they had already begun discussing in 1834 and '35. As before, the question was not finding issues worthy of their attention—the problems stood out as sharply and intractably as ever—but choosing which ones to tackle and agreeing on ways of approaching them.

It was a situation which would have tested the unity of any movement, but to the abolitionists, divided as they already were, it brought a sense of peculiar bafflement. Most were agreed that the two pressing issues were the Atlantic slave trade and American slavery. But there were also such questions as native slavery in British India, slavery in the colonies of various European powers, Arab slavery and slave trading,

[31] *Anti-Slavery Society Minute Books*, 13–16 November 1837, MSS. Rhodes House, Oxford; *British Emancipator*, December 1837.
[32] For details of the committee's finances see *British Emancipator* (1837–40).

British consumption of slave produce, and the holding of slaves by British nationals abroad. The list was almost infinitely extendible. And even when it was narrowed down to a single issue there was no guaranteeing that any two abolitionists would see eye to eye on what needed to be done.

The result, predictably, was a proliferation of new organizations. In 1839 alone three new central committees were established: Buxton's African Civilization Society, Sturge's British and Foreign Anti-Slavery Society, and Joseph Pease's and George Thompson's British India Society. The movement's provincial supporters were understandably non-plussed. Some, unable to decide which of these bodies to support, pursued independent courses of their own, so complicating matters yet further. At the time it was possible to claim that these developments demonstrated a healthy broadening of the movement; in retrospect it looks more as though it was falling apart.[33]

Still, a measure of cohesion might have been maintained if these new policies had produced practical results. To the general public the most impressive looking of these new bodies was the African Civilization Society. It was also the one which, in terms of structure, came closest to being a political pressure group in the narrow sense of depending on the support of a small but influential clique within Westminster. There was nothing narrow, however, about Buxton's aims. Since his retirement from parliament in 1837 he had devoted himself to studying the workings of the African slave trade and had quickly reached the conclusion that Britain's traditional method of combating it by means of naval patrols was ineffective. So great was the profit to be made from a single voyage to Cuba or Brazil that however much effort was put into blockading the African coast enough slavers would always get through to make the attempt worthwhile. The proper point at which to attack the trade, therefore, was not on the coast but at its place of origin within the African interior. Britain's object should be to get the Africans themselves to give up the traffic by persuading them that selling ivory or palm oil was not only morally more desirable but financially more profitable than selling one another. The first step was to sponsor a pilot project by planting a settlement on the upper reaches of the Niger. From this other projects would follow.[34]

Whatever else may be said about Buxton's scheme, it was not lacking in boldness. The most impressive feature of it, however, was the list of those prepared to lend it their support. At its head stood Prince Albert, who agreed to become the Society's patron and president. There

[33] For a more detailed account of anti-slavery activities in these years see H. Temperley, *British Antislavery 1833–1870* (London, 1972).
[34] Buxton, pp. 344–61.

followed a catalogue of archbishops, dukes, marquises, earls, bishops, MPs and, at the very bottom, a handful of prominent Quakers. These, collectively, constituted the officers of the Society. When Buxton had first approached the Melbourne cabinet with his scheme its response had been to suggest modifying it in such a way as to make it innocuous. But the Whig's position in parliament was weak. Confronted by the formidable array of establishment support Buxton commanded, it promptly gave way and agreed to place the necessary vessels and personnel at his disposal.[35]

The Niger expedition, which set sail from Devonport on 12 May 1841, ended in total fiasco. The three vessels, built specifically for the purpose at a cost of £100,000, reached the Niger safely enough. But once on the river, fever began its ravages and one after another they were obliged to turn back. Forty-four of the 303 passengers and crew who set out died of fever and nine others from miscellaneous causes. Many of those who escaped death were severely debilitated. 'We might indeed be considered as having been in a battle,' wrote one survivor. 'We in fact only retreated with strength enough to carry away our *wounded*.' The last remaining hope disappeared when, in the summer of 1842, a scratch crew went back to see how the model farm, which had been planted at the confluence of the Niger and the Benue, was faring. It was found that the superintendent had been murdered and that the settlers, most of whom had been recruited in Sierra Leone, had begun preying on the surrounding tribes and that slavery—or something very like it—had been established. The farm was accordingly abandoned.[36]

It was a failure that cost the abolitionists dearly. The subsequent parliamentary enquiry confirmed the impression that the whole project had been ill-conceived. Heartbroken at the collapse of his plans, Buxton retired from public life. The African Civilization Society wound up its affairs quickly and discreetly. But the memory remained. Ten years later, when Dickens needed a project to match the absurdity of Mrs Jellyby he chose the settlement of 'Borrioboula Gha on the left bank of the Niger' where 'the climate [was] the finest in the world.'

Meanwhile, the other branches of the movement had also run into trouble. The British India Society[37] had begun its career by boldly claiming that the ending of the African slave trade and the overthrow of

[35] J. Gallagher, 'Fowell Buxton and the New African Policy, 1838–1842', *Cambridge Historical Journal*, 10, 1950–52, pp. 36–58.

[36] William Allen and T. R. H. Thomson, *A Narrative of the Expedition . . . to the River Niger in 1841* (2 volumes, London, 1848).

[37] The British India Society was launched at a public meeting held in Freemasons Hall, 6 July 1839. For an account of its activities see *British India Advocate* (London, 1841–2), and John Hyslop Bell, *British Folks and British India Fifty Years Ago: Joseph Pease and his Contemporaries* (London, 1891).

American slavery were dependent on reforming the administration of India. In support of this unlikely contention it produced figures purporting to show that the cost of maintaining a slave in America was five times that of employing a free labourer in Bengal. Once the agricultural potential of India had been realized the whole structure of New World slavery would come tumbling to the ground. These notions gave rise to a good deal of speculation but not many took them very seriously and a few wondered just how free a Bengali labourer whose earnings were so small might be. By 1842 interest in this particular line of endeavour had waned.

Sturge's British and Foreign Anti-Slavery Society proved more enduring. Indeed, allowing for miscellaneous amalgamations and changes of name, it still exists. Initially, support for it came mainly from those who had earlier backed the radical branch of the movement. A large proportion of these were Quakers. Of the original thirty members of the metropolitan committee fifteen were members of the Society of Friends. Most of the rest were dissenters of one persuasion or another.[38] Much the same holds true of provincial organizations, of which there were still some seventy in existence. A few gave their allegiance to Buxton or Thompson or followed independent courses of their own. But most agreed to become auxiliaries of the British and Foreign Anti-Slavery Society. Since the failure of the Buxtonites to help in the apprenticeship agitation the radicals had virtually taken over the popular movement.

To the extent that the Society acted as a watchdog whose responsibility it was to keep an eye on British policy, this support was important. During the 1840s it was employed in harrying successive governments over such matters as freedmen's rights in the West Indies, the regulation of the traffic in indentured labourers to the British colonies, and the right of American fugitives to take refuge in Canada. The Society's principal aim, however, was to foster the growth of anti-slavery movements abroad. Unlike Buxton, Sturge had no faith in African schemes, or, for that matter, in the government's policy of seeking to suppress the slave trade by means of Britain's naval strength—a policy to which, as a pacifist, he also had strong moral objections. In his view, the only way of ending the trade was by abolishing slavery itself. To this end he looked to the establishment of anti-slavery organizations overseas, encouraged and sustained by support from Britain.

As a first step, the Society set about organizing a world convention.[39]

[38] The occupations, religious affiliations and previous anti-slavery connections of committee members are given in H. Temperley, 'The British and Foreign Anti-Slavery Society, 1839–1868' (Yale Ph.D. dissertation, 1961), appendices 1 and 2.

[39] British and Foreign Anti-Slavery Society, *Proceedings of the General Anti-Slavery Convention Called by the Committee of the British and Foreign Anti-Slavery Society, 12 June to 23 June, 1840* (London, 1841).

This gathering, which assembled in London in the summer of 1840, attracted a good deal of attention. It was the most formidable array of abolitionist talent ever brought together. More than fifty delegates attended from the United States, and there were sizeable contingents from the continent and the West Indies. Its early proceedings were slightly marred by a wrangle which developed over the seating of American women delegates, but otherwise all went smoothly. Handsome tributes were paid to the British for having taken the lead in the struggle against slavery and for continuing their efforts now that their own house had been set in order. Altogether it seemed an auspicious beginning.

Within a matter of weeks, however, the Society was in serious trouble. The problem was sugar, or more precisely the decision of the Melbourne government to modify the discriminatory duties which gave colonial producers an effective monopoly of the British market. Traditionally, Britain had got her sugar from the West Indies, but in the 1820s and '30s her market had been opened to Mauritian and East Indian producers also. In terms of price and quality these colonial sugars had compared not unfavourably with those produced elsewhere, so that Britain had been able to supply not only her own needs but those of much of Europe as well. Even without the tariff system it is unlikely that very much foreign produced sugar would have found its way on to the British market.

But by 1840 things had changed. Sugar consumption in Britain had gone up while colonial production had been going down. Partly it was a matter of worn out lands and a shortage of labour. But emancipation had not helped. In many cases the Negroes had responded to emancipation by moving off the plantations. As a result, the sugar exports of Jamaica had been cut by half. This was in marked contrast to what was happening in Cuba and Brazil where, with the help of massive importations of slaves, production was rising rapidly. British producers simply could not compete.

As might be expected, the rising price of sugar in Britain was a source of grievance, particularly when it became known that prices elsewhere were falling. Such discrepancies would have been easier to bear had they arisen from the government's legitimate need for revenue. But this was patently not the case. It was the planters, not the exchequer, who profited. Like the Corn Laws, with which they inevitably became associated in the popular mind, the sugar duties presented a clear-cut case of legislation designed to benefit one section of the population at the expense of the rest.

The Sturgites were perfectly well aware of these aspects of the problem. Sturge himself had been a founder member of the Anti-Corn Law League and his colleagues were, virtually to a man, free-traders. What gave them pause, in this instance, was the intimate connection between sugar and slavery. If reducing the tariff on foreign sugar meant throwing open the British market to slave-grown sugar—which was clearly what it *did* mean—then they could hardly refuse to speak out against it. What was involved however, was much more than the undesirability of consuming 'blood-stained produce'. As they saw it, there was also the future of the West Indies at stake. They did not care at all about the prosperity of the planters, whom they would have been happy to see go bankrupt, but they did care very much about what happened to the freedmen. The economic ruin of the colonies was not reconcilable with their own aim to make them a show piece. The over-riding issue, however, was the impulse which such a decision would give to the slave trade. It was a simple matter of supply and demand. When the world demand for sugar rose, prices increased, the need for labour grew, and the slave trade expanded; when it fell, prices dropped, the need for labour declined, and the slave trade lagged. So, by opening her ports to Brazilian and Cuban sugar, Britain would be buying produce paid for by the lives of some hundreds of thousands of Africans.

It is hard to see what the Society could have done but oppose the free-traders on this particular issue. Nevertheless it was a decision that tore the movement apart. In all the major industrial centres the auxiliary societies rebelled. Within the metropolitan committee itself there was dissension resulting in members being drummed out. Outsiders were were amazed to see what they had taken to be a liberal organization, apparently engaged in lobbying on behalf of West Indian planters and Tory protectionists. The situation was made the more difficult for the Society by the way in which former opponents, availing themselves of the abolitionists arguments, hastened to proclaim themselves converts to the cause. Altogether it looked as if the abolitionists had got themselves into some very odd company.

The effects on the movement were exacerbated by the fact that the controversy dragged on for so long. Had the Whigs succeeded in carrying their motion in 1841 the destruction would have been considerable, but there would have been enough of a movement left to be worth patching together at the end. As it was, the struggle continued until 1846 when the Whigs, once more in office, pushed through a measure even harsher than the one the Society had originally opposed in that, instead of merely reducing the margin of colonial preference, it abolished it altogether. The Society derived some satisfaction from the fact that it had helped delay the admission of slave-grown sugar and thereby the date at

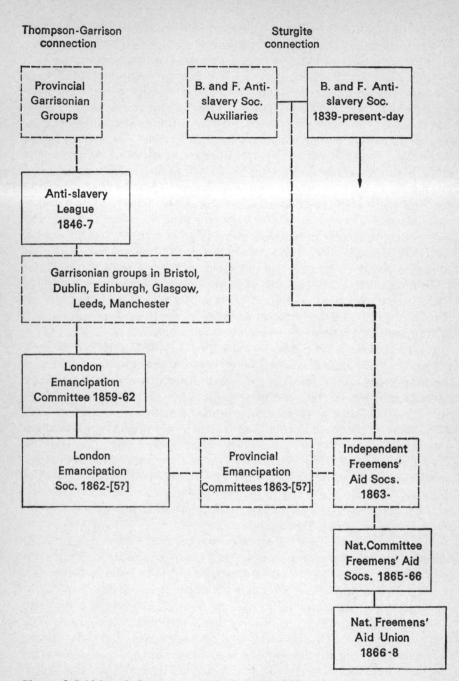

Figure 2 *British anti-slavery organizations, 1840–1868*

which the predicted expansion of the slave trade occurred. But, in the late '40s, with the slave trade at double its previous level and its own organization in ruins, this was meagre consolation.[40]

Its stand over the sugar duties was not the only issue which lost the Society support during these years. It had also, through no fault of its own, become the object of bitter attacks from rival anti-slavery groups. These difficulties stemmed from an essentially American feud caused by the increasingly radical pronouncements of Garrison and his supporters on matters only marginally related to the cause and their refusal to relinquish the high ground of moral principle by assisting in the political campaign against slavery. Although only a minority of American abolitionists supported him, Garrison had managed to take over the national organization, which he proceeded to use as a platform to denounce all who disagreed with him. The British and Foreign Anti-Slavery Society became embroiled in this controversy as a result of the World Convention at which it supported the main body of American delegates by refusing to seat the Garrisonian women. The high feeling this aroused would doubtless soon have subsided had it not been for visits to Britain by Garrisonian agents, mostly soliciting funds, who toured the country denouncing not only American slaveholders but their alleged allies, the members of the British and Foreign Anti-Slavery Society. The problem became more complicated when a number of provincial organizations, the most notably being those in Glasgow, Edinburgh, Dublin and Bristol, were converted to Garrisonianism and took up the cry. It would appear that Garrisonianism held a particular attraction for Unitarians, but it also received the support of a number of groups and individuals who, again for reasons mostly unconnected with the cause, simply did not like the London Quakers.[41]

Garrison, in fact, had carried the 'higher law' argument through to the point where he refused to have anything to do with politics at all. Few members of the general public actually believed that the British and Foreign Anti-Slavery Society by supporting those American abolitionists who believed in working through political channels, had made itself 'a bulwark of American slavery'. But the internal dissension which such charges engendered helped convince many that the cause was no longer worthy of their support.

Thus, by the 1850s, anti-slavery was no longer the political force it

[40] Temperley, *British Antislavery*, pp. 137–67.
[41] *British Antislavery*, pp. 191–247. These Garrisonian feuds are described in detail in Louis Billington 'Some Connections Between British and American Reform Movements, 1830–1860, with Special Reference to the Anti-Slavery Movement' (unpublished M.A. dissertation, University of Bristol, 1966) and C. Duncan Rice, 'The Scottish Factor in the Fight Against American Slavery' (unpublished Ph.D. dissertation, University of Edinburgh, 1969).

had once been. That there was still a fair amount of genuine anti-slavery feeling in the country was revealed by the enthusiastic response given to Harriet Beecher Stowe and other abolitionist visitors. People who showed no interest in supporting anti-slavery organizations in Britain responded readily to the solicitations of foreigners.

During the 1860s the movement showed some signs of revival. Support for the Unionist cause in the American Civil War was expressed through George Thompson and F. W. Chesson's[42] London Emancipation committee[43] and its numerous provincial affiliates. Much of this activity, however, stemmed from a desire to counteract the propagandistic efforts of the various pro-Confederate groups which, during the early stages of the war, had sprung up around the country, rather than from any deep commitment to anti-slavery. The Quakers, whose concern over American slavery *was* genuine, were prevented by their pacifist principles from engaging in these activities. However they played a prominent part in the subsequent freedmen's aid movement, which between 1864 and 1868, managed to collect some £120,000 for the support and re-settlement of Negroes in the American South.[44]

This extraordinary burst of generosity effectively marks the end of the British anti-slavery movement, at least as a popular cause. The British and Foreign Anti-Slavery Society continued its operations up to the end of the century and beyond. The main focus of its attention was now Africa. From time to time spokesmen in parliament were heard demanding the further extension of British rule or the removal of this or that administrative anomaly. By and large, however, it had become an in-

[42] Frederick William Chesson (1833–88) was George Thompson's son-in-law. In 1851 he founded the Manchester Anti-Slavery Union and launched the *Anti-Slavery Watchman*. As a Garrisonian he disapproved of the policies of the British and Foreign Anti-Slavery Society and when the M.A.-S.U. agreed to sponsor an anti-Garrisonian lecturer he resigned and set about establishing a rival organization, the North of England Anti-Slavery and India Reform League. From 1855 until 1888 he was Secretary of the Aborigines Protection Society.

[43] The London Emancipation Committee was a Garrisonian organization founded by Chesson and Thompson in 1859. There had been two earlier attempts (in 1846 and 1852) to establish metropolitan Garrisonian bodies. Like its predecessors, this one would no doubt soon have collapsed had it not been for the American Civil War. In 1862, following Lincoln's Preliminary Emancipation Proclamation, it was reorganized as the London Emancipation Society and during the last two years of the war was actively engaged in sponsoring pro-Union activity in Britain.

[44] Thomas Phillips to General O. O. Howard, 7 July 1868, British and Foreign Anti-Slavery Society Papers, MSS., Rhodes House, Oxford. By the end of the Civil War there were some fifty freedmen's aid organizations in Britain. The dominant figure in the enterprise was Joseph Sturge's son-in-law, Arthur Albright (1811–1900), a Birmingham Quaker. In May 1865 an attempt was made to pool resources by establishing the National committee of British Freedmen's Aid Societies, which gave way the following year to the National Freedmen's Aid Union (1866–8). For an account of their activities see Christine Bolt, *The Anti-Slavery Movement and Reconstruction* (London, 1969).

formation gathering agency. Auxiliaries no longer played any part in its affairs. The amount of paper work handled by its secretary grew enormously. Members still felt that they were performing a useful function and took pride in the fact that they still could, on occasion, shame the government into action. But, as a *popular* movement, anti-slavery was dead.

Further Reading

The best general accounts of British anti-slavery activity up to 1833 are still F. J. Klingberg's *The Anti-Slavery Movement in England* (New Haven, 1926) and Sir Reginald Coupland's *The British Anti-Slavery Movement* (London, 1933). However neither has much to say about the way anti-slavery efforts were organized at the grass roots level. So far no detailed treatment of this subject has appeared in print, although it is fairly extensively dealt with in the Hunt and Lipscomb theses cited in my footnotes. Klingberg and Coupland are also weak on the economic background to abolition. This aspect is taken up by Eric Williams in *Capitalism and Slavery* (Chapel Hill, 1944) who asserts that economic considerations largely determined British policy. That Williams's claims are exaggerated, and his scholarship often defective, is shown in Roger Anstey '*Capitalism and Slavery*: A Critique', *Economic History Review*, 21 (1968), 307–20. Developments after 1833 are covered in Howard Temperley, *British Antislavery, 1833–1870* (London, 1972), which also had a good deal to say about the American connection.

The influence of anti-slavery ideas on the making of colonial policy and their reception in the colonies are described in W. L. Mathieson's *British Slavery and its Abolition, 1823–1838* (London, 1926); *British Slave Emancipation, 1838–1849* (London, 1932); *The Sugar Colonies and Governor Eyre* (London, 1936); W. L. Burn's, *Emancipation and Apprenticeship in the British West Indies* (London, 1937), and Philip Curtin's, *Two Jamaicas: The Role of Ideas in a Tropical Colony, 1830–1865* (Cambridge, Mass., 1955). The other major governmental concern of these years, the suppression of the Atlantic slave trade, is dealt with in W. L. Mathieson's *Great Britain and the Slave Trade, 1839–1865* (London, 1929) and Christopher Lloyd's *The Navy and the Slave Trade: the Suppression of the African Slave Trade in the Nineteenth Century* (London, 1949).

3
The Philosophic Radicals
William Thomas

'A Radical party which does not rest upon the masses, is no better than a nonentity.' Most people would agree with the opinion, but a few would be surprised to know its author, and still more the occasion. For it was written by J. S. Mill in 1837, in the *London and Westminster Review*.[1] Mill and his friends in parliament had just been discouraged by the results of the general election, and in a few years, disillusioned with politics and alarmed by Chartism, they retired from parliament. Mill's words were intended as a rallying cry, but now read like an epitaph. The radicals he exhorted never had provided a voice for the masses in parliament. The reformed parliament, five years old when Mill wrote, proved resistant to the formation of a mass party, and began shortly to experience the 'pressure from without' in a form more intense than could have been conceived by the unreformed legislature which went before. The philosophic radicals were left trying to advance popular measures in a hostile atmosphere. Mill, in the same article, said they were the men, who, until universal suffrage was possible, wanted to do everything for the good of the working classes which would be needed if it were realized.[2] It is not clear how many of them would have agreed with this description. At any rate, it did not impress the working classes; while the upper classes were downright hostile. The group was ground between the upper and nether millstones of the two great parties, without even the gratification of popular sympathy.

This failure was an important factor in the revival of popular agitation outside parliament in the late 1830s. But it has been little studied or even acknowledged. One reason for this neglect is that historians have persisted in seeing the philosophic radicals as theorists rather than actors; as formulators of a policy which others applied, rather than as politicians in their own right. This habit of mind has a long history. Gladstonian liberals, perplexed by disagreements within their own

[1] *L[ondon] & W[estminster] R[eview]* volume vi, October 1837, p. 16.
[2] *Ibid.*, p. 18.

ranks, tended to exaggerate the doctrinal purity and practical single-mindedness of their forerunners of the age of Grey and Peel. Of course men as divergent in outlook as John Morley and J. F. Stephen, H. S. Maine and A. V. Dicey, chose to stress different parts of the utilitarian writings in their search for the essence of liberalism.[3] But they all agreed, with Acton's phrase, 'to go behind the men and grasp ideas', and this meant studying not the philosophic radicals in their short-lived political careers, but philosophic radicalism as a continuous doctrine. Such failure as they admitted to seeing, was the effect of inner contradictions in the creed, not of political obstacles to its operation. And what began as a decorous sort of political polemic passed into historical scholarship. Halévy gave his authority to the scattered and impressionistic suggestions of Morley, Maine and others, that the philosophic radicals were the men who gave the Victorian Liberal party, if not its leadership, at least its programme and its real claims to popular allegiance.[4] The failure of the men was finally merged and lost in the success of the creed.

For our purposes, the most important point is that the philosophic radicals whom Mill was urging on in 1837 were not exclusively or even necessarily followers of Bentham and James Mill. The name had a more modest function, and a still more modest success. It was not even meant to apply exclusively to the adherents of a particular philosophy.[5] It is

[3] The literature on this topic is vast. For a few samples, see John Morley's 'Valedictory' article in *Fortnightly Review* volume xxxii. no. 90, October 1882, p. 521; H. S. Maine's 'Radical Patriarchalism' and 'Radicalism Old and New', in *St James's Gazette*, 18 June 1880, pp. 259–60, and 25 January 1881, pp. 11–12. Leslie Stephen discusses his brother's utilitarianism in the *Life of Sir James Fitzjames Stephen* (2nd edn 1895), pp. 306–40. A. V. Dicey's *Lectures on the Relation between Law and Public Opinion in England during the Nineteenth Century* (1905), ignores a caution of Leslie Stephen's and boldly, and wrongly, equates Benthamism with 'individualism'. It has become, far more than the more accurate work of Stephen, the text for much subsequent writing on Bentham's influence on Victorian legislation.

[4] E. Halévy's *The Growth of Philosophic Radicalism* (trans. Mary Morris 1928) included in that term many doctrines, notably Ricardo's economic theory and Malthus's theory of population, which were not the peculiar property of John Mill and his circle, but were held by many Whigs and even liberal Tories. He also neglected much of the Scottish enlightenment, dealing with Hume and Smith, but ignoring John Millar, Adam Ferguson and William Robertson. He thus tended to exaggerate the influence of Bentham and his followers, if only by underrating other sources of liberal thought, and did little to qualify the claims made, with much less learning, by Dicey. Following Halévy and Dicey, students of nineteenth century government are still strangely preoccupied with finding 'Benthamites' behind every hedge. For a recent example, see Professor S. E. Finer's 'The Transmission of Benthamite Ideas, 1820–50' in G. Sutherland (ed.), *Studies in the Growth of Nineteenth Century Government* (1972), pp. 11–32.

[5] J. Hamburger's *Intellectuals in Politics: J. S. Mill and the Philosophic Radicals* (New Haven and London, 1965) is the only study of the political careers of the group. Professor Hamburger stresses their commitment to a unifying 'ideology', but to do this he pushes Bentham into the background and gives James Mill the chief influence on the group.

true that the men who drew most heavily upon the writings and teach-
ings of Bentham and James Mill formed the nucleus of the group.
George Grote, J. A. Roebuck, and John Mill himself were 'orthodox'
utilitarians who had taken part in the first propaganda in the *Westminster Review* and the *Parliamentary History and Review* and they strove to
make their political activities harmonize with their political theory.
Their careers can hardly be described without a full consideration of the
ideas of their preceptors.[6] But even these most loyal of the followers of
Bentham and James Mill carried the philosophy in different directions,
according to temperament and circumstances; Grote into the history of
ancient Greece; John Mill into an abstract analysis of the methods of the
social sciences; Roebuck into more active agitation than either. Not all
the members of the circle made such full acknowledgment of the influence of Bentham and Mill, however, and some who did remained
outside active politics. John Austin, whom Roebuck called 'the first
head among us',[7] was satisfied by the Reform Act, and drawn increasingly into an admiration of the political system of Prussia. His wife, the
'dear Mütterlein' of John Mill's earlier letters, described herself defi-
antly as 'a Radical and an Absolutist'.[8] Others joined the group apparently without being subjected to an ideological test. Charles Buller[9]
and J. T. Leader[10] were both men of means whose speeches show very

[6] John Mill, at a time when he was rather inclined to call the older members of
the utilitarian circle rather narrow, said that Grote's opinions were narrower than
most, and largely indebted to the teaching of James Mill; see F. E. Mineka (ed.),
Earlier Letters of J. S. Mill (1963) i, 170–71. A. Momigliano (*Studies in Historiography*
[1966], p. 63) greets this opinion with incredulity; but while it may not apply to the
composition of *The History of Greece*, of Grote's opinions to 1833 it seems to me substantially true. Mill had allowed that Roebuck by that time was rid of his 'strait
jacket' (*Earlier Letters*, i. 87).

[7] Bodleian Library, MS. Eng. lett. c. 295 fo 171, J. A. Roebuck to Henrietta
Falconer (his future wife), 26 October 1833. John Austin (1790–1859), author of
The Province of Jurisprudence Determined (1832); appointed, after an unsuccessful period
as Professor at the new London University, to Brougham's Criminal Law Commission, from which he also resigned. A scrupulous man, he became more conservative
as he grew older and received a sharply unsympathetic portrait in John Mill's
Autobiography.

[8] Carlyle MSS., National Library of Scotland, MS. 1774, ff. 32–3, letter to Jane
Carlyle, 25 December 1832. She made the same claim to Brougham, only this time
omitted the radicalism; see Brougham MSS., University College, London, letter of
25 May 1835. Sarah Austin (1793–1867) was the translator of Goethe, Falk and
Ranke. Her brief biography is in Janet Ross, *Three Generations of Englishwomen* (1892).

[9] Charles Buller (1806–48) was descended from a family of Cornish gentry:
educated at Edinburgh and Cambridge; between the two periods he was a pupil of
Carlyle, who pronounced him 'the genialest radical I have ever met'. Macaulay
thought his speeches marred by 'too strong a propensity for jokes'.

[10] John Temple Leader (1810–1903) shared with Burdett not only the famous
Westminster by-election of 1837 but also the fact that he was educated at Christ
Church. In 1842 he moved the hearing of the Chartist petitioners at the bar of the
House. He left England in 1844 for Cannes and finally settled in Florence and wrote
a biography of the English *condottiere* Sir John Hawkwood. His *Rough and Rambling*

little of the doctrinal loyalty of Roebuck to the writings of the elder Mill.
Sir William Molesworth joined Grote out of admiration for his speeches
in the first session of the reformed parliament.[11] Socially, he belonged to
the same class as Leader and Buller, and Roebuck welcomed his addition to the group because in such an aristocratic country as England it
was important to have among them 'a *rich* man, of good standing and
rank'.[12] Molesworth was much more doctrinaire than the other two, but
even he found it hard to blend broad acres and deep study, and in his
early political career wavered between being a subversive theorist and
an aristocratic *frondeur*. The result was that even his friends could not
take him seriously. Other members of the group in parliament like
William Clay,[19] Benjamin Hawes[14] and Henry Warburton,[15] further
diluted the doctrinal purity of the original sect or coterie which had in
the 1820s run (or ruined) the first *Westminster Review* and given so stark
and unyielding an impression of their views in the London Debating
Society. The real training in utilitarian principles had, in fact, preceded
political prominence, and the later philosophic radicals, like raw con-
scripts in war, were hastily trained and superficially versed in the
parade-ground drill of the regulars. They also had less staying power.
John Mill's name for them, itself a symptom of the disunity of the parliamentary radicals after 1832, was evidently meant to invite unity without
abandoning the essential motive which he thought should be common
to all radicals. He described the various 'schools' of radicals:

> There are the historical radicals, who demand popular institutions as
> the inheritance of Englishmen, transmitted to us from the Saxons or
> the barons of Runnymeade. There are the metaphysical radicals, who
> hold the principles of democracy not as means to good government,
> but as corollaries from some unreal abstraction—from 'natural

Notes, chiefly of my Early Life (Florence 1899) contains less information than the notice
in the DNB Supplement.
   11 Sir William Molesworth to Lady Molesworth (his mother), 5 March 1833, MS.
in private hands; Harriet Grote, *The Philosophical Radicals of 1832* (1866), p. 1. This
is a memoir of Molesworth, written after his death (in 1855) and interspersed with
Mrs Grote's own piquant comments. Mrs Fawcett's *Life* (1901), is the only full
biography.
   12 R. E. Leader, *Autobiography and Letters of J. A. Roebuck* (1897), p. 81.
   13 William Clay (1791–1869), MP for Tower Hamlets from 1832 to 1857; Secretary
to the Board of Control 1839; baronet 1841.
   14 Benjamin Hawes (1797–1862), MP for Lambeth 1832–47, for Kinsale 1848–52;
in 1846 he became Under-Secretary of State for Colonies; K.C.B. 1856.
   15 Henry Warburton (1784?–1858), son of a timber-merchant; educated Eton and
Trinity College, Cambridge. A friend of Ricardo and of Althorp, and an habitué of
the 'Grote conclave'. He resigned his seat at Bridport (see below) in 1841 because of
his colleague's bribery. He sent the circulars to O'Connell which brought the Irish
party to the meeting at Lichfield House where 'the compact' was concluded. Retired
from politics 1847.

liberty', or 'natural rights'. There are the radicals of occasion and circumstance, who are radicals because they disapprove the measures of the government for the time being. There are, lastly, the radicals of position, who are radicals, as somebody said, because they are not lords. Those whom, in contradistinction to these, we call philosophic radicals, are those who in politics observe the common practice of philosophers—that is, who, when they are discussing means, begin by considering the end, and when they desire to produce effects, think of causes. These persons became radicals, because they saw immense practical evils existing in the government and social condition of this country; and because the same examination which showed them the evils, showed also that the cause of those evils was the aristocratic principle in our government—the subjection of the many to the comparatively few, who had an interest . . . in perpetuating those evils. . . . the motto of their radicalism was, enmity to the Aristocratical principle.[16]

General though this was, the name was not enthusiastically received by those to whom it was meant to apply, least of all by the journalist whose work Mill had been reviewing.[17] It provoked some ponderous humour in the House of Commons and even the liberal press, and caused some embarrassment to the men themselves.[18]

The philosophic radicals used to be thought to have owed their cohesion as a party to their common adherence to an essentially simple doctrine, and their decline to an inner crisis of confidence in that doctrine.[19] This view, which seems to be based on a rather partial reading of J. S. Mill's *Autobiography*, obscures another fact about them: that in so far as they formed a party, it was not because of their theory, but in spite of it. They were deeply influenced by the view common in the eighteenth century, given practical force by the Fathers of the American republic, and repeated by many different kinds of English radical since the reign of Queen Anne, that party was inherently mischievous, because it demanded a sacrifice of a man's integrity and independence.[20] But

16 *L. & W. R.*, v and xxvii, April–July 1837, p. 67.
17 Albany Fonblanque (1793–1872), editor of *The Examiner*. He had not been enthusiastic about an earlier name 'philosophical Reformers'. Cf. *Examiner*, 10 May 1835 and, in criticism of Mill's review, 28 January 1837, p. 50, and 4 February 1838, pp. 65–6. Mill's half of the correspondence which followed is in *Earlier Letters*, ii, pp. 369–77. There he insisted that he had applied the term to 'the thinking radicals generally'.
18 *P[arliamentary] D[ebates]*, 3rd series, xl, pp. 398–9 (E. L. Bulwer, Grote 23 January 1838); 618, 623 (Sir G. Sinclair and J. Hume, 29 January 1838); *M[orning] C[hronicle]* 29, 30 January 1838.
19 E.g. A. D. Lindsay, *The Modern Democratic State*, vol i (1943), p. 136; G. H. Sabine, *History of Political Theory* (3rd edn. 1952), p. 565.
20 For a fine account of eighteenth century ideas on party, to which I am much indebted, see R. Hofstadter, *The Idea of a Party System* (Berkeley, 1969), chapters 1 and 2.

while other English radicals tended to make exceptions to excuse those parties with which they had historical and sentimental affinities, the philosophic radicals were more uncompromising, and condemned party from first principles. James Mill, who did most to give the group its theory and peculiar idiom, held that any representative system was defective if it gave power to a group of men who had interests at variance with those of the rest of the community. 'Party is only necessary for concert in evil, and never did exist for any other purpose.'[21] He did not rule out the possibility that by education and the acquisition of correct principles, groups of men could unite to further the general interest, without incurring the reproach of party motives. But in general he held that individual altruism was rare, and that the enlightened man who joined a group came to obey the selfish interests of the group.[22] Members of parliament were most subject to this rule of group behaviour; and their propensity to engross power and therewith 'the means of satisfying their desires' must always be subject to checks. The checks he proposed were that they be subject to the censure of a free press, and that they be answerable for their conduct to an electorate wide enough to have no interests at variance with the interest of the whole of society. The first condition enabled him to admit the advantages of group action in cases where men worked fearlessly and in public for causes they knew would stand up to scrutiny. A group like the Saints, who worked for the abolition of slavery, or Mill's friends Place and Hume, who worked for the repeal of the Combination Laws, came into this category and were permitted. The second condition did not necessarily involve giving the vote to the ignorant and disorderly classes, but it emphatically disqualified for public trust men whose political power depended on evading popular checks at elections. It disqualified the Whigs, a party which seemed to Mill's friends to be always avid for office but only occasionally keen on reform, and even in its arguments for reform, inclined to favour representation by classes and to distrust a uniform suffrage.[23] As Grote put it, in a pamphlet heavily indebted to the elder Mill's writings, party considered as 'a means of enhancing, by discipline and concert, the powers of a given number', was good if the ends it pursued were good; but once the ends were gained the union ceased to be legitimate. This implied that the Whigs had a function in opposition which they forfeited as soon as they were in office.

[21] Quoted in J. Hamburger, *Intellectuals in Politics*, p. 57.
[22] W[estminster] R[eview], volume i, no. 1, January 1824, pp. 216–17.
[23] The statement of Whig views on reform which the utilitarians treated as typical of the party's thinking was Mackintosh's article on Universal Suffrage in the *Edinburgh Review*, volume xxxi, no. 61, December 1818, pp. 165–203. For James Mill's most forceful attack on Whig theory, see *W.R.*, volume iv., no. 7 (July 1825), pp. 194–233.

> While the Government is constituted as it is now [1821], a party to oppose it in the Parliament is an excellent thing; but, when that party enlarges its views farther, and claims for itself the same unrestricted licence of doing evil, it may then be pronounced unequivocally noxious.[24]

For this reason Mill and his followers in the 1820s put more trust in the spread of education and the rising moral tone of the society they saw around them, than in the relative strengths of the Ministry or the opposition.

The common acceptance of Ricardian economics which seemed to late Victorian liberals to make allies of utilitarians and Whigs, was not at this early stage enough to draw them together.[25] This was partly because in the 1820s liberal economic measures came from Tory ministers, and the Whig opposition had no skilled political economist to equal Huskisson in the House of Commons.[26] But it was also because James Mill's teaching infused a strong dose of puritan feeling into his disciples' view of the science. They were, in intention at least, innocent of the imputation made by later socialist writers that they provided the justification for the predatory appetites of a capitalist middle class. Rather they used the new science as a paradigm of social enquiry, an exact discipline which advanced no particular interests but enabled its initiates to see the good of society more accurately than other men, and proved that the problems of politics and legislation could be reduced to a few simple certainties, and taught to the people. They drew from it an ideal of a decentralized society, regulated according to the simple principles of the natural order; and all they asked of statesmen was a willingness to abolish such archaic rules and privileges as stopped those principles from working unclogged for the public good. It did not matter to them that the first signs of such a willingness came from Tories, or that after 1830, popular measures were shunned by Tories and taken up by Whigs. What mattered was the fact that the true principles on which they rested were becoming more and more widely accepted.

This emphasis helps explain that neglect, which is so marked and in-

[24] *Statement of the Question of Parliamentary Reform* (1821), pp. 29–30 n.
[25] Cf. Professor Finer's assertion (Sutherland, *Studies in Growth*, p. 25), that in political economy there was 'little to choose between the *Westminster* and the *Edinburgh* as vehicles for Benthamite opinion'. This not only ignores the considerable differences between Mill and McCulloch (the *Edinburgh*'s chief writer on political economy) in interpreting Ricardo's views, but underrates the mutual antagonism to which the two journals consistently gave way. For a discussion on Mill's (and McCulloch's) debts to Ricardo, see D. Winch (ed.), *James Mill: Selected Economic Writings* (1966), esp. pp. 178–202.
[26] Francis Horner, the Whig spokesman on economic questions, had died in 1817; his loss was not supplied by Alexander Baring, Sir Henry Parnell or even Lord Althorp.

deed forbidding a feature of utilitarian writings about politics, of the details of usage, convention, precedent and law, which make up so much of the subject-matter of political discussion and constitutional history. They regarded the theory of the balanced constitution as so much cant; a view which had some truth; but with the cant they also ignored some important changes in the relationship of King, Lords and Commons, and great residual powers in each. In the pamphlet I have quoted Grote asserts that there has been 'no very remarkable change' in the constitution since 1793.[27] He was writing in the year after the Queen's Trial. Their extant writings in the 1820s give very little attention to the way in which both government and opposition were becoming more professional as legislation became more complicated and less localized. The debate on the influence of the Crown had no significance for them save that it touched their views on taxation. They did not, it seems, discriminate between the Ministry and the civil service, between major office holders and subordinate permanent officials—a strange omission, considering both the Mills were what old-fashioned radicals would have called placemen. They held a theory of representation which gave scant attention to the House of Lords, and treated the strong pull which the peerage exercised on a romantic age chiefly as a deplorable threat to public morals.

It may be they underrated these developments because they saw them as the petty concerns of an office-seeking aristocracy, and trivial alongside the great contemporary developments in morals and education. But their neglect of them does mean that when the reform agitation cast them into politics, they came on stage like actors who had not learnt their parts, and that once there, they were often confused and tongue-tied by what the other actors did. The doctrinaires among them were the most maladroit, and those least committed to utilitarian dogmas the most adaptable. But in particular, they all in varying degrees misunderstood the strength and tenacity of the Whig tradition, and the support which Whig ideas of moderate reform and religious tolerance had always commanded and would continue to command among the propertied classes like themselves. The Reform Bill, which gave life back to the Whig party, and even conferred a sort of honorary Whiggism on those who had been outside the party, embodied ideas which had been mulled over in Whig circles since the time of Fox and Burke, and rejected utilitarian and other ideas alien to the party's thinking.[28] But in 1830, James Mill's followers, having given more energy in the previous decade

[27] *Statement of the Question of Parliamentary Reform*, p. 15.

[28] As early as 1812 John Allen, Lord Holland's librarian and friend of Lord John Russell, wrote a pamphlet for the Spanish Liberals called *Suggestions to the Cortes*. Its proposals are strikingly similar to those embodied in the Reform Bill twenty years later.

to exposing Whig pretensions than Tory achievements, tended to see the Grey Ministry merely as a branch of the aristocracy which had been converted to a respect for the popular will. Consequently they supported the Whig Reform Bill for the oddest reasons. They loathed the aristocracy, which the Bill did so much to mollify and placate. They had condemned the 'class system' of representation which was the essence of the new franchises. They wanted secret voting which the Whigs had always opposed and now withheld. They tolerated imperfections in the final bill as the start of further reforms, which the Whigs had deliberately inserted to discourage further reforms. And most important for our purposes, they expected an end of party from a measure which polarized political opinion in the House of Commons, and, if it did not create a two party system immediately, at least made it very hard for a member to avoid committing himself either for or against reform.[29] They travelled through the reform agitation like passengers who prefer to sit with their backs to the engine, and have to be told by those opposite them that they have arrived.

Other radicals, drawing on the anti-party traditions of eighteenth century radicalism, or hoping that a new era of economy and retrenchment would destroy 'the factions' by removing places and pensions from their reach, or simply buoyed up by the euphoric conviction that reform had ushered in a new era, were equally reluctant to admit that the victory of reform must be consolidated, and the victors organized and disciplined. Their reluctance may account for that astonishing collapse of the reformers' majority between 1832 and 1837. When the Reform Act was law, the Grey government expected grateful support in return for its sacrifices. Accustomed to the idea that divergent interests were brought into harmonious co-operation by the spoils of office, Ministers thought they could go on, as governments of departments usually had gone on, without a clearly formulated legislative policy or much formal liaison with their supporters outside the merely social cohesion of the clubs. The radical members on the other hand felt that they represented not a new interest but a new age. They called themselves 'the Movement', a name which exactly expressed their sense of the irresistible momentum of reform. Time was to show that they had little common purpose on any issues which did not tap their superfluity of righteous feeling. They were often pledged to a variety of incompatible ideals: Cobbett to the annihilation of 'the Thing'; Attwood to currency reform; O'Connell to repeal; nearly all to making the reform of the representation a first step to something larger. They did not see the results of the first elections under the Reform Act as a victory for 'the liberal party',

[29] N. Gash, *Reaction and Reconstruction in English Politics 1832 to 1852* (Oxford, 1965), pp. 126–30.

but as a victory at the expense of party of any sort. They opposed the re-election of a Tory Speaker, Manners-Sutton, not so much because he was a Tory (for many admitted he had been a good Speaker despite this handicap) as because the reformed House must not have a Speaker associated with an era that was past.[30] The government did little to channel the righteous feeling of the Movement to its own advantage, but still managed to salvage a reforming reputation. Though there were occasions when all radicals could unite to oppose Ministers as a Movement, there were more when they could support them as individuals. If there was little sign of a united Liberal party, there was still less of a separate radical one.

The Movement had its first serious check in November 1834, when William IV dismissed the Whig Ministry led, since Grey's retirement, by Melbourne. Radicals were badly shaken by Peel's short Ministry which followed. The Lichfield House Compact, by which radicals, Whigs and Irish combined to bring Peel down, is a less famous constitutional landmark than the Tamworth Manifesto, but in the evolution of party it may have been more decisive.[31] In the Manifesto Peel tried to detach the Whigs from the radicals with an appeal to all politicians, of whatever party, who valued order and stability. It was a traditionalist appeal against the polarization of opinions which had resulted from the reform agitation. But at Lichfield House the different shades of reformer agreed (whether they realized it or not at the time) to set their individual opinions on one side for the sake of overthrowing Peel. The agreement in practice reversed the idea which had informed so much criticism of the Grey Ministry, that principle was more important than party.

Few radicals realized this at the time. Their overriding concern was to get rid of Peel. They took little account of the fact that the Tories were in discipline and organization far ahead. The Tories, out of sympathy with the new electorate, had a much sharper sense of their common interest at the polls. It was noticed that they were better at whipping-in and drilling their members, but this was put down by the radical press to the desperate death-throes of a 'faction'. The radicals themselves began with no sense of a common party interest, took a long time to develop one, and had a diffuse conception of the popular will which sometimes ignored local attitudes and needs.[32] Peel's defeat in April

[30] *P.D.*, 3rd series, volume xv., pp. 35–85. O'Connell asked the House if they should 'allow the spirit of toryism which we thought extinct, to revive'. A. Aspinall, 'Le Marchant's Reports of Debates in the House of Commons, 1833', *English Historical Review*, volume lviii (1943), p. 81.
[31] A. D. Macintyre, *The Liberator: Daniel O'Connell and the Irish Party, 1830–1847* (1965), p. 145.
[32] See for instance, M[orning] C[hronicle], January 1835; *Examiner*, 4 January 1835, p. 2.

1835 was achieved by a cumbersome alliance of three 'sections', Whigs, Irish, and other radicals, co-ordinated in an office in Cleveland Square.[33] This was a clearing-house of information about the constituencies, and had no formal authority over individuals. But it involved a pooling of interests which was an important step to the development of a Liberal party.

The curious thing about the philosophic radicals' role after Peel's first ministry is that while other radicals realized for the first time that the reform cause was fragile and demanded co-operation between all shades of reformers, they for the first time began to draw apart.[34] Between the elections of 1835 and 1837 they became known as the 'violent party', prepared to wreck the Melbourne ministry for the sake of their own reforms, especially the ballot. Former Movement men were drawn into supporting the Ministry, and even the Irish under O'Connell, the most disciplined of the 'sections', shielded an administration which seemed to have lost all reformist zeal. Only the philosophic radicals (with here and there a stray ally from other groups) seemed ready to carry to its practical conclusions their view that party was 'faction' and the Whigs no better than the Tories.

In this they claimed to have the support of popular opinion, but the places for which they sat do not suggest that they had much first hand experience of it. Molesworth sat from 1832 to 1837 for East Cornwall, owing his seat to his family interest in the county, however much he might seek other means of distinction. Even when he transferred to Leeds in 1837, after vainly trying to be adopted by the Westminster radicals, he showed an aristocratic impatience of his constituents' opinions, found the constraints of the 'Bainesocracy' (the local following of his fellow member Edward Baines) rather uncongenial and soon retired.[35] His friend J. T. Leader entered parliament in 1835 for Bridgwater, which had about 500 electors.[36] Charles Buller sat in 1830 for the family borough of West Looe, which was in Schedule A, but in 1832 he was returned for Liskeard, a single-member constituency with only 300 electors, of whom about a third polled at that election. Warburton sat from 1826 to 1841 for the small and corrupt borough of Bridport, a two-member constituency which the Reform Act increased to 500. His col-

[33] For pre-election forecasts of the Liberal strength, see *Spectator*, 6 December 1834, p. 1160; and 3 January 1835, p. i.

[34] James Mill in an article on 'The State of the Nation', *London Review*, i, April 1835, pp. 1–24, urged them to keep an independent role. Cf. J. Hamburger, *Intellectuals in Politics*, pp. 136–43.

[35] Mrs Fawcett, *The Life of Sir William Molesworth*, pp. 215–19.

[36] It is true that J. T. Leader was returned in 1837 for Westminster, but this was in a general election. The radical interest there had since 1807 been weak at by-elections and strong at general elections, probably because at the latter the politically influential were out of town and preoccupied with elections in the country.

league in 1832 was John Romilly, Whig by descent and utilitarian by conviction. Edward Strutt, the dullest of the group and the first to be raised to the peerage, sat with a Whig colleague for Derby, with about a thousand registered electors. None of the philosophic radicals sat for a borough in Schedule C or D of the Reform Act in the first reformed parliament, and they remained rather out of touch with the outlook of the new bourgeoisie of the industrial towns. Urban constituents, indeed, did not necessarily mean extreme politics. The metropolitan Members who belonged to the group more by their parliamentary conduct than their adoption of its theory, like William Clay and Benjamin Hawes, were certainly not the most idiosyncratic or extreme of radical MPs. Even Joseph Hume,[37] the veteran radical MP of the utilitarian circle, and an indefatigable vote-loser in the House of Commons, illustrates this. Both he and Warburton had had their seats threatened in January 1835. Warburton's colleague Romilly had been displaced by the Tory Horace Twiss. Hume's seat for the urbanized county of Middlesex had been shared with the Whig Byng, but a young and unknown Tory, Wood, had cut down their majority considerably.[38] After 1835 Warburton turned moderate, playing a well-known part in the sealing of the Lichfield House compact, and thereafter moderating the zeal of the younger philosophic radicals. Hume's radicalism remained outspoken through the following two sessions of parliament, and it seems to have imperilled his seat. He declared full support for the Ministry only in 1837, apparently too late, for he was defeated at the general election, and only remained in parliament because he was returned through O'Connell's influence for Kilkenny, the first utilitarian to become a joint in the famous 'tail'.

Of the inner circle of James Mill's followers only two sat for large constituencies after 1832. George Grote sat for the City of London. But the reforming tide which swept him to the top of the poll in 1832 receded thereafter, as the opposition organized the livery against him, and in 1835 he was fourth on the City poll.[39] His economic orthodoxy, and his refusal to join the National Political Union were not enough to save him with his constituents, who seem no exception to the tendency in the metropolis towards moderate and unadventurous politics. He was,

[37] Joseph Hume (1777–1855) trained as a surgeon in Aberdeen and Edinburgh; in 1797 took service under the East India Company, making £40,000 by 1808, when he returned home. MP for Weymouth 1812 as a Tory; for Border burghs 1818 as a Whig and a member of 'the mountain'; for Middlesex 1830–37. A friend of Bentham and James Mill, he identified himself with the utilitarians, but he was not skilled at expounding his principles, and prone to verbal gaffes which only his stolid perseverance and imperviousness to mockery overcame. He never (in spite of DNB) led the radical party, and did not earn the respect of the younger philosophic radicals.
[38] *M.C.*, 17 January 1835.
[39] *M.C.*, 9 January 1835.

as we shall presently see, not the man to use popular support in the service of a party.

The other was J. A. Roebuck, who was not only the most doctrinaire of James Mill's followers, but was much more outspokenly radical than Grote. He was returned in 1832 for Bath, which had been a corporation borough until the Reform Act gave it an electorate of about 3,000. Roebuck had some of the instincts of a revolutionary demagogue. Parallels with revolutionary France were natural to him.[40] He had a devouring ambition and a strong will, and he drove himself sometimes to the verge of collapse. Least of all his friends did he feel grateful to the Whigs for the work of parliamentary reform. He thought there was a natural antagonism between aristocracy and democracy, which would eventually oblige the two aristocratic parties to forget their differences and merge in the face of a common danger from the People.[41] Then he saw himself leading the popular party over their ruins. When he first represented Bath, he thought he had such a popular party at his back. In a sense he did, for his candidature had been supported by a strong Political Union in the city, as well as by liberals of the professional classes, and in 1832 his supporters defeated a Whig, not a Tory, candidate. The alliance held through the election of 1835, and Roebuck probably felt that his seat gave him a better claim to lead the radical party in parliament than any of the philosophic radicals who sat for smaller places, or shared them with Whigs. He certainly thought that Grote, in spite of his wealth and the prestige of being member for the City of London, squandered his chances of leading the group, with his hesitant and apologetic outlook and his recurrent pessimism.[42] He himself was for grasping the nettle. If the Ministry after 1835 would make no further reforms in the representative system, the radicals should use their parliamentary strength to force them either to propose radical measures or accept defeat. Roebuck gathered his forces for a demonstration of radical strength at the end of 1836.[43] It was to take the form of a dinner in Bath, at which prominent radicals would set out their terms for further support of the Ministry. It was the first practical result of a conscious effort to become a separate party. But it failed to attract a wide range of radical support. Roebuck was joined by Molesworth and Leader. Grote held aloof. The metropolitan members joined in a counter-demonstration of moderate-radical or even Whig opinion, a dinner of the Middlesex electors at Drury Lane.

[40] B. M. Add. MSS. 37949, ff. 295–6, Roebuck to Place, 29 November 1832; Roebuck–Falconer letters, ff. 225–6, 19 November 1833.

[41] *P.D.* 3rd series, volume xv (5 February 1833), pp. 198–202.

[42] Roebuck–Falconer letters, ff. 230–31, 22 November 1833; ff. 232, 23 November 1833; ff. 238, 27/28 November 1833; ff. 266, 9 December 1833.

[43] Napier MSS., Bodleian Library, MS. Eng. lett.d. 245, ff. 48–9, Roebuck to Col. W. Napier, 2 November 1836; ff. 50–52, same to the same, 7 November 1836.

Place, taking Roebuck's part, called this a 'Whig feast'.[44] But it saw a general affirmation of support for the Ministry from radical MPs, and even a remarkable speech from Hume in praise of the reforming record of the House of Russell.[45] Grote atoned for his attendance, according to his wife, with much anguish and lack of sleep, but that he went at all shows how little he and his friends could agree.[46] The Middlesex dinner marked a further stage in the assimilation of the parliamentary radicals to a larger Liberal party embracing different shades of reforming opinion, but to the philosophic radicals it marked the beginning of the end.

Molesworth called the Middlesex dinner 'a Whig scheme to exclude Roebuck & myself' and separated from the Grotes, at least for a time.[47] Roebuck condemned the whole affair as playing the Whigs' game, and when parliament met he took his isolation from his fellow radicals as a sign that he was right and they were wrong.[48] He still behaved as if the stand of one popular MP would discredit them all. But his position was not as secure as he supposed. There were other factors which prevented him from becoming in fact what in imagination he aspired to be, a popular leader; and they illustrate how hard it was for a philosophic radical to acquire genuine popular following. There was first of all the legacy of theory. Like most utilitarians Roebuck spoke of 'the People' as a faceless and voiceless abstraction, the only part of the community incapable of following the selfish interests of a class. In the thick of the first Bath election, he quickly assumed that his opponent represented aristocratic interests and he himself the whole community. He gave pledges at the hustings, but they were on large national issues not local ones.[49] Two years' service of the citizens of Bath did not alter this. In the 1835 election he told his audience: 'You are not acting for yourselves alone, nor for your families alone, nor for this city alone, nor for the people of Great Britain, but for all who inhabit the face of the Globe.'[50] He assumed that the abstract 'People' would always follow an enlightened lead, and his own idea for a constituency organization was the foundation of a school which he rather naïvely hoped would engage the efforts of all religious sects.[51] When the Poor Law came to Bath and was bitterly opposed by some of his supporters, and he was forced to choose between

[44] B.M. Add. MSS. 35150, ff. 216–19, Parkes to Place, 8 January 1837.
[45] *M.C.*, 24 January 1837.
[46] Add. MSS. 35150, ff. 234–4, Mrs Grote to Place, 27/28 January 1837.
[47] Sir W. Molesworth to Lady Molesworth, n.d. January/February 1837, MS. in private hands.
[48] Napier MSS., ff. 59–60, Roebuck to Colonel W. Napier, 6 February 1837.
[49] Bath Public Library, Scrapbook kept by Thomas Falconer of the 1832 election: placard d. 1 September 1832.
[50] *Bath Chronicle*, 5 January 1835.
[51] Roebuck–Falconer letters, ff. 11–15, 13 August 1833.

offending them and upholding a measure which he thought rested on correct principles, he did the latter.[52] In an area with high unemployment, the precondition of strong Chartist feeling, this was not a popular move, and it widened the split among his supporters and hastened his defeat. He himself ensured that defeat by his outspoken opposition to Sabbatarian legislation which, it was said, alienated the Methodists from his following. In his final speech admitting defeat he remained convinced of his own rightness. 'I have done my duty by you,' he told his constituents, 'but you have not done yours by me.'[53]

This was not the headlong self-immolation of an ideologue, however. The utilitarians' rarefied conception of the popular will has been contrasted with 'their meagre involvement with the actual populace'.[54] But the two things were causally connected. Even Roebuck, who knew more of popular opinion than most of his friends, could not have overcome the obstacles, both of law and of convention, to building up a constituency party. Of convention, because he certainly modelled his canvass on the example of radical Westminster, and that had been an organization which had aimed to rid the electors of the disgrace of being represented by either of the aristocratic parties.[55] Of law, because the Reform Act did not alter two of the legal barriers which, in the old regime, had separated an MP from his constituents. Legislation against bribery and the danger of a contested return if bribery was proved, had long been a reason why a candidate should refrain from interfering in the machinery which returned him, especially in boroughs, where venality was more common than in counties. The property qualification required of a candidate for parliament further widened the gulf between a Member and his constituents since it usually prevented the organizers, who knew local needs and conditions best, from standing themselves. In these respects, Roebuck's début was not unlike that of the radical Members for Westminster a generation before, and at times his attitude to his constituents might have been modelled on the advice which Burdett had given Hobhouse in 1819: 'these men must not make a puppet of you, and the sooner they know that, the better'.[56] From the start, he assumed his supporters depended on him, and not the other way around. 'At this

---

[52] *Bath & Cheltenham Gazette*, 3 January 1837; *Bath Journal*, 9 January 1837. Cf. Add. MSS. 35150, ff. 197–200, Roebuck to Place, 4 January 1837.

[53] *Spectator*, 29 July 1837; *Bath & Cheltenham Gazette*, 25 July 1837.

[54] J. Hamburger, *Intellectuals in Politics*, p. 55.

[55] The Whig candidate in 1832 was H. W. Hobhouse, brother of the Member for Westminster, J. C. Hobhouse. Sir Francis Burdett spoke in his support, but (in contrast to the Westminster election of 1819) opposed the giving of pledges. Roebuck asked Place for information for use against the Hobhouse party from the records of Westminster contests which Place kept. See Add. MSS. 37949, ff. 278—9 (19 September 1832).

[56] Add. MSS. 56540, J. C. Hobhouse's diary entry for 20 October 1819.

moment order reigns in Bath because I wish it,' he declared in September 1832. 'The people are completely at my command—a more unanimous feeling I never saw.'[57]

In one respect, the Reform Act wrought a crucial change in the relations of a member to his electorate. It may be debatable whether the five years after 1832 saw the disappearance of the independent member in the House of Commons; but it seems very likely that they saw the end of the independent voter. The change is particularly vivid in the case of two member constituencies like Bath, where each voter cast two votes. In such a case, open voting called for a special strategy. An elector might be asked to cast both his votes for two allied candidates, or else 'plump' for one, and refrain from using the other vote at all. If party feeling was intense, cross-voting, the casting of the two votes for candidates of different parties, would be reduced. In that case, any party organization in a borough might either start two candidates to catch both the votes of each elector; or else one candidate, and ask electors to 'plump' for him alone. The first course meant that the two candidates should agree, or at least not disagree with one another in their appeal to the electors. As early as 1832, Roebuck's supporters thought it best that he should run in harness with the local liberal. He chafed at the compromise this involved, for he was much more outspokenly radical than his colleague in his parliamentary conduct. In 1835 the Bath Tories started one candidate and asked for 'plumpers' and as a result ran Roebuck and his colleague quite close. By 1837, emboldened by the split which had appeared between moderate and radical on the opposite side, they started two candidates, and asked for double votes. The Bath liberals seem to have understood the threat better than Roebuck did, and to have urged him to drop his attacks on the Whig Ministry if he wanted to save his seat.[58] He refused to do so; and the election of 1837, which saw a dramatic reduction of cross-voting, showed that even the most popular radical candidate must observe liberal solidarity at the polls or be defeated.[59] Perhaps the moderation of the metropolitan radicals, the ill-fitting Whiggism of Hume, and the scrupulous wavering of Grote, were due to the fact that they had all in their different ways learned the same lesson earlier than Roebuck.

One man, who had a more acute appreciation of the behaviour of the new electorate than most of his contemporaries, has left letters which give an admirable picture both of the philosophic radicals' decline and the growth of party consciousness in the ten years after 1830. Joseph

[57] Add. MSS. 37949, ff. 282–3; J. A. Roebuck to Place, 29 September 1832.
[58] This seems to me the point of Roebuck's remark written after the election that, had he 'joined the Ministry and sold the People' he might have secured his seat. Add. MSS. 35151, ff. 17–18, letter to Place, 18 September 1837.
[59] Bath P.L. Poll Book of 1837 election.

Parkes became in that period a reluctant party man. Like many brought up in the sober and frugal traditions of dissent, he had looked forward to reform, because it would bring, among other things, an end to party. In 1833 he thought the Whigs must take the lead in further reforms or else break up—as he was inclined to think the Tories already had broken up.[60] But there the resemblance with the philosophic radicals ends, and to treat Parkes as a member of their group only confuses their role in the development of party.[61] For both by upbringing, study and profession he was more drawn to the Whig tradition than the utilitarian. The utilitarians were interested in the past only as a quarry of general laws and practical precepts. Parkes had an antiquarian bent and loved the past, like a romantic, for its own sake. His early writing shows strong affinities with the historic outlook of such Whigs as Mackintosh and John Allen.[62] His work as a provincial attorney before 1830 brought him a knowledge of the realities of electoral politics, especially in the Midlands, such as no philosophic radical possessed. None of them had dipped his hands so deep into the electoral malpractices of the unreformed system.[63] His historical and his professional interests made Parkes take a sober view of men's capacity for or perseverance in improvement, and counteracted the family inheritance of idealism and hope. The rapid alternation of enthusiasm and calculation in his letters make him a very important witness of the process I am trying to describe.

Parkes's expectations of the general election of 1835 were those of a 'Movement' man, tempered with a shrewd respect for the latent power of the aristocratic parties. Like other radicals he was shaken by Tory gains. Unlike many of them, he saw immediately that they meant that reformers could not do without the electoral influence of wealth, especially landed wealth. Thereafter, as Toryism revived, his energies were given to holding together Whigs and radicals, moderates and doctrinaires.[64]

[60] Staffs R.O. Hatherton MSS., Parkes to E. J. Littleton, 2 January 1833.

[61] Cf. J. Hamburger, *James Mill and the Art of Revolution* (Yale, 1963), pp. 32–3, where Parkes is (with little supporting evidence) treated as a disciple of James Mill; and the same author's *Intellectuals in Politics* (already cited, pp. 180–89) where the supposed discipleship leads to some difficulty in explaining Parkes's divergence from Grote and the other philosophic radicals.

[62] Notably his *History of the Court of Chancery* (1826), and his pamphlets, on *The Governing Charter of the Borough of Warwick . . . with a letter to the Burgesses on the Past and Present State of the Corporation* (1827) and *The Prerogative of Creating Peers* (1832). The last quoted pamphlets once owned by Sir Robert Walpole which had come into Parkes's possession.

[63] See especially his evidence before the House of Commons Select Committee on Bribery, March–August 1835, *P.P.*, 1835, volume viii, pp. 92–3.

[64] This aspect of Parkes's career is underrated in the only biographical study, Jessie Buckley's *Joseph Parkes of Birmingham* (1926). Cf. W. L. Burn's assessment, *The Age of Equipoise* (1964), pp. 74–5.

His task got harder as the Ministry's reforming zeal cooled. As Secretary to the Commission which prepared it, he had seen the difficulties in the way of a thorough Municipal Reform Bill. It had been delayed a whole session by the by-election defeat of Campbell, the Attorney-General.[65] When it was presented as a bill, after Peel's first Ministry, the reformers' majority was much reduced. Parkes knew that, in the circumstances, it could not be a very radical measure, and he managed quite successfully to counter the doctrinaires' criticism of its many shortcomings by greatly exaggerating its remoter benefits.[66] From 1836 he had no such resource, and his alarm grew, at the younger philosophic radicals' apparent determination to upset the Ministry. His case for moderation and co-operation was utterly opposed to their case for further organic reform. They thought (of course with variations according to position and temperament) that the Ministry could still gain an accession of strength if it confidently advocated further reforms in the representation, because, as John Mill asserted even after the elections of 1837, the country was 'moderate radical'.[67] Parkes on the other hand knew how small a proportion of the radically-inclined classes in the towns had been enfranchized at all, and how easily their electoral influence was outweighed by the venal and craven electors in numerous small boroughs, by the freemen in large ones and by the landed interest everywhere. He had never ignored the mixed character of the coalition which had passed the Reform Act, and the drift of the landed aristocracy from the Reform cause did not surprise him. Had he been more confident of the strength of radicalism in the country, or at least in the representative system, he might have looked forward to a Whig-Tory merger, as Roebuck and Molesworth did. But he had no such confidence. Indeed, as a dissenter, he could not rid himself of a deep suspicion of the Tory party as the party of religious intolerance, a fact which would always distinguish them from the Whigs. In 1834, using his experience on the Corporation Commission, he had helped set up the Cleveland Square office, among other things, to collect information about the localities and help prevent the common cause from being damaged by wasteful contests in which Whigs and radicals competed for Liberal votes.[68] At the same time he wrote leaders in the *Morning Chronicle* calling for Whig

[65] At Dudley.
[66] Brougham MSS., Parkes to Brougham, 20 August 1835. For Parkes's articles embodying his belief that the House of Commons, if 'well *hunted* will bag the fox' (i.e. accept the Bill as amended by the Lords) see especially, *M.C.*, 22 August 1835, 'What have the Lords Done?' and 7 September 1835, letter signed 'A Veteran Reformer (Aged 85)'—both bearing the inimitable stamp of Parkes's eloquence.
[67] *L. & W.R.*, volume vi, October 1837, p. 8.
[68] Lambton MSS., Parkes gave a day-by-day commentary to Durham throughout December and January 1835. See especially letters of 22 December 1834 and 18 January 1835.

and radical co-operation.[69] He cannot have been unconnected with the fact that when Roebuck and Molesworth began their breakaway movement late in 1836, the *Chronicle* rejoiced at their isolation and called their views 'the Bath mania'.[70] Soon after, he railed at them in a letter to the Whig Edward Ellice, in which he voiced his main worry, that the Liberals could not afford to show their disunity at the hustings, should the King's death bring a dissolution of Parliament.

> Caught in disunion at a dissolution of Parlt. *Whigs* will not fight the Counties, who alone can get seats there—Tories will split in between City & Boro polls of Whigs & Radicals & the Constituencies will be still further debased by a desperate expenditure of Tory money throughout the Country. Further, the best men & many among the Liberals in all 3 Kingdoms will retire from Parlt. in disgust, already God knows an onerous & costly duty. D—n & Bl—t their [i.e. Roebuck's and his friends'] exquisite Tom foolery. To play such a suicidal game when we are the only country in Europe enjoying a *practical* Republic, daily improving—when there is palpably no other game on the cards, but to keep the two sections of the Hereditary Peerage poised against each other—when the issue with the Lords for next Session stands so well, if we are united; & when if the Tory Peers & Court drive the Ministry out next Spring, we can pull through a Dissolution decently well & stronger,—be the Parlt dissolved by whom it may. . . .[71]

Parkes's difficulty was that he could not get all the philosophic radicals to appreciate the problem as a matter of votes in the constituencies.

The small part which party played in their political theory, and the variety of doors through which they entered political life need not have prevented the philosophic radicals from acting as a party in debate. There have been parties, especially before the advent of a mass electorate, which have come together with fewer agreed principles, more divergent interests and less common feeling than the young politicians who gathered at Mrs Grote's house in Dulwich Wood or went to the soirées of Mrs Buller and Mrs Austin. And it remains a problem, after their differences have been stressed, why they did not pull together more effectively in a parliament where sympathy for their aspirations, though waning, was still strong, where the ministerial forces were stretched

[69] *Ibid.*, Parkes to Durham, 22, 27 December 1834; 18 January 1835; *M.C.* leaders of 22 and 27 December 1835, both by Parkes.
[70] *M.C.*, 12 January 1837.
[71] Lambton MSS., Parkes to Ellice, 8 January 1837.

often to breaking point, and where the leader of the ascendant party played a waiting game.

They had considerable advantages, which gave them prominence in the reformed House of Commons. In 1838 a liberal journalist noticed that in general the radical MP was 'rarely an ambitious cadet of good family, put into parliament to keep up the family interest, and borrowing a family qualification from his father or brother', but rather 'a man of mature age;—a merchant—a retired manufacturer of large capital, who comes into parliament at the close, not at the commencement, of an industrious and honourable career.'[72] Such men were unlikely to be fluent in speech or at ease in the forms of the House, and though often of great administrative experience, did not take to political office. The philosophic radicals comprised a few such men, like Warburton and Hawes, but those of them who came into the public eye, had entered parliament relatively young. The same writer went on to note, with an air of relief, that what he called the Ultra-radical party in England, unlike 'the discontented Democrats of other countries', were men of great fortune; and he instanced Molesworth, Leader, Pattison, Grote, and Hume. These men were 'Ultras' because they were more articulate, less overawed by their audience, and less patently the spokesman of particular economic interests. Why then, did they not behave as a party in the House?

Probably because they were independent. They were, in the best sense, amateurs in politics. Some of them hankered after literature and scholarship hardly less ardently than Althorp hankered after his estate.[73] And having an alternative pursuit which beckoned them, they tended to lack the instinctive competitiveness of the professional politician, who enjoys struggle for its own sake. Before 1830, the traditional parties had recruited such men from the law. But utilitarians, following Bentham, were hostile to 'Judge & Co.' and so debarred from their emoluments. The careers of a Lyndhurst, a Brougham, or even such advocates of law reform as Horner and Romilly, were not for them. Even Roebuck, whose property qualification at Bath had been provided by Leader, thought he could earn his living by writing, rather than from the law. That was tedious and demeaning work, 'grimgribber' as Bentham had called it, which would hardly have a respected place in a reformed society. 'I do not much admire putting myself into a passion, & professing a violent interest for every fellow who pays me a fee',[74] he told

---

[72] *Monthly Chronicle*, volume i, June 1838, p. 342, 'On Public Opinion'; Cf. J. Vincent's analysis of the radicals of a later generation, *The Formation of the Liberal Party* (1966), pp. 28–35.

[73] Obvious examples are Grote and Molesworth, but even Roebuck kept longing for literary fame, and indeed earned more by his pen than his profession.

[74] Roebuck–Falconer letters, ff. 221–2, 16 November 1833.

his future wife. In a later letter he told her: 'It would seem ordained by fate, that all my success in life should be the result of my own unaided exertions.'[75]

Believing this, he thought taking office under the Whig government would be a living death. So did others. Buller, perhaps because he lived up to his income, was by the end of 1836 inclined to make excuses with his radical friends for the policies of the government. But when Molesworth heard, through Buller's mother, that her son might take office, he exploded.

... They [the Whigs] will never give him any thing & if they would he would only damage himself for the sake of that which can only be of the most temporary duration. Apostacy is bad enough a moral prostitution, but why openly proclaim the willingness to commit either sort of it? do it if you cant help it but hold your tongue.[76]

Buller reconciled his radicalism and his wish to keep the Ministry in, by joining Durham's mission to Canada, and was disowned in the House of Commons by Leader.[77] But Buller was only submitting to a process which was reducing the effectiveness of the private member in every way. Even under the relaxed guidance of Melbourne, Ministers commanded resources of expertise which made them more than a match for radical critics of general policy. Individual radicals who persevered in causes from the floor of the House, had to allow a kind of division of labour to prevail, and tended to become specialists in a particular field of legislation: Molesworth in transportation and emigration, Buller in the regulation of controverted elections; and even Grote in advocating the ballot acquired the reputation of being a man of one measure. Those who tried like Hume or Roebuck, to keep up the criticism of all aspects of government policy, lost stature with the great body of members who remained uncommitted on general issues. Hume became the butt of the Tory press for his obsession with trivial economies. Roebuck's nickname, 'Tear 'em,' was a sign that his indiscriminate ferocity had its comic side.

Having a certain aristocratic contempt of the traditional means by which the political novice made his way to fame, it is not surprising that the philosophic radicals could never agree to sink their individual wills in obedience to a common leader, or that when they admitted the need to form a party, they should have thought a leader more important than

[75] *Ibid.*, f. 255, 4 December 1833.
[76] Sir W. Molesworth to Lady Molesworth, 15 October 1836. MS. in private hands.
[77] *P.D.*, 3rd series, volume xliv, pp. 1242–50; 1295, 14 and 15 August, 1838.

an organization. Following such a leader was something they could never do. Grote's position and high moral stature set him above the other philosophic radicals. His wife had the charm and the energy to be a hostess to a party, a radical Lady Holland. The 'Grote conclave' gathered talent, and Grote could have been its director had he wished. In addition, he might have exercised some influence in the larger Liberal party. When the Reform Association was founded after the election of 1835, its funds were put in his bank.[78] Influential editors like Fonblanque and Rintoul were willing to put their papers at his disposal. But nothing came of it. Grote's mind was rigid and doctrinaire but his will was easily influenced. Both Cobden and Parkes noticed that he lacked 'devil'. He could on occasion impress the House of Commons with a speech full of grave moral indignation, but he could not play upon the different interests in it, nor use them to forward his cause. He conscientiously believed it was the House's duty 'whenever a question arose between the interest of any one class of persons and the interest of the public' to decide in favour of the public.[79] In this spirit he pressed his annual motion for the ballot, regardless of whether his allies were country gentlemen who wanted the ballot with the existing qualification, moderate radicals who wanted it with household suffrage, advocates of harmony like Parkes who wanted it declared an open question chiefly to allay radical hostility, or Chartists who thought it less important than universal suffrage and shorter parliaments.[80] The ballot might have become irresistible as the common demand of many interests: it actually became an open question through the stubbornness of Queen Victoria in retaining a weak Ministry after the 'Bedchamber crisis'. But that compromise was hardly a sign of the strength of the advocates of secret voting.

A party of writers and philosophers trying to be politicians might be expected to have been stronger in its periodicals than in parliament. It has even been implied that the tactical doctrines of the party were propounded in its journals, where, presumably, the disagreements of personality and parliamentary conduct did not penetrate.[81] It is true that

[78] *M.C.*, 21 May 1835. Grote was also a member of the thirty-six-strong committee of management, and one of six on the finance committee of the Reform Association. *Ibid.*, 29 May 1835.
[79] *M.C.*, 26 April 1838, the debate of the previous night on Talfourd's Copyright Bill.
[80] By 1838, a division was appearing between middle class liberals who wanted the ballot without suffrage extension, and Chartists who put the wider suffrage first because they saw the ballot as a middle class ruse for keeping the electorate as it was. The *Leeds Mercury* and *The Scotsman* took the first course, Feargus O'Connor and others the second. Thus Bulwer could declare 'Universal suffrage is the question of the democracy, but ballot is essentially the question of the middle class.' (*M.C.*, 28 February 1838, quoting an article from *Monthly Chronicle*.) For Parkes's views, see his letter to Ellice of 8 January 1837 in Lambton MSS.
[81] J. Hamburger, *Intellectuals in Politics*, chapter 4, esp. pp. 128-36.

the philosophic radicals always assumed that they had the advantage in argument over their contemporary critics, and that their characteristic reaction to the disunity of the radicals in parliament was to pool their efforts in a new periodical. When the *Edinburgh* and the *Quarterly* were read as expressing the views of their respective parties, a radical review might claim to perform the same function for the radicals. But in fact the group's ventures were never properly supported, and there are good reasons to believe that they were no less subject to the economic pressures which were making other liberal journals reflect more and more the drift of the propertied classes away from radicalism during the 1830s.

The *London Review* had been planned in 1833, but money difficulties and what John Mill called 'the incapacity of the radicals to co-operate' held it up. It was launched when Molesworth decided to finance it himself in June 1834.[82] But its editorial arrangements were an unsatisfactory compromise between his inability and Mill's official reluctance to take the public responsibility for the review. A subordinate was the nominal, John Mill the efficient editor, and Molesworth held the purse-strings. This was not a recipe for a clear doctrine of party tactics or even a decided editorial line. The political articles did little more than lament the lack of leadership in the radical ranks. Mill's own intention was to introduce variety among the contributions which would relieve the dogmatic utilitarianism of the old *Westminster Review*, but he could hardly do this openly till his father had died in 1836.[83] Molesworth did not agree with such a policy and denied in the management what Mill strove for in the editorial part of the concern. On the dubious principle of strengthening the new venture by propping it with an old and declining one, he absorbed the *Westminster Review*.[84] The result did not satisfy him either, and by August 1837 he was glad to arrange that Mill should take over the review as soon as its annual deficit was reduced.[85]

Roebuck disapproved of John Mill's editorship, but his own venture, the *Pamphlets for the People*, was scarcely more successful. Like the *London Review*, the *Pamphlets* were born in a project (in this case the short-lived Society for the Diffusion of Moral and Political Knowledge) in which the participants failed to honour their first enthusiasm.[86] The financial

---

[82] *Earlier Letters of J. S. Mill*, volume i, pp. 216, 225; Molesworth's views are touched on in Mrs Grote, *Philosophical Radicals of 1832*, pp. 9–10.

[83] J. Stillinger (ed.), *J. S. Mill's Autobiography* (Oxford, 1971), p. 123.

[84] Sir W. Molesworth to T. Woolcombe (his agent) n.d. (1837), MS. in private hands.

[85] *Earlier Letters of J. S. Mill*, volume ii, pp. 388, 672; and the letter of 29 August 1837 in *Mill News-Letter*, volume vi, no. 1 (Autumn, 1970).

[86] *Pamphlets for the People*, no. 1, 'On the Means of Conveying Information to the People', p. 1. For Place's view of their financial prospects and note on their failure to pay their way, Add. MSS. 35150, ff. 59–60. Grote wrote to *The Times* on 20 June 1835 denying his connection with the *Pamphlets*.

support Roebuck had hoped for from Grote and other rich men of the party seems not to have materialized, and Roebuck wrote most of each number himself. They therefore tended to be, at their best a highly prejudiced and personal commentary on the week's events, and at worst a hortatory letter to the Bath electors. Their editor certainly did not take care to have them widely accepted. His antagonists were mostly men who might have become allies. A brush with *The Times* was followed by an open apology to Albany Fonblanque of the *Examiner* and a duel with the editor of the *Morning Chronicle*, John Black.[87] Such quarrels must have had much to do with the financial failure of the pamphlets, for they were ably argued and pungently written. By February 1836 when he gave them up, Roebuck's health had worsened, and his disagreements with his friends had made him very isolated. 'He is a fire ship' said Joseph Parkes, 'which will never sail in convoy.'[88]

It is not clear who carried the financial burden of the *Pamphlets for the People*. But falling sales were not confined to periodicals which the philosophic radicals projected by themselves. *The Spectator*, which had supported Molesworth and Roebuck in their criticism of the Whig government in 1837, was by the election of that year in difficult straits, and its editor Rintoul anxious to find a buyer.[89] By this time the Grotes, to whom it was natural to turn, apparently found it natural to decline. Mrs. Grote's perception of the risks was acute, and overrode Rintoul's hint that, unless a radical bought it, the paper would fall into the hands of the Tories. She told Place that 'the party at my back' would take that risk rather than buy Rintoul with his debts and thus 'feed the cow for others to milk'.[90] Grote's election scrutiny promised to be costly, and the additional expense of rescuing Rintoul would be too much.

The philosophic radicals had been occasional contributors to Fonblanque's *Examiner*, which had always had money difficulties, in spite of the fact that it was less ambitious in its news coverage than the *Spectator*, and seems to have been largely written by Fonblanque himself.[91] At any rate, Fonblanque was more susceptible to the flattery of the party in

[87] *P.D.*, 3rd series, volume xxviii, pp. 784–5, 15 June 1835; *The Times*, 18 June 1835; *Pamphlets for the People*, no. 4 (on 'The Dorchester Labourers'), pp. 15–16. For the quarrel with Black, see Leader, *Roebuck*, pp. 190–93, and Charles Mackay, *Forty Years' Recollections* (1877), volume i, pp. 89–90.

[88] Quoted in S. J. Reid, *Life and Letters of the First Earl of Durham* (1906), volume i, p. 105. MS. not traced.

[89] R. S. Rintoul (1787–1858) began his connection with journalism as printer of the *Dundee Advertiser*. Came to London in 1826, and became founder-editor of *The Spectator* 1828–58. Parkes thought him 'an incomparable editor', and his paper was certainly brilliantly edited and well written.

[90] Add. MSS. 35150, ff. 279–80.

[91] *England under Seven Administrations* (1837) reprints many of Fonblanque's leading articles in the *Examiner*, but the 3 volumes may well show his swing to moderation, since the most extreme leaders are not reprinted.

power, and more immediately aware of the falling off in sales which followed from a particular editorial line. By 1835 he was noticeably more sympathetic to the Whigs than to the radicals. He had taken the part of Lord Durham against the Melbourne cabinet, but when Durham returned from St Petersburg and recommended support for the Ministry, Fonblanque fell in with his advice.[92] Ellice arranged an appropriate reward. In 1837 H. L. Bulwer examined Fonblanque's debts, and with Ellice's help a subscription was raised in Whig circles to pay them and set the *Examiner* to paying its way.[93] From then on, Fonblanque's criticism of his former radical friends became more outspoken, until even the tolerant John Mill was moved to protest at the unfairness of his articles.

Ellice represents Whiggism at its most cynical. His political allegiance was sharpened by the shrewd calculation of a man with large financial interests in several countries. To him, the stability of the Melbourne government rested on its capacity to outlast its rivals and to wear out its critics. All he wanted of a government which he supported was what Parkes despairingly called 'keeping the offices'.

The Ministers will be able to maintain themselves through the Session [Ellice told Durham in May 1837]—& the only danger is from these mad & absurd radicals, who will not be taught wisdom, by the admitted change in the publick opinion towards their doctrines, & themselves. Their papers fall off in circulation—they have the plainest demonstrations in the late elections, of the alarm felt at their conduct in Parlia[men]t—they see, they are setting up the Tories—& yet imagine that a change of Govt so far from being an evil, would be an absolute advantage to the popular party.[94]

To Ellice such an attitude (expressed by mid-1837 by Roebuck and Molesworth and supported by the *Spectator*) was merely unprofitable. But to them, his alternative was much more disgraceful, since it involved a sacrifice of all the principles which had led them into politics in the first place.

The main reason why the Whigs and the philosophic radicals never agreed upon a common policy or helped to form a united Liberal party

[92] Fonblanque was cool, verging on hostility, in his comments on Molesworth's 'Terms of Alliance between Radicals and Whigs' in the *Examiner*, 8 January 1837; he rebutted critical comments on his editorial policy since 1835 which were made by John Mill in *L. & W.R.* (*Examiner*, 16 April 1837); and when many radicals were openly disappointed by Durham's open letter to Russell Bowlby, he defended it (*Examiner*, 16 July 1837). By the end of the year the *Examiner* was able to enlarge its size.

[93] Lambton MSS., Edward Ellice to Lord Durham, 7 March 1837.

[94] *Ibid.*, Ellice to Durham, 28 May 1837.

before 1840 was that their demands were mutually exclusive. The Whigs whether they had popular principles or not, had traditionally been excluded from power by the Crown, not put in power by the people. Their return to office in 1835 did not alter this habit of mind. They looked on their alliance with the radicals and Irish as a bargain which set no precedent and implied no permanent promises on their side. After 1835 they accepted radical criticisms as a reversion to type of men who had always been more difficult to please than any other group in politics.[95] They felt no disgrace in having to defeat radical criticisms with Tory votes. The philosophic radicals on the other hand inherited a different stereotype, according to which the Whigs had always professed popular sympathies merely to get into power, so that they could act in defiance of the people once there. They could not have swallowed their suspicions of the members of the Grey government in 1830 to 1832, had they not felt that they were themselves being borne on by a flood-tide of popular feeling against which neither of the traditional parties could long hold out, whatever efforts they might make to do so. In a word, they could not believe the meaning of 'Finality', and were very shocked when Russell, apparently taking advantage of the defeats of the elections of 1837, spelled it out for them.[96] Until then their demands of the Whig governments of Grey and Melbourne had been based on the assumption that the tide of reform feeling could not recede. When it did, they were forced to choose between trying to rouse popular feeling against the government and retiring from politics to wait for better times. On the whole, they were not in favour of popular agitation for its own sake. Even Roebuck, who after exclusion from parliament was most willing to co-operate with future Chartists, was restive when agitations were led by men more ignorant than himself. But the others felt no temptation to 'wield the fierce democracy'.[97] The humiliating thing about the 'Finality' declaration was its accurate assessment of their powers of protest. They retired disillusioned, more by the Ministry's obdurate passivity than the people's discontents. Thus Grote, in a letter to Austin early in 1838:

The degeneracy of the Liberal party and their passive acquiescence in everything, good or bad, which emanates from the present Ministry, puts the accomplishment of any political good out of the question, and it is not at all worth while to undergo the fatigue of a nightly attendance in Parliament for the simple purpose of sustaining *Whig*

[95] E.g. *Monteagle Papers*, National Library of Ireland; Charles Wood to Thomas Spring Rice, 3 February 1835.
[96] *P.D.*, 3rd series, volume xxxix, pp. 65–73 (20 November 1837).
[97] Roebuck-Falconer letters, ff. 258, 7 December 1833.

Conservatism again *Tory* Conservatism. I now look wistfully back to my unfinished Greek History. . . .[98]

At the same time Molesworth began his edition of Hobbes. Soon after Mill left the editorship of the *London and Westminster Review* and began in earnest the *System of Logic*. Buller joined the Ministry rather than see a division in which he and Grote would be left to 'tell' Molesworth. Roebuck went on circuit with more zeal than formerly. The group had ceased to have any collective purposes before the Newport rising in November 1839.

This was not the defeat of a party, but it was the elimination of a type of politician. More learned than the patrician demagogue of the Burdett era, less practical than the hard-headed agitators of the Anti-Corn Law League, they were too public-spirited to consider themselves an interest and too divergent in opinion to form a party. Those who retired from politics did so not merely from despair at altering the system but also from the fear that it would alter them. Those who remained were absorbed. Nor was this a tragedy, for themselves or for the future Liberal party. In the cases where it mattered, they retired to more congenial company and to tasks to which they were more suited, and were able to make better contributions to the literature of liberalism because they enjoyed the unforced leisure of private life. Their philosophy was devised in the study and to the study most of them returned. As an episode in the history of party, they merely show how resistant the reformed parliament continued to be to the sort of pressures which brought reform about, and how easily the two major parties, after an initial failure of nerve, were able to defer the acquisition of a popular appeal.

Further Reading

The best account of the ideas of Bentham, James Mill and Ricardo is still Élie Halévy's *Growth of Philosophic Radicalism* (trans. Mary Morris, 1928.) But the very qualities which make that a fine analysis of the ideological inheritance of the philosophic radicals—its zest and imaginative commitment—make Halévy a less reliable judge of English party politics in the 1830s. In volumes 2 and 3 of his *History of the English People* (trans. E. I. Watkin, 1949, reprinted 1961) he exaggerates the impact and representativeness of the philosophic radicals as politicians, and needs to be corrected, or at least redressed, by Professor Gash's *Reaction and Reconstruction in English Politics, 1832 to 1852* (1965). The most recent studies of the philosophic radicals as a group are J. Hamburger's *James*

[98] Harriet Grote, *Philosophical Radicals of 1832*, p. 41.

Mill and the Art of Revolution (1963) and *Intellectuals in Politics: J. S. Mill and the Philosophic Radicals* (1965). Both convey the severity of political sociology without its data, using much journalism and correspondence, but ignoring poll books, divisions lists, and even important parliamentary reports. Even the shortest bibliography should mention H. J. Hanham's new edition of *Charles Dod's Electoral Facts 1832–1852 Impartially Stated* (1972) though the editor's excellent introduction deals chiefly with a period after the philosophic radicals had left the scene. The lives of individual members of the group are unsatisfactory. All save J. S. Mill moved to the right as they grew older, and were disinclined or unable to recall fully their early struggles; while Mill himself allowed his own account of them in the *Autobiography* to be affected by his later views. M. St. J. Packe's *Life of J. S. Mill* (1954), adds vividness to Mill's own dry description but is unoriginal on the politics of the 1830s. There are no biographies of Charles Buller, Joseph Hume or J. T. Leader. As a biographer Mrs Grote was a ruthless user of asterisks. Only in her privately printed memoir of Molesworth, *The Philosophical Radicals of 1832* (1866) does one glimpse her flair for character-study. Her *Personal Life of George Grote* (1873) discreetly condenses the historian's political failure. Mrs Fawcett's *Sir William Molesworth* (1901) uses the former but like R. E. Leader's *Autobiography and Letters of J. A. Roebuck* (1896), only with more excuse, it is thin. Jessie Buckley's *Joseph Parkes of Birmingham* (1926) depends chiefly on Parkes's letters to Lord Durham and Francis Place and so exaggerates Parkes's radicalism, but it conveys the flavour of his personality well. Janet Ross's *Three Generations of Englishwomen* (1893) gives some material on the Austins. The journalism of the group is important and hardly studied, but for the main events and issues which affected the *Examiner* and the *London & Westminster* the best guide is F. E. Mineka's edition of *The Earlier Letters of J. S. Mill 1812–1848* (1963) This should be supplemented by Carlyle's observations, both in J. A. Froude's biography and in his letters to J. S. Mill in A. Carlyle (ed.), *Letters of Thomas Carlyle to J. S. Mill, John Sterling and Robert Browning* (1923).

4

The Suffrage Movement

Alexander Wilson

From the parliamentary motions in 1819 and 1821 of Sir Francis Burdett and Lords John Russell and Durham, the suffrage question was the prime concern of nineteenth century pressure from without. The struggles preceding the Reform Acts of 1832 and 1867 on the one hand, and Chartism on the other, have appropriately received most attention. But other aspects of the suffrage movement, the Complete Suffrage Union of the 1840s led by Joseph Sturge, the New Reform Movement and parliamentary and financial reform associations centred on Joseph Hume, Cobden and Bright in the late 1840s and early 1850s on the other, have been neglected rather more than their ineffectiveness deserves.

The ineffectiveness itself is surprising since the reformed parliament included up to a hundred radicals in the 1830s on whom the Whig government depended;[1] and working class radicals in their turn were reluctant enough revolutionaries who appreciated that radical reform required an alliance with middle class reformers. But parliamentary radicals were divided among themselves,[2] alienated by Chartist talk of physical force, and above all lacking coherent leadership. Once 'Radical Jack' Durham had in 1835 been discreetly removed to St Petersburg, thence to Canada in 1838, followed by his death in 1840, there was no one acceptable to both middle and working class radicals. Daniel O'Connell's attacks on trade unionism in 1837–8 were unforgivable, Thomas Attwood, Hume, Walmsley[3] and Cobden wanted a wider franchise to reduce aristocratic privilege and erode aristocratic power. Military spending would be curbed, taxes diminished, industry and commerce stimulated; and the rightful position of the industrial and

[1] See W. Thomas, 'The Philosophic Radicals', chapter 3, above.

[2] Their causes included currency reform, disestablishment of the Church, repeal of the Irish union, Corn Law repeal, peace movement, national education to name but a few.

[3] Sir Joshua Walmsley, 1794–1871, Liverpool corn merchant, founder of the National Reform Association, MP for Bolton and Leicester.

commercial wealth-owning and professional classes of Britain secured. But they had no great trust in the masses. Revealingly, they considered that the redistribution of seats and therefore of power to the large industrial towns was at least as important as manhood suffrage. Nor did they possess the demagogic skills of Feargus O'Connor, who could win and hold working class loyalty whatever the crisis. Yet O'Connor in turn they distrusted for he was erratic, extravagant, and idiosyncratic. Unable to lead a radical alliance himself, he would prevent any middle class radical from doing so. And so the radicals lived for several decades with a stubborn dilemma. Being men of reason and respectability, they were loath to commit themselves to 'unreasonable' demands. Yet unless they could show moral fervour and a clear commitment to universal suffrage, they would be denied the working class support that was essential for outside pressure. Not until John Bright built up a relation of trust between the parliamentary radicals, their middle class extramural supporters and the emerging holders of power within organized labour, would there be a further and substantial instalment of reform.

All shades and class of reformer had come together in the Friends of the People in the 1790s, the Hampden Clubs of 1816, and the struggles of 1819–20. It was a harmony carried forward to the early stages of the Reform Bill, when working class radicals took their lead from Attwood and Place. The discipline of the mass processions and open air demonstrations which the political unions organized at Birmingham, Manchester, and other major towns on the one hand, and the riots at Bristol, Nottingham, and Derby after the Lords rejected the Reform Bill in October 1831 on the other, had a powerful impact on parliamentary proceedings.

But although working class radicals were willing to accept the Whig bill as a first instalment towards political justice, increasingly during the winter of 1831–2 they came to demand universal suffrage. The rift within the radical alliance widened and denunciations of the Whig Ministry grew as the Irish coercion act and the new Poor Law were followed by the treatment of the Dorchester labourers in 1834 and the Glasgow cotton spinners in 1838. Moderate middle class radicals, alarmed by the vehemence of anti-Whig sentiment, became increasingly fearful of a Tory-radical alliance.

The task of healing this rift was taken up in 1837 simultaneously but independently by the mainly middle class Birmingham Political Union and the mainly working class London Working Men's Association. The BPU's original programme of household suffrage, ballot, triennial parliaments, payment of MPs, and the abolition of the property qualification for MPs, was widened in December 1837 to meet the working class demand for universal suffrage. Meanwhile the LWMA under Lovett's[4] secretaryship was slowly preparing the document which was to be published in May 1838 as the People's Charter.

Chartism, however, became a movement from outside parliament which lacked pressure from within. Although it covered the country with a network of associations far more thoroughly than had the political unions in 1831–2, although its demands had long been part of the radical programme, and although O'Connell, Hume, Roebuck and Attwood played some part in launching it, they quickly withdrew. Many Chartists continued to seek middle class support and one solution, which was tried in a few towns like Glasgow and Leeds, was to form universal suffrage associations of electors. In November 1839, after six weeks of effort, the Glasgow association, for example, had obtained 275 paid-up members, which represented about 5 per cent of the electorate. But middle class radicals found their lingering sympathies dispersed with talk of ulterior measures and torchlight processions. The Chartists for their part were deeply split over strategy and were never able to resolve their own attitude to overtures from middle class reformers, particularly on the questions of Corn Law repeal and suffrage extension. To most Chartists, the manufacturer and the merchant were more the industrial opponents than the political partners of working men. In parliament and in town councils, they had come to be influential, yet they had done little to soften the repression of Chartism in the winter of 1839–40. If they now professed sympathy for the people on the Corn Laws, it was assumed they sought merely to lower wages. Nevertheless, many Chartists, especially in Scotland, were still 'out-and-out Repealers' and to them it was axiomatic that the first action of a parliament elected by universal suffrage would be Corn Law repeal. The rank and file of both agitations overlapped in 1838, and the *Northern Star*, the *True Scotsman* and the *Scottish Patriot*, as well as numerous Chartist banners, all included Corn Law repeal among their aims.[5]

Chartist attitudes, however, began to harden. As early as the summer of 1838, the *Birmingham Journal*, speaking for the BPU, told unions not to be misled by 'symptomatic grievances'. Such 'little goes as anti-corn law associations' should be left to the less clear-sighted.[6] This advice was soon translated into Chartist attacks on repeal as a Whig plot to divert the people from Chartism. Repeal meetings were captured or disrupted and repealers found themselves forced to charge admission fees if they were to retain control over their meetings. Occasionally there were local

---

[4] See D. Large, 'William Lovett', chapter 5, below.
[5] See my *Chartist Movement in Scotland* (Manchester 1970), chapter 12; *Northern Star*, 24 March 1838; *True Scotsman*, 20 October 1838; *Scottish Patriot*, 6 July 1839.
[6] *Birmingham Journal*, 28 July, 15 September 1838.

agreements to compromise so that joint petitions for repeal and universal suffrage could be adopted, and on the strength of this the League began to feel its way towards combining a programme of parliamentary reform with free trade. O'Connell along with Hume, Roebuck, Sharman Crawford, and other parliamentary radicals, had come to favour a union of middle and working class radicals around household suffrage, and after a delay during which much good will was lost the plan for a major conference was announced by the Leeds Reform Association in the *Leeds Times* in September 1840. In the premises of J. G. Marshall, a well-known radical mill-owner, and under the leadership of Hume, O'Connell, Perronet Thompson and Crawford, a programme would be devised to reconcile middle and working class reformers.

Harney and O'Connor would have none of it. Harney since the spring had been stumping Scotland denouncing the 'Household Suffrage Humbug' and exposing 'the real nature' of Anti-Corn Law motions. Now they reminded Chartists that O'Connell was 'a shuffler and a double-dealer'; and they instructed Chartist delegates to oppose anything less than universal suffrage. Despite the efforts of the *Northern Star* to treat the Leeds conference as a huge joke, and helped by the absence of O'Connell, Joseph Hume and the Chartist James Moir were able to make conciliatory moves. The conference ended with the adoption of their joint resolution 'that the united efforts of all reformers ought to be directed to obtain such a further enlargement of the franchise as should make the interests of the representatives identical with those of the whole community.'[7]

But the Leeds conference failed either to persuade the parliamentary radicals to take up suffrage extension, or to mend the division within Chartist ranks between moderates and hard-liners, a division soon to be enlarged when the New Move of William Lovett and John Collins, with its emphasis on educational activity and its welcome for middle class co-operation, failed to carry the O'Connorite majority. Local supporters of the New Move were denounced as heretics.[8] Hostilities were exacerbated still further when the O'Connorites worked to help the Tories and defeat the Whigs at the general elections of July 1841. If as a result many intelligent Chartists had come to favour reunion with middle class radicals, it was equally clear that such a policy would never be endorsed by the whole of the Chartist body.

The next phase of the suffrage movement was not long delayed. Against a sombre background of economic recession and mounting unemployment, which seemed to emphasize the interdependence of

[7] *Leeds Times*, 15 September 1840; *Northern Star*, 2, 16 January 1841.
[8] *Northern Star*, 8, 22, 29 May 1841.

middle and working classes in the manufacturing areas, and with the cause of repeal making little headway in parliament, there emerged a new radical partnership, guided by the Reverend Edward Miall, editor of the *Nonconformist*,[9] and Joseph Sturge, a Birmingham corn factor, Quaker, philanthropist, and city alderman, widely admired for his efforts to emancipate the slaves in the West Indies.[10] In October and November 1841, the *Nonconformist* published a series of articles by Sturge on the benefits, moral, political and economic, which would come from a 'Reconciliation between the Middle and Labouring Classes' and their admission to the franchise. Miall simultaneously addressed his editorials to the Anti-Corn Law League conference assembling in Manchester 'to summon all classes to one mighty effort for freedom' under the banner of COMPLETE SUFFRAGE.[11] The conference, with its formal business completed, empowered Sturge and Sharman Crawford to draw up a document for middle class radicals to sign which would serve as the basis for a motion in parliament:

Deeply impressed with conviction of the evils arising from class legislation, and of the sufferings thereby inflicted upon our industrious fellow-subjects, the undersigned affirm that a large majority of the people of this country are unjustly excluded from that fair, full and free exercise of the legislative franchise to which they are entitled by the great principles of Christian equity, and also by the British Constitution, for 'no subject of England can be constrained to pay any aids or taxes . . . but such as are imposed by his own consent, or that of his representative in Parliament.'[12]

The Sturge declaration was introduced at a Convention of the League in Edinburgh, and adopted at a series of enthusiastic meetings in Edinburgh, Glasgow and Birmingham in January 1842, where the formation was approved of a 'cordial union of middle and working classes'.[13] At the highly significant meeting at the Crown and Anchor in London on 11 February 1842 the declaration was supported not only by middle class radicals, Sharman Crawford, John Bright, George Thompson, Archibald Prentice, Lawrence Heyworth, and repealers

[9] *Nonconformist* was published weekly in London from 1841 to 1900. Its first number of 14 April announced that it would 'represent principles, not a class', that it would be founded on the New Testament, and would advocate 'fair and full representation of all'.

[10] See Howard Temperley, *'Anti-Slavery'*, p. 45.

[11] *Nonconformist*, volume i, pp. 552, 616.

[12] Crawford's motion was presented on 28 August 1841 and obtained forty-one votes.

[13] *Nonconformist*, volume II, pp. 3, 35–40, 55, 68–9; H. Richard, *Memoirs of Joseph Sturge*, 1864, p. 302.

from Edinburgh, Paisley, Forfar, Dublin, Manchester, Sheffield, Liverpool, and Birmingham, but also by Henry Hetherington and William Lovett. If Mr Sturge and his friends would 'inquire into the Charter as a whole,' Lovett said, 'he should be prepared to give up points that were proved to be non-essential, and by those means there would be a chance of a cordial union between the middle and working classes.[14]

Such a prospect was most encouraging, but it immediately raised obvious problems. The closer they drew to Lovett and moderate Chartists, the less support Sturge could expect from the Council of the League and Cobden, who feared and probably rightly that such an alliance would hinder rather than help repeal. 'We must keep the League as a body wholly distinct from the suffrage movement,' Cobden wrote to its chairman, George Wilson, in February, while at the same time rejecting the pressure of E. W. Watkin, the organizer of the Manchester Operative Anti-Corn Law Association for an entente with the Chartists. The O'Connorites, he argued, had 'no organization, no pecuniary resources, no moral influence'.[15] The other danger was that any alliance of complete suffrage leaders with Lovett would bring down the wrath of the *Northern Star*. Although many provincial Chartists found complete suffrage congenial, the movement was quickly named 'The Plague' and its Chartist supporters were denounced as 'Complete Suffrage Humbugs' and dispossessed of office. In many Chartist localities, the result was civil war.[16]

Despite these difficulties, the movement made considerable progress in the early months of 1842, culminating in the arrangements for a conference in Birmingham on 5 April. Provisional committees, consisting mainly of middle class councillors, clergymen, small businessmen, and Chartists, had been elected in many towns to collect signatures for the Sturge declaration and to choose delegates to the conference. By March the *Nonconformist* was reporting complete suffrage associations in most large towns from Aberdeen to Plymouth, and detecting 'an astonishing change' in middle class attitudes to suffrage extension.[17]

More than a hundred delegates from fifty-one places met at Birmingham from 5 to 8 April, among them nine members of the 1839 Chartist General Convention, most notably Lovett, Collins, O'Brien, Vincent, and Lowery. As few O'Connorites who had been deputed to attend were permitted to take their seats,[18] and as there was a strong middle

[14] *Nonconformist*, volume II, pp. 108–9.

[15] J. Morley, *Life of Richard Cobden*, 1903, pp. 229–30; E. W. Watkin, *Alderman Cobden of Manchester*, 1891, pp. 82–3.

[16] *Northern Star*, 22, 29 January; 5, 19, 26 February; 12, 26 March 1842.

[17] *Nonconformist*, volume II, pp. 139–40, 184, 186, 198.

[18] O'Connor called a public meeting in Birmingham on the opening day of the conference to attack Sturge and the 'Complete Humbug' movement.

class contingent which included Sharman Crawford, John Bright, and Archibald Prentice, the future historian of the League, the conference remained throughout in the safe hands of its chairman, Joseph Sturge. But the Chartists dictated its terms. The original resolution to make representation co-extensive with taxation was dropped in favour of one conceding the franchise as a natural right, while another in favour of freedom of elections became the more explicit demand for the secret ballot. John Bright's motion for shorter (triennial) parliaments was defeated by another for annual parliaments, and one by one the six major points of the Charter were adopted as conference policy. But Lovett and O'Brien failed to have the Charter adopted in its entirety, since Sturge knew

> ... there was great alarm excited at the name of the charter, on account of the improper conduct of some persons bearing the name of chartists. Few could conceive the difficulties there were in getting people to reason calmly upon the subject. He had thought that if they could agree to the first four points it would be desirable to have another conference rather than go into further detail. They had, however, proceeded beyond it ... but he trusted that the good temper which had been hitherto exhibited would continue to be displayed. ... There were a number of chartists as anxious as the middle classes to get rid of the name. Persons, however, should not look at the name but at the thing.

Lovett, who had intended to propose the adoption of the Charter, accepted that 'the conduct of individuals had rendered the name of the Charter unpopular' and instead moved that a further conference should be called to work out the proposals in detail. The final day was spent in forming 'The National Complete Suffrage Union', agreeing its objects and rules, the issue of tracts and the appointment of missionaries, and the election of a general council whose forty-eight members included Lovett, Vincent, Collins, and fourteen Birmingham men.[19]

The complete suffrage conference had moved remarkably close to the Chartist platform, and although O'Connor ensured that O'Brien and R. K. Philp were voted off the executive of the National Charter Association, it was O'Connor who was forced to follow the rank and file and

[19] *Nonconformist*, volume II, pp. 234–44. Several delegates remained in Birmingham to prepare a public report of their conference, to a meeting in the Town Hall on 11 April. Middle class spokesmen bore testimony to the honesty and ability of the Chartists. O'Brien confessed that he had entertained grave forebodings before the conference, but he had never been present at 'an assembly where he witnessed so little malice, uncharitableness, or desire for self interest'. It deserved the support of 'every honest chartist in the kingdom'. *Nonconformist*, p. 231.

modify his position. He supported Sturge in the corrupt Nottingham by-election against John Walter of *The Times*, and published a series of letters to the 'Industrious Portion of the Middling Classes' during the summer, showing that middle class assistance was essential for working class reforms.

Over the summer, the council of the CSU met weekly in Birmingham to establish its organization, gathering support for Sharman Crawford's parliamentary motions,[20] sending out missionaries into the provinces,[21] and endorsing parliamentary candidates.[22] Minor worries included their legal status within the Corresponding Societies Act, and the slenderness of funds.[23] Major worries came in August 1842 with extensive strikes in Lancashire, Yorkshire, Staffordshire, and Lanarkshire, culminating in the Plug Plots. Chartists, repealers, and even the inoffensive complete suffragists were all in turn accused of inciting the disturbances so damaging to class relations; and a 'special extraordinary' meeting of the CSU's council on 12 September[24] reaffirmed its commitment to strictly peaceable and Christian measures, and urged the immediate formation of local committees for canvassing electors and registering supporters. The council then proceeded to arrange a national conference in Birmingham on 27 December 'for the purpose of deciding on an act of parliament, for securing the just representation of the whole people; and for determining on such peaceful, legal and constitutional means as may cause it to become the law of these realms'. In the election of representatives

... all party spirit must be excluded, all efforts for forcing individual views through the power of number, must be avoided. A victory obtained by such intolerant, overbearing policy would be defeat to our object—that of having a fairly constituted national conference—a body in whom all shades of reformers among the middle and working classes may place confidence. ...

[20] Crawford's second motion for 'full, fair and free representation' was presented on 21 April and was lost by 67 votes to 226; a month later he again divided the House but obtained only 21 votes.
[21] Henry Vincent and Robert Somers toured Scotland and the north-east, Charles Clarke and Henry Solly the west and south-west, the Reverend Thomas Spencer appointed himself to the Midlands. Vincent moved on to work in East Anglia and Samuel Smiles was recruited for Yorkshire. Apart from meetings, they formed associations and established local committees.
[22] Vincent stood at the Ipswich and George Thompson at the Southampton by-elections, Sturge at Nottingham.
[23] In the twelve months from April 1842, subscriptions came to £155, donations to £303, and there were outstanding accounts requiring a further £270.
[24] The 12 September meeting was attended by Lovett from London, John Dunlop from Edinburgh and Lawrence Heyworth from Liverpool, and strong contingents from Birmingham and Nottingham. O'Connell, Miall and Bright sent letters of support as did fifty other towns.

Half of the representatives were to be chosen by electors, the other hal
by non-electors. 'The two classes are not to interfere with each other's
meetings, otherwise the election shall be declared void.'[25]

During September, CSU temperance banquets, public meetings, and
lecture tours multiplied under the encouragement of progressive clergy,
magistrates, and former prominent Chartists. Scotland was particularly
receptive to their efforts.[26] In October and November the council
strengthened its communications by dividing the country into ten districts, each with their corresponding superintendents; and promoted
complete suffrage candidates in municipal elections with a fair degree
of success.[27] And elections began to be held for delegates to December's
conference. It was soon clear that they would not be as amicable as
Sturge and Lovett hoped. Birmingham was embarrassed to find that
O'Connor was one of its three electors' representatives; and in over
thirty towns, including Leicester, Glasgow, Paisley, Manchester,
Coventry, Bradford, Bury, South Shields, Bristol, and London, meetings
were 'packed', disturbed, and disrupted.[28] For the most part, Chartists
had their own way.

As reports of elections came in to the council, it was clear that despite
their carefully agreed arrangements to ensure equal representation for
both electors and non-electors, the aggressiveness of O'Connor's followers, coupled with the weakness of Lovett's National Association and

[25] *Nonconformist*, volume II, pp. 570–72, 591, 618–19. Towns of less than 5,000 could
send 2, larger towns 4 delegates. London, Edinburgh, Birmingham, Manchester,
Glasgow and Liverpool could send 6.
[26] Outside Birmingham, the CSU in 1842 was strongest in Edinburgh, Glasgow,
Nottingham, Newcastle, Leicester, Leeds, Aberdeen, Sheffield, Bristol, Cheltenham,
Paisley and Bradford in approximately that order. Glasgow had over a thousand
electors enrolled.
[27] Five candidates were elected in Nottingham, Glasgow, Falkirk and Sunderland,
six in Cupar, eight in Leeds and Derby, and sixteen in Birmingham.
[28] *Nonconformist*, volume II, pp. 796–7, 811–12, 828, 842–5, 859–60, 870. In Manchester the Chartists elected their own nominees after clearing the hall, armed with
pokers and bludgeons. In Newcastle, the chairman was bullied into declaring for the
Chartist candidates and refusing the complete suffrage demands for a poll, which was
taken at a further meeting several days later. In Leicester the police were called when
the Chartists prevented electors entering the hall; at Bristol there was also uproar
until they were left in possession of the hall. In Bradford the Chartists insisted on
electing three of their nominees despite their previous agreement to elect two. At
Arbroath where separate meetings were held to elect the 4 delegates, the Chartists
elected 4 and the suffragists 2. In London, 16 places were allocated to the NCA, 6 to
Lovett's National Association, 4 to the Metropolitan Reform Association, and just
2 to the CSU. At Glasgow, Loughborough, Coventry, Bury, Leicester, Warrington,
South Shields, Elderslie and Hawick, the Chartists allowed the election only of 'out
and out' Chartists. Some thirty to forty towns had disputed elections; but Sturge
could console himself with the fact that harmony had prevailed at thirty other
elections and there were no reports of serious difficulties at a further thirty-five. More
than thirty Birmingham men were elected to represent towns, mainly in Scotland
and the North, about which they knew little, to save expense.

the apathy or consternation of many of the middle class supporters was resulting in a conference mix they might not be able to control. Bright resigned from the council as early as 5 December, but Sturge continued hopeful.

When the conference began on Tuesday 27 December, almost four hundred delegates, many with disputed credentials, demanded to participate; and the council reluctantly accepted the conference's decision that a committee of nine should scrutinize credentials. The committee itself was manned mainly by O'Connorites; virtually everyone was allowed to sit, and as a result the complete suffragists were in a vulnerable minority. Only with the help of all the supporters of Lovett, O'Brien, and Collins, could they hope to achieve parity with the O'Connorite Chartists of the National Charter Association.

In these circumstances, the council was extremely foolish to press a group of four resolutions on its first day, before they had agreed their procedure with Lovett.[29] As they were already committed by the previous conference to the six points, Sturge and his colleagues now tried to embody them within a bill of rights which would have the treble advantage of being in appropriate form to present to parliament, of honouring their obligations to their Chartist friends while avoiding the O'Connorite overtones of the Charter 'name and all' which were so offensive to middle class supporters. The Bill of Rights was more innocent than its ninety-nine clauses suggested. It simply spelled out in considerable detail the mode of implementing the six principles agreed in April, such as MPs to be paid at £500 p.a., the allocation of parliamentary seats, and registration and electoral procedures. But delegates had not even seen an abstract of it, and in the acrimonious atmosphere following the elections, they were unlikely to take it on trust. Lovett, the author of the People's Charter, felt compelled to move that the Charter should be accorded equal standing with the Bill of Rights as the basis for discussion. As the previous conference had agreed that the Charter would be considered along with any other document, Lovett's motion was reasonable as well as understandable. But the council for the first time proved inflexible. Having chosen to maintain their grounds, making it an issue of principle on which the fate of the convention hung, the council was less than fortunate in its spokesmen. Chartists claimed that the middle classes were yet again betraying working men, while Dr Ritchie, Lawrence Heyworth, and Sturge impatiently stated that they were conceding all and receiving nothing in return. In their view,

[29] These resolutions adopted the principles agreed in April; disclaimed all interference with existing organizations; declared that conference would consider all documents laid before it; and that the Bill of Rights presented by the council should serve as the basis of discussion.

the council had convened the conference and it should either assert its authority or remain independent. Ritchie argued that if anything went out from the conference under the name of 'charter' it would defeat the objects they had in view. Heyworth, under the strain of the uproar, lost his self-control and while claiming to respect Chartist principles accused its leaders of tyranny.[30] To O'Connor's delight, the Sturgeites had unwittingly manoeuvred Lovett and almost all the Chartists into one camp, and they thereupon lost the division on the bill against the Charter by 94 votes to 193. Sturge and his friends withdrew, promptly reconvening themselves in a nearby Temperance hotel. They appear to have been curiously insensitive to the effect of their proposals on Lovett and the moderate Chartists. Rather they seemed to welcome the chance to withdraw from a compromising relationship which was threatening their public image; and they went eagerly about their next business, debating whether they had the right to exclude the majority and constitute themselves the conference, getting approval for their bill from the conference rump, and adopting a plan of organization and 'educational effort' from Henry Vincent.[31]

A lengthy explanation of the council's attitude came from its secretary, William Morgan.[32]

The policy of the adherents of Mr Feargus O'Connor has been such, that union with them upon their own terms must have been productive of defeat of the great object. . . . The advocates of the people's charter had no right to assume to that document a prior claim over all other documents . . . inasmuch as those principles have been incorporated in numerous schemes of parliamentary reform, long before the people's charter was proposed. . . . The recognition of the charter as a model of reform would have been fatal to the efforts of the Complete Suffrage Union to create an independent and enlightened public opinion in favour of the representation of the people in parliament. The very claim for its pre-eminence, viz., 'that in its advocacy vast numbers have suffered imprisonment, transportation and death', constitutes with thousands, a reason for identifying it with anarchy and confusion, and refusing to hear a discussion upon it. . . . The proposal of the council . . . presented no barrier to free discussion of the various plans of parliamentary reform which might be submitted to the conference. . . . The amendment was equivalent to a

[30] *Nonconformist*, volume II, pp. 873–9.
[31] A plan of public meetings in every town to support the bill, canvassing of electors, and a pledge to disseminate sound political knowledge, while spreading sobriety, peace and toleration. *Nonconformist*, volume III, pp. 4–5.
[32] *Nonconformist*, volume III, p. 20.

vote of want of confidence in the council of the Complete Suffrage Union.

The verdict of Edward Miall was similar. If the council's tactics had been indiscreet, the blame for the fiasco could nonetheless be equally placed on the 'large section of men sent thither by unfair means, for the purpose, not of deliberation, but of imperious dictation', and on the 'better-disposed but equally impracticable, leaders of chartism'. But although the movement had not escaped without some immediate damage, the danger was now over. 'A premature attempt at union has been terminated in throwing off . . . a vast mass of worthlessness, of narrow-minded bigotry, of selfishness and vanity.' The Complete Suffrage Movement 'henceforth unburdened by the follies and the crimes of prominent chartist agitators, will step forward with . . . fresher and clearer spirits'.[33]

Several towns, including Aberdeen, Cambridge, Worcester, and most Scottish towns, applauded the decisions of their delegates to withdraw with Sturge from the conference. But despite the energetic lecture tours of Vincent, who in 1843 visited at least thirty-five towns, Spencer who lectured in a further twenty, and Beggs who found 'quite a rage' for his lectures in the Midlands, the movement was clearly on the decline. Few new associations came into existence in 1843, apart from those in Norwich, Stockport, Truro, and Abergavenny; and the *Nonconformist* found itself relying on wordy and repetitive addresses to Joseph Sturge, and wordy and repetitive accounts of its lecturers' tours, to fill its columns.

The council in its turn devoted itself to bringing the Bill of Rights before parliament,[34] organizing election committees and parliamentary candidates,[35] and sustaining the propaganda of its lecturers with tracts and pamphlets.[36] In November, the council was delighted to report that the movement was now extensively supported by the press, and listed some thirty-one sympathetic papers and journals, including London's *Morning Advertiser*. With the Bill of Rights temporarily laid aside,

[33] *Nonconformist*, volume III, p. 8.

[34] Crawford and T. S. Duncombe, the Chartist champion, were to present it in parliament, and an abstract of it was sent to all MPs, and liberal editors; it was postponed from 23 February to 9 March and then to 16 March but the House was counted out. Eventually Crawford carried out his pledge on 18 May and 20 June.

[35] Election committees were set up in Leeds and Newcastle, T. Gisborne was successful at Nottingham, Vincent lost 71 to 113 at Tavistock, Bright lost 401 to 504 at Durham.

[36] These included 'A Defence of the Working Classes' by Sharman Crawford, 'The People's Rights and how to get them' by Thomas Spencer, and a lecture by the Reverend J. E. Giles to the Leeds Complete Suffrage Association. Several societies distributed tracts locally. *Nonconformist*, volume III, pp. 102, 234.

Sharman Crawford suggested that radical MPs should engage in fili-
buster, moving amendments to the Queen's Speech and appropriate
financial items, since the people had the constitutional right to voice
their grievances before voting supplies.[37] This 'Supply Movement and
Redress of Grievances' injected new life into the ebbing movement, and
Sturge and secretary Wilson toured the Bath area, Yorkshire, and the
Midlands. Promises of support came in from over fifty towns, and on
31 January 1844 seventy representatives from more than twenty towns,
assembled in London to give their final approval to the plan and wait
upon their MPs.[38] With the opening of parliament on 1 February,
Crawford duly moved his amendment, and followed this with a further
division on the 6th, but his vote had dropped from 29 to 22, and it was
clear that their effect on the Government was minimal.[39] So the council
issued a spate of addresses, and worked to return Vincent at Kilmarnock
and Sturge at Birmingham, where they succeeded only in splitting the
liberal vote and rousing liberal ire.

When the council reported on the preceding six months activity on
17 February 1845, its main themes were slavery in the USA, the need
for a domestic parliament in Ireland, and Sturge's discussion with the
Scottish complete suffragists on their response to local Chartists, whom
he had met during his customary end-of-season tour at Christmas. But
there was less and less activity to report. Towards the end of the year,
the council devoted much time to their relations with the free trade
movement and the danger of famine in Ireland. By 1846, though several
local associations still survived, only Leicester, Finsbury, and Edinburgh
continued to report regular council meetings.[40] The Metropolitan Complete Suffrage Movement, formed in November 1844 mainly to provide
column inches for the *Nonconformist* and the *Morning Advertiser*, held a
few meetings, but for the rest they were an extension of Henry Vincent's
lectures. Even here, Vincent had added popular education, religious
liberty, and particularly temperance to his repertoire to retain an
audience.

The Complete Suffrage Movement had never resolved its position
between the League on the one hand and Chartism on the other. When

[37] *Nonconformist*, volume III, pp. 660, 708–9. Duncombe was slightly scornful,
Lovett welcoming, and he followed with an address from his National Association.
[38] *Nonconformist*, volume IV, pp. 20, 35–7, 47.
[39] Crawford brought about five divisions but his support dwindled to eight.
[40] In 1844 and still more in 1845, the volume of activity fell very low. The total
number of meetings (reported in the *Nonconformist*) in 1842 was 410, 125 in 1843, 80 in
1844, 22 in 1845. This excludes lectures which were held at some 58 places in 1843,
46 in 1844, 27 in 1845, 15 in 1846. No public meetings were reported in 1844 from
Aberdeen, Bradford, Manchester, Paisley and Newcastle; and only one from
Nottingham, Bristol, Sheffield and Finsbury. Edinburgh dropped from 22 in 1842 to
7 in 1844.

the League had been in the doldrums, an alliance with suffrage extension could have proved attractive, but this the O'Connorite Chartists
would not permit; the result was to split the Chartist movement and
denude it of many of its local leaders. Once the League was moving
from strength to strength, there was little the CSU could offer it. And
so radicals within parliament dispersed their energies in a multitude of
worthy but secondary causes, such as the crusade against the Established Church, bishops, Church rates, religious tests; against infringe-
ments of private liberty, capital punishment, flogging, militia, slavery;
against aristocratic privilege and government mismanagement, primogeniture, pensions, tithes, corn laws, factory legislation, newspaper tax,
and income tax. The CSU had tried but failed to reunite middle and
working class radicals on the basis of the major demands of the Charter
and free trade.

The excitement of the French Revolution in February 1848 and the
comfort that it brought to power a Chamber of patently middle class
deputies elected by universal suffrage on the one hand, and the depression at home and troubles in Ireland on the other, ensured that the
first signs of Chartist revival would be met by middle class moves for
a radical alliance. Even the fiasco of Kennington Common in April did
nothing to damp the sudden middle class enthusiasm for suffrage extension. Early in March there was talk of plans by Cobden, Bright, and
Hume to form a 'People's League' to reform parliament and reduce
taxation;[41] Bright in particular had his aim primarily on a redistribution
of parliamentary seats. Other essential parts of the programme were the
ballot and shorter parliaments.

The customary machinery swung into action. Provisional committees
of electors were appointed, meetings arranged, mayors, MPs, pro-
fessors, provosts, and churchmen were approached to act as chairmen,
and resolutions were adopted. The intentions of Joseph Hume were
elaborated in the resolution adopted at the Middlesex county meeting
on 17 May:

That to secure the stability of the throne, public order and content-
ment, the constitutional rights of the people, equalization of taxation,
economy of the public expenditure, just laws, and good government,
it is indispensable that the elective franchise should be extended to

[41] Cornewall Lewis wrote to Sir James Graham on 20 April, 'If the bulk of the
upper and middle classes cannot continue to keep on good terms for the next six
months, a few ambitious and vindictive men may call in the assistance of the working
classes in the large towns and overthrow everything. I hear that Bright proposes that
the Metropolis should return fifty to sixty members, and by universal or household
suffrage.' (S. Maccoby, *English Radicalism, 1832–52* (1935), p. 287.) Cobden, as before,
had misgivings.

all men who are registered as residents for a limited time; that the duration of parliament should not exceed three years; that votes should be taken by ballot; and that there should be more equal apportionment of members to population.[42]

Occasionally, it was resolved as in 1832 to abstain from consuming taxed luxuries and to eschew violence. The degree of suffrage extension was allowed to remain an open question. Some meetings, particularly the Scottish ones, demanded universal suffrage; others favoured the 'full, fair and free representation' formulated by the CSU. Meetings infiltrated by the Chartists, though orderly enough, usually mentioned the Charter, as at Edinburgh on 21 April. This welcomed an extension of the suffrage, the reduction of taxation and the People's League as a means of 'effecting a union of working and middle classes on the principle of equal and just representation as set forth in the People's Charter—with such alterations and amendments as may appear necessary.'[43] But Cobden and O'Connor continued to snipe at each other, and Lord John Russell judged correctly that this enthusiasm lacked roots. There was little excitement in the country when Hume eventually presented his motion on 20 June that the suffrage should be given to all rate-payers. He mustered only 86 votes, and few radicals professed indignation at Russell's assessment that 'while erroneous and mischievous views of capital, of labour, and of property' were threatening danger, it was not the time to consider great changes. Minor amendments could be dealt with in the 'perhaps not distant' future.[44]

In a few towns, the new electoral associations continued to select, pledge, and support candidates, and in Glasgow's municipal elections the former Chartist, James Moir, was returned at the head of the poll. More significant was the establishment by Sir Joshua Walmsley and Lawrence Heyworth of the Liverpool Financial Reform Association, and its efforts to promote similar bodies in Manchester, London, Glasgow, and Edinburgh. Cobden provided them with proposals to cut the votes for army, navy and ordnance from £18·5 million to £10 million; to abolish duties on butter, cheese, timber, malt, paper, soap, hops, window tax, and advertisement duty; and to reduce the duty on tea to 1s. per pound.[45]

Such a limited programme failed to enthuse John Bright, who brought pressure to bear on Cobden to link financial with parliamentary reform in a new 'Common's League', to be led by the reformers of

[42] Maccoby, pp. 287–8.
[43] *The Scotsman*, 22 April, 6 May, 17 June 1848.
[44] *The Scotsman*, 24 June 1848.
[45] *Glasgow Examiner*, 23 September, 9 December 1848; Morley, pp. 495–9.

Manchester. Cobden's hesitations were overcome,[46] and he, Bright and George Wilson, chairman of the old League, launched the new League in Manchester and the north in January 1849. Several thousand supporters were enrolled, but the Commons League was virtually stillborn. For while Bright wanted a suffrage extension campaign centred on Lancashire and Yorkshire, Cobden wanted a London based association for financial reform, concentrating its local energies on creating 40s. freeholders.[47]

The idea of linking financial and parliamentary reform was more sensible than Cobden allowed, and although his freehold land agitation kept active in London, Sheffield and particularly Birmingham, it was Hume's and Walmsley's movement for parliamentary and financial reform that made more progress in 1849 and 1850. Supporting societies were established in London, Birmingham, Manchester, Sheffield, Leeds, and the other major English and Scottish towns. Their public meetings increasingly demonstrated strong radical sympathies for the continental liberals in Rome, Baden, and Hungary. O'Connor stopped abusing Cobden and began to associate himself with the movement, seeing in it a way to revive Chartism. 'Therefore,' he appealed to his 'Old Guards'

> I ask you in the name of honour, justice, patriotism and the CHARTER, to join the new Parliamentary Reform Association, heart and soul, as the only means of breaking down . . . that feudal system which has so long held you as bondsmen in fetters . . . (what was needed now was) UNION between the veritable middle classes and the working classes.[48]

But if O'Connor, and certain leading Chartists such as Thomas Clarke and George Reynolds, supported Hume and Walmsley, Cobden remained cool and resisted Bright's persuasion to lend his name and supporters.[49]

[46] Cobden preferred the Liverpool Association to any Commons League. They could not 'ignore the existence of the Liverpool movement. However defective in men and money at present, they are in as good a position as we were a year after the League was formed; and they have far more hold upon the public mind than we had even after three years' agitation'. (Morley, pp. 495–9.)

[47] See David Martin, 'Land Reform', p. 151.

[48] *Northern Star*, 13, 20 October; 10 November 1849.

[49] 'I do not object to Walmsley's proceedings', Cobden replied on 1 October. 'I have subscribed my mite to his association and cheered him on. He has rendered this good service . . . that he has brought middle-class people and Chartists together without setting them by the ears, and although he has rather shocked some moderate Liberals by his broad doctrines, he has carried others unconsciously with him. But . . . I have not disguised from him that mere demonstrations without an organized system of working will do nothing towards effecting a change in the representation. That can only be done in the registration courts, and above all by the forty shilling votes in the counties.' (Morley, pp. 515–17.)

Walmsley, George Thompson, and O'Connor[50] together toured Scotland in the autumn of 1849, acquiring the support of former Chartists, councillors, and MPs. This was followed by a fund-raising meeting in London in January 1850 which brought in £1,500 towards a target figure of £10,000 for the year. All seemed hopeful, but soon their Chartist allies were again involved in internal strife sparked off by Harney's criticisms of the Parliamentary and Financial Reform Association. The early months of 1850 were devoted to preparing for a three day conference of the association, in April. It was to be the most impressive suffrage reform conference since that of Sturge in 1842. One hundred and thirty delegates, including Hume, Walmsley, O'Connor, Reynolds, Cobden, and Bright, came from all over the country.

Yet it is difficult to see that this almost endless round of meetings, 'banquets', and conferences, had much effect on the thinking and voting of the House of Commons. The radical motions each year of Hume, Berkeley, and Locke King on suffrage extension and the ballot seemed useful only to remind ministers of the total voting strength of the parliamentary radicals. Nor did reform meetings appear to affect ministerial calculations and promises. The radical press obtained useful copy for its large readership, and local reformers kept their organization in trim, but beyond that the PFRA seemed incapable of going. It had still not won over the main body of Chartist opinion, despite O'Connor's support.[51] Inside parliament, their greatest triumph was the promise extracted from Russell, during Locke King's county franchise debate on 20 February 1851, to introduce a measure of reform in the next session.

Nor had Bright won over the other key figure in any reform alliance, Richard Cobden. On 29 September he wrote to Bright that he could not

> . . . see any indications of a breeze in the direction of Reform. People are too well-to-do in the world to agitate for anything . . . I am willing to do my share in the House or out of it, as an individual; but when you suggest a Conference under the auspices of Wilson and ourselves in Manchester, it is well to consider whether we may not be under the risk of deceiving ourselves. . . . If we move together at the head of an organization, it will be assumed that we are going to bring the League following us. . . . Do not deceive yourself; the same men will not fight the battle of Parliamentary Reform.[52]

50 Commented the *Northern Star* (12 January 1850), 'May the walls of exclusion soon be thrown down by the united efforts of the National Reform Association and the Chartists . . . Mr O'Connor cannot confer a greater benefit on the middle and labouring classes than by forming a link between both, on which they can repose confidence.'

51 When Holyoake tried to persuade the Chartist convention to co-operate with all reformers, he was defeated by Ernest Jones' argument that the PFRA would enfranchise only the aristocracy of labour. (*Northern Star*, 5, 12 April 1851).

52 Morley, pp. 557–8.

However, he did agree to come to a large meeting of the Friends of Parliamentary Reform in the Free Trade Hall, Manchester, on 3 December, to consider their response to Russell's promised Bill. Bright's proposals—the franchise to all ratepaying occupants, ballots, shorter parliaments, no property qualifications, no constituencies of more than 5,000 electors, and a redistribution of seats—were adopted almost unanimously.

Both Cobden and Bright had some justification for their different attitudes. Russell's Reform Bill of 9 February 1852 did substantially increase the franchise, and abolished the property qualifications for MPs. The radicals were highly critical of it, but failed to modify it. Ironically, Russell's Ministry fell only a few days later when radicals and Tories attacked his defence policies; and a Tory ministry was established whose first pronouncements on 27 March, favouring a duty on corn, finally stirred Cobden into action.[53] He and Wilson quickly revived the League in Manchester.

Meanwhile Hume, Walmsley, and Thompson tried yet again to re-unite radicals and Chartists, and to this end convened a 'conference of Delegates and Leading Reformers' in St Martin's Hall, London. Hume, its chairman, called on delegates to accept a compromise without giving up the full opinions they professed. G. J. Holyoake, on behalf of the National Charter Association, supported the appeal, Earnest Jones would not, and the meeting ended in uproar.[54] But in Glasgow, Birmingham, and Manchester, local Chartists aligned themselves with middle class radicals. Hume and Walmsley organized numerous meetings in 1852 which though too late for either Russell's Reform Bill of 9 February or Hume's motion of 25 March,[55] probably helped to ensure the return of radical candidates in the general elections in July. Even then, the radicals seemed unable to bring pressure from without on ministerial attitudes. The former *Northern Star* published the obituary of the PFRA in the autumn of 1852:

The Parliamentary Reform Association is a large body. It has too that recommendation which is of such great importance. . . . It is respectable. Its leaders are men of wealth and station who have the opportunity of speaking their opinions before assembled legislators. The funds which are applied to promote its objects . . . are considerable. Some hundreds of meetings have been held throughout the country, at which the crack orators of the party have spoken. Addresses have

[53] Morley, p. 576.
[54] *Nonconformist*, 3 March 1852, pp. 164–5.
[55] Hume's motion was for household and lodger franchise, the ballot and triennial parliaments. It was lost by 89 to 244.

been issued, and newspaper advocates have not been wanting. With a good cause straightforwardly put and consistently expounded, such materials could hardly fail to command success. Yet the Parliamentary Association has done as little, perhaps less in proportion to its means and opportunities, as any other political body. Much noise and little work has been the order of the day. They have sounded the trumpet, but they have not fought the battle.[56]

Certainly Cobden had been right in his analysis that there was no enthusiasm for parliamentary reform outside the working classes; but this the leaders of the PFRA knew perfectly well. Where they failed was to win sufficient middle class men to their ranks to impress both working class politicians and members of parliament.

It was not that the radicals could not have obtained a further instalment of reform before 1867, for with their support Russell could have carried his modest Bills of February 1852, February 1854, or March 1860.[57] Nor was it simply a matter of ill-luck that foreign affairs dominated politics since even Palmerston, Disraeli, and Derby, paid lip service to parliamentary reform on occasion. But the proposals were modest and did little to redistribute seats; and it was clear to Palmerston for one that 'all such changes as were desirable have been long since effected'.[58]

Despite foreign distractions, such as the Crimean war, the Italian struggles for independence and unification, the American civil war, and the suppression of Polish autonomy, the same groups of reformers kept the suffrage question alive throughout the 1850s and 1860s; but their activities were desultory and until 1866 exceedingly respectable. In 1855 their new move was to form the Administrative Reform Association, with Layard as its parliamentary spokesman.[59] However there was little electoral support for radical advocacy of peace and administrative reform and Milner, Gibson, Layard, Cobden, and Bright all lost their seats in the general elections of March 1857.

More typically there were again attempts at the end of 1857 for a 'thorough union between the middle and working classes' in anticipa-

[56] *The Star of Freedom*, 18 September 1852.
[57] Russell offered a £6 borough franchise (£5 in 1852), and a £10 county franchise (£20 in 1852), with a slight redistribution of seats (none in 1852, 49 in 1854 and 25 in 1860). Lord Aberdeen had promised in December 1852 that his new ministry would not exclude from its consideration 'an amendment of the representative system, undertaken without haste or rashness'. (J. Irving, *The Annals of our Time* (1876), pp. 347–8.)
[58] Irving, p. 672.
[59] See Olive Anderson, 'The Administrative Reform Association', chapter 11, below.

tion of Palmerston introducing a reform bill in the next session. The result was the London Reform Association in November which produced an address signed by thirty-six MPs and 240 well known reformers which was circulated and adopted at numerous meetings in Yorkshire, Lancashire, London, Norwich, Worcester, Glasgow, and Carlisle. And again typically, some of these meetings were captured by Chartists for manhood suffrage.[60] As the national Chartist conference had recently adopted a resolution by Ernest Jones calling for union with middle class reformers on the basis of manhood suffrage, about 100 representatives of the Reform Association met the Chartist delegates on 11 February 1858, in St Martin's Hall, London, to set up a joint committee. Samuel Morley, Ernest Jones, and G. J. Holyoake made conciliatory speeches but again the radical alliance could generate no enthusiasm in the country at large.[61] Even if Palmerston's ministry had not fallen on 19 February, it is unlikely that his promised reform bill would have amounted to much. As one radical editor put it:

It is but evident that he will have but little pressure from without to compel a proper measure. The country is at present politically dead. Political parties are defunct, and isolated reformers have but little influence. . . . Food is cheap, and till lately employment was abundant. . . .[62]

The progress of the London Reform Association was reviewed by its secretary, Edward Pryce, at its conference in November 1858. Birmingham, Manchester, Liverpool, Newcastle, Edinburgh, and Glasgow all had strong movements; the parliamentary motions of Locke King, Caird, Berkeley, Fox, and others had kept the issue alive in the Commons; property qualifications for MPs had been abolished and they had successfully divided the House in favour of a £10 occupational franchise for the counties. Bright, who had only recently emerged from political retirement, agreed to introduce a reform bill in the coming session, and he asked that local associations be formed in support, funds raised, meetings held, and petitions signed.

There was considerable significance in the choice of John Bright, and Roebuck's graceful withdrawal of his own claims to lead the radical alliance. Although Bright's leadership was not yet undisputed,[63] he was now to determine its direction and its tone. Less influenced than

[60] *Nonconformist*, 1858, pp. 10, 11.
[61] *Nonconformist*, 1858, pp. 108, 134.
[62] *Glasgow Examiner*, 9 January 1858.
[63] The Northern Reform Association, led by Newcastle's Joseph Cowen, MP, was not easily reconciled to Bright's moderate programme, and for several years tried to persuade George Thompson MP to act as the champion of advanced liberals.

formerly by Cobden, and coming gradually to an understanding with trade union leaders, Bright could develop the combined strategy which had been missing in 1842 and 1849. At Bradford on 17 January he outlined his bill: a ratepayers franchise, the disenfranchisement of fifty-six boroughs, the loss of an MP from a further thirty, and redistribution of these seats to the cities and large boroughs.[64] Meetings at Manchester and Glasgow suggested that such a bill would be acceptable to the working classes if Bright lent his name to it; and reform meetings, in which former Chartists were present, were held at Leicester, Norwich, Paisley, and Portsmouth.

In the confused political situation of 1859 all seemed hopeful, since first the Derby-Disraeli minority ministry was pledged to modest reform, then Russell to a 'sound, moderate and constitutional measure of reform', and finally Gladstone that among the new Palmerstonian ministry's 'early as well as its very gravest duties will be the proposal of a Reform bill.'[65] But while the new Liberal government dragged its feet, advanced Liberals turned their attention to Mazzini and Garibaldi, and Cobden advised Bright to be 'more exclusively a House of Commons man', and drop provincial reform agitation.[66] By the time Russell introduced the government's bill on 1 March 1860, public interest was so slender and the debates so languid that the bill was withdrawn in June. Bright and his colleagues were temporarily more intent on teaching the House of Lords a lesson for rejecting the Paper Duty repeal clause in the budget, than in improving Russell's bill.

1861 was another barren year for the reform cause. Locke King's annual motion for reducing the county franchise was again narrowly defeated, Baines's motion for reducing the borough franchise to £6 was heavily lost, and Bright continued to fulminate against the aristocracy. In November the Leeds Reform Association tried to break this apathy and plans were laid for a National Reform conference in London in May 1862; but despite local efforts to arrange regular organization, they could arouse no popular feeling.[67]

Two years later the reform scene appeared virtually unchanged. In parliament, Berkeley's motion for the ballot was lost by 212 to 123, and Locke King's County Franchise Bill suffered its usual narrow defeat. Palmerston's confidence that constitutional change was neither desired nor desirable seemed unshaken. But a month later in May 1864 when Baines introduced his bill to lower the borough franchise, Gladstone

---

[64] *Nonconformist*, 1858, pp. 1013–15; Irving, p. 533.
[65] Disraeli's bill offered a £10 county franchise and a new borough franchise based on personal property, pensions, savings, education and profession.
[66] Morley, pp. 813–14; Cowen collection, 704, 795, 919, 990.
[67] *Glasgow Examiner*, 23 November, 14 December 1861; *Glasgow Sentinel*, 17, 24 February 1862.

surprised the House by drawing the opposite conclusion: because there was no public agitation, it was therefore safe to make large concessions. Despite the conversion of his Chancellor to reform, Palmerston would not budge; and eight months later Bright impatiently asserted that England could not be said to be free until representatives of all Englishmen were admitted to Parliament.[68]

This led to talk of a new reform movement, and early in March 1865 there was a conference of working class reformers in St Martin's Hall, London, which as in 1858, was followed by an exploratory meeting with middle class reformers from the National Reform Union. Bright, Ayrton, and Morley advocated household suffrage, but Taylor, Lawson, and Edmond Beales, who was president of the mainly working class National Reform League,[69] sided with Odger, Conolly, Potter, and other working class representatives in refusing to enter any movement for less than manhood suffrage protected by the ballot. This programme was presented to a national reform conference in Manchester on 15 and 16 May, sponsored by the National Reform Union. Its 650 delegates from 170 towns included some of the best known survivors of the suffrage movements of the previous thirty years. It was agreed that the forthcoming elections should return a parliament pledged this time to reform. In his July election address, Bright accused the Palmerston administration of violating its 1859 election pledges and predicted that the Ministry would 'soon totter to its fall; but the question of reform lives, and at the moment in the eyes of its opponents takes a more distinct shape than at any other period since the passing of the bill of 1832'.[70] After the elections he was awaiting only the end of Palmerston's 'official life'.

So when Palmerston died on 18 October, Bright and his colleagues quickly renewed their reform activity, and before the end of the year held meetings in most major towns. Much of their energy was devoted to capturing Gladstone whose readiness to support reform had damaged him in the Oxford and South Lancashire elections, and who was now receiving petitions and deputations from working men. With Russell as premier, it now looked at last as if the forces within parliament would be strong enough to ensure reform, provided that there was sufficient

[68] *Nonconformist*, 1865, pp. 71, 74–5.
[69] The National Reform Union, which had been formed in 1864, consisted of more than 130 branches throughout the country, but largely in the North and Midlands. It was firmly under the influence of John Bright. The National Reform League was formed in 1865, out of the 'Trade Union Manhood Suffrage and Vote by Ballot Association', which had been set up in 1862 by trade union leaders who were impatient at the readiness of Bright and middle class radicals to compromise on household suffrage. Several well-to-do radicals, such as Morley, Lawson, Salt and Taylor, gave financial support to both organizations, which were both rivals and allies.
[70] Irving, pp. 708–9.

pressure from without. The Queen's speech promised 'such improvements in the laws which regulate the right of voting . . . as may strengthen our free institutions'. And although Gladstone's bill of 12 March 1866 fell short of Bright's hopes, he promised it his support as 'a simple and honest measure'. He fiercely attacked Horsman and Lowe for splitting the Liberals, and became still more worried when the Conservatives decided to oppose the bill. At Manchester, Bright urged the immediate organization of meetings and petitions and wrote to a Birmingham reform meeting on 26 March:

> Parliament is never hearty for reform. . . . It does not like the franchise bill now upon its table. . . . But notwithstanding such a Parliament, this bill will pass if Birmingham and other towns do their duty. . . . If Parliament-street from Charing Cross to the venerable Abbey were filled with men seeking a Reform Bill, as it was two years ago with men come to do honour to an illustrious Italian, these slanderers of their countrymen would learn to be civil.[71]

In the subsequent wave of meetings, Gladstone declared in Liverpool that the government had crossed the Rubicon. It would now stand or fall by its bill, but he warned his audience that 'it is not in our power to secure the passing of the measure; that rests more with you, and more with those you represent'.[72] The defection of Lowe and his Abdullamites forced the government's resignation on 25 June.

This roused the radicals and the National Reform League, and on 29 June they met in Trafalgar Square to censure Russell for resigning without seeking a dissolution. A second demonstration was held in Trafalgar Square on 2 July, and a mass demonstration was proposed for Hyde Park on 23 July. This was forbidden by the Home Secretary on 19 July, so the League leaders ceremoniously marched to the park's gates; they were refused entry, and the crowd rioted. Reform demonstrations were now planned throughout the country by organizations linked to the League and the Union.

Bright, Beales, and Jones, with an entourage of Reform League and Union notables, moved from one demonstration to the next, speaking to 200,000 in Birmingham in August, on to massive meetings in Manchester, Leeds, Glasgow, Edinburgh, and finally back to London in December. Trade unionists were prominent both on the platform and in the processions.

[71] Irving, pp. 725, 728–30. The Government bill provided for a £14 county franchise, and a £7 borough franchise, with various concessions for compound householders and lodgers. A separate bill for the redistribution of 49 seats, and Scottish and Irish reform bills were introduced on 7 May.

[72] Irving, pp. 731–6, 743; *Nonconformist*, 1866, pp. 438, 517, 613.

The strength of these demonstrations appears to have swayed Derby and Disraeli into their decision to introduce yet another reform measure in the next parliamentary session, a 'real and satisfactory bill'. Disraeli introduced it on 18 March 1867, but although it seemed to offer household suffrage, it excluded the compounders and offset its liberal effects with restrictions designed to favour the more conservative sections of society. Gladstone was highly critical, and Bright argued that there was not a single proposition in the bill that 'any real earnest, intelligent reformer would consent to'.[73] The Reform League again called a meeting in Hyde Park for 6 May. The Home Secretary swore in great numbers of special constables and the government eventually decided not to suppress the meeting unless disorder occurred. The radicals were at last applying pressure with some degree of success both within and without parliament. During the ensuing parliamentary debates on the bill, the radicals won several important concessions. Compound householders were no longer to be excluded, and a further twelve seats were obtained for redistribution by raising the minimum size for a two member borough to 10,000. The government was also forced to withdraw its proposals for educational and property qualifications. Meanwhile outside parliament, the National Reform Union mounted the largest demonstration ever held in Manchester, and in London the League used its strength to overawe the Lords during their deliberations in July and early August. A few days later, the bill received the royal assent.

Once again the Tories had followed the course of bending before the storm and beating a graceful retreat when their opponents could show overwhelming force and determination. But neither they nor Whig administrations showed any sign of being impressed by much less than complete solidarity within the ranks of the radicals. The radicals for their part were left with some lingering doubts about the extent of their suffrage victory. 'We may go forward,' wrote Miall, '—the Reform Act of 1867 may and probably will be supplemented by further radical changes before the lapse of many years.'[74] Indeed, after nearly forty years of agitation and organization, the radicals had still not obtained anything approaching manhood suffrage, nor the ballot, nor a reasonably fair distribution of seats, nor even triennial parliaments. And while the 1867 Reform Act allowed them to win several additional seats in the following election, the failure of Edmond Beales and Ernest Jones to win places in the reformed parliament recalled the unsuccessful attempts of earlier spokesmen of the people's right, such as Dr John Taylor, Joseph

[73] Gladstone decided to transform the bill by a series of resolutions and withdrew from the leadership of the Liberal party when his policy was not accepted by his colleagues.

[74] *Nonconformist*, 1867, p. 686.

Sturge, and Henry Vincent, to represent their supporters without parliament. The radicals had numbered constantly between fifty and one hundred and very often had held the balance of power, a position they had failed to exploit. For Cobden, Hume, Attwood, and most of their colleagues, basically distrusted the masses; and were themselves concerned less with manhood suffrage than with promoting industry and commerce and eroding aristocratic power; concerned less with trebling the electorate than with redistributing parliamentary seats to the industrial towns.

Further Reading

John Cannon's *Parliamentary Reform 1640–1832* (1973) provides a survey for the period before 1832. On the 1832 Reform Act itself there is an extensive literature, headed by Michael Brock's *The Great Reform Act* (1973) and Norman Gash's *Politics in the Age of Peel* (1953); two articles which have reinterpreted the nature of the Act, D. C. Moore's, 'The Other Face of Reform', *Victorian Studies* 1961, and 'Concession or Cure', *Historical Journal*, 1966. Professor Asa Briggs has examined the background of the reform movement in two articles in the *Cambridge Historical Journal* for 1948 and 1952. N. McCord's article, 'Some difficulties of parliamentary reform', in the *Historical Journal* 1967, and Professor Hanham's Historical Association pamphlet, 'The reformed Electoral System 1832–1914', open up the wider issues.

There is no adequate modern account of the suffrage question in the 1840s, independent of its Chartist version. For the 1850s, F. Gillespie's classic, *Labour and Politics in England, 1850–1867* (1927), has not been displaced; though F. Herrick's 'The Second Reform Movement, 1850–1865', *Journal of the History of Ideas*, 1948, is useful. The literature begins again with 1867, R. Harrison's *Before the Socialists*, 1965; M. Cowling's *1867* (1967), and F. B. Smith, *The Making of the Second Reform Act* (1966).

5

William Lovett

David Large

William Lovett's autobiography[1] has made the outline of his career well known. Born in Newlyn in 1800[2] his childhood, like others in his circle, was marked with harshness[3] and no job awaited him after his apprenticeship to a drunken master ropemaker. He migrated to London, a penniless young man, managed to make a living as a cabinet maker, embarked on strenuous self-education and was attracted first to Owenite co-operation and then also to radical political reform in the heady days preceding and during the crisis of the first Reform Bill. Subsequently in 1836 he founded the London Working Men's Association, progenitor of the famous People's Charter, and served as secretary of the first Chartist National Convention in 1839 until arrested and lodged in Warwick gaol following rioting in Birmingham's Bull Ring for which he was held responsible. On release he sought, but largely failed, to steer the Chartist leadership into concentrating on the moral and educational advance of working men, a cause which increasingly preoccupied him in later life and led him to join liberal–radical crusades for peace, land reform, teetotalism and so forth in which his role was that of a follower rather than a teacher.

Three questions in particular are worth exploring: what did Lovett stand for? What means did he use to achieve his aims? What was the nature of the support he aroused?

What was the quality and content of Lovett's radicalism? Although

[1] *Life and Struggles of William Lovett in his pursuit of Bread, Knowledge and Freedom* (1876). Reprinted in 1920 in two volumes with an introduction by R. H. Tawney and again in 1967 omitting the last three chapters.

[2] He was baptized on 25 May in St Paul's Church (J. J. Beckerlegge, *William Lovett of Newlyn* (1948), p. 4).

[3] His father was drowned before his birth; his mother, Keziah, at one time supported life by odd jobs such as selling fish in Penzance market. William regarded her second marriage as very unhappy and lived with his grandmother whom he supported by his own pitifully small earnings, cf. Hetherington whose father was a prosperous tailor who gave up his business, bought a pub and drank himself into a premature grave leaving a widow overwhelmed by misery, debt and four children. (Holyoake MSS. in Holyoake House, Manchester.)

he began his career as a political Owenite and ended it as a liberal radical it is as well to emphasize the consistent and enduring elements in his radicalism. Throughout his life Lovett was deeply influenced by his thorough soaking in his early days as a member of the Radical Reform Association (RRA)[4] in that traditional radicalism matured by Paine, Carlile, Cobbett, and Hunt which vehemently denounced aristocracy, monopoly, taxes and corruption. It asserted that the rights of the millions must be safeguarded 'by the restoration of Universal Suffrage and Annual Parliaments with the protection of Vote by the Ballot'.[5] If one turns from the first to the last of the political associations with which Lovett was actively connected, the People's League established in 1848,[6] one finds him still sawing away along the same lines. In the addresses which he prepared for it the diseases of society are still 'over-burthening taxation', 'extravagant expenditure' imposed by 'the overwhelming power of aristocratic nominees' in parliament and the only effective cure is 'the equal and just representation of the whole people'[7] though by now there is a detailed parliamentary bill prepared for achieving this object, the celebrated People's Charter. In short to Lovett until his dying day the real enemy remained the aristocracy not the middle class manufacturer. Right down to the very last pages of the running diary that makes up the last chapters of his autobiography he keeps up the attack: the aristocracy has robbed the industrious, artisan, and manu-

[4] The RRA was formed in July 1829. To begin with it held monthly meetings at the London Mechanics Institute to popularize the cause of radical parliamentary reform. Hunt and Cobbett, though only briefly, supported it but its proceedings became increasingly dominated by Lovett, Hetherington, Cleave, Watson and Warden. An attempt to unite RRA supporters with middle class radicals in a Metropolitan Political Union in 1830 failed. The RRA preserved its separate identity and held its own mass meeting on Kennington Common in October 1830 and now met weekly at the Rotunda in Blackfriars Road. Here, thanks to the July revolution in France, the utmost excitement prevailed: the tricolour was regularly sported, the formation of a National Guard was demanded and threats that forcible action would be taken to assert the people's rights were heard. All this was intermingled with the demands of traditional radicalism. By December 1830, however, the RRA had dissolved in a welter of dissension between those such as Hunt who drew back from adopting a revolutionary stance and those such as Lovett, Watson and Carlile who taunted Hunt as a traitor to the radical cause.

[5] To quote the RRA's address to the people of the United Kingdom in 1829 signed by its secretary, Lovett's friend Hetherington. (*Weekly Free Press*, 24 October 1829.)

[6] The People's League aimed at uniting all radicals, middle and working class, behind a programme of the Charter, reduced government spending and the abolition of indirect taxes in favour of progressive direct taxation on property. It was dissolved in September 1849 after being sharply attacked by Feargus O'Connor and Ernest Jones and failing to gain the support of parliamentary radicals such as Hume and Cobden. Its few hundred supporters included nonconformist radicals such as Edward Miall and Thomas Beggs and Chartists such as Lovett and Robert Lowery, its first secretary, by now increasingly identified with crusades such as that for teetotalism. (*Life and Struggles*, pp. 335-49.)

[7] *Life and Struggles*, p. 338.

facturer alike, of their political rights, has monopolized ownership of the land and far from being a cultivated elite is given up to betting, racing, and shooting.[8]

The second enduring element in Lovett's radicalism was, of course, his struggle 'in pursuit of knowledge'. It sprang from his experiences in the 1820s, the truly formative decade in his life. As he related in classic pages in his autobiography, driven by an acute consciousness of the defects of his early education, he was then 'awakened to a new mental existence' by joining a small literary association, attending lectures at the London Mechanics Institute and frequenting the London coffee shops where Richard Carlile and the old revolutionary Gale Jones held forth.[9] The awakening went deep with Lovett. It led him into radical politics, Owenism, and repudiation of the Methodism in which he had been reared. Nevertheless, although he was sufficiently influenced by Carlile's infidel doctrines to champion him in 1830 and break with Hunt on this score[10] he did not really involve himself deeply in free thought. Unlike his friends Hetherington and Watson he took no part in the atheist mission to England of the 1840s. The morality of Methodism he never repudiated, witness his puritan character structure. One cannot imagine the sober, honest, and respectable Lovett deserting his wife and driving her literally insane by deposing her in favour of a servant girl as John Cleave did.[11] In reality Lovett resembled those Leicester Chartists of dissenting background[12] who believed in 'a very plain, simple and practical Christianity' devoid of credal beliefs, conceding the right of private judgment and free from all priestly 'mercenary idlers'. To Lovett the twin duties of man were quite simply 'to love God and to do unto all men as he would wish them to do unto him'.[13]

But above all the experience of the 1820s provided him with a substitute religion—the gospel of knowledge. You carried out your twin duties by acquiring knowledge; you differentiated yourself from the savage by studying His creation and this was one reason for Lovett's emphasis on studying geology, zoology, and astronomy—that 'region of enquiry above all others in which the human mind has been expanded to the achievement of its grandest and proudest triumphs', as he put it.[14]

---

[8] *Ibid.*, pp. 343–4, 406, 427, 440. [9] *Life and Struggles*, pp. 34–6.

[10] H.O. 64/11, informer's report of 20 November 1830.

[11] Carlile MSS., 15 January 1840; some confirmation of the none too reliable Carlile is provided by Place's remark in a letter in June 1840 to Lovett then in Warwick gaol, 'Cleave has conducted himself towards his wife and daughters in a manner too disgraceful to be written about.' (*Place Newspaper collection*, set 55, f. 555.)

[12] For them see J. F. C. Harrison, 'Chartism in Leicester' in A. Briggs (ed.), *Chartist Studies* (1959), p. 140.

[13] To quote his specimen lesson card on the DUTIES of man appended to W. Lovett and J. Collins, *Chartism, a new organization for the people* (1969 edn.), pp. 123–4.

[14] *Life and Struggles*, pp. 376–7.

Unlike those self-made literary men, Thomas Cooper and Henry Vincent, Lovett had little of the Romantic in him but much of the Enlightenment: knowledge promotes the happiness of all was his constant refrain. Knowledge would destroy the ignorance that led to crime, vice, intemperance, brutality, prostitution, and all the evils of a society that condemned the millions to poverty while exalting the few to power and wealth. Education was 'a universal instrument for advancing the dignity of man'. It would teach the millions their political rights and how to attain them through union and organization by which alone the true power of the working class would be demonstrated.[15]

Throughout his life, for there was little that was new in spirit about his 'new move'[16] in 1840–41, Lovett remained convinced that if only all obstacles could be removed, all could follow his path and acquire life-giving Knowledge and thus society would be transformed. Hence his fierce hostility to the Taxes on Knowledge, to education dominated by dissent or establishment or government controlled in the Prussian sense, or viewed as 'a boon to be sparingly conferred on the multitude'. Lovett uncompromisingly proclaimed the *right* of everyone to education. And, as is well known, in his *Chartism* (1840), he elaborated plans for achieving this through a system of infant, preparatory, and high schools, teachers' training schools and so forth which demonstrated his relief in the benefits of organization for the working classes, his 'enlightened' views on educational practice, his faith in the democratic management of schools, and his enthusiasm for mutual self-help. Although he owed much to Owen's example in all this Lovett certainly displayed a genuinely radical, even original, vision.

However when one turns to Lovett's other struggle, that for bread, or

---

[15] See especially his Address on education composed for the LWMA in 1837 for which see *ibid.*, pp. 135–46.

[16] The term 'the new move' was bestowed by the *Northern Star* on Lovett's proposal in March 1841, originally propounded in his *Chartism*, that a National Association embracing all Chartists should be formed 'to create an enlightened opinion in favour of the Charter' and to launch a general scheme of education. Since the Chartists had already evolved an increasingly flourishing national organization, the National Charter Association (NCA) Lovett's proposal was bound to seem a 'new' move to supplant that body. Feargus O'Connor and leading figures in the NCA's metropolitan localities (e.g. Henry Ross) sharply attacked the proposal on this score and branded it as an unholy conspiracy between Lovett and O'Connell, Hume and Roebuck to split the Chartists, destroy the NCA and the *Northern Star* and substitute household for universal suffrage as the main aim of the movement. O'Connor also saw the new move as more subtly destructive of Chartism: 'Knowledge Chartism', to use his term, 'impliedly acknowledges a standard of learning as a necessary qualification to entitle a man to his political rights' and teetotal Chartism (which Lovett also supported) was open to the objection 'that all who do not join it, will be considered unworthy of their civil rights'. (*Northern Star*, 3, 10, 24 April 1841.) Lovett, none the less, went ahead with forming his National Association which attempted to put his educational ideals into practice.

in other words his attitude to what can loosely be termed the anti-capitalist strand in radical thinking as exemplified by Owen or the early English socialists and later by Bronterre O'Brien, Julian Harney, and Ernest Jones, there is no consistent thread. Owenism, for example, he came vehemently to reject[17] even though he had played a major role in propagating it among working people. As secretary of the British Association for the Promotion of Co-operative Knowledge (BAPCK) he was the leading spirit in a body which, along with William Pare's First Birmingham Co-operative Society, Dr King's Brighton Society, and the Manchester and Salford Association for the Promotion of Co-operative Knowledge were primarily responsible for spreading co-operative principles to a degree which, it is arguable, overshadowed the campaign in the early thirties for ultra-radical political reform.[18] By October 1830 the BAPCK claimed to be in touch with 400 to 500 societies[19] advocating co-operative trading and production as a means of accumulating finance to create communities based on co-operation rather than competition and in which the worker as the sole producer of wealth should reap the whole reward of his labour. Lovett's circle, unlike many 'pure' Owenites certainly saw no conflict between political radicalism and Owenism. Indeed under their leadership the BAPCK linked the two together in novel fashion by sponsoring public meetings to back the unstamped press campaign or simultaneously to commend universal suffrage and co-operative principles.[20]

Why, then, did Lovett, unlike Hetherington, discard Owenism? No doubt his hostile reaction to Owen's authoritarian streak, the withering of the co-operative societies, and the failure of the attempts at community building played a part but the fundamental reason appears to be that Lovett in the last resort did not reject but accepted the industrial system of the day and the ideology of individual striving on which it was built. He was in the long run more impressed than depressed by its material results and in the end like any good liberal he concluded that they had been brought about 'by the hope of wealth, fame, or station, keeping up

---

[17] *Life and Struggles*, pp. 42–5, 429–30.

[18] The BAPCK defined its aims at its third quarterly meeting as being 'to promote Knowledge of Co-operation and of the best way to form co-operative associations, to establish exchanges between co-operative societies or the sale of their produce through bazaars and to publish such knowledge in cheap tracts' (*The London Co-operative Magazine*, volume iv, p. 27, 27 February 1830). It was founded on 11 May 1829 originally as The London Association . . . by members of the London Co-operative Trading Association who ran a store in Red Lion Square which Lovett took care of from Christmas 1829. The store was intended to raise funds for the project of founding a co-operative community which was the *raison d'être* of the Trading Association's parent body The London Co-operative Society founded in 1824.

[19] *Magazine of Useful Knowledge and Co-operative Miscellany*, 29 October 1830.

[20] *Ibid.*, 13 November 1830; W. Carpenter, *Political Letters*, 11 November 1830; *Weekly Free Press*, 10 April 1830.

man's energies to the tension point'. Furthermore there was in Lovett a strong streak of individualism. It was not perhaps surprising that this should be so: his personal experience was one long essay in self-help. He had lived at one time for weeks on end on 'a penny loaf a day and drink from the most convenient pump' but had achieved sufficient success through his own efforts to qualify for joining the Cabinet-Makers Society and eventually being chosen their president.[21] His residual Methodism predisposed him to respect individual efforts at self-improvement rather than putting *all* his faith in communal arrangements to perfect human character on Owenite lines. Place was certainly right to report that Lovett's 'feelings for his fellow workmen are intense'[22] nor did he ever lose sight of their contribution to the development of Victorian Britain.[23] But he lacked the intellectual power, literary ability, and imaginative emotion that enabled Bronterre O'Brien and those who followed him, such as Harney, to create out of such sympathies a new vision that shifted the analysis away from Lovett's attack on the old corruption of aristocratic society to a new one that focused on the fraud and force used by the union of the monopolists of both land and money by which the useful classes were plundered through rent, profit, interest, and taxes for the benefit of the useless. Much of this new analysis was designed to confront popularized political economy of the Place or Charles Knight kind head on[24] and Lovett was not uninfluenced by it. He rejected some of the nostrums of the political economists—for example, emigration as a remedy for population pressure and low wages.[25] He can be found repeating some of the slogans of the new analysis especially in the early '30s[26] and Place duly underlined disapprovingly such of them as crept into the addresses Lovett wrote for the

[21] *Life and Struggles*, pp. 24–33 for Lovett's struggle to become a cabinet-maker.
[22] *Place Papers*, B.M. Add. MS. 27791, f. 241, 6 October 1836.
[23] 'Our trade and manufacturers,' he wrote in the late sixties, 'exhibit their inventive and constructive power and attest their skill, ability and plodding industry throughout the length and breadth of the land.' (*Life and Struggles*, p. 408.) Nevertheless it should be noted that Lovett like Place rarely strayed from his customary habitat of the districts lying between Bloomsbury and the Strand. While Hetherington, Cleave and Vincent embarked on venturesome journeys all over the country Lovett stayed behind to mind the shop. His experience of industrialism was second hand which, incidentally, may help to explain why Hetherington was more deeply impressed than Lovett by the evils of industrialism, that 'competitive, scrambling, selfish system ... by which all men are trained to be slaves, hypocrites or criminals' (Hetherington's last will and testament, conveniently reprinted in M. Morris (ed.), *From Cobbett to the Chartists* (1951), pp. 237–9).
[24] For a valuable account of the new analysis see P. Hollis, *The Pauper Press* (1970), chapter vii and for O'Brien see A. Plummer, *Bronterre* (1971).
[25] See, e.g., his speech on this to the BAPCK in January 1831 (*Penny Papers*, 15 January 1831; W. Carpenter, *Political Letters*, 13 January 1831).
[26] E.g. he upheld the view that labour not land was the true source of wealth (*Weekly Free Press*, 24 July 1830).

LWMA.[27] But even Place could find no enduring acceptance by Lovett of the new analysis and significantly by 1836 he writes that Lovett had to some extent relinquished his absurd notions concerning the distribution and production of wealth and had wholly given up Owenism.[28] The truth is that the old analysis which Lovett embraced in the '20s co-existed with the new in the '30s and remained highly influential as study of the unstamped press shows. Lovett was one of those who helped to keep it this way. He was prepared to protest over concrete issues arising from industrialism and add them to the old analysis[29] but he never took over in any coherent fashion O'Brien's devastating vision.

In some respects Lovett's radicalism was highly traditional: the LWMA's *Rotten House of Commons* might have been compiled by T. H. B. Oldfield in Regency days or appeared as a *piece justicative* for Wilke's speech on parliamentary reform in 1776. In other respects it looked far into the future—his educational ideals with their emphasis on finding methods to promote the self-activity of the child, as opposed to a Gradgrind belief in the virtue of driving facts into its head, and his vision of education as a great creative power by which man makes himself, and in doing so changes himself, commend him to 'progressive' educationists today.[30]

How did he seek to achieve his ends? What techniques and tactics did he resort to?

Some comparison with Place is almost forced on one. Both were deficient in certain political gifts which dictated the role they played. Both were easily outshone by others, notably by Feargus O'Connor, as public speakers in an age that attached great importance to the art. Neither were lively or even moderately accomplished writers. Indeed Lovett regarded the pedestrian and Casaubon-like Place as his superior in this respect, inviting him, for example, in 1836, to polish up his narrative of the NUWC 'in your own style'.[31] Some might doubt whether Place had one. Nevertheless both were indispensable to their organizations as men of business. R. G. Gammage singled out Lovett as the ablest member of the LWMA in this respect.[32] Both had a great urge to draw up rules,

[27] E.g., in that to the working classes of Belgium where it is asserted that the working classes 'being the *producers of wealth*, have *the first claim* to its enjoyment'. For this address see *Life and Struggles*, pp. 98–102 and for an example of Place's disapproving annotations see *Place Papers*, B. M. Add. MS. 27835, f. 251.

[28] *Place Papers*, B.M. Add. MS. 27791, f. 242, 6 October 1836.

[29] For a discussion of the impact of the new analysis see P. Hollis, *op. cit.*, chapter viii.

[30] See, e.g., B. Simon, *Studies in the History of Education, 1780–1870* (1960), pp. 258–66 and for the ideas themselves see especially Lovett's *Chartism*.

[31] *Place Papers*, B.M. Add. MS. 27822, f. 15, Lovett to Place, 26 July 1836.

[32] R. G. Gammage, *History of the Chartist movement, 1837–1854* (1894), p. 10.

objects, addresses, petitions to parliament or paragraphs for the press. Place was certainly better equipped for such work as was shown by the help he was to Lovett in putting the LWMA's six points into the exact- ing technical form of the parliamentary bill which became known as the Charter.[33] By nature the post of secretary fell to them, the role of indis- pensable man behind the scenes. Indeed it has been said of Lovett that so little did he relish the drama of politics that while he certainly had a political commitment he was no politician.[34] Both Lovett and Place, in sharp contrast to O'Connor, believed that moral reform must parallel, even precede, political reform. To both, improvement for the working class meant the acquisition by individual working men of the so called bourgeois virtues of sobriety, thrift, knowledge, and so forth. The quality of community life was as important if not more important than constitutional arrangements, or so it seemed increasingly to Lovett from the days of the 'new move' onwards.

Nevertheless the comparison between Lovett and Place can be pressed too far. In spite of mutual respect and co-operation at particular times such as in efforts to raise cash to assist the publishers of the un- stamped or in building up the LWMA in its early days,[35] there were substantial differences in their outlook. Even when their relationship was at its most cordial in 1836 Place wrote condescendingly about how unfortunate it was that Lovett had not prospered as much as he had, had not acquired so much education, had not 'associated with persons of greater acquirements' (i.e. with Place's revered Benthamite friends), was too immersed in 'small particulars' and above all had been foolish enough to fall for the 'absurd notions' of Robert Owen and the 'not less absurd' idea that 'the whole should belong to those by whose labour it was produced'. In short in Place's view Lovett would not be a really useful member of society until he became a political economist like him- self.[36] In 1836 Place had some hope that this would happen and in the long run his faith was not misplaced. But by 1838 his expectation was dashed. Lovett's circle were attracting his shrillest disapproval for their enthusiastic endorsement of the BPU's National Petition; 'a piece of absurdity, full of anomalies and false statements' in Place's view. For Place but not for Lovett the whole gathering movement supporting Birmingham's Petition and London's Charter became mischievous non-

[33] D. J. Rowe, 'The London Working Men's Association and the "People's Charter" ', in *Past and Present*, no. 36, April 1967, pp. 81–5, for a full examination of Place's role.

[34] A. Briggs's introduction to 1969 edn. of Lovett's *Chartism*, p. 20 and cf. G. D. H. Cole's conclusion in his essay on Lovett in his *Chartist Portraits* (1941), p. 62.

[35] D. J. Rowe, *op. cit.*, has explored and emphasized this co-operation, perhaps unduly.

[36] *Place Papers*, B.M. Add. MS. 27791, ff. 241–2.

sense since it embraced a whole gamut of further demands for better wages, shorter working hours, abolition of the new Poor Law, reform of the currency on Attwoodian lines, and so forth which Place's political economy could not stomach but which could be tagged on to Lovett's traditional political radicalism.[37]

Furthermore they differed over tactics. Place's ideal campaign was one of 'long continued, steady, patiently liberal conduct, accepting and using every kind of assistance' so that credit was won in the press, among MPs and the public. The great error was mistaking the noise an organization made as evidence of power and of believing that reform would be obtained rapidly and *in toto*. In his own clumsy words, 'one must creep and then go'.[38] No doubt in later life the Lovett who laboured away as an educator writing books on elementary astronomy, geology, and physiology, welcomed and wrote for the prohibitionist movement,[39] joined the Anti-Slavery League,[40] the Land Tenure Reform Association,[41]

[37] For Place's views see especially *Place newspaper collection*, set 56, volume i, f. 10 of the introduction.

[38] *Place Papers*, B.M. Add. MS. 27819, ff. 47, 50–51.

[39] See B. H. Harrison, 'State Intervention and Moral Reform', p. 298. Lovett was a member of the United Kingdom Alliance from its inception in 1853. In 1870 under the pseudonym of 'An Old Reformer' he wrote several articles for its organ *Alliance News* (16 April, 18 June, 9 July 1870) declaring that 'the greatest and most needed of all reforms is the removal of the great demoralising curse of our country . . . the insane desire . . . for intoxicating drinks.' He anathematized music halls, 'thickly planted gin palaces', 'stately public houses' and the spread of wine selling by pastry cooks, confectioners and grocers, pleading for total abstinence. A paper by him on the same theme emphasizing 'the waste of capital in drink and the harm it did the working class' was read before the annual congress of the National Association for the Promotion of Social Science held at Newcastle-on-Tyne in 1870 (see 'The Liquor Traffic', *Transactions*, pp. 546–7), a great working class question by William Levitt [*sic*]. Lovett also preached against drink in the *Bee-hive* (see 1 August 1868).

[40] See H. Temperley, 'Anti-Slavery', p. 48, above. The Anti-Slavery League was an attempt to create a national organization in Britain of those who sympathised with William Lloyd Garrison's 'real, thorough Abolitionist view' of the American slavery question. Its supporters denounced the more august British and Foreign Anti-Slavery Society for being insufficiently militant. It was launched in 1846 as a result of a visit to England by Garrison. Lovett became a member of the League's Council and wrote to Garrison saying he saw slavery 'as one link in the great chain of oppression' (Lovett to Garrison, 1 March 1847, *Garrison Papers*). No doubt Lovett and other English radicals such as George Thompson, Vincent, Arthur O'Neil and W. H. Ashurst who were active in the League were attracted by the American's unconcealed contempt for the British monarchy, aristocracy and Anglican clergy which upset middle class sensibilities and thus helped to ensure that the League was short-lived. For its history see H. Temperley, *British Anti-slavery, 1833–70* (1972), pp. 215–20 and L. Billington, *Some connections between British and American reform movements, 1830–1860* (Bristol, M.A. Thesis, 1966), chapter viii.

[41] For land reform, see D. Martin, chapter 6, below. The Land Tenure Reform Association, launched in 1869 and surviving to the mid-seventies was led by John Stuart Mill supported by prominent Liberals such as Fawcett, John Morley and Dilke. George Howell, secretary of the Reform League, was appointed as its financial agent with the aim of attracting support from working men. He succeeded in the case of Lovett but the Association's programme of abolishing primogeniture, removing all

the Anti-Game Law League,[42] and the Working Men's Peace Association[43] and advocated public parks and public housing and so forth[44] would have agreed with Place. He came to believe more and more strongly as time passed that the power of example set by a working class that was sober, respectable, self-reliant, and above all educated was the best means of winning acceptance by the rest of the community of their just claims to full citizenship. The general tenor of his *Life and*

hindrances to the free transfer of land, and, eventually, the taxing of land values, failed to attract either a mass following or the adherence of the land nationalizers of the Land and Labour League. (See F. M. Leventhal, *Respectable Radical*, pp. 136–7 for Howell's role; for Mill's activities see M. St. John Packe, *The Life of John Stuart Mill* (1954), pp. 490–91; J. S. Mill, *Dissertations and Discussions* (1875), volume iv, pp. 239–302; H. S. R. Elliot, *The Letters of John Stuart Mill* (1910), volume ii, pp. 214–15, 263, 313–15, 336.)

[42] Lovett's interest in this cause probably began in the 1840s when he acted as publisher for *Howitt's journal of literature and popular progress*. In 1847 this carried an extensive series of articles which attempted to revive interest in John Bright's agitation for the total abolition of the unspeakably harsh laws for preserving game (for these see C. Kirby, 'The attack on the English Game Laws in the forties', in *Journal of Modern History*, volume iv (1932), p. 34, note 57); for *Howitt's journal*, with which Samuel Smiles as well as Lovett was associated, see M. Howitt (ed.), *Mary Howitt, an autobiography* (1889, ii, 42–3). The cause remained an item in the liberal–radical programme after Bright's campaign had failed (see, e.g., Passmore Edward's election address at Truro in 1868 quoted as representative in S. Maccobby, *English Radicalism, 1853–1886* (1938), p. 106). Lovett himself called for game-law abolition in the *Bee-hive* in 1868 (18 July) recommending looking at Howett's letters on the subject in the *Star* and other papers. For the Anti-Game Law League itself see *Anti-Game Law Circular and Organ of the Anti-Game League* which ran from 17 August 1872–31 December 1872. The League sought to rally support for an abolition bill introduced in the House of Commons in 1872 by, among others, P. A. Taylor, whom Lovett had long known.

[43] Lovett's concern for promoting international peace can be traced in the 1840s, e.g. in his *Address from the members of the National Association to the working classes of France on the subject of war* (1844), which *inter alia* advocated holding a conference of nations annually to settle disputes by arbitration. The Working Men's Peace Association was founded in 1870 at the time of the Franco-Prussian War by W. R. Cremer who had been first English secretary of the first international, active in the Reform League and a prominent trade-unionist. It was composed chiefly of old Chartists like Lovett and Cremer's friends in the Reform League. It was subsidized by the old-established, respectable, Quaker-inspired Peace Society led by Henry Richard, MP, and supported by prominent Liberals such as Samuel Morley the millionaire manufacturer and MP. The Association sought to have established a High Court of Nations to act as an arbitrator in international disputes and eventually gave birth to the International Arbitration League. (See Howard Evans, *Sir Randal Cremer* (1909), chapter viii; many references to Cremer's activities in H. Collins and C. Abramsky, *Karl Marx and the British Labour movement* (1965), and an assessment of the Association's role in the European peace movement; F. S. L. Lyons, *Internationalism in Europe, 1815–1914* (1963), pp. 320–21.)

[44] For his advocacy of free open spaces and government aid for improving working class housing see *Bee-hive*, 25 July 1868. Lovett was also a member of the National Sunday League, launched in 1855, which attracted support from London artisans, intellectuals such as John Stuart Mill and secularists in its endeavours to secure a relaxation of rigid sabbatarianism in order to encourage working class self-education on their only day of rest. (See B. Harrison, 'Religion and Recreation in England', in *Past and Present*, no. 38, pp. 109–11.)

Struggles does indeed lead one to suppose that he was consistently the classical example of the gradualist moral force man ever fated to see his causes wrecked by 'the hot brained few' and 'the physical force mania' whipped up by O'Connor, Stephens, and Oastler. However, in the '30s, Lovett frequently diverged from Place's conception of how to conduct pressure group politics. He was less of a gradualist moral force man and less consistent about political tactics than his autobiography suggests. His impatience with gradualism is apparent during the Reform Bill crisis, for although, unlike Hetherington, he enrolled with supporters of the Whig Bill in Place's National Political Union nevertheless at the crunch-point he refused to remain in it, as some of the NUWC did, unless its middle class members committed themselves to universal suffrage which only a minority led by Roebuck wished it to do.[45] And it is fairly clear that in the May days of 1832 he rejected the idea that the government Bill was a welcome step to total reform and stood firm for the extreme solution of universal suffrage.[46] Likewise, to Place's disgust, Lovett's LWMA in 1837–8 departed from the 'quiet, sensible manner' of its early days and endorsed the tactics of the mass petition, the mass meeting, the general strike, and the national convention, or in other words, making a big noise to achieve a rapid and total reform. And, lastly, can one imagine Place, the inventor of the baton charge,[47] being arrested and gaoled for a year as Lovett was in 1839 for placarding a highly excitable Birmingham with a notice charging its Council with using 'a bloodthirsty and unconstitutional force [of police] from London' to suppress public meetings in the Bullring?[48]

In reality Lovett was not wholly consistent in his attitude to the tactics of the big noise. In August 1831 and again in the spring of 1833 he opposed plans by militants such as Benbow, Petrie, Preston and Lee for holding a national convention sponsored by the NUWC,[49] although he was to act as secretary of the Chartist National Convention in 1839.

[45] Most of the key documents concerning the NPU can be found in D. J. Rowe (ed.), *London Radicalism, 1830–1843* (London Record Society, 1970), although a careful reading of *The Radical Reformer* provides a useful supplement particularly on the activities of those NUWC members who, unlike Lovett, stayed in the NPU unavailingly trying to persuade it to embrace universal suffrage.

[46] A. Briggs, *The Age of Improvement*, p. 257 speaks of 'the leaders of the Rotunda joining hands with Place' in May 1832 but on the other hand the police informer wrote, 'Benbow, Cooper, Watson and Lovett always denounce the Bill and say they must have the Ballot, Equal Laws and Equal Rights and to get it they will have to fight for it' (H.O. 64/12, reports of 12, 17 May 1832) and Place himself testified that the unions of the working classes made no efforts to promote the passing of the Bill in London, Manchester, Bristol and other places (*Place Papers*, B.M. Add. MS. 27792, f. 15.)

[47] According to C. Reith, *A short history of the police*, p. 54.

[48] *Life and Struggles*, pp. 217–19.

[49] H.O. 64/12, report of 16 January 1832; *Poor Man's Guardian*, 3 September 1831; *Republican*, 17 September 1831; *Life and Struggles*, pp. 68–9, 83.

Likewise he would not support Benbow's notion of a grand national holiday, or general strike, in 1831, but he was certainly party to having the idea submitted to Chartist supporters as a possible ulterior measure should the Commons reject their petition in 1839.[50] Also in its early days Lovett's London Working Men's Association did not seek to win support through mass meetings yet eventually Lovett was to take great pride in the numbers whom it gathered at its meeting at Palace Yard, Westminster, to choose London's delegates to the National Convention.[51]

On the other hand he was reasonably consistent in his attitude to law-breaking and the use of force. He would have no truck with secret conspiratorial proceedings, such as some of the Manchester allies of the NUWC appeared to favour. Even Benbow agreed with him on this.[52] Also, apart from challenging the law over service in the militia[53] and aiding those who illegally published and distributed the unstamped press, he was careful to keep within the law when it came to holding public meetings or national conventions, on occasion seeking legal advice when in doubt.[54] On resort to arms his view in the '30s seems to have been consistent. He did not deprecate any mention of physical force. Indeed in 1830 a police informer, not given seemingly to exaggeration since he measured men's violence by the standards of the Cato Street conspirators, described Lovett as 'a dangerous man' who had delivered 'a very strong and traitorous speech' in which 'he urged the unions to arm themselves' and declared 'that the only question now between the people and the aristocracy was whether they would allow the latter any longer to plunder them of their bread and perish or unite and fight to put them down'. Lovett's conclusion was that 'He for one would fight.'[55] But as this and similar if less lurid speeches made in the NUWC[56] shows, Lovett took the line that the people had a right to arm themselves and fight in *self-defence* against aristocratic oppression, a view he was to champion again in 1839 when, in the Convention, against the votes of more moderate delegates, he seconded an address advising the people to arm because the Whig government was behaving unconstitutionally by seeking to put down Chartist meetings by proclamation

[50] *Life and Struggles*, pp. 207–15.
[51] *Ibid.*, pp. 181–2.
[52] H.O. 64/26, 1831 bundle, Benbow to Ashmore, 17 December 1831, declaring that he hated secrecy and did not want underhand means but was 'always for bold measures'.
[53] *Life and Struggles*, pp. 65–7.
[54] E.g. he sought such advice over the National Convention in 1839.
[55] H.O. 64/11, report of November 1830.
[56] E.g. his declaration in November 1831 that 'the question was whether the people would die for want of bread or fight for it; he for one would rather fight . . . (*Poor Man's Guardian*, 26 November 1831).

which was not law.[57] Certainly he put his first trust in rational argument
and the power of 'enlightened and moral public opinion' as expressed in
a numerously signed National Petition. Certainly, too, his definition of
what constituted aggression that might legitimately call forth armed
resistance was a narrow one, narrower than that of Ernest Jones, for
example. Also he believed that he was only asserting the old radical
notion of the ancient and constitutional right of the Englishman to bear
arms for his own protection which no less a person than prime minister
Melbourne conceded, albeit in private. But he strongly deprecated the
public exhibition of arms, plans for the *offensive* use of them, and constant
bluster about physical force. Lovett's views really place him in an intermediate position between O'Brien or Stephens who can on occasion be
found unequivocally praising violence or those such as some of the
Scottish Chartists who unequivocally rejected it.[58] It is noteworthy that
in his bitter denunciations of O'Connor he goes out of the way to dis-
claim attacking those who sincerely believed that liberty could only be
won by force and were ready to die for the cause. In Lovett's eyes
O'Connor did not belong to this camp: he was a mere blusterer about
physical force. His chief crime for Lovett was that he destroyed democracy in the movement by demanding uncritical worship of himself and
stirring up by deceit and lies hatred and intolerance of all who disagreed
with him.[59]

O'Connor was, of course, the prime but by no means the only example
of a major problem of political tactics for working men like Lovett.
On whom should they rely for leadership? On themselves or on the
Hunts, Cobbetts, Attwoods, O'Connells, or O'Connors of the world?
Lovett was acutely aware of the dilemma involved: only too often
to rely on working folk was to forfeit the widespread support that
a name could arouse, while to accept a name was to risk being sold
down the river of compromise or having to bob along in the
wake of the great man's personal crotchet. Lovett found no solution
to this problem. All the great names proved unsatisfactory: Cobbett
was insufficiently radical for him in 1829;[60] Hunt too cowardly in

[57] F. C. Mather, *Public order in the age of the Chartists* (1959), p. 8. Lovett himself did
not mention this in his *Life and Struggles*.

[58] F. C. Mather, *Chartism* (Historical Association pamphlet, 1965), pp. 15–17, for
some wise observations on the over simple classification of Chartists into moral and
physical force advocates.

[59] See particularly his *Letter from Mr. Lovett to Messrs. Donaldson and Mason containing
his reasons for refusing to be nominated Secretary of the National Charter Association* (1843), the
substance of which is given in *Life and Struggles*, pp. 294–7.

[60] *Life and Struggles*, p. 55, fails to make clear that in the quarrel between Hunt and
Cobbett, Lovett certainly sided with Hunt and this meant embracing a sharper
version of political radicalism than Cobbett would accept since, amidst the sordid
quarrel with Daniel French, which was the occasion for Cobbett's quitting the RRA,
there can be detected his distaste for its toleration of such ultra-radical notions as

1830;[61] Attwood's BPU would only support the Whig Reform Bill and when it did embrace universal suffrage in 1837 its leaders withdrew from the Chartist Convention disgusted that Birmingham's currency reform was not acceptable; O'Connell 'dragged the people of England and Ireland through the quagmire of Whiggery for years' by his 'miserable instalment principle'[62] and, as for O'Connor, words almost failed Lovett. No wonder he encouraged working men to provide their own leadership.

The leadership issue, however, was only one aspect of a crucial question for all radical politicians in early Victorian Britain: what relationship should exist between middle and working class pressure for reform? Lovett's brand of radicalism put him in an equivocal position *vis à vis* middle class radicalism as represented by Joseph Hume in the '30s or Joseph Sturge in the '40s. On many individual issues co-operation occurred but time and time again during Lovett's career it broke down. Hunt's attempt in 1830 to create a Metropolitan Political Union (MPU) in imitation of the Birmingham Political Union to unite the middle and working classes of London as a pressure group favouring 'an effectual reform of parliament', although it led to Lovett for the first time into co-operating with the MPs Joseph Hume, John Wood, Otway Cave, and Daniel O'Connell, eventually collapsed. The root cause was that Hume and his friends interpreted 'effectual reform' as meaning household suffrage while Lovett stood firm by the RRA's commitment to universal suffrage, annual parliaments, and the ballot.[63] As already mentioned Lovett also withdrew from Place's NPU in 1831 for basically the same reason: it would not accept universal suffrage, and for Lovett this showed that the middle classes only wanted to make the working classes 'tools of their purposes'.[64] It was precisely this fear that dominated the LWMA's dealings with the radical MPs supposedly sympathetic to its six point programme. For example it flatly rejected

abolition of the monarchy and the House of Lords and its willingness to accept as members old revolutionaries such as Gale Jones. For this see *Weekly Free Press*, 26 September 1829 and G. D. H. Cole, *Life of William Cobbett* (1947), p. 314.

[61] H.O. 40/25, report of 15 November 1830 shows Lovett, Watson and Cleave sharply criticizing Hunt on this score. Hetherington remained sympathetic to him as late as July 1831 (H.O. 64/11, report of 5 July 1831).

[62] *Life and Struggles*, pp. 288–93, for Lovett's comprehensive indictment of O'Connell.

[63] Lovett and his circle were clearly on their guard throughout in joining the MPU. They kept the RRA in being wholly separate from it. The MPU was plainly falling apart on the reform issue *before* news of the July Revolution reached London and delivered the *coup de grâce* by galvanizing Lovett's circle into a quasi-revolutionary fervour of sporting the tricolour and declaring that France had taught tyranny a lesson and set England an example, all of which was too much for middle class moderate reformers to stomach. (For the whole episode see *The Weekly Free Press*, February–July 1830, supplemented by *Place Papers*, B.M. Add. MS. 27789, ff. 137, 145, and Add. MS. 27822, ff. 11–14, and *Life and Struggles*, pp. 56–7.)

[64] *The Times*, 1 November 1831, records these words of Lovett's at the mass meeting chaired by Burdett for the public launching of the NPU.

O'Connell's plea that it should accept the help of all who were ready 'to support *any* part of the improvements it demanded' and dissolve itself in favour of a broader based organization.[65]

Most strikingly, when all seemed set fair in 1841–2 for closer co-operation by Lovett with middle class reformers, all turned to dust and ashes. His year in Warwick gaol had partly broken his independent spirit and agonized reflection on 'the discord and folly' which he believed had marred the Chartist movement so far, induced him to look more kindly on such co-operation,[66] particularly since middle class reformers were extending the hand of friendship. Lovett was encouraged by the financial support for his National Association given by leading middle class London radicals,[67] by Joseph Sturge's initiative in seeking support from the Anti-Corn Law League's membership for 'a fair, full and free exercise of the franchise'[68] and by the formation by Place and P. A. Taylor of the Metropolitan Reform Association which sought 'the Charter under another name'.[69] The last straw, as ever for Lovett, was O'Connor. Feargus's refusal to withdraw his charge that the National Association was in collusion with O'Connell caused the Association to reverse its decision to support the NCA's second National Petition and instead to seek co-operation with Sturge.[70] For a while, as the first Birmingham conference of April 1842 showed, Lovett and Sturge appeared to shake hands, as the *Nonconformist* put it, on a basis of mutual acceptance of the six points of the Charter although not as yet on the document itself.[71]

[65] *Life and Struggles*, pp. 283–4.

[66] This emerges clearly from the extensive correspondence Lovett carried on with Place during his spell in Warwick gaol. He came to rest his hopes, as he put it, on 'the virtuous exceptions' among the masses of the middle classes who 'were wedded to the absurdities of the present system', allied with 'the reflecting part of my own class'. (*Place Newspaper collection*, set 55, especially Lovett to Place, 19 May, 1 June 1840, ff. 546–7, 568–70.)

[67] See *First Annual Report of the National Association* (1843), and *Receipts and Expenditure of the National Association, 22 February 1842–24 June 1843*, which in spite of the title includes a list of subscribers prior to these dates which includes J. T. Leader, Warburton, Earl Radnor, Sir John Easthope, George Grote, Brougham, T. S. Duncombe, Charles Buller, C. P. Villiers, Benjamin Wood, John Stuart Mill, Otway Cave, General Evans, etc.

[68] For the origin of this initiative in November 1841 see H. Richard, *Memoir of Joseph Sturge* (1864), pp. 311–12; and A. Wilson, 'The Suffrage Question', pp. 84 f., above.

[69] This has attracted little attention in print: *Place Papers*, B.M. Add. M.S. 27810 provides good documentation.

[70] B.M. Add. MS. 37774, Minutes of the National Association, v. 16 and f. 17. The Association decided to issue an Address to the middle classes (for the text see *Life and Struggles*, pp. 260–63) 'to come with us and declare at once for the Charter' and to send a Remonstrance to the House of Commons.

[71] For the proceedings see *Report of Proceedings of the Middle and Working Classes at Birmingham*, April 5 1842 and three following days (London, 1842); the *Nonconformist*, 6, 13 April 1842; H. Richard, *op. cit.* pp. 303–5; *Life and Struggles*, pp. 274–5; Rev. H. Solly, *These eighty years*, i, pp. 375–83.

But all came to nothing when they met at Birmingham again in December 1842. Throughout, middle class radicals showed every sign of shrinking from calling themselves Chartists,[72] while Lovett remained convinced that *his* Charter alone was the only instrument which would guarantee that universal suffrage would be fully enacted. The Bill of Rights produced by Sturge's supporters at the second conference he regarded as defective in this respect. Also it took no account of the popular support the Charter already commanded and, furthermore, Lovett believed that he was the victim of sharp practice in that the Bill of Rights had been drawn up without reference to him.[73] There were, of course, other reasons why no middle and working class alliance emerged in 1842,[74] but it was plain that there was no shifting Lovett on the supreme priority of the vote for the millions; middle class reformers had to accept that if they were to be acceptable to him. Not too many passed the test.

Yet on a wide variety of other matters co-operation was possible. Hume, for example, presented Lovett's petition of 1829 for Sunday opening of the British Museum and other places of 'national recreation' by which the working classes were to be saved from the demon drink; he backed Lovett's protest over the seizure of his household goods for refusing to serve in the militia; he had won Lovett's sympathy for his part in repealing the Combination Laws and championing in the Commons the abolition of the taxes on knowledge and flogging in the armed services as well as a reduction in the army's size and cost, to mention but three causes vehemently supported by Lovett. Indeed the full story of co-operation between Lovett and parliamentary radicals such as Hume, Roebuck, Wakley, or Leader is as long and complicated as the tale of the limitations of such co-operation and cannot be told here. It reveals some of the affinities that link Lovett the Chartist of the '30s with Lovett the latter-day liberal, who in his autobiography would say of Hume that 'no

---

[72] See, e.g., Bright's worry that if a second conference was held to discuss detailed proposals (i.e. the Charter) the precarious unity achieved in April 1842 would be destroyed (*Bright Papers*, B.M. Add. MS. 47663F, Bright to Lovett).

[73] For the second conference at which Lovett, seconded, ironically, by O'Connor, moved that the basis of discussion should be the Charter and the middle class delegates eventually trooped out to meet on their own after being outvoted, see the *Nonconformist*, 31 December 1842, special supplement; H. Spencer, *An autobiography*, i, pp. 217–22; H. Richard, *op. cit.*, pp. 315–18; Rev. H. Solly, *op. cit.*, i, pp. 406–9; *Life and Struggles*, pp. 282–5; *The life of Thomas Cooper by himself*, pp. 220–28.

[74] E.g., neither Sturge nor Lovett were able to attract substantial support away from the alternative leadership offered by Cobden and O'Connor respectively. Indeed O'Connor's attitude was probably decisive: following the Plug riots he was furious that government should prosecute him rather than the Leaguers, hence he sought to smash the Complete Suffrage Movement by taking over the second conference and packing it with his own supporters. In a sense Lovett did O'Connor's work for him by insisting that complete suffrage must mean the Charter and thus bringing about the collapse of the conference.

man was ever more persevering in seeking to carry the principles of
reform into every department of state'.[75]

What support did Lovett and his circle arouse? This can be measured
to some extent by the size of the membership of the associations they led,
by the scale and number of the indoor public meetings, branch meetings
and outdoor demonstrations they could muster in the metropolis and by
the connections they were able to build up with like-minded bodies in the
provinces. No precise figures can be given for RRA membership although clearly it was a matter of hundreds not thousands. The highest
membership figure Lovett reported as secretary of the BAPCK seems to
be 738 in July 1830.[76] The maximum membership of the NUWC was
probably about 3,000.[77] The most recent enumeration of the LWMA
shows that during its three year existence (1836–9) it admitted 291 full
members.[78] Lovett's national association gathered in no more than three
or four hundred at its most flourishing[79] and his People's League, he tells
us, 'some few hundreds joined'.[80] In short mass membership was not
achieved: true it was not always sought, particularly, of course, in the
case of the LWMA but even when it was sought, as in the case of the
NUWC, it did not materialize.

Calculations of attendance at meetings in the '30s and '40s are bedevilled by controversy arising from the difficulty of obtaining reliable
information. Nevertheless given the importance of 'the platform' in
exerting pressure some attempt must be made to measure how far Lovett
was able to use it. The evidence shows that the RRA succeeded in the
first requisite of a platform campaign, that of holding *regular* public
meetings. Attendance at these, however, fluctuated sharply. To begin
with while Cobbett and Hunt were present these seem to have attracted
2,000 to 3,000 'gentlemen, merchants, artisans and mechanics', so

[75] *Life and Struggles*, pp. 283–4; the connections between Chartists and liberals are
explored in B. Harrison, and P. Hollis, 'Chartism, Liberalism and the life of Robert
Lowery', in *E.H.R.*, volume LXXXII (1967), pp. 503, 535.

[76] *The Weekly Free Press*, 24 July 1830.

[77] The NUWC was divided into classes of twenty-five numbered consecutively and
the highest figure allocated to a class appears to have been 117 given to one formed in
October 1832. Some classes, it is true, notably James Watson's to which Lovett belonged, had then double the accepted figure but these were offset by others known to
have fallen below twenty-five. Three thousand was the figure accepted by the *Report
from the Select Committee on the Cold Bath Fields Meeting, P.P.*, 1833, volume XIII (718);
H.O. 64/12 report of 2 October 1832 for the 117th class; that of 12 September
1832 gives a particularly clear account of the process of forming classes of twenty-
five.

[78] I. Prothero, 'Chartism in London', in *Past and Present*, no. 44, August 1969,
Appendix II.

[79] *First Annual Report of the National Association* (1843).

[80] *Life and Struggles*, p. 340.

Cobbett claimed.[81] But significantly, when the big names were absent and Lovett's circle was in charge numbers fell off sharply as was freely admitted early in 1830.[82] The electrifying effect of the French July revolution nevertheless led to a substantial revival at the now weekly meetings held at the celebrated Rotunda.[83] Also before its collapse in December 1830 the RRA at least displayed a capacity to bring people out on the streets and to create enormous alarm in the mind of the authorities and respectables. Its Kennington Common meeting in October 1830, it claimed, had an audience of 9,000 to 10,000 working people.[84] Also, although the RRA pretty clearly made no attempt to organize a 'demo', or an attack on the new police, still less an armed insurrection on 9 November 1830 when Wellington, fearing precisely this, cancelled the King's customary annual visit to the City, authority's spies spoke of an audience of 2,000 at the Rotunda with three times as many gathered outside. On the evening of that day an experienced informer declared that 'he had been a great deal among the people in the streets for the last twelve years and have mixed in all number of societies, but I never before saw so many persons of all classes so thickly crowded'.[85]

Like the RRA the NUWC established weekly general meetings. And, since a police informer secured the job of counting entrants precision about attendance is possible. In the first year these numbered around 800 although, significantly enough if a well known guest speaker—O'Connell or Hunt—was present, or the political situation unusually tense, this figure would be swelled by additional hundreds unable to get in, at least not until the meeting place of the Institution in Theobald's Road was enlarged in the summer of 1832 to hold 2,000.[86] Outdoor demonstrations were plainly limited in number by lack of cash for printing notices. Indeed it was only the fortunate coincidence of Julian Hibbert's £5 gift on his resignation and officialdom's announcement of its day of fasting to ward off cholera which enabled the NUWC to mount their celebrated counter-demonstration.[87] This was certainly imposing. Lovett, Watson, Benbow, and the just released Hetherington marched at the head of a procession which virtually all press reports put

[81] *The Weekly Free Press*, 12 September 1829; *Pol. Register*, volume 68, 12 September 1829.
[82] *The Weekly Free Press*, 6 February 1830, especially Hetherington's speech. This was one of the factors that led Lovett's circle to venture co-operation with middle class radicals in forming the Metropolitan Political Union.
[83] *Ibid.*, 10, 17 July 1830.
[84] *Ibid.*, 2 October 1830.
[85] H.O. 40/25, for a collection of reports on the RRA at this time.
[86] H.O. 64/11, report of 10 May 1831, for the informer's convincing defence of his attendance figures. H.O. 64/12, report of 10 June 1832, for the enlarging of the hall and an example of a larger gathering drawn by a name.
[87] H.O. 64/12, reports of 2, 6, 7 February.

at 20,000 to 25,000 with about 100,000 lining the streets to watch.[88] But this was almost certainly far and away the NUWC's largest open air 'demo'.[89] No doubt the NUWC alarmed the authorities although in reality it was rarely able to demonstrate a capacity to rally large numbers. Where the NUWC scored over both the RRA and the LWMA was first in having in the proliferating unstamped press an effective publicity machine and secondly in developing in its well known class system a network of local meetings often held weekly in private houses for political education and tactical discussion. In Lovett's class, led by James Watson, the police spy who also belonged to it found himself listening to a reading aloud of a couple of chapters of Godwin's *Political Justice* followed by 'a long conversation on what the union should do on the General Fast Day'.[90] A little earlier he had reported, 'Watson has a great quantity of old books by him, by Paine, Sherwin, Carlile, and others which he lends us to read from Sunday to Sunday'[91]—an interesting confirmation of the major role played by the classics of the older radical tradition in moulding the outlook of Lovett and his circle.

Most probably Lovett's experience of Watson's class suggested the character which he gave the LWMA of a small group of carefully chosen men dedicated to mutual instruction rather than mass agitation. Later it did, however, seek popular support by holding its first public meeting in February 1837. But in London it scarcely turned itself into a major force for mobilizing opinion. Its public meetings were few; it did not stimulate the emergence of like-minded bodies so that in January 1839 on the eve of the National Convention there were only five Chartist organizations in the whole of the capital,[92] and, in spite of some urgings from Hetherington and others, it did not abandon its policy of keeping its own numbers small. Its most considerable effort in London was its carefully stage-managed Palace Yard meeting in 1838 at which eight delegates selected by it rather than Harney's rival London Democratic

[88] *The Times*, 22 March 1832; *The Observer*, 25 March 1832; *Morning Chronicle*, 23 March 1832; *Poor Man's Guardian*, 24 March 1832; *Cosmopolite*, 25 March 1832.

[89] Five thousand were reported by a friendly witness to have formed its contingent at the funeral of Thomas Hardy, veteran founder of the London Corresponding Society, in October 1832; the police reports on its meeting at Kennington Common to protest against flogging in the armed services in June 1832 and of another in March 1833 to denounce the 'military despotism' of the Whig's Irish policy, put attendance at 3,000 and 7,000 respectively (*Cosmopolite*, 20 October 1832; H.O. 64/13 contains lengthy reports on both these occasions). Cf. *The Working Man's Friend*, 3 August 1833, which claimed an attendance of 3,000 for the NUWC's public celebration of the third anniversary of the July revolution in France.

[90] H.O. 64/12, report of 20 February 1832. The police spy, it seems, was Abel Hall, who was in the Cato Street conspiracy, but avoided trial and was co-opted by the police as an informer on the Bow Street payroll. (I am grateful to Dr I. Prothero, of Manchester, for this information.)

[91] *Ibid.*, report of 13 February 1832.   [92] I. Prothero, *op. cit.*, p. 77.

Association to represent London at the Convention were chosen. The meeting certainly collected a sizeable audience—30,000 if one included all who came and went during its five hours duration, 15,000 if one counted the maximum present at any one time.[93] Such figures, however, were markedly smaller than the comparable meetings to elect delegates held in Birmingham, Kersal Moor in Lancashire or Peep Moor in the West Riding.

The LWMA was seen to greater advantage if one turns to its provincial connections and compares them with the less impressive efforts in this direction of the RRA and the NUWC. The RRA had little contact with provincial organizations of the same persuasion: it received news of such bodies at Paisley, Brighton, Chichester, Newcastle, and Leeds which last was probably the best supported. It was led by the veteran radical bookseller James Mann who was made an honorary member of the RRA. But if an estimate of the circulation of *The Leeds Patriot*, edited by Mann's collaborator John Foster, as being 600—or even the 1,200 claimed by Foster himself—is correct, then support for RRA principles cannot have been great. Elsewhere, in Manchester, for example, there was little or no sign of a revival of political radicalism among working people in 1829–30.[94]

The NUWC, however, had supporters in the provinces on a greater scale. From the pages of the *Poor Man's Guardian* can be traced thirty-two local NUWC organizations.[95] Almost certainly, except in Lancashire, these consisted of a small core of leaders, often sellers or publishers of the unstamped press, such as John Chappell in Bristol, or leading co-operators such as William Pare in Birmingham[96] who were supported by hundreds rather than thousands. Almost everywhere they were heavily outnumbered by supporters of the Reform Bill[97] except in Lan-

---

[93] Lovett MSS. (Birmingham Reference Library), volume 1, ff. 242–52; R. C. Gammage, *op. cit.*, pp. 47–53.

[94] Apart from reports in *The Weekly Free Press* see for Leeds, A. S. Turberville and F. Beckwith, 'Leeds and parliamentary reform, 1820–1832', in *The Thoresby Miscellany*, volume XII (1954); A. Briggs, The background of the parliamentary reform movement in three English cities', in *The Cambridge Historical Journal*, volume X (1952); D. Read, *Press and People, 1790–1850*, pp. 181, 210; and for the situation in Manchester J. M. Main, *The Parliamentary reform movement in Manchester, 1825–1832* (B.Litt. thesis Oxford, 1952).

[95] A. Briggs (ed.), *Chartist Studies*, p. 18, note 2.

[96] Pare's connections with the Lovett circle had been established through the BAPCK.

[97] E.g., when in July 1831 Hetherington visited Coventry about 200 turned up to hear him preach universal suffrage while 3,400 were signing a petition asking parliament to delay no longer in passing the Whig Bill. In the Midlands it was only after the Bill had become law that some significant increase in sympathy for the NUWC can be discerned in the links established between it and the new Midland union of the working classes who contemptuously thought 'Mr Attwood is asleep and does not go far enough.'

cashire, where the NUWC had links with a mixed collection of veteran radicals of Peterloo, such as the Rev. Joseph Harrison of Stockport and the leaders of the Lancashire political unions of the working classes such as Firebrand Nathan Broadhurst, Edward Curran, and William Ashmore. These last were sufficiently powerful to smash up the great meeting at Camp Fields called by the respectables to protest against the Lords rejection of the Reform Bill in October 1831 and in the May days of 1832 strong enough to commit 'the moderates to a public declaration of the *right* of universal suffrage' as one disconsolate supporter of the Whig Bill put it.[98]

Indeed the NUWC's connections with the provinces were more substantial and complicated than is often thought. And when the LWMA began to foster working men's Associations up and down the country in 1836–7 on a substantially greater scale than the earlier bodies had achieved it built in part at least and where appropriate on NUWC foundations. As Gammage remarked of one of their missionary tours, 'it was not his mission to create new elements but to cement those already in existence.' Detailed local research shows that the leading spirits in local NUWC organizations emerged again to play their part in the new WMAs. The precise number of these with whom Lovett was in touch is difficult to establish. It was probably around 135–150 rather than the 250 which appears in one of Place's accounts.[99] Their character varied considerably. Some like the Ipswich WMA clearly bore out Gammage's description of their recruiting a considerable number of voters, sufficient to give them some weight in local politics. Others like that of Leeds, collected together an impressive band of leaders long active in many fields of working class activity such as Joshua Hobson, J. F. Bray, George White, and David Green; others sprang from close friends of Lovett's circle such as the first WMA in South Wales, that formed by Hugh Williams, a solicitor, at Carmarthen early in 1837; yet others began independently of the London association from the actions of much humbler folk such as the two shoemakers and a plasterer who took the lead at Bath and eventually welcomed Vincent to the city.[100]

Important though the WMA's were in bringing together radicals in their localities and in gathering approval for Birmingham's National Petition and the LWMA's Charter there were major limitations to the support won in the provinces. The LWMA's missionaries were far from

[98] A. E. Watkin (ed.), *Absalom Watkin, extracts from his journal, 1814–1856*, pp. 159–62.

[99] One hundred and thirty-five secretaries of provincial societies joined Lovett in appealing to the Irish to rally to the Charter rather than O'Connell late in 1838 (*Place Papers*, BM. Add. MS. 27835, ff. 89–90).

[100] For these examples see A. Briggs (ed.), *Chartist Studies*, pp. 66–71, 150, 175, 220–21; R. G. Gammage, *op. cit.*, p. 8.

universally successful. For instance in 1837 its missionary Hetherington failed to win acceptance at Dewsbury and Bolton[101] as Henry Vincent failed to do in some western districts. In general it gained little or no support north of a line running from Stockport via Leeds to Hull and in large tracts of rural southern, western, and eastern England. Most important limitation of all, of course, was that in 1838 its provincial support was first overshadowed by the powerful rising tide of the revived BPU and then by Feargus O'Connor's excitable campaign. By the time the National Convention met, Lovett's circle had lost most of the support it had won outside London without having established a major following in the capital itself.

After his imprisonment Lovett never again had a following of any note. London Chartism, reaching its peaks in 1842 and 1848, owed little to his leadership. His National Association gained no significant provincial following and in London was completely overshadowed by the NCA with which he would have nothing to do.[102] The associations in which Lovett was prominent were far from the only bodies of importance involving working men. There were whole fields of activity in which his role was of minor significance. For instance, in many London parishes there were groups of shopkeepers and working men who campaigned against select vestries, church rates, assessed taxes, the establishment of Poor Law Boards of Guardians and so on, often combining this with traditional political radicalism, Lovett's circle did not stand aloof from such agitations but their role was essentially auxiliary to that of local leaders, such as Thomas Murphy in St Pancras, John Savage in Marylebone, or George Rogers, the tobacconist, in Bloomsbury.[103] Likewise the London Irish made their contribution to metropolitan radical politics but as an independent force having their own organizations and treating with the Lovett circle on equal terms.[104] Also, among the trade societies

[101] Lovett MSS., volume i, f. 109 ff., for a collection of newspaper cuttings on Hetherington's 1837 tour.

[102] I. Prothero, *op. cit.*, p. 78.

[103] No very satisfactory examination of these parish campaigns has yet been made but F. H. W. Sheppard, *Local government in St. Marylebone, 1688–1835*, chapter XVI and D. J. Rowe, *Radicalism in London, 1829–1841* (M.A. thesis, Southampton 1965), chapter II are useful for the early '30s. I. Prothero, *op. cit.* has valuable details on local leaders in the later '30s and early '40s for whom Lovett was no leader.

[104] E.g., in September 1832 their Anti-Union Society approached the NUWC with a proposal that the two bodies should unite in agitation for Repeal of the Union and against the Whig's Irish policy. When this came about the NUWC in 1833 came close to being an auxiliary of O'Connell's campaign against Whig coercion rather than a promoter of causes dear to Lovett. Also, when the London Irish became divided in 1835–6 into an O'Connellite majority and a more radical O'Connorite minority, the LWMA found itself sympathizing with the policies of the minority, but in Lovett's case especially, quite unable to stomach its leader, 'the great I AM of politics'. No wonder, in spite of John Cleave's foot in both camps, the LWMA had little following among the London Irish: the autonomous politics of the Irish precluded this.

Lovett enjoyed only a limited influence. He acted as secretary to the committee that sought to organize nationwide protests on behalf of the Tolpuddle 'martyrs' in 1834 and to the general committee of the London trades formed to watch over their interests during the parliamentary investigation in 1838 into trade unions arising from the Glasgow cotton spinners' case. But in the remarkable efflorescence among tailors, shoemakers, silk-weavers, and builders which in 1834 produced the Consolidated Trades Union and the Builders Union Lovett's circle was left on the sidelines vainly urging that agitating for the vote should take priority over industrial syndicalism.[105]

Turning, finally, to the social composition of the organizations in which Lovett was concerned nothing useful can be said about the RRA beyond Place's general comment that it was increasingly dominated by working men.[106] As for the NUWC painful collection of references in the unstamped press and the reports of police spies can unearth just over 360 names of its 3,000 or so members and of these about seventy can have occupations fitted to them. Inevitably this is a sample heavily biased towards those most prominent as speakers, officers, central committee members, and class leaders. As far as these were concerned a pattern emerges of a mixture of maverick gentlemen,[107] professional men,[108] shopkeepers,[109] small masters,[110] men from the 'aristocratic' trades[111] together with some from trades lower down in the social hierarchy[112] and a few of very humble occupations.[113] As for the LWMA on which the data is exceptionally good since the careful Lovett recorded the occupation of each new member as he was admitted, Dr Prothero's valuable analysis shows that 12 per cent of its members were not manual workers at all and that compared with the General Council of the NCA it contained a higher proportion of the best paid, best organized trades such as compositors, bookbinders, clock and watchmakers, and a smaller proportion of trades lower down the social scale such as tailors, shoemakers, the building trades and silk weavers. True it did contain

[105] W. H. Oliver made this clear in his *Organization and ideas behind the efforts to achieve a general union of the working classes in the early 1830s* (D.Phil. Oxford, 1954).
[106] *Place Papers*, B.M. Add. MS. 27789, f. 137.
[107] E.g., Julian Hibbert and 'honest' Jack Lawless.
[108] E.g., Daniel French and James Lorimer, both barristers; Drs Lynch and Dermot; Webb and Hargrove, surgeons; George Faull, an accountant and, inevitably, the Reverend Dr Wade of Warwick.
[109] E.g., Wyse, 'a respectable fishmonger', John Savage, a Marylebone draper, John Cleave and James Watson, booksellers and publishers.
[110] E.g., Henry Medlar, a master carpenter who had 'some good property', Benjamin Warden, a master saddler and Henry Hetherington, a master printer.
[111] E.g., Lovett himself.   [112] E.g., nine silk weavers.
[113] E.g., O'Keefe, an Irish labourer G. Hawkins, unemployed, James Williams noted by an informer as 'very poor' and Kingsmill similarly described as 'nailleterate [sic] shoemaker'.

men of this kind in poor circumstances such as Richard Cray, a semi-literate silk weaver who told Roebuck that he could 'bring whitness (*sic*) to prove that I am obliged to work 16 hours a day for 7s. 6d. a weak (*sic*)'.[114] But in essence the LWMA was a small, exclusive body bringing together men from the aristocratic trades and a small number of 'middle men'. It should be contrasted both with the Consolidated Trades Union and the NCA whose membership was more clearly the mass of men involved in the great variety of less well rewarded and organized trades.

To conclude: as a pressure group leader Lovett was scarcely a success. He chalked up no clear cut victories in legislation to establish equal rights for the million. There were sharp limits to the support he aroused. He was no leader of the mass of the unskilled and casual poor of Mayhew's London. Even among the artisans his influence seems to have been confined to the most 'aristocratic' of the trades. It is not altogether surprising that this should be so: major problems faced working men seeking to act together politically especially in early- and mid-Victorian London.[115] Some of these arose simply out of social and economic circumstance. Finding reliable treasurers,[116] methodical secretaries, reasonably educated men to edit periodicals, cash to pay printers, travel expenses of a missionary tour, the hire-price of a meeting place, was inevitably difficult in circles lacking the business experience, cash and formal education enjoyed by a middle class radical.[117] Then there was

[114] C. Richards (pseudonym for Richard Cray) to J. A. Roebuck, 5 September 1835 (*Place Newspaper collection*, set 52, ff. 91–4).

[115] Many factors inhibited the formation of mass based political organizations: the sheer size of London's population and built up area posed a severe problem of communicating a message; the very diversity of the occupations of her inhabitants and their division into numerous variegated communities militated against class solidarity and cushioned the effect of down turns in business activity which often triggered off political activity elsewhere. Lovett was active in the silver rather than the golden age of the London artisan: from the '30s onwards the artisan's position was being progressively undermined, the silk weavers were painfully crushed by the ending of protection, the watchmakers decimated by foreign competition, the shipbuilding trades overwhelmed by technological change and so on. For further points see D. J. Rowe, 'The failure of London Chartism', in *Historical Journal*, xi (1968), pp. 472–87, and G. Stedman Jones, *Outcast London* (1971), *passim*.

[116] E.g., the NUWC suffered from the embezzlement of its funds by the journeyman currier James Osborn (H.O. 64/12, reports of 1, 20 December 1832).

[117] Richard Cray, a member of the LWMA, has left a vivid impression of the problems facing a politically conscious Spitalfields weaver: replying to a typically smug homily from Place urging working people to stand on their own two feet, he wrote 'there is Hundreds in the Silk Trade that don't know a Single Letter. you speak of Clubs, I am of your Opinion there. But how is Trade Clubs to be supported at the Low Price Paid for Labour for in the first Place they must have a Room to meet in and if you go to a Public House wich I detest and have the use of there Room they Expect for you to spend money there and I whas Obliged to drop the Trade Union Because I could not afford to pay 3 pence per Weak for I very often find it hard to pay Threhafpence for a Pamphlet on Saturday' [*sic*] (*Place Newspaper collection*, set 52, ff. 99–101, Cray to Place, n.d., 1835).

the special difficulty of the widespread hostility towards working class activists of those wielding power in society. Few working class organizations in early Victorian Britain were not penetrated by spies in the pay of the police or magistrates. Few leaders identified with the working classes failed to end up before judges or magistrates followed by gaol or sometimes worse. The law was not their friend: it allowed, for instance, the Whigs to persecute the working man's cheap press and after 1836 it forced up the price beyond the reach of many while the papers of the middle and upper classes were able to voice heterodox opinions on religion. Most employers, too, frowned severely upon working class political activity.[118] The would be organizer of such action inhabited a harsher world than that known by a Cobden or Sturge unless he could establish his respectability. To do so, though, ultimately involved conciliating middle class radicalism by accepting its behaviour, norms, and values. Certainly there were considerable numbers of sober minded Chartists up and down the country who were prepared to travel this road in the forties and fifties particularly once the tumult and violence of the first phase of the movement was seen to be counter-productive. Nevertheless to do so meant risking losing more widespread support among the working class by failing to make a powerful enough emotional appeal to their sense of being deprived of their just rights by an oppressive political and economic system. This was Lovett's fate in the forties.

Nevertheless he did make a contribution to the evolution of pressure from without on parliament and government. It was a fourfold one. His insistence that working men could and should conduct their own affairs, that they should challenge unjust laws, press parliament, Ministers, and even the Queen for their rights and that they were as capable as any of the middle or upper class of arguing a case and preparing legislation was certainly a contribution to increasing the dignity and political consciousness of many a working man. Then, too, the bodies with which he was involved developed techniques of organization and propaganda of considerable sophistication. The class organization of the NUWC, the use of the Victim Fund to sustain casualties in the war of the unstamped, of missionaries to tour the provinces both by the NUWC and the LWMA and of research, however primitive, to give weight to publications, as occurred in producing the LWMA's *Rotten House of Commons*, are just a few examples of this. Next, as we have seen, Lovett's campaign for the improvement of the working man through acquiring knowledge, involved

---

[118] E.g., Lovett's colleague Hetherington reported that when he visited the Strutt's Belper in 1839 to hold a Chartist meeting in the market place he found that the famous manufacturer had tried to prevent his employees attending by locking them in the mills which he had fortified with cannon (*The Charter*, 28 April 1839).

a genuinely radical vision and was probably his most distinctive characteristic as a leader. And, finally, as he came gradually to adopt a more conciliatory attitude to middle class radicalism, he made his contribution, albeit more as a follower than a leader, to the alliance of middle class radicals and the artisan aristocracy that emerged as such an important force in mid-Victorian public life.

Further Reading

The Lovett MSS. in the Birmingham Reference Library contain newspaper clippings and some manuscript material. The *Place Papers* and newspaper collection, the minute books of the LWMA, the Chartist National Convention and Lovett's National Association, all in the BM, are of first rate importance as is also the unstamped and Chartist press. *The Home Office papers* in the PRO are equally important particularly for the early 1830s. Besides his *Life and Struggles* and *Chartism* Lovett published a considerable number of addresses composed on behalf of the various associations with which he was connected, several textbooks on elementary science, a poem entitled *Women's Mission* (1856) advocating equality of rights for men and women, and his *Social and Political Morality* (1853).

No adequate biography of Lovett exists. There are brief studies by Barbara Hammond (Fabian pamphlet, no. 199, 1922), G. D. H. Cole, *Chartist Portraits* (1941), chapter I, J. J. Beckerlegge (1948), and A. Briggs (1969) as introduction to a reprint of Lovett's *Chartism*. Also there are no satisfactory single-volume narrative histories of either the extra parliamentary agitation during the Reform Bill crisis or of the Chartist movement. The standard older accounts such as J. R. M. Butler's, *The Passing of the Great Reform Bill* (1914), J. West, *A history of the Chartist movement* (1920), and M. Hovell, *The Chartist movement* (1925) have many weaknesses and have been overtaken by a mass of recent work a guide to which for Chartism is provided by F. C. Mather, *Chartism* (Historical Association pamphlet, 1965). The articles by D. J. Rowe, I. Prothero, and B. Harrison and P. Hollis referred to in the footnotes indicate the direction of the most recent work. E. P. Thompson's, *Making of the English working class* (revised edn 1968), provides an unsurpassed study *inter alia* of the golden age of metropolitan radicalism between 1790 and 1832: chapter 16 is particularly important for Lovett's earlier years. Valuable contributions to an understanding of working class radicalism in Lovett's time have been made by J. Hamburger, *James Mill and the art of revolution* (1963), P. Hollis, *The Pauper Press* (1970), J. H. Wiener, *The war of the unstamped* (1969), A. Briggs (ed.), *Chartist Studies* (1959), and J. F. C. Harrison, *Robert Owen and the Owenites in Britain and America* (1969).

6

Land Reform[1]

David Martin

When in 1834 John Stuart Mill wrote simply 'Land is power', he was expressing a view accepted not only by reformers, but by the landed interest itself.[2] The ownership of land had for many centuries provided the economic basis for the political influence and social prestige enjoyed by the English ruling class, and that class, whether Whig or Tory, resisted all attempts to undermine its position. A century after it was coined, Bolingbroke's aphorism, 'the landed men are the true owners of our political vessel', was still the opinion of the landed interest and those who spoke on its behalf.[3] In the 1790s radical ideas were countered by Burke's case for the oligarchic rule of a landed class, while the government determinedly rooted out seditious propaganda.[4] Half a century later, the Corn Law agitation produced another crop of conservative arguments. Disraeli elaborated the value of a 'territorial aristocracy',[5] and J. W. Croker simplified the issue to a single question:

> ... the great question which agitates society in this country—disguise itself how it may—is the struggle—not between Democracy and Monarchy, nor between Democracy and Aristocracy, but between Democracy and PROPERTY ... the broad fact [is] that Property is the foundation of all government and Landed Property is the foundation

[1] I am grateful to Professor John Saville for his comments on an earlier draft of this paper.

[2] [J. S. Mill], 'Notes on the Newspapers', *Monthly Repository*, volume 8 (1834), p. 244.

[3] 'Some Reflections on the Present State of the Nation', *The Works of the late Right Honourable St. John, Lord Viscount Bolingbroke* (5 volumes, 1754), volume 3, p. 174.

[4] As Lord Braxfield insisted at the trial of Thomas Muir: 'A Government in every country should be just like a corporation; and in this country it was made up of the landed interest, which alone has a right to be represented; as for the rabble, who have nothing but personal property, what hold has the nation on them? What security for the payment of their taxes? They may pack up all their property on their backs, and leave the country in the twinkling of an eye, but landed property cannot be removed.' T. B. Howell, *A Complete Collection of State Trials* (1817), volume 23, column 231.

[5] See, e.g., his speech before the House of Commons on 4 May 1846, Hansard, volume 86, esp. column 87.

of all property; and therefore it is that with a natural instinct, as the wolf attacks the fold, all revolutionists attack landed property.[6]

However, the landed interest was not monolithic. On the Corn Laws, for example, several landlords agreed with Lord Fitzwilliam who supported repeal.[7] And while many may have envied the stable hierarchy under which their feudal ancestors lived, others accepted that Peel was right when he spoke in the Tamworth Manifesto of 'the correction of proved abuses and the redress of real grievances'. At the same time there was a general conviction that Peel was also right when he emphasized 'respect for ancient rights, and the deference to prescriptive authority'. The 1832 Reform Act did not, in the short term, upset the authority of the landed classes; in rural areas the system of deference continued, and in some respects the power of land owners increased.[8] In national government, too, landed magnates held all the principal offices, and few of them had any doubts about their fitness to rule—even Disraeli's Lord St Aldegonde, 'a republican of the reddest dye', opposed all privileges except those of dukes, and favoured the equal division of all property except land.[9]

On one minor aspect of the land question the landed interest was quite sharply divided: mixed opinions were held on the allotment system, under which small plots of land were made available for renting by agricultural labourers. The advocates of this system emphasized that the plots would be of such a size as to lend themselves to spade cultivation— usually less than an acre.[10] Opposition came generally from the farming class who believed that even a small amount of land would make the labourer too independent and give him ideas above his station.[11] But

[6] [J. W. Croker], 'Democracy', *Quarterly Review*, volume 85 (1849), pp. 292–3.

[7] David Spring, 'Earl Fitzwilliam and the Corn Laws', *American Historical Review*, volume 59 (1954), pp. 287–304.

[8] For example, the amended Poor Law of 1834, it has been argued recently, gave greater control to local landlords, Anthony Brundage, 'The Landed Interest and the New Poor Law: a reappraisal of the revolution in government', *English Historical Review*, volume 87 (1972), pp. 27–48.

[9] *Lothair* (1870), chapter 21.

[10] Superficially, there are similarities between allotments and Owen's village communities. But Owenites denied that the 'cottage system' had anything in common with their co-operative schemes. The case is rather that both emerged from a complex pattern of agricultural change, and the resulting debate about the merits of large and small farms and related questions. Similarly, the advocacy of allotments by middle class philanthropists, the movement for home colonization and O'Connor's Land Plan were all responses to intense economic and social changes. Some of the immense volume of literature is discussed by A. Plummer, 'Spade Husbandry during the Industrial Revolution', *Journal of the South-West Essex Technical College and School of Art*, volume 1 (1942), pp. 84–96.

[11] For instances of farmers' opposition to allotments, see *Report from the S.C. on Agriculture*, 1833 (V), Q.12086 and *Report from the S.C. on Labouring Poor* (Allotments of Land), 1843 (VII), Q.1242.

some larger landlords, often supported by their local clergy, experimented with allotment schemes and tried to persuade others that the system was a good one. It was argued that the possession of a little land removed labourers from parish relief, encouraged habits of thrift and obedience, and reduced poaching and drunkenness. They were also seen as an insurance against unrest, and this view was strengthened after the 'Swing' riots of 1830, as it was commonly held that areas in which allotments were widespread had been less turbulent than those counties where the labourer was without access to the land.[12]

The Labourers' Friend Society was established in the early 1830s to make the case for allotments better known. Its monthly journal, the *Labourers' Friend Magazine*, consisted almost exclusively of examples of schemes and advice upon practical problems. As a pressure group, however, it reflected ruling class attitudes; its patron was the King and its vice-presidents included many titled landlords.[13]

The allotment system originated mainly as a solution to the disruptive effects of the last stage of enclosure and the problem of rural underemployment. Intimately bound up with the Poor Law questions as a means of reducing the burden of rates, it tended to decline as the management of the Poor Law improved, and with the more regular wage-employment of the agricultural labourer.[14] The greater part of the debate took place between large landlords, members of the gentry and squirearchy, tenant farmers, and Anglican clergymen. Among reformers, some saw benefits in the system, but most were sceptical or opposed to it.[15] In terms of the whole picture the allotment issue was of

[12] For example, see 'A. Solicitor' [Thomas Archer], *A Plan for relieving the Pressure of the Poor Rates, affording Employment to the Agricultural Poor, and improving their Condition* (1832), p. 54, and evidence of Richard Pollen, J.P., in *Report from the S.C. of the House of Lords on the Poor Laws*, 1831, p. 53. This committee, which sat under the chairmanship of the Marquis of Salisbury, was particularly interested in the provision of allotments. From the minutes of evidence, it appears that the distribution of allotments was rather patchy, but most widespread in the south-eastern counties of England. Of the witnesses, several were clergymen who advocated allotments, while Earl Stanhope, a member of the committee, also spoke in favour, as did Thomas Estcourt, MP.

[13] Details of the society's programme can be found in *The Labourers' Friend: A Selection from the Publications of the Labourers' Friend Society, showing the Utility and National Advantage of Allotting Land for Cottage Husbandry* (1835). See also D. C. Barnett, 'Allotments and the Problem of Rural Poverty' in E. L. Jones and G. E. Mingay (eds.), *Land, Labour and Population in the Industrial Revolution* (1967), pp. 162–83.

[14] The issue did flicker on until the late nineteenth century, particularly in the form of the 'three acres and a cow' agitation; see Frederic Impey, *Three Acres and a Cow: Successful Small Holdings and Peasant Proprietors* [1886], and J. Frome Wilkinson, 'Pages from the History of Allotments', *Contemporary Review*, vol. 65 (1894), for contemporary arguments, and also Henry Pelling, *Popular Politics and Society in Late Victorian Britain* (1968), pp. 6–7.

[15] For examples of opposition see [Thomas Chalmers], 'Causes and Cure of Pauperism', *Edinburgh Review*, volume 29 (1818), p. 272; George Ensor, *The Poor and*

minor importance, though it does help to illustrate a difference of attitude among landowners. Almost all substantial owners of real property were agreed that an essential ingredient of a stable society was a territorial aristocracy: a class that would safeguard the constitution by providing government, both nationally and locally, and by having a dominant voice in the Church, the Army, and the Law. They were for the most part convinced that reformers were out to subvert this time-honoured system, and some thought it unwise to allow any concessions, not even allotments. Others were less inflexible, perhaps a few agreed with Coleridge that landholders had to perform duties as well as enjoy a special status. But virtually all regarded their land as conferring on them a title to govern, and having a well-developed group consciousness, they in turn used their legislative power to preserve their status.

Radical views on land were more varied. Though all radicals generally accepted that the land monopoly and the power it conferred upon a relatively small class were barriers to social and political progress, in terms of both their ideology and their plans for reform, there were considerable divisions. The term 'land reform' embraced a host of related issues ranging from moderate proposals for administrative improvement to common ownership; class relationships based on property were central in both the Chartist movement and the Anti-Corn Law campaign, and the issue was a key part in the development of radical-liberal politics in the years before the second Reform Act. Before going on to examine the movement for land reform in the decades after the great Reform Act, it is necessary to sketch in the development of earlier radical ideas, beginning first with those most commonly held by men identified with the working class movement.

Unlike most other nineteenth century reform movements, the 'land question' had deep roots. Though founded on a myth, the idea of the 'Norman Yoke', under which Saxon liberties had been extinguished, was deeply embedded in popular consciousness.[16] It was a major influence on radical ideology, for if the people had lost certain rights, then their object was clearly to restore them: as a correspondent to Hetherington's *Poor Man's Guardian* insisted, 'no personal liberty or happiness for the people, can exist, until at least there is no individual property in the soil',[17] Often radical ideas about land consisted of several strands. The concept of the Norman Yoke and simplistic appeals to natural rights

---

Their Relief (1823), p. 87; [J. S. Mill], 'The Claims of Labour', *Edinburgh Review*, volume 81 (1845), p. 524. Supporters of the system included William Allen, *Colonies at Home . . .*, (Lindfield, 1832); W. T. Thornton, *Over-Population and its Remedy* (1846), pp. 335–8.

[16] Christopher Hill, 'The Norman Yoke', in *Puritanism and Revolution* (1958), pp. 50–122.

[17] *Poor Man's Guardian*, 20 August 1831, p. 54.

were of long standing, but many theories current in the mid decades of the nineteenth century originated in the 1790s. Under the impact of the French Revolution, libertarian thought in Britain was greatly stimulated. Most striking, perhaps, was the enormous circulation of *Rights of Man* which advanced the authority of the people rather than of governments.[18] In *Agrarian Justice* (1797) Paine dealt specifically with the problem of landed property. He proposed that the dispossessed should be compensated not by a restoration of the land, but from a fund raised from an inheritance tax on property. To conservatives the scheme was at one with his other ideas, but for Thomas Spence, Paine did not go far enough. Since his arrival in London in the early 1790s, Spence had energetically spread his plan for 'parochial partnerships in land', by which he meant communally-owned small farms organized on a parish basis. Repetitively, he hammered at the evils produced by private landlordism, and how the 'spoilers' should have their 'ill-gotten lands' taken from them to set the world 'free from all exactions, imposts, and abuses'.[19] His propaganda ranged from token coins to chalked notices, and though the posters and broadsheets he issued were usually too ephemeral to have survived, his message was widely-disseminated and familiar to Londoners. Spence drew on the long history of land radicalism and after his death in 1814 his gospel was spread by others.[20]

Robert Owen was often described as Spence's successor. In 1817 the *Black Dwarf* pointed to the irony of Spence's fate compared with the approval Owen was enjoying.[21] Owen's projects for 'villages of co-operation' were temporarily fashionable among prominent and respectable persons who regarded his ideas as primarily philanthropic. His schemes suggested a way of reducing pauperism and thus the poor rate;

[18] Other writers, less widely read than Paine, were sometimes regarded as more dangerous; William Godwin's *Political Justice*, for instance, was condemned by the social conservative Arthur Young for 'options more paradoxical; bolder assertions; morals more depraved; and impudence more unblushing' than the contents of Paine's work: 'All Property invested in Land, whether by Landlords or Tenants, attacked by Reformers,' *Annals of Agriculture*, volume 21 (1793), p. 176.
[19] *The End of Oppression* ... (1795). Similar passages are to be found in his other works; Spence's strictures on *Agrarian Justice* appeared in *The Rights of Infants* ... (1797).
[20] Cobbett in a letter of 1822 observed, 'We have all seen for years past written on the walls in and near London those words "Spence's Plan",' quoted by P. M. Kemp-Ashraf in P. M. Kemp-Ashraf and Jack Mitchell (eds.), *Essays in Honour of William Gallacher* (Berlin, 1966), p. 354. Much of the literature on Spence is cited in this valuable essay. See also Olive D. Rudkin, *Thomas Spence and His Connections* (1927); James Eayrs, 'The Political Ideas of the English Agrarians, 1775–1815', *Canadian Journal of Economics and Political Science*, volume 18 (1952), pp. 287–302.
[21] Frank Podmore, *Robert Owen: A Biography* (1906), p. 232; see also J. F. C. Harrison, *Robert Owen and the Owenites in Britain and America: The Quest for the New Moral World* (1969), p. 56. But for the most part, radicals decried Owen's schemes as potentially harmful to the poor.

but he fell foul of the political economists when Torrens made a devastating critique of his plan.[22] His dreams of community building were broken on the wheel of orthodox political economy, and after Ricardo spoke against his proposals in the Commons in December 1819, the mainstream of economic thought accorded virtually no attention to Owenite schemes. But Owen's later ideas did sustain a working class co-operative movement, built around co-operative stores, congresses and labour exchanges, which in turn flowed into trade union attempts to create a general union in the mid-1830s. Owenism touched one of the deepest responses of the poor, the dream that they might again have some stake in the land, but as E. P. Thompson has argued, by renouncing the expropriation of the great landowners it suffered from a 'vitiating weakness'.[23]

Among Owen's critics was Cobbett who earlier denounced his plans for pauper management, and then attacked him as a 'half-mad and beastly fellow' for advocating contraception.[24] While Owen looked forward to the millennium when rational man had garnered the fruits of the Enlightenment, Cobbett found his inspiration in a lost Golden Age. Cobbett told of a time when King Alfred, perhaps 'the greatest man that ever lived', ruled a race of freedom-loving Saxons.[25] He blamed the Norman Conquest for breaking up this old society, and the Reformation for creating a deeper misery among the poor. But—and the contradiction is typical of Cobbett—he also insisted that there had been a large class of contented and independent yeomanry as late as the 1770s: it was only within the last fifty years, he wrote in 1835, that the 'monstrous encroachments of the aristocracy and usurers' had taken place.[26] Cobbett thundered at the 'Old Corruption' until his attack on jobbery, monopoly, and privilege was deeply implanted in the consciousness of his followers. He also voiced what was to be a continuing attack by working class radicals—opposition to political economy. Malthus, Ricardo, and the 'Scotch feelosofers' were partly responsible for society's ills and had helped to deepen the misery of the labourer: 'if we could make the enumeration, we should, I am convinced, find, that paper

[22] [Robert Torrens], 'Mr. Owen's plan for relieving the National Distress', *Edinburgh Review*, volume 32 (1819), pp. 453–77.
[23] E. P. Thompson, *The Making of the English Working Class* (1963), p. 886. For the experimental communities established by followers of Owen, see Harrison, *op. cit.*, esp. pp. 163–92.
[24] G. D. H. and Margaret Cole (eds.), *Rural Rides* (3 volumes, 1930), volume 2, p. 404. Many Owenites saw artificial birth control as necessary to maintain the stability of agrarian communities.
[25] *A History of the Protestant Reformation in England and Ireland* (2 volumes, 1829), volume 1, paragraph 147.
[26] *Legacy to Labourers: What is the Right which the Lords, Baronets, and Squires have to the Lands of England?* (3rd edn., 1835), p. 6.

money, large farms, fine houses, pauperism, hangings, transportation, leprosy, scrofula, and insanity, have all *gone on increasing regularly to-gether.*[27] Apart from his role as a moral critic of new economic ideas, Cobbett for the most part represented an older radical tradition. He looked back to a mythical society where small independent landowners and self-respecting peasants led simple, vigorous lives, practising the honest virtues of brewing, breadmaking, and cow-keeping. Though he made few specific proposals for land reform, he did sustain the legend of lost rights, and in the 1830s and '40s his ideas, mixed in with those of Owen, Paine, Spence, Cartwright, Godwin, and others, were spread in modified and distorted forms. Although incorporated into newer analyses of the working class predicament, land thus remained, even in an increasingly urbanized society, a major radical preoccupation.

There was little class co-operation on the land question for bourgeois ideology was largely distinct from that of the working class. At times there was considerable middle class hostility towards the old landed interest, but after 1832 it was effectively channelled only into the campaign of the Anti-Corn Law League. And this was a movement with a strong economic basis that reflected middle class interests. With Britain's industrial and commercial expansion, merchants and factory masters grew increasingly prosperous. This meant, firstly, that through marriage and the purchase of estates the wealthiest of them became absorbed into the upper class, and secondly, there grew a deep conviction of the need to maintain a free market—a belief that found intellectual expression in political economy and utilitarianism. These two newer modes of thought provided only a limited degree of support for land reform, and in some respects tended to justify the prevailing system of ownership.

By the 1830s conventional political economy offered a theoretical case that could be applied to the existing tripartite division of large landlord, tenant farmer, and landless labourer. Although Adam Smith in the *Wealth of Nations* had not only condemned primogeniture but had favoured small farms as against large,[28] later economists adopted a different approach. Arthur Young, for example, employed his considerable reputation as an authority on agriculture to state the case for the large farm, and his view was shared by many others.[29] In the late eighteenth century the principal argument stressed the greater efficiency of the large farm in producing the food demanded by a rising population.

[27] 'To Mr. Coke on the Question of Large Farms and Small Farms and on the Fall of the System out of which they have arisen', *Political Register*, 26 May 1821.

[28] *Wealth of Nations* (1776), book 3, chapters 2 and 4. Smith, however, did not define a small property in terms of acres.

[29] Instances are given by Hermann Levy, *Large and Small Holdings* (1911, translated by Ruth Kenyon), pp. 20 f.

Such a view did not go unchallenged, but opponents usually adopted a moralistic approach in the 'Deserted Village' tradition.[30] In the early nineteenth century Malthus argued that if landed property was distributed too widely, over-population and all its attendant evils would result.[31] A few years later McCulloch produced an influential essay that combined the two questions of efficiency and population in a trenchant denial that small farms or even allotments had any value whatever.[32] The essay had the approval of David Ricardo who read it in proof stage,[33] and its economic arguments were accepted by those who, on other questions, may have had progressive ideas. Among these was Bentham, the recognized father of utilitarian thought.

Bentham was a decided opponent of the aristocratic element in society, rhetorically asking, 'be it pot or be it kingdom, that which occupies the top of it, is it not the scum?'.[34] The concept of a hereditary peerage was alien to his views, but he was not prepared to overturn the system of landed property which formed the basis of aristocratic power. On one occasion he stated that very great proprietors often cared little about improving their estates, but went on to say, 'let it not be supposed that I recommend agrarian laws and forced divisions: this would be to cut off an arm in order to avoid a scratch.'[35] Any scheme of land reform that would tend to increase the power of the government was also resisted by Bentham and his followers.[36] Bentham was, moreover, persuaded by the economic arguments in favour of large farms. In 'Of the Levelling System' he contended that 'farms, large or small, would suffer much in value by being broken down into smaller ones',[37] and ironically, at the time of Arthur Young's conversion to peasant proprietorship, Bentham wrote suggesting that he was most fitted to apply 'the advantages of the *large scale* principle . . . to *agricultural* establishments'.[38]

[30] *Ibid.*, especially pp. 38–41; see also A. H. Johnson, *The Disappearance of the Small Landowner* (Oxford, 1909), chapter 5. Ironically, in later life Arthur Young became a convert to the moral virtues of small farms, but his arguments made little headway, see J. R. Poynter, *Society and Pauperism* (1969), pp. 98–105.

[31] A good statement of Malthus's views are contained in the controversy he had with Young over the size of farms: T. R. Malthus, *An Essay on the Principle of Population* (2nd edn., 1803), pp. 570–80, (3rd edn., 1806), pp. 528–47.

[32] 'Cottage System', *Encyclopaedia Britannica Supplement* (Edinburgh, 1824), volume 3. See also D. P. O'Brien, *J. R. McCulloch: A Study in Classical Economics* (1970), pp. 282–3.

[33] Ricardo to McCulloch, 24 November 1818, in P. Sraffa (ed.), *The Works and Correspondence of David Ricardo* (10 volumes, Cambridge, 1951–5), volume 7, p. 337.

[34] John Bowring (ed.), *The Works of Jeremy Bentham* (11 volumes, Edinburgh, 1838–43), volume 9, p. 57.

[35] *Ibid.*, volume 3, p. 69.

[36] Elie Halévy, *The Growth of Philosophic Radicalism* (1952 edn., translated by Mary Morris), p. 314.

[37] Bowring, *op. cit.*, volume 1, p. 359.

[38] Bentham to Young, 8 July 1801, quoted *ibid.*, volume 10, p. 374.

Thus the philosophical justification of *laissez faire* economics also lent itself to non-interference with the organization of agriculture, and, by extension, farmers and landlords. There was only one aspect of the question where Benthamites did call for change, and here again free market considerations provide the reason; there was strong opposition to the laws of inheritance, particularly the custom and practice of primogeniture. The law of primogeniture directed that the landed possessions of a person dying intestate should be exclusively the property of the eldest son or the eldest male heir. Many reformers regarded this as treating landowners differently to the rest of the community, but if the law had been abolished there would probably have been no more than a marginal effect on the size of estates. Large landlords almost invariably willed their estates to their eldest son in order to preserve them intact, and this custom would have continued. It was uncommon for a substantial holder of land to trust merely to the law of primogeniture, and he often settled entails on his estate as a further guarantee of its survival, not only in the hands of his eldest son, but also to his first male grandson, who might be unborn when his inheritance was arranged.[39]

But reformers were slow to realize the true operation of the law. To both sides it had a symbolic importance; the privileged position of the eldest son was at the root of the hereditary system, while such artificial devices were intolerable to Benthamites—in James Mill's words they were 'mischievous in every way'.[40] In 1836 William Ewart introduced a bill to abolish primogeniture, the first of a series of attempts to change the law. But as often as the radical group in the Commons brought forward legislation, they aroused opposition that was always too strong. Even when reformers protested that they wished only to end an anomaly and to prevent an occasional injustice, conservatives were likely to respond in sweeping terms and denounce any legal changes as 'most insidious and most dangerous to the institutions of the country'.[41]

The case against primogeniture was often couched in libertarian

[39] Eileen Spring, 'The Settlement of Land in Nineteenth-Century England', *American Journal of Legal History*, volume 8 (1964), esp. pp. 210–12; see also Arthur Underhill, 'Changes in the Law of Real Property', in *A Century of Law Reform* (1901). It was a commonplace for radicals to suggest that the legal interest was opposed to reforming the law because it did so well out of it.

[40] P.Q. [James Mill], 'Aristocracy', *London Review*, volume 2 (1836), p. 285. For Bentham's criticisms of primogeniture, Bowring, *op. cit.*, volume 9, pp. 17–18; W. Stark (ed.), *Jeremy Bentham's Economic Writings* (3 volumes, 1952–4), volume 1, pp. 328–32. The best single statement of the utilitarian view is [John Austin], 'Disposition of Property by Will—Primogeniture', *Westminster Review*, volume 2 (1824), pp. 503–53.

[41] Lord Campbell, quoted by P. J. Locke King, *Injustice of the Law of Succession to the Real Property of Intestates* (1854), p. 34. For the campaign in Parliament against primogeniture, see F. M. L. Thompson, 'Land and Politics in England in the Nineteenth Century', *Transactions of the Royal Historical Society*, volume 15 (1965), pp. 26–30.

terms: land was a factor of production and should not be subject to restrictive measures that interfered with the free working of the market. Such a philosophy, however, also precluded legislation that insisted upon estates being divided among all, or at least some of the children, in a similar way to the operation of the law in France under the Code Napoleon. Utilitarians could not countenance interference with the rights of property,[42] and so were left in the ineffectual position of opposing the law while admitting that the custom would operate with similar effects, but being prevented by their doctrines from advocating legislation to disallow the custom. Because of the difficulty of formulating specific remedies, primogeniture and entail were never sound planks in the campaign for land reform, and much energy was dissipated in vain attempts to erect a solid case for reforming this area of land law. Only as a subject of polemic did primogeniture generate opposition against the landed interest. Thus, for example, 'Timothy Winterbottom' assailed the 'hereditary peerage, and the clan-like aristocracy supported by primogeniture, [which] form a kind of artificial scum on the surface of society, and unworthily usurp the place which, according to the natural order of things, would be occupied by more deserving and useful objects, taken from among our wealthy and intelligent merchants and manufacturers, who are thus depressed below their proper station.'[43]

When members of the middle class felt they were being denied their rightful place in society they were at their most indignant, and on these occasions could be outspoken. J. L. Mallet recorded one such instance during a debate in the semi-private Political Economy Club on the question 'Ought a compulsory provision against destitution to exist wherever there is exclusive property in land?' The proposer was James Hume, Secretary to the Board of Trade, and Mallet's account illustrates how the middle class reformer sometimes came near to the working class tradition: 'Mr Hume is a man of sense and talent; and who disavows any opinions in common with the Schools of Godwin or Owen, but whose abhorrence of the aristocracy and landlords and monopolisers of property often brings him on the confines of those wild regions.'[44] Concealed by the pseudonym John Hampden Junior, the Quaker journalist

---

[42] J. S. Mill, for example, in his attack on landlords quoted above, made clear that 'their property must be protected because all property must be protected.' 'Notes on the Newspapers', *loc. cit.*, p. 235.

[43] Timothy Winterbottom, *A Letter to Isaac Tomkins, and Peter Jenkins on Primogeniture* (1835), pp. 9–10. Winterbottom was commenting on a pseudonymous pamphlet by Henry Brougham, *A Sketch of the Aristocracy of England* (1835) by 'Isaac Tomkins, Gent. and Mr. Peter Jenkins'. Brougham, Lord Chancellor from 1830 to 1834, but excluded from Melbourne's second administration, was passing through a radical phase. His criticisms of the aristocracy had James Mill's approval: see Alexander Bain, *James Mill: A Biography* (1882), p. 360.

[44] Diary of J. L. Mallet (March 1835), printed in *Political Economy Club . . .*

William Howitt also borrowed working class rhetoric when tracing the aristocracy back to the invasion of a bastard king and his lawless adventurers.[45] Howitt was one of many liberal journalists who provided a more or less systematic attack on the landed interest; others, such as Albany Fonblanque, W. J. Fox, and William Tait, represented a largely middle class readership which identified substantial owners of land with Toryism and monopoly.

In the 1830s, J. S. Mill spoke from this position. He acknowledged that the 'English government is an oligarchy of landholders', whose 'fancies go before all other people's most substantial interests', but believed that a sufficient body of reformers could be mustered to push through changes.[46] Mill looked chiefly to the middle classes, the people whose 'most essential interests are made to give way to the idlest fears, the most silly prejudices of the landowners',[47] while also hoping for working class support. He argued that given a popular leader, the forces of reform could be rallied; but his nominee, Lord Durham, refused to assume the role of leader, and in any case few reformers had much enthusiasm for him.[48] For a time Mill was optimistic, but in calmer moments he recognized the divisions between the 'divers schools of radicals' of which the philosophic radicals was only one.[49] While hoping for a rebirth of the concerted action that had helped to secure the Reform Act, he had to acknowledge the existence of several currents of thought. There were not only divisions between the middle and working class movements, but

Proceedings . . . , volume 6 (1921), p. 266. James Hume should be distinguished from the radical Member of Parliament Joseph Hume, although both were critics of aristocratic privilege and opponents of the Corn Laws.

[45] [William Howitt], *The Aristocracy of England: A History for the People*, by 'John Hampden Junior'. (2nd edn., 1846), p. 21. For another vigorous exposition of the 'Norman Yoke', John Noakes, *The Right of the Aristocracy to the Soil, considered* (1847); see also Olive Anderson, 'The Political Uses of History in Mid Nineteenth-Century England', *Past and Present*, no. 36 (1967), esp. pp. 99–102.

[46] J. S. Mill, 'Reorganization of the Reform Party', *Westminster Review*, volume 32 (1839), p. 479.

[47] *Ibid.*, p. 485.

[48] See W. Thomas, 'The Philosophic Radicals', chapter 3, above, and A. Wilson, 'The Suffrage Movement', p. 80, above; see also Joseph Hamburger, *Intellectuals in Politics: John Stuart Mill and the Philosophic Radicals* (New Haven, 1965), pp. 234–5. These manoeuvres caused the government little concern. Melbourne informed Queen Victoria in May 1839 that 'The radicals have neither ability, honesty, nor numbers. They have no leaders of any character. Lord Durham was raised, one hardly knows how, into something of a factitious importance by his own extreme opinions, by the panegyrics of those who thought he would serve them as an instrument, and by the management of the Press.' A. C. Benson and Viscount Esher (eds.), *The Letters of Queen Victoria* (3 volumes, 1907), volume 1, p. 195.

[49] [J. S. Mill], 'Fonblanque's England under Seven Administrations', *Westminster Review*, volume 27 (1837), p. 67. Mill also discussed the different types of radical in a letter to Albany Fonblanque, 30 January 1838, in F. E. Mineka, *The Earlier Letters of John Stuart Mill 1812–1848* (2 volumes, Toronto, 1963), volume 2, p. 370.

also different opinions within these two broad groups. While in general terms opposed to the power of the great landed magnates, their diagnoses and remedies were often at odds.

Many of these ideological differences emerged during the late 1830s and 1840s when in the parallel movements for Corn Law repeal and the People's Charter, land reform began to find political expression. Among middle class radicals there was a growing conviction that the Reform Act of 1832 had left the power of the landed interest largely intact. Much of this sense of dissatisfaction began to crystallize around the Corn Laws which symbolized in both a political and economic sense the supremacy of aristocratic government. The Anti-Corn Law League, as is well known, principally represented the middle class manufacturing interests; its supporters saw freer trade as part of the shift of power from the older aristocracy. For the most part the League based its case on economic grounds. If the Corn Laws were repealed, then, it was argued, Britain's increasing population would be supported by the expansion of overseas trade, which would also create greater prosperity. But the Corn Laws were said to deny the foreigner a market for his agricultural produce, thus forcing him to establish his own manufacturing industries, which would compete with the British trader.[50] While at home, the corn laws meant that 'The great bulk of the people, the customers of each other, and of all the other classes are becoming too poor to purchase, and thus they cease to consume, and profits are destroyed.'[51] The question also had a moral aspect, that of fostering international goodwill, as conflicts were less likely to break out between nations which depended upon trade with each other. To Cobden especially, Corn Law repeal represented a step in the advance of civilization, part of his wider philosophy of progress; as he wrote to Joseph Sturge, 'In fact, all good things pull together. Free Trade, peace, financial reform, equitable taxation, all are co-operating towards a common object.'[52]

As a matter of strategy the leaders of the League concentrated on the single issue of Corn Law repeal, and refused to allow the intrusion of wider political questions. They were also determined not to lose the support of the more cautious who shied away from anything that appeared disreputable. Thus, for example, when in May 1839, George

[50] John Morley, *The Life of Richard Cobden* (2 volumes, 1896 edn.), volume 1, pp. 141–2; see also Cobden on 'the law which interferes with the wisdom of the Divine Providence, and substitutes the law of wicked men for the law of nature.' John Bright and J. E. Thorold Rogers (eds.), *Speeches on Questions of Public Policy by Richard Cobden* (2 volumes, 1870), volume 1, p. 68.

[51] Letter sent to MPs in June 1842, quoted Archibald Prentice, *History of the Anti-Corn-Law League* (2 volumes, 1853), volume 1, p. 336.

[52] John McGilchrist, *Richard Cobden, the Apostle of Free Trade* (1865), p. 161.

Greig, the secretary of the Leeds Anti-Corn Law Association, launched into an attack on the 'gluttons and debauchees' who comprised the landed aristocracy, his opinion met with the *Northern Star's* approval, but caused anxiety to the League Council.[53]

At first the League attempted to proceed as a pressure group in certain limited directions. In canvassing MPs and bringing together leaders of business, it followed a Whiggish approach that emphasized the concession of proved grievances instead of calling upon popular agitation. The failure of these methods led to a widening of its propaganda. In January 1841 it supported J.B. ('Corn Law') Smith in a by-election at Walsall against Captain Gladstone, the Tory candidate. After a hard-fought campaign, in which both sides practised bribery and corruption and Chartist leaders were induced to support Gladstone, Smith came narrowly within winning the seat. As much of the Whig–Liberal press had opposed the League's intervention, the result was regarded as a vindication of independent electoral activity by repealers, and the experience of Walsall strengthened the tactics of 'pressure from without'.[54] Immediately, however, there was no great upsurge in the League's campaign, and by the middle of 1842 doubts had arisen about its future.[55] Its leaders rose to the challenge and organized a full programme of speaking and collecting campaigns. By the autumn of 1842 some 2,000 lectures had been delivered under League auspices and over five million anti-Corn Law tracts distributed, in 1843 its staff of 800 sent out nine million tracts, and matched this deluge of literature with speaking tours, petitions, deputations, and the publication of full subscription lists in the *League* newspaper, which was launched in September 1843.[56] Its techniques were, in Cobden's words, those of an 'eminently . . . middle-class agitation'. The League was carried on 'by those means by which the middle-class usually carries on its movements. We have had our meetings of dissenting ministers; we have obtained the co-operation of the ladies; we have resorted to tea-parties, and taken those pacific means for carrying out our views, which mark us rather as a middle-class set of agitators.'[57]

[53] Norman McCord, *The Anti-Corn Law League 1838–1846* (1968 edn.), p. 59.

[54] Dissatisfaction with the Whig approach to reform was expressed by Prentice after the Walsall election: 'The cry of "Keep out the tories", has had its day, and is no longer available. The people are no longer to be brought to the aid of men who will do nothing for them.' Prentice, *op. cit.*, volume 1, p. 184.

[55] One hostile critic virtually wrote it off: 'The cry, "Down with the food laws!" did not rally the insurgents; and the *"pressure from without"*, with which they had hoped to coerce Government, the people refused to execute.' [J. W. Croker], 'Anti-Corn-Law Agitation', *Quarterly Review*, volume 71 (1842), p. 297.

[56] Prentice, *op. cit.*, volume 2, pp. 394 ff.; G. M. Trevelyan, *The Life of John Bright* (1913), p. 91. See also C. R. Fay, *The Corn Laws and Social England* (Cambridge, 1932), pp. 91–6.

[57] Morley, *op. cit.*, volume 1, p. 249.

On redoubling its efforts, the League increasingly began to take its campaign into the counties, despite the difficulties and even dangers created by hostile audiences. In so doing, it made an explicit attempt to undermine the system of land ownership that was both the basis of and reason for protection. League publicists tried to divide the landed interest by showing the tenant farmer that he was really the rural equivalent of the urban middle class. Speakers urged that there was a major distinction between the landed and agricultural interests.[58] From about the middle of 1843 an effort was made to win the support of farmers over the issue of the game laws which were characterized as a flagrant abuse of aristocratic privilege. Bright in particular took an active part in this aspect of the League's propaganda work, and instigated the appointment of a House of Commons Select Committee in 1845. But, while urban audiences may have been roused to indignation by tales of poaching incidents and the destruction of 'the people's food' by vermin, the League made little headway where it was most eager to succeed.[59] The farmer remained for the most part protectionist; working to small margins, he was 'terrified at what might be the result if repeal were passed.'[60] Moreover, landlords expected their tenants to share their political commitments; there was always the threat of eviction or the refusal to renew a lease, and in the years after the Reform Act it was still not uncommon for tenants to receive written advice from the landlord's agent at election time naming the candidate who ought to be supported.[61] At the parliamentary level, defenders of the landed interest, such as Bentinck, claimed that there was no case for interfering with contracts freely entered into by tenants who knew that their landlord was a preserver of game, and Bright, with his own philosophy of *laissez faire*, never came to terms with this argument.[62]

There was another way in which the League endeavoured to cut into the electoral strength of the landed interest. After Walsall, it contested a number of seats where there was no candidate with a repeal platform. This led to the manipulation of voters' qualifications to disqualify protectionists and to register all free traders on registers of electors. Through this process the League came to employ a large staff practised in the creation of new voters. From late 1844 the League assisted supporters to purchase 40s. freeholds, especially in south Lancashire and the West

[58] Asa Briggs, 'The Language of "Class" in Early Nineteenth-Century England', in Asa Briggs and John Saville (eds.), *Essays in Labour History* (1960), p. 60.

[59] Chester Kirby, 'The Attack on the English Game Laws in the Forties', *Journal of Modern History*, volume 4 (1932), pp. 23 f.

[60] G. Kitson Clark, *The Making of Victorian England* (1962), p. 8.

[61] Norman Gash, *Politics in the Age of Peel* (1953), p. 181.

[62] Kirby, *loc. cit.*, p. 29. The game laws remained part of the radical armoury, becoming as the *Quarterly Review* complained, the demagogue's 'stock subject of class abuse'. [Theodore Thring], 'Game and the Game Laws', volume 122 (1867), p. 136.

Riding where quite a significant impact was made on the pattern of political representation. As the owners of these freeholds were qualified to vote in parliamentary elections, Cobden urged the wider acquisition of the franchise by these means to force the monopolists to 'give us corn in order to save a great deal more'.[63] To begin with, intending purchasers of freeholds could obtain advice from the League but had to make their own arrangements to obtain land. In October 1845, however, Cobden suggested that the League should purchase an estate in which shares could be sold to create a large block of votes in one area. The scheme did not materialize before the League was wound up, though a few years later Cobden returned to the idea as a means of land reform.[64]

Active supporters of the anti-Corn Law movement were never so numerous as the speeches of its leaders sometimes suggested, nor had the League even the tacit support of many middle class radicals. In particular those based in London had reservations about both its aims and its methods. A certain amount of jealousy may account for the aloofness of the London radicals, for the Anti-Corn Law Association, formed in London in 1836, and with Grote, Molesworth, Hume, and Roebuck among its leaders, had failed to get off the ground.[65] To others, the League appeared to embody values in which self-interest and materialism were dominant.[66] Mill was one of the most prominent of the London radicals to oppose the assertions of the entrepreneur and factory master—men who measured 'the merit of all things by their tendency to increase the number of steam engines, and make human beings as good machines and therefore as mere machines as those'.[67] Though withdrawn into private life in the 1840s, Mill was a keen observer of public affairs. He believed Corn Law repeal to be inevitable, but showed more interest in the Chartist movement, subscribing to a testimonial for Lovett in December 1847 and referring favourably in his *Principles* to the Chartist land colony at Rickmansworth.[68] In the early years of Chartism, several

[63] Prentice, *op. cit.*, volume 2, p. 261.

[64] Morley, *op. cit.*, volume 1, pp. 305–6. See below, pp. 150–52.

[65] Morley, *op. cit.*, volume 1, p. 143; see also William D. Grampp, *The Manchester School of Economics* (Stanford, 1960), pp. 8–9.

[66] Cobden was too honest to deny the point observing in 1843: 'most of us entered upon this struggle with the belief that we had some distinct class-interest in the question, and that we should carry it as a manifestation of our will in this district, [Manchester] against the will and consent of other portions of the community'. Morley, *op. cit.*, volume 1, p. 141.

[67] J. S. Mill to Sarah Austin, 26 February 1844, quoted Mineka, *op. cit.*, volume 2, p. 662. Mill harboured his antagonism for many years, in 1859 he wrote of 'such people as Bright, the mere demagogue and courtier of the majority'. Mill to Edwin Chadwick, 20 December 1859, in Hugh S. R. Elliot (ed.), *The Letters of John Stuart Mill* (2 volumes, 1910), volume 1, p. 233.

[68] J. S. Mill, *Principles of Political Economy* (W. J. Ashley edn., 1909), p. 336. Mill

of the metropolitan reformers encouraged its moderate leaders, with Lovett especially enjoying much favour.[69] William Howitt was another who explicitly rejected the League in favour of Chartism; he wrote to Harney that 'my opinion and yours is identical as to Cobden and all the Millocrats, and the Millocrats know it since I declined to act with them in the League'.[70]

The contemptuous generic terms 'millocrats' and 'shopocrats' accurately summarize the predominant interests within the Anti-Corn Law League. Aided by historical circumstance, the League was the most successful example of a movement created in order to apply extra-parliamentary pressure upon the government of the country. It succeeded not only against vested interests, but also in the face of indifference as many middle class radicals who believed in free trade in corn were suspicious of the motives behind the League's agitation. But, while there are grounds for regarding the repeal of the Corn Laws as heralding 'the victory of the manufacturing capitalist . . . over the landed aristocracy',[71] it did not mark the victory of the land reform movement. Agriculture was not ruined as protectionists had predicted it would be, so the great landowners were not forced to sell their estates; the Conservative Party was divided, but the radicals in Parliament were unable to win further reforms; while after repeal, reformers often relaxed their efforts. Cobden complained that once the 'gross pocket question was settled' many League supporters fell away and even became Tories.[72]

After Corn Law repeal the machine that Cobden had helped to create was dismantled. The demand for a single political reform had been a source of strength to the League, but by concentrating on one issue it meant that, with repeal, its programme had been realized. After

gave a detailed account of peasant proprietorships which he advocated as a solution to the Irish problem; but though he re-opened what most economists had regarded as a settled question they were never established on any scale in the British Isles.

[69] See D. Large, 'William Lovett', p. 118. Among Lovett's early supporters were 'virtually all the intellectual liberals', Julius West, *A History of the Chartist Movement* (1920), p. 160. Predictably, the Working Men's Association was denounced by the more extreme radicals. The *Northern Star* described Lovett and his followers as 'no better than the tools of Place, Grote, Hume, Brougham, and the other leaders of the Malthusian party'. Quoted by Graham Wallas, *The Life of Francis Place* (1925 edn.), p. 373.

[70] Howitt to G. J. Harney, 16 August 1846, in F. G. and R. M. Black (eds.), *The Harney Papers* (Assen, 1969), pp. 24–5.

[71] Frederick Engels, 1892 preface to *The Condition of the Working Class in England in 1844* (trans. F. K. Wischnewetzky, 1892), p. xii. The class interpretation of repeal which regarded 1846 as the bourgeoisie's year of triumph has recently found a number of critics, including Betty Kemp, who in 'Reflections on the Repeal of the Corn Laws,' *Victorian Studies*, volume 5 (1961–2), has argued that Peel in fact outwitted the League politically, and D. C. Moore, whose 'The Corn Laws and High Farming', *Economic History Review*, 2nd series, volume 18 (1965), attempts to show that Peel realized that repeal was to the economic advantage of the landed interest.

[72] Quoted by Goldwin Smith, *Reminiscences* (New York, 1910), p. 216.

the success of the League, Cobden and Bright began to cast around for another cause that would rally the forces of progress against established interests. Cobden inclined towards continuing with the creation of 40s. freeholds, but Bright did not see such a scheme enfranchising sufficient voters to alter the balance of representation. In the late 1840s a 'Commons League' was proposed to advance the demand for financial and parliamentary reform, but they were unable to agree on its organization: Bright wanted to base it in Lancashire and Yorkshire, Cobden believed they should look to London for support. Nor were they in one mind about a programme, and the 'Commons League' never got off the ground as a successor to the Anti-Corn Law League.[73]

Just as an attack on the landed interest was implicit in the agitation of the Anti-Corn Law League, Chartism too had a firm anti-landlord basis. Chartism drew together several different movements, but all emphasized the injustice of a small class owning most of the land. Often having rural origins, working class radicals understood the land-hunger of the English labourer, and his nostalgia for a half-mythical past. Many were familiar with the views of Spence, Cobbett, and other agrarian radicals, and regarded the possession of land as the means of gaining economic independence, self-respect, and employment for those who would otherwise overstock the industrial labour market. However, the Chartists, with the exception of a few moderates, operated independently of the Leaguers, or actively opposed them. Place, who was hoping to wire-pull yet another campaign, had to report:

The leaders [of the London working population]—those among them who do pay attention to public matters, are one and all at emnity with every other class of society. True it is as they allege they have been cajoled and then abandoned by the middle class as often as they have acted with them, but their opinions are pushed to extremes and are mischievous prejudices. They call the middle class—'Shopocrats' —Usurers, (all profit being usury)—money-mongers—Tyrants and oppressors of the working people, and they link the middle class with the Aristocracy under the dignified appellation of 'Murderers of Society'—'Murderers of the People'.[74]

Especially in its early years, the League came into direct conflict with militant Chartists bent on breaking up its meetings.[75] Though often

[73] Morley, *op. cit.*, volume 2, pp. 37 f. For details of financial reform as a vehicle of middle class radicalism, see W. N. Calkins, 'A Victorian Free Trade Lobby', *Economic History Review*, 2nd series, volume 13 (1960–61).

[74] Place to Cobden, 4 March 1840, B.M. Add. MSS. 35151, IV, f. 233b.

[75] For example, see Prentice, *op. cit.*, volume 1, pp. 116–17; Place to T. P. Thompson, 10 March 1840, B.M. Add. MSS. 35151, IV, f. 234b, for a fracas at which Hetherington was the ringleader.

showing a condescending attitude towards the working class, a number of League leaders did try to reach an understanding and a basis for united action. But there was little co-operation apart from exceptional cases, for example at Derby where a successful meeting was probably due to working class hostility towards the Duke of Devonshire, the prominent local landowner.[76] Most Chartists argued that the real campaign was for the suffrage, and on this question there was some co-operation with middle class reformers, but the mistrust of the O'Brien school was so great that it argued the case that free trade would bring disadvantages to the working class by increasing the power of the 'great monied class' over the 'producing class'.[77] The League responded on one occasion by scheming for a Chartist meeting to be physically wrecked,[78] but later it began to control entry to its meetings by the issue of tickets, despite the Chartist accusation that this was done to stifle debate.

Chartism was never an organized movement to the extent of the Anti-Corn Law League; the six points of the Charter were a means to an end rather than an end in themselves, and that end was to create a political democracy. Once this had been won, the repossession of the land for the people was expected to follow. There remained, however, the unanswered question of how 'the people's farm' would be managed. J. B. O'Brien was the strongest protagonist in favour of nationalization (together with a reform of credit and currency systems), while Feargus O'Connor fixed upon a form of peasant proprietorship. Some Chartists argued that small farms could be established immediately, before political reform had been achieved, and the 'Land Plan' was introduced by O'Connor in 1843 after the failure of the second National Petition.[79] O'Connor became absolutely committed to the plan, 'my honour, my character, my very existence', he wrote, was involved in its success.[80] In the *Northern Star* he expounded lengthy arguments to show the viability of his scheme, and before the Chartist convention of April 1845 he advanced figures to demonstrate that a man could support a wife and three children on four acres and have a surplus of £100. Not all of the working class would become small landowners, but O'Connor reasoned,

[76] Lucy Brown, 'The Chartists and the Anti-Corn Law League', in Asa Briggs (ed.), *Chartist Studies* (1959), p. 358.

[77] R. G. Gammage, *History of the Chartist Movement* (1894 edn.), p. 103; see also J. B. O'Brien, 'A few Words to the Anti-Corn Law Agitators', *English Chartist Circular*, volume 1, no. 7 (1844), p. 26.

[78] Donald Read and Eric Glasgow, *Feargus O'Connor: Irishman and Chartist* (1961), pp. 93–4.

[79] O'Connor's *A Practical work on the Management of Small Farms* began to appear in penny numbers on 8 July 1843. O'Connor had long been sympathetic towards schemes involving spade husbandry which he had earlier advocated as a remedy for Irish poverty; see Read and Glasgow, *op. cit.*, pp. 108–9.

[80] *Northern Star and National Trades Journal*, 26 July 1845.

those who did would benefit the remainder by making labour more scarce and thus raising wages.[81] The Land Plan had numerous disciples among the working class, for it appeared to provide the means of breaking the old land monopoly, and, even if only in a limited way, it promised to restore the land to the people. It offered not only economic independence and an escape from the hardships of industrial life, but also made an emotional appeal to a consciousness that recalled a golden age of yeoman farming.

The O'Brienites, however, feared that small farmers would adopt reactionary attitudes, making it impossible ever to bring the land into common ownership, and so they preferred that the people's farm be rented. The social stability of the peasant class was frequently asserted by writers who had studied European societies, and O'Connor's scheme was viewed in this light by the *Leeds Mercury*, which declared that the possession of land by Chartists would give them 'an increased interest in the tranquility and good order of society, and make them anxious to preserve whatever is valuable in the government and institutions of the country.'[82] In the face of such a possibility, O'Brien campaigned against the scheme, contending that those who joined it were betraying their own order. The plan was attacked as divisive, and even condemned as 'a government plot to stifle in embryo our movement for the nationalization of land and property'.[83] Unlike Owenite schemes, which sought to establish village communities based upon shared effort, O'Connor's land colonies were designed to create independent peasant holdings and had no socialist ideology. But both types of settlement shared an idealistic enthusiasm that was insufficient to overcome practical difficulties.[84] Despite O'Brienite criticisms, there were many subscribers to O'Connor's projects, and this basic division in Chartism remained unsolved until the collapse of O'Connor's freehold schemes, by which time Chartism as a national movement was largely a spent force. The remaining hardcore of Chartist leaders continued to advocate public ownership of the land; 'the final and complete nationalization of the land' was called for at the 1851 Chartist convention.[85] Although in the 1850s their

[81] *Ibid.*, 26 April 1845.
[82] *Leeds Mercury*, 23 September 1843, quoted by W. H. G. Armytage, 'The Chartist Land Colonies 1846–1848', *Agricultural History*, volume 32 (1958), p. 88.
[83] *National Reformer and Manx Weekly Review*, 14 May 1847.
[84] For a good factual account, Joy MacAskill, 'The Chartist Land Plan' in Briggs, *op. cit.*, pp. 304–41. In 1846, O'Connor settled Herringsgate, near Watford (later called O'Connorville), and Lowbands near Gloucester, in 1847 Snig's End, near Lowbands, and Minster Lovell (near Witney), later renamed Charterville. With a membership of 70,000, drawn from southern market towns as well as the industrial north, the National Land Company probably settled less than 300 of them. The soil was often poor, the settlers inexperienced and isolated, and the finances increasingly unsound. The Company was wound up in 1850–51.
[85] E. Eldon Barry, *Nationalisation in British Politics: the Historical Background* (1965), p. 39.

audiences had dwindled, O'Brien, Harney, and Jones all retained land nationalization as part of their policy.[86] They helped to keep alive the spark that was to be fanned by Henry George; in 1850 for example, the Chartist and engraver W. J. Linton, called upon reformers to 'raise the cry of *a land tax in the place of all other taxes*; and rouse the whole empire to contest with landlordism. This is the true way in which the People may repossess the land.'[87] With the failure of the Land Plan some of O'Connor's followers drifted into temperance and journalism, while Owenism and the freehold land movement gave others a link with the idea of land reform.

Though Chartism dwindled in the late 1840s, land radicalism found further expression when Cobden took up the 40s. freehold movement as a vehicle of reform. Some years previously the Anti-Corn Law League had advised individuals how they could obtain the franchise by purchasing freehold properties. Another scheme, devised mainly by John Taylor, a Birmingham radical, found a way round the restrictions of the 1836 Building Societies Act which did not allow building societies to own land. In 1847 Taylor helped to form the Birmingham Freehold Land Society 'for the purpose of procuring qualifications in the County for the representation of North Warwickshire'.[88] This scheme had an advantage over the one undertaken by the League as through it land was bought at wholesale prices, to be divided into small plots which were sold without profit, and this was within the law as technically the society was advancing money to purchasers. The scheme operated so that a qualification to vote could be secured for less than £20. The Birmingham society was closely associated with the temperance movement of which Taylor—a reformed drinker—was a local leader. The improvident lower orders were enjoined to regard the society as a means of moral regeneration, urged on by Taylor who calculated that 'every time a man drinks a quart of ale he engulphs at the same time a yard of solid earth'.[89]

In 1847 four freehold land societies were formed. After a further six years 113 had been established, made up of sixty-nine provincial socie-

[86] Alfred Plummer, *Bronterre: a Political Biography of Bronterre O'Brien 1804–1864* (1971), p. 220; A. R. Schoyen, *The Chartist Challenge: a Portrait of George Julian Harney* (1958), p. 197; John Saville, *Ernest Jones, Chartist* (1952), pp. 152–7.

[87] W. J. Linton, *The People's Land and an easy way to recover it* (1850), p. 6.

[88] George Elkington, *The National Building Societies: 1849–1934* (Cambridge, 1935), p. 3. For some details of the origins of Taylor's schemes see S. D. Chapman and J. N. Bartlett, 'The contribution of Building Clubs and Freehold Land Society to Working-class Housing in Birmingham', in S. D. Chapman (ed.), *The History of Working Class Housing* (Newton Abbot, 1971), pp. 240–1.

[89] W. Ewing Ritchie, *Freehold Land Societies: Their History, Present Position, and Claims* (1853), p. 19. For other links between the freehold land movement and temperance see Brian Harrison, *Drink and the Victorians: The Temperance Question in England 1815–1872* (1971), pp. 174–6, 288.

ties and forty-four in London.[90] Their leaders were usually middle class
in origin and generally adopted as a model an already established
society. In Bradford, for example, Titus Salt, the mayor, became president, with W. E. Forster as vice-president, of the Bradford Freehold
Land and Building Society, which was established in June 1849. Its
prospectus emphasized the success of the Birmingham society, and
declared its 'Grand Objects . . . are to Improve the Social, Promote the
Moral, and Exalt the Political Condition of the Unenfranchised Millions'.[91]

The first society to be formed in London was the National Freehold
Land Society, an offshoot of the Metropolitan Parliamentary and
Financial Reform Association.[92] Among a number of radical MPs who
gave their support was Cobden who envisaged the creation of a 'phalanx
of forty shilling freeholders'. Because the 'citadel of privilege' was 'so
terribly strong, owing to the concentrated masses of property in the
hands of the comparatively few', he planned to enlist the help of a portion of the working class.[93] He detailed his proposals at a meeting of the
National Freehold Land Society held in November 1849 at the London
Tavern. His object, he told the audience, was to place 'as much political
power as he could in the hands of the middle and industrious classes'.
The members of the society could not be called red republicans or revolutionists; they were, he emphasized, simply 'trying to bring back to the
people some of their ancient rights and privileges. They were digging
into four centuries at least to find the origins of this freehold franchise'.[94]
He announced, too, his willingness to serve with the freehold movement
for as long a period as he had spent in the anti-Corn Law agitation.

In the outcome he had not the opportunity, though initial prospects
were promising. On 1 January 1850 the *Freeholder* was launched as the
movement's journal, and its pages were filled with details of numerous
societies that had sprung up. Quite soon, however, what had been the
secondary function of the societies, the business side, came to the fore;
after only one year's experience, the National Freehold Land Society
noted that its commercial activities were likely to overshadow its political role. Some of the societies that had mushroomed failed through fraud

[90] E. J. Cleary, *The Building Society Movement* (1965), p. 51.
[91] Ezra Naylor, *Bradford Building Societies from 1823* (Bradford, 1908), p. 66. For the
freehold land movement in the Sheffield area, where enfranchisement of non-electors
again provided the impetus, see E. M. Gaskell, 'Yorkshire Estate Development and
the Freehold Land Societies in the Nineteenth Century', *Yorkshire Archaeological
Journal*, volume 43 (1971), esp. pp. 159–61.
[92] Seymour J. Price, *Building Societies: Their Origin and History* (1958), p. 127; see
also H. J. Dyos, *Victorian Suburb* (Leicester, 1961), pp. 116–17.
[93] Cobden to Bright, 1 October 1849, quoted Morley, *op. cit.*, volume 2, p.
53.
[94] *The Times*, 27 November 1849.

or incompetence,[95] and this probably encouraged greater caution among other organizers.[96] Nor was it possible to ensure that newly-enfranchised voters held fast to their former beliefs. Just as some Owenites lost sight of the new moral world and some land colonists forgot the Charter, there were defectors among the 40s. freeholders. Some ceased to be concerned about political questions, and, even more disappointingly for the Liberals, others changed their allegiance and started to vote Tory. In 1852 the Conservative Freehold Land Society was formed as a rival to the Liberal organizations, and in August of that year the *Freeholder* had to close down after incurring heavy losses. Those societies that continued soon lost their political complexion and became simply the forerunners of the building societies of the present day.

The Crimean War drew the attention of radicals from domestic matters, and then Palmerston's administration became another barrier to reform. On the institution of landed property Palmerston would allow no concessions; when it was suggested that probate duty might be extended to real property, he vetoed the proposal on the grounds that 'hereditary succession to unbroken masses of landed property [is] absolutely necessary for the maintenance of the British constitution'.[97] The great majority of Conservatives agreed with such a view, and so did the Whig magnates, while Gladstone, though a convinced financial reformer, also shared many of the attitudes of the large landed proprietor.[98] Cobden found it 'astonishing that the people at large are so tacit in their submission to the perpetuation of the feudal system in this country as it affects the property in land'.[99] He explained their submission by the prosperity of the manufacturing system and the outlet for population provided by Britain's colonies. And there are grounds for accepting this as part of the explanation of why no effective movement for land reform emerged, for the social groups who had provided the finance that made the organization of the Anti-Corn Law League possible enjoyed, for the most part, an economically enhanced position after repeal, and this tended to blunt their political ambitions.

[95] For the case of Birmingham see G. J. Johnson, 'On the Benefit Building and Freehold Land Societies of Birmingham', *Journal of the Statistical Society of London*, volume 28 (1865), p. 510. Taylor's society was successful, but here too the commercial aspect soon predominated.

[96] There were warnings too that the freehold societies might go the way of the Chartist land scheme; see W. R. Greg, 'Investments for the Working Classes', *Edinburgh Review*, volume 95 (1852), pp. 431 f.

[97] Palmerston to Cranworth, 10 December 1856, B.M. Add. MSS. 48580, f. 332. See also Palmerston to Westbury, 1865, in Thomas Arthur Nash, *The Life of Richard Lord Westbury* (2 volumes, 1888), p. 94.

[98] John Vincent, *The Formation of the Liberal Party, 1857–1868* (1966), pp. 212 f.

[99] Cobden to White, 22 November 1857, Morley, *op. cit.*, volume 2, p. 215.

The 1850s was thus a lean decade for radicals. In the ten years after the dissolution of the Anti-Corn Law League, Cobden and Bright passed from being leaders of a great popular movement to a position of relative isolation, and in the general election of March 1857 both lost their seats.[100] If the ruling class had jettisoned the Corn Laws in order to assuage the rising tide of radicalism, it could regard its strategy as vindicated.

In 1859 Cobden was returned to the House of Commons as Member for Rochdale, and despite the failure of the 40s. freehold movement to realize its early promise, he did not allow the question of land reform to rest. He still regarded it as an essential part of radical liberalism, and as a means of facilitating social and political reform in general. During the 1860s the land question again came to the fore. The returns of the 1861 census showed that only 30,766 persons had described themselves as proprietors of land.[101] This figure became widely quoted by reformers, although the more moderate of them would add that the true figure was probably appreciably higher.[102] Reflecting this renewal of interest in the land question, in November 1864 Cobden addressed a packed meeting of his constituents in which he called for a league for free trade in land.[103] The expression 'free trade in land' was by then at least thirty years old and had certainly entered into common currency in the 1840s.[104] Cobden was thus drawing upon the long tradition of land radicalism, and also harking back in the last few months of his life—he died in 1865—to the successful struggles of the Anti-Corn Law League, and offering a cause for popular support which the Commons League and 40s. freehold movement had failed to provide. In his speech at Rochdale he held fast to the same principles that he had believed might guide those earlier movements. Just fifteen years earlier at the London Tavern, he had expressed the hope of seeing the time 'when land would be as easily transferred as railway shares or Consols'.[105] He continued to stress free

[100] For an account of their careers during these years see N. McCord, 'Cobden and Bright in Politics, 1846–1857', in Robert Robson (ed.), *Ideas and Institutions of Victorian Britain* (1967), pp. 85–114.

[101] *Census of England and Wales: Population Tables*, volume 2 (1863), p. xxxv.

[102] For example, Charles Neate, *The History and Uses of the Law of Entail and Settlement* (1865), p. 40. Neate was a barrister and MP for Oxford.

[103] *Rochdale Observer*, 26 November 1864; also Morley, *op. cit.*, volume 2, pp. 455–7. Reports of the speech show Cobden to have been at his most eloquent, and for several years reformers referred to it in reverential terms; see, for example, Arthur Arnold, 'Free Trade in Land', *Contemporary Review*, volume 20 (1872), pp. 880–81.

[104] In 1830 an advocate of allotments called for 'a free trade in land and cottages', [Edward Edwards], 'The Influence of Free Trade upon the condition of the Labouring Classes', *Blackwood's Magazine*, volume 27 (1830), p. 568; Edwards, however, was an old-fashioned Tory. For a concise statement from a liberal position, see 'The Monopoly of Land', *Tait's Edinburgh Magazine*, volume 15 (1848), p. 418, and also James Beal, *Free Trade in Land* (1855).

[105] *The Times*, 27 November 1849.

market conditions: 'I would take Adam Smith in hand—I would not go beyond him, I would have no politics in it—and I would have a League for free trade in land just as we had a League for free trade in corn.'[106] As at the London Tavern, he dissociated his proposal from 'revolutionary, Radical or Chartist notion[s]' in order to emphasize the economic side of the issue.[107]

By implying that the League would not have a political motivation, Cobden was being somewhat disingenuous for the land question was, as it had long been, a key part of his political platform. Land reformers, quickly seized upon the wider aspects of Cobden's speech, and tended to discount the essentially *laissez faire* basis of his arguments. In an editorial the Liberal *Rochdale Observer* thought the suggestion of a new League bore the stamp of a 'practical and sagacious intellect', but went on to raise the obvious problem of the dominance of the landed interest in Parliament: the 30,000 owners of the land also controlled the legislature, and it would be 'utopian' not to expect them to put their own interests first.[108]

The main short term effect of Cobden's speech was to add weight to the demand for a wider franchise; the cry of land reform accentuated the separateness of the ruling class while helping to increase the pressure for parliamentary reform. In the debate surrounding the second Reform Act, Liberal authors claimed that the 'chief obstacle to progress is the *political* power of the Territorial Aristocracy',[109] and spoke of a 'vast cousinhood' of 500 MPs who represented land.[110]

Nor was the attack abated by the Reform Act of 1867. To some radicals the extension of the franchise was seen as an opportunity for making the Liberal party a combative and reforming body in which there would be little place for the patrician Whigs. The land question was one means of welding new votes to liberalism, and several radical MPs took it up. In 1869 the Land Tenure Reform Association held its inaugural confer-

[106] *Rochdale Observer*, 26 November 1864. Conservatives also adopted the rhetoric of *laissez faire*; Cecil, for example, defended entails as 'the dying man's right of free bequest, or the living man's right of free contract' [Robert Cecil], 'The Programme of the Radicals', *Quarterly Review*, volume 135 (1873), p. 563.

[107] *Ibid*. A good exposition of Cobden's views on the land question was given by his son-in-law, James E. Thorold Rogers, *Cobden and Modern Political Opinion* (1873), chapter 3.

[108] 'Mr. Cobden's Proposed League for Free Trade in Land', *Rochdale Observer*, 10 December 1864. An important side issue from the renewed interest in land reform was the founding of preservation societies to protect the remaining commons, such as Hampstead Heath, from builders, in the mid 1860s. The Commons Preservation Society was founded in 1865; and thirty years later, the National Trust.

[109] A. O. Rutson in the symposium *Essays on Reform* (1967), p. 291.

[110] Bernard Cracroft, *ibid*., p. 165. For a fuller statement of a Liberal programme for land reform, see W. L. Newman, 'The Land Laws', in *Questions for a Reformed Parliament* (1867), chapter 4; see also William Fowler, *Thoughts on 'Free Trade in Land'* (1869).

ence, after its organizers had sent out invitations on notepaper headed with Cobden's phrase calling for a league for free trade in land. The LTRA was largely a middle class body which called for the abolition of primogeniture, easier land transfer, a wider distribution of ownership and taxation of the unearned increment.[111] Mill, one of its leading supporters, tried to gain working class members, but the LTRA programme, which excluded nationalization, was considered too moderate by many radicals. A rival body, the Land and Labour League, formed in the autumn of 1869, did call for nationalization, and drew support that was largely working class in origin. Some respectable radicals, such as Howell, Cremer and Applegarth, worked with the LTRA, while one of its council members was the veteran Chartist Henry Vincent.[112] When Mill nudged the LTRA a little to the left, he lost some of his middle class supporters, without achieving more than LTRA attendance at the Land and Labour League's inaugural meeting.[113]

After Mill's death in 1873, the LTRA faded away, a fate shared also by the Land and Labour League. Nevertheless, the land question continued to be a subject of vigorous debate until the turn of the century and beyond. The publication of the 'New Domesday Book' in the mid-1870s produced a spate of radical compilations which showed how few in numbers were the great landowners of Britain,[114] particularly when compared with the Continent. A. R. Wallace's *Land Nationalization* appeared in 1882, and in the same year Hyndman reprinted Spence's tract of 1775, pointing out that it was 'specially worthy of attention at the present time' as a 'practical and thoroughly English proposal'.[115] The advent of Henry George placed the question in a sharper focus,[116] while Chamberlain made land part of his radical platform, most explicitly when he created a furore with his 'ransom' speech of 1885.[117] In the 1880s two more organizations were formed to press for change, the English Land Restoration League and the Land Nationalization

[111] For the programme of the LTRA, *The Bee-hive*, 11 September 1869, see also *Programme of the Land Tenure Reform Association, with an Explanatory Statement by John Stuart Mill* (1871).

[112] Brian Harrison, 'Henry Vincent', in Joyce M. Bellamy and John Saville (eds.), *Dictionary of Labour Biography*, volume 1 (1972), p. 332.

[113] Barry, *op. cit.*, pp. 51–2; see also R. Harrison, 'The Land and Labour League (Some new light on Working Class Politics in the Eighteen Seventies)', *Bulletin of the International Institute of Social History*, volume 8 (1953).

[114] In particular, Joseph Kay, *Free Trade in Land* (1879), with a Preface by John Bright; Arthur Arnold, *Free Land* (1880); George C. Brodrick, *English Land and English Landlords* (1881). Brodrick estimated that half of England and Wales was held by less than 4,000 owners, who possessed 1,000 acres or more.

[115] H. M. Hyndman, Introduction to *The Nationalization of the Land in 1775 and 1882* (1882), p. 4.

[116] For an assessment of George's importance see John Saville, 'Henry George and the British Labour Movement', *Science and Society*, volume 24 (1960).

[117] J. L. Garvin, *The Life of Joseph Chamberlain*, volume 1 (1932), pp. 549 ff.

Society, and a quarter of a century later, audiences were still being brought to the boil by denunciations of the land monopoly, most effectively by Lloyd George and his rhetorical question, 'who made 10,000 people owners of the soil and the rest of us trespassers in the land of our birth?'[118]

In many respects, the post-1870 debate was covering again and again the ground that has been surveyed in this essay. Questions concerning entails and primogeniture, allotments and peasant proprietorships, the 'land monopoly' and 'free trade in land' and the political and social power of the landed interest had all been raised in the middle decades of the century or earlier, and, despite urbanization, reform continued to be seen almost invariably in a rural context. What was known simply as the 'Land Question' was in fact an amorphous and many-sided issue upon which reformers had a wide range of opinions.

To some extent it is true, as Professor Thompson has maintained, that the agitation for land reform was a 'political talisman', a symbolic issue around which reformers could rally, as, too, could Conservatives to whom land was the basis of the old order.[119] But this is only a part of the picture and fails to take account of the wider question: why did the radical groups not coalesce in order to demand change? A full answer to this question would have to consider the broader character of nineteenth-century radicalism. But the land issue does help to illuminate the larger problem of the relationship between various reforming elements. Opposition to the prevailing system of land ownership acted as a sort of core to movements like Chartism and Corn Law repeal. By providing a basis for agitation in both counties and towns and cities it played an important part in advanced politics. But while there was general agreement on the need for reform, a programme acceptable to all radicals did not emerge. Class antagonisms sharpened the problem, but essentially the contradiction between the libertarian approach typified by the slogan 'free trade in land', and the movement towards greater public control could not be resolved.[120]

On the other side of the agitation, landowners were much more agreed

[118] *The Times*, 11 October 1909. It was left mainly to the few that followed Marx and Engels to argue that the manufacturers and owners of capital had become the real enemies of the working class. This was the basis of Marx's attack on Henry George, who he accused of the 'repulsive presumption and arrogance that distinguish all such panacea-mongers' and of being theoretically '*total arrière*' in putting forward an idea that originated with 'the earliest *radical* disciples of Ricardo'. Marx to Frederick Sorge, 20 June 1881 quoted in Alexander Trachtenberg (ed.), *Letters to Americans 1848–1895* (New York, 1963 edn.), pp. 127–9.
[119] F. M. L. Thompson, *loc. cit.*, p. 39.
[120] For the application of a similar argument, see A. V. Dicey, 'The Paradox of the Land Law', *Law Quarterly Review*, volume 83 (1905). Dicey also pointed out that in the case of the land laws, great technical problems made amendment difficult.

on their aims than were radicals, and even though the outworks of the old order had to be sacrificed, land was the citadel to be conceded last. Up to 1867 the landed interest had dominated parliament, and even after it outweighed by far any other single interest. By the 1880s, moreover, it had been joined by an ally, for many businessmen, whose fathers could well have been supporters of the Anti-Corn Law League, began to suspect that land reform might introduce a socialistic wedge that would lead to interference with the right of capital and other forms of property.[121] Thus the rearguard action fought by the owners of land became stiffened by the owners of capital, so that in the present century the landed interest, though eclipsed and weakened, has been able to out-survive all but the stragglers of land radicalism.

Further Reading

Despite the importance attached to the land question in the nineteenth century, there is no modern study evaluating its many-sided and complex significance. F. M. L. Thompson, 'Land and Politics in England in the Nineteenth Century', *Transactions of the Royal Historical Society*, 5th series, volume 15 (1965), surveys some aspects, but, in a challenging essay, he sometimes prefers to dwell on a paradox at the expense of analysis. The same author's *English Landed Society in the Nineteenth Century* (1963) is concerned with the institution and administration of the landed estate rather than its radical critics.

Certain features of the land question have been examined, usually in isolation. The allotment issue is discussed by D. C. Barnett, 'Allotments and the Problem of Rural Poverty, 1780–1840', in E. L. Jones and G. E. Mingay (eds.), *Land, Labour and Population in the Industrial Revolution* (1967) and by Newlin R. Smith, *Land for the Small Man: English and Welsh Experience with Publicly-Supplied Small Holdings, 1860–1937* (New York, 1946). Primogeniture and entails are explained by Eileen Spring, 'The Settlement of Land in Nineteenth-Century England', *American Journal of Legal History*, volume 8 (1964). The Freehold Land Society movement is briefly referred to by E. J. Cleary, *The Building Society Movement* (1965). Radical arguments against the game laws have been studied by Chester Kirby, 'The Attack on the English Game Laws in the Forties', *Journal of Modern History*, volume 4 (1932). Kirby shows how an attempt was made to incorporate the game laws into the agitation of the

---

[121] F. M. L. Thompson, *English Landed Society in the Nineteenth Century* (1963), pp. 284–5. See also Harold Perkin, *The Origins of Modern English Society 1780–1880* (1969), pp. 452–3; since the present essay was written, Professor Perkin has expanded this argument in 'Land Reform and Class Conflict in Victorian Britain', in J. Butt and I. F. Clarke (eds.), *The Victorians and Social Protest: A Symposium* (Newton Abbot, 1973).

Anti-Corn Law League. In its broader significance, the League was a manifestation of middle class hostility towards landlordism; this is brought out in John Morley, *The Life of Richard Cobden* (1881), which, though uncritical towards its hero, can still be read with profit. The development of the League has been unravelled by Norman McCord, *The Anti-Corn Law League 1838–1846* (1958), while William O. Aydelotte, 'The Country Gentlemen and the Repeal of the Corn Laws', *English Historical Review*, volume 77 (1967), supports the view that 1846 did not mark a defeat for the landed interest, but merely a timely retreat.

The issue of land also made a distinct contribution to Chartism. The nationalization aspect is outlined by E. Eldon Barry, *Nationalization in British Politics: The Historical Background* (1965), chapter 1. There is a more substantial literature on the Land Plan; most of it is referred to in the course of a sympathetic treatment of O'Connor's schemes by John Saville in his introduction to the 1969 reprint of R. G. Gammage, *The History of the Chartist Movement*. Alice Mary Hadfield, *The Chartist Land Company* (Newton Abbot, 1970) is principally descriptive. For the Land and Labour League, see R. Harrison's essay of that title in *Bulletin of the International Institute of Social History*, volume 8 (1953), and Barry, chapter 2, which also contains a short account of the Land Tenure Reform Association.

Contemporary material on the land question is considerable. Some sources are mentioned by O. R. McGregor in his Introduction to the 1961 edition of Lord Ernle, *English Farming Past and Present*. The bibliographies of three unpublished theses also give a selection of material: Joy MacAskill, 'The Treatment of "Land" in English Social and Political Theory, 1840–1885', (Oxford B.Litt., 1959); A. J. Peacock, 'Land Reform 1880–1919: A Study of the Activities of the English Land Restoration League and the Land Nationalization Society', (Southampton M.A., 1961); D. E. Martin, 'Economic and Social Attitudes to Landed Property in England, 1790–1850, with particular reference to John Stuart Mill' (Hull Ph.D., 1972).

7

Shaftesbury[1]

Geoffrey B. A. M. Finlayson

If birth, family background and education are ever any guide to a man's future career, for Anthony Ashley Cooper, Seventh Earl of Shaftesbury,[2] they pointed to a life in political and governing circles. Born in 1801, Shaftesbury had an impeccably aristocratic and strongly political pedigree[3] and his early years, if harsh in their lack of parental affection, were spent amidst the traditional setting of an aristocratic way of life. Shaftesbury's education at Harrow and Christ Church was, moreover, highly conventional, and in 1826 he embarked upon the career normal for a young man of his social standing by entering parliament; he was returned in the Tory interest for Woodstock, the pocket borough of the Marlborough family. In 1828, a further step was taken when he was appointed to office by Wellington, serving as a Commissioner at the India Board of Control until Wellington's resignation in 1830. At the General Election of that year, he was elected for Dorchester, thereby continuing a long family association with that borough. Thus although he had doubts and misgivings about his aptitude for political and public life, Shaftesbury's course seemed well set. And in 1830 he married.[4] His bride was Lady Emily Cowper, daughter of the fifth Earl Cowper and, on her mother's side, grand-daughter of the first Viscount Melbourne.

[1] I should like to thank Professor G. F. A. Best of the University of Sussex and Miss Felicity Ranger of the Historical Manuscripts Commission for assistance which has greatly facilitated my research, and Dr A. G. R. Smith of the University of Glasgow for reading and commenting on this essay.

[2] Shaftesbury inherited the title on the death of his father, the sixth earl, in 1851. Before this, he was known as Lord Ashley, but it makes for greater clarity to refer to him as 'Shaftesbury' throughout this essay.

[3] On his father's side, Shaftesbury was heir to the title founded in 1672 by the celebrated politician of Charles II's reign. Subsequent holders of the title were not especially noted for their political skills, but the sixth earl, Cropley Ashley, represented the borough of Dorchester from 1790 to 1811, when he succeeded to the earldom. He was appointed permanent chairman of committees in the Lords in 1814 and held this position until shortly before his death. Shaftesbury's mother was a daughter of the fourth Duke of Marlborough.

[4] Shaftesbury's search for a wife had been conducted with zeal and seriousness and had not been without its disappointments. (See G. F. A. Best, *Shaftesbury* (1964), pp. 22–9.)

The fact that he was marrying into a family with such strong Whig connections gave Shaftesbury some twinges of conscience; but it was a marriage much in keeping with the tenor of his life. All the signs were, therefore, that a political career in aristocratic circles lay ahead.

The early signs, however, proved misleading; the first thirty years of Shaftesbury's life were to bear little relation to the next fifty. With the exception of some eighteen months, he did, indeed, remain in parliament for the rest of his life. He was returned for Dorset at the General Election of 1831 and retained the seat until 1846, when he resigned it owing to his conversion to Corn Law repeal. In 1847, he was, however, elected for Bath, which he represented until he entered the Lords on his father's death in 1851. Nevertheless, his career did not follow a conventional political pattern. He came to concern himself with a host of activities which were far removed from official political pursuits and which were, indeed, to place him outside the ruling ranks of the Tory party. Again, although his aristocratic connections were retained and, if anything, strengthened by the marriage of his widowed mother-in-law, Lady Cowper, to Palmerston in 1839, his interests developed in directions which took him far beyond the circle of aristocratic society and which, indeed, led to a rupture of the admittedly fragile bonds with his father. One of the most natural 'insiders' of the nineteenth century became one of its most noted 'outsiders'; and it was in the 1830s, when the future promised quite otherwise, that the beginnings of this process may be discerned with the stirring of the two forces which were to undergird his life and, in time, to dictate his future.

The first of these was paternalism. It was not altogether new, for in the late '20s, Shaftesbury had shown an interest in the less fortunate sections of society: in 1828, he had taken up the question of lunacy, one which was to remain an active concern for the rest of his life.[5] In the early '30s, however, he fell increasingly under the influence of the Tory paternalist school of thought and became a regular correspondent of one

[5] Shaftesbury seconded proposals put forward by Robert Gordon, a Dorset magistrate, in 1828 to amend the lunacy laws (Hansard, *Parl. Debates*, 3rd ser., xviii, 575–85). These laws, dating from the late eighteenth century, had attempted to regulate and control the setting up of madhouses, but had been defective in implementation. Two acts followed Gordon's proposals: the County Lunatic Asylums Act (1828), which encouraged (with little effect) local JPs to establish county asylums; and the more important Madhouse Act of the same year. Shaftesbury was closely involved in the implementation of the latter act, for he was one of the fifteen commissioners appointed under it to license and visit Metropolitan private madhouses. The Act was later repealed, but the Metropolitan Commissioners continued in existence under subsequent legislation (and Shaftesbury remained a Commissioner) until they were replaced in 1845 by the Board of Commissioners in Lunacy. Shaftesbury was chairman of the Board from its establishment until his death in 1885. (See below footnote 27 and see also W. Ll. Parry Jones, *The Trade in Lunacy* (1972), pp. 6–20.)

of its leading exponents and publicists, Robert Southey. He was thus exposed to the central points of the school's teaching: its distrust of any change in the political structure and dislike of material values and competitive conduct; its ideal of a stable and harmonious society, bound together by mutual obligations and attachments between rich and poor; its belief that only by showing care and concern for the poor could the rich hope to survive. Shaftesbury clearly made good progress; in January, 1832, Southey wrote approvingly to him:

> I agree with you that the state of the poor cannot be discussed too much, for till it is improved physically and morally and religiously we shall be in more danger from them than the West Indian planters are from their slaves.[6]

Thus the first seeds of Shaftesbury's paternalism were sown; and soon the first fruit was to appear when, in 1833, he espoused the cause to obtain a ten hour day in factories. Agitation to reduce factory hours of work had first become evident in the 1810s, but it was only after 1830 that a concerted campaign came into being in the form of the Ten Hours Movement. It owed much to the leadership of Richard Oastler,[7] a steward on an estate near Huddersfield, who became converted to the cause after hearing of the conditions of child labour in neighbouring mills. Soon there developed a well-organized pressure group; local short-time committees were formed, great meetings were held, petitions to parliament presented and attempts made to obtain the support of a member of parliament to introduce a bill which would limit the working day to ten hours.[8] Shaftesbury's association with all this was, in a sense, strange and it was also rather accidental. On his own admission, he knew nothing of the subject and had almost certainly never seen a factory. Further, it was only on the defeat at the 1832 General Election of Michael Sadler,[9] who had introduced a ten hour bill on behalf of the

[6] E. Hodder, *The Life and Work of the Seventh Earl of Shaftesbury K.G.* (3 volumes, 1886–7), volume 1, p. 129. (Hereafter referred to as 'Hodder' with appropriate volume and page number.)

[7] For his biography, see C. Driver, *Tory Radical. The Life of Richard Oastler* (Oxford, 1946).

[8] J. T. Ward, *The Factory Movement, 1830–1855* (1962), pp. 32–55. See also J. T. Ward (ed.), *Popular Movements, c. 1830–1850* (1970), pp. 65–7.

[9] Michael T. Sadler (1780–1835) was member for Newark, a resident of Leeds and a friend of Oastler, with whom he shared Tory paternalist ideas. His Bill, introduced in December 1831 and read for the first time in January 1832, prohibited any work under the age of nine and night work under the age of twenty-one, and limited hours of work between the ages of nine and eighteen to ten hours a day or forty-eight hours a week. At its second reading in March 1832, it was referred to a Select Committee, which met under the chairmanship of Sadler. Before he had any opportunity to take the matter further in parliament, Sadler was defeated at Leeds in December 1832, having fought the election on the issue of ten hours. (M. W. Thomas, *The Early Factory Legislation* (Leigh-on-Sea, 1948), pp. 37–42.)

Movement in 1831, that an approach was made to Shaftesbury; and this was only after several other members had been asked and had refused to take up the cause. Shaftesbury himself was surprised when invited by the Movement to re-introduce Sadler's bill.[10] He had, it appears, written to Sadler on the latter's defeat offering his services in presenting petitions or in any other small work, but he had received no reply and had forgotten the matter.[11] The prospect of playing such a prominent role as the Movement's request clearly implied filled him with apprehension and alarm; and it was only after further thought that he finally decided to proceed with Sadler's bill rather than let it fall for want of support.[12] The precise reasons for his decision are hard to determine; but it was partly due to his growing commitment to Tory paternalism. Here, indeed, was an opportunity to limit the activities of the mill-owners, many of whom he regarded as blind to their social obligations; it was also a means of affording relief, as he was later to put it, to 'those miserable victims of the most abominable system that had ever prevailed in any civilised country'.[13] The words were strongly reminiscent of those used by his mentor, Southey, who had, in fact, been in correspondence with Shaftesbury about the factory system at the time of the Movement's invitation and who wrote to congratulate him on his decision to accept it: 'Thousands of thousands will bless you for taking up the cause ...,' Southey wrote. 'I do not believe that anything more inhuman than the [factory] system has ever disgraced human nature, in any age or country. ...'[14] Shaftesbury had, indeed, proved a faithful disciple.

If his introduction of the ten hours bill in March 1833[15] marked the

[10] The invitation was delivered by the Reverend G. S. Bull, a prominent member of the Ten Hour Movement, who was introduced to Shaftesbury by Sir Andrew Agnew, Tory member for Wigtownshire. For Bull's career, see J. C. Gill, *The Ten Hours Parson* (1959) and the same author's *Parson Bull of Byerley* (1963).

[11] Hodder, volume I, p. 148.

[12] Shaftesbury was under pressure for a quick reply, since the Movement feared that Lord Morpeth, member for the West Riding, was about to introduce a Bill which would have given an eleven hour day.

[13] Hansard, *Parl. Debates*, 3rd ser., xliii, 969.   [14] Hodder, volume I, p. 157.

[15] Hansard, *Parl. Debates*, 3rd ser., xvi, 199. The Bill followed Sadler's proposal for a ten hour day between the ages of nine and eighteen. The matter was, however, further delayed by the appointment of a Royal Commission in April 1833 (*ibid.*, xvii, 113), which recommended in its Report of June, 1833 that protection should cease at the age of thirteen (see M. W. Thomas, *op. cit.*, pp. 46–60). Shaftesbury's Bill received its second reading in June 1833 (Hansard, *Parl. Debates*, 3rd ser., xviii, 915), but in committee in July, the ten hours clause was heavily defeated (*ibid.*, xix, 913), and Shaftesbury surrendered his Bill into the hands of Althorp, the Whig Home Secretary. As passed, the Factory Act of 1833 prohibited work under the age of nine and night work under the age of eighteen, and limited hours of work between the ages of nine and thirteen to forty-eight a week, or nine in any one day; and between the ages of thirteen and eighteen to not more than sixty-nine a week or twelve in any one day. Inspectors were appointed to implement the act. Despite the fact that the act gave

effective beginning of Shaftesbury's paternalistic career, the other great
influence on his life was soon to become evident: evangelicalism. In
many respects, this was an individualistic form of religious belief. The
evangelical was acutely aware of the presence of God in his life and the
purpose of God for his life. Yet the very fact that his religious experience
was so direct and personal made him want, indeed burn, to share it with
others. He was constrained to go out into all the world to preach the
Gospel and to bring men, even, and perhaps especially, the most destitute and down-trodden of men, to a saving knowledge of God. Further,
the evangelical's time, talents and possessions were not to be regarded
as a means to secure his own pleasure and profit; rather they were to be
held in trust as gifts from God and used to promote a society which
would honour His name and be pleasing in His sight. Thus evangelical
religion, if rooted in an intensely personal experience, could and did
have considerable social repercussions. Both aspects, private and public,
appeared in Shaftesbury in the mid-thirties. Exactly when and where
he 'caught' his evangelicalism is not clear; in the late '20s, he had
already shown considerable interest in religion and certainly was regarded, and regarded himself, as a Christian. There appears to have
been no dramatic 'Damascus Road' conversion to which so many
evangelicals testified; but there was evidence in 1834 of a deepening
awareness of the things of the spirit and a stronger trust in the guiding
hand of God. In July of that year, he wrote:

> To all subjects I prefer theology. Finance, corn laws, foreign policy
> or poor laws would give me more public usefulness, but they would
> not give me more private happiness. I shall be content henceforward
> to float down the stream of time, and put ashore at any point whither
> the Almighty in His wisdom may command me.[16]

Further, his comments later in the same month made it clear that the
more public aspects of his new-found faith did not escape him. When it
was rumoured in the summer of 1834 that Peel might be invited to form
a ministry, Shaftesbury complained that he neither saw nor heard 'any
symptom of awakened religion among those who aspire to be our
rulers'; and, he added, 'what security does any other principle afford?'[17]
Evangelical principles were thus the sole guarantee for the proper
conduct of political and public life.

some protection up to the age of eighteen, and thus went further than the recommendation of the Royal Commission, it was a great disappointment to the Ten Hour
Movement.
[16] Lord Shaftesbury's Diary (hereafter referred to as 'SHA/PD/appropriate volume
number'), SHA/PD/1, 3 July 1834. (I quote from the Diary by permission of the
Trustees of the Broadlands Archives.)
[17] *Ibid.*, 14 July, 1834.

In time, the impulses of paternalism and evangelicalism were to gather strength and were, indeed, to reinforce each other. To Shaftesbury's nascent spirit of 'noblesse oblige' was added a growing sensitivity to the claims of a practical and vital religion upon his life and a feeling of stewardship to use aright the blessings which he had received from God. And as these influences came increasingly to involve him in schemes for the physical and spiritual welfare of his fellow men, Shaftesbury became ever more aware that he was being carried away from the conventional occupations of the political and social world into which he had been born. The beginnings of this process should not, however, be over-dramatized, for when he took up the cause of factory reform in 1833, it seems unlikely that he grasped the bearing which this would have on his future career.[18] To Tory paternalists such as Oastler, Sadler, Shaftesbury, and indeed to the group which later went under the name of 'Young England', the way for the Tory party to recoup its fortunes after the disasters of the 1832 General Election was to effect an alliance between the aristocracy and the people and thereby to offset what they saw as the sinister Whig–middle class entente created by the Reform Act. It was a policy which tended to exaggerate the political gains made by the middle classes in 1832; and it failed to take account of the fact that the people had made virtually no gains at all and were, therefore, of no value as allies.[19] Nevertheless, factory reform, even if in itself an obscure cause, could form part of such a programme; it would enlist the support of the people against the Whigs and their manufacturing, mill-owning friends. Exactly when Shaftesbury realized that the Tory paternalist thesis did not, in fact, accord with official Tory policy is difficult to say. He held office during Peel's ministry of 1834–5 at the Board of Admiralty, but he was sorely disappointed by the offer of such a lowly post: '... what a humiliation for an ambitious man!' he wrote.[20] Worse was, however, to come, for in 1839 and again in 1841, he was offered even more minor office in the Queen's Household. These offers, the first at the time of the Bedchamber crisis and the second on the return of the Tories to power were, he felt, quite unworthy of him and very poor reward for his paternalistic efforts, which he regarded as having contributed to the Tory recovery. The 1839 offer was grudgingly and reluctantly accepted, but since Peel did not attain office, came to nothing; when it was repeated in 1841, it was refused. 'Thus the decisive step is taken,' Shaftesbury wrote, 'and I have chosen that course which will exclude me, perhaps for ever, from a share in the official

[18] Hodder, volume I, pp. 149–50, tends to exaggerate the extent to which Shaftesbury realized in 1833 that his sponsoring of the ten hour bill marked the 'parting of the ways' in his career.

[19] See R. Blake, *The Conservative Party from Peel to Churchill* (1970), pp. 24–5.

[20] SHA/PD/1, 22 December 1834.

government of this Kingdom.'[21] It may be that unless Peel had been willing to concede ten hours, Shaftesbury would have refused any office, great or small: this is what he claimed in 1841. But he certainly expected Peel to make a promising and attractive offer, even if only to give him the opportunity of turning it down. The fact that such a meagre offer was made showed him that his services were little estimated by the Tory leaders and that his involvement with the Ten Hours Movement and the agitation surrounding it found little favour with Peel. It was a painful and wounding discovery: 'a plain, cruel, unnecessary insult', Shaftesbury wrote of the 1841 offer.[22]

After 1841, Shaftesbury became ever more firmly wedded to his career of paternalistic and evangelical concern. Time and again during the Peel ministry of 1841–6, he urged the need for legislation to improve social conditions and to spread wholesome influences among the people. Thus in 1842, he sought to rouse the conscience of the House to a reform of conditions in mines:[23] in 1843, he warned his fellow members of the crime, delinquency, and disorder induced by lack of proper provision for education and moved an address to the Crown praying Her Majesty 'to take into her instant and serious consideration the best means of diffusing the benefits and blessings of a moral and religious education amongst the working classes of the people';[24] and he continued to press the claims of the Ten Hour Movement for a reduction of hours in factories.[25] He also condemned any practices which he regarded as an

[21] SHA/PD/2, 4 September 1841.
[22] SHA/PD/2, 3 September 1841.
[23] Shaftesbury's speech of June 1842 (Hansard, *Parl. Debates*, 3rd ser., lxiii, 1320–52) was based on the Report, issued in May 1842, of the Commission on Child Employment which he himself had initiated in August 1840. 'It is not possible', Shaftesbury said, 'for any man, whatever be his station, if he have but a heart within his bosom, to read the details of this awful document without a combined feeling of shame, terror and indignation . . .' (*ibid.*, 1321). The major proposals of his Colliery Bill were the total exclusion of women from employment in mines and the exclusion of boys under the age of thirteen. The former proposal stood part of the Act of 1842, but the minimum age for the employment of boys was reduced to ten by a Lords' amendment, which Shaftesbury reluctantly accepted. (*ibid.*, lxv, 1098.)
[24] *Ibid.*, lxvii, 47–75. Shaftesbury had opposed the Whig proposals of 1839 whereby a Committee of the Privy Council was to administer grants made for educational purposes mainly on the grounds that this would weaken the control and influence of the Church of England over education (*ibid.*, xlviii, 268–84). He was prepared to accept the educational clauses of the Factory Bill introduced by Graham, the Tory Home Secretary, in 1843 which gave the Church of England, if not a monopoly in the running of the proposed grant-aided factory schools, at least a large say; but when dissenter opposition caused the abandonment of the clauses, Shaftesbury felt that any such scheme for 'combined education' between dissenters and Anglicans should not be repeated (SHA/PD/3, 16 June 1843).
[25] Shaftesbury acquiesced in the proposals embodied in the Factory Bill introduced by Graham in 1843. These would have reduced the minimum age for work to eight, but would also have limited the working day between the ages of eight and thirteen to six and a half hours. He would, however, have preferred a further limitation in the

affront to public or national morality. Thus in 1843, he presented petitions against the Opium Trade on behalf of various missionary societies and denounced the trade as 'utterly inconsistent with the honour and duties of a Christian Kingdom'.[26] Such activities meant that Shaftesbury increasingly adopted a free-lance role in politics, and although this did not preclude a measure of co-operation with the government on some issues,[27] for the most part Shaftesbury became more and more conscious of his estrangement from the Tory leadership. He felt that the government betrayed a lamentable lack of concern for social and moral improvement and he complained that his efforts over mines and factory reform and the Opium question met with indifference or positive resistance. Although he came finally to take the view that Corn Law repeal was necessary and desirable,[28] he was totally unimpressed by Peel's plans for economic expansion based on a freeing of trade. In some of his criticisms, Shaftesbury was rather petulant and unfair. If social reform was not a hallmark of Peelite Conservatism, the record of the 1841–6 government was not totally barren in this respect; and Peel's economic liberalism was certainly designed in part to ease the 'Condition of England Question' by creating the conditions for greater all-round prosperity. But to Shaftesbury, it was dull, soulless, and materialistic.

hours of labour. (Hansard, *Parl. Debates*, 3rd ser., lxvii, 424.) When this Bill was abandoned and the government introduced a similar measure in 1844, Shaftesbury attempted to introduce amendments which would have secured a ten hour day, but was finally defeated on a threat of resignation by the government. (See M. W. Thomas, *op. cit.*, pp. 201–8.) The 1844 Act reduced the minimum age for work to eight and limited the working day between the ages of eight and thirteen to six and a half hours. Twelve hours a day, or sixty-nine a week, were to remain the hours of work between the ages of thirteen and eighteen, but women were also to be restricted to these hours (*ibid.*, pp. 209–10).

[26] Hansard, *Parl. Debates*, 3rd ser., lxviii, 362 ff.

[27] One of the most notable instances was in June 1845, when, at the government's request, Shaftesbury introduced two bills on lunacy, which were seconded by Graham (*ibid.*, lxxxi, 180 ff). Both passed later in the year. The first provided for the establishment of the Board of Commissioners in Lunacy, a permanent body which replaced the Metropolitan Commissioners (see above footnote 5), with wide powers of inspection over all licensed madhouses; it also introduced more secure safeguards in the certification of the insane. The second provided for an extension of county asylums and increased accommodation in them. (See W. Ll. Parry Jones, *op. cit.*, p. 20 and also K. Jones, *Mental Health and Social Policy, 1885–1959* (1960), pp. 8–10.) As chairman of the Board, Shaftesbury presided over its weekly meetings. He visited institutions in person until about 1850; thereafter, his visits were only on special occasions. (G.F.A. Best, *op. cit.*, p. 49.)

[28] By 1845–6, Shaftesbury no longer thought that Protection was indispensable to the landed interest. He felt that Corn Law repeal would force the aristocracy to improve their estates, or, as he put it 'do their duty by their estates and the people on them'. If they did this, they would 'be richer and more powerful than ever'. (SHA/PD/4, 27 January 1846.) Since he thought that there had been an understanding with his constituents that he would support Protection, he felt it necessary to resign his seat in January 1846.

'Imports and Exports; here is Peel's philosophy!', he wrote, 'there it begins and there it ends!'[29] With this, and, in particular, with Peel's continued hostility to 'ten hours', Shaftesbury could find little common ground, and he gradually and painfully became reconciled to his role as an 'outsider'. His career, he became convinced, lay 'among the questions and labours of *social* interests';[30] nothing would induce him 'to surrender these social and moral questions'.[31]

If Shaftesbury thus became increasingly aware of his political alienation from his own party, he also came to feel a sense of isolation in public life. 'I confess I feel sadly alone,' he wrote in 1842. 'I am like a pelican in the wilderness, or a sparrow on the housetops. . . .'[32] In 1845, he wrote that 'by taking this course of declaring and endeavouring to alleviate the wrongs of working people, I have made many enemies and shaken the confidence of many friends';[33] and he wondered if Wilberforce would have had success in his labours had they been 'engaged in the domestic vineyard, and in the discovery and removal of abuses and shame'.[34] He became finally estranged from his father, who strongly disapproved of his conduct and, in particular, of a speech of 1843 in which he turned his attention to the responsibilities of landed proprietors towards their workers. 'He has said he detests my public life,' Shaftesbury wrote in 1844;[35] and in 1845:

I am now a sufferer in domestic relations and I am excluded from my father's house, in no slight degree because I was known to have maintained the cause of the agricultural labourer. No one but myself can estimate the amount of toil by day and by night, of fears and disappointments, of prayers and tears, of repugnances contended against and overcome.[36]

At certain times, indeed, Shaftesbury was tempted to give up his public life. 'I am growing tired of public life,' he wrote in 1845, 'and specially of this pelican life, in the wilderness, alone to feed others and never myself.'[37] After he resigned his seat in 1846, he had doubts about returning to parliament and thus exposing himself to the misunderstandings and abuses which he had suffered. The Hammonds, indeed, see this period of retirement from parliament as the turning point in his

[29] *Ibid.*, 6 September 1842.
[30] SHA/PD/3, 24 January 1845.
[31] *Ibid.*, 1 February 1845.
[32] SHA/PD/2, 3 February 1842.
[33] SHA/PD/3, 11 January 1845.
[34] SHA/PD/4, 23 December 1845.
[35] SHA/PD/3, 16 December 1844.
[36] *Ibid.*, 11 January 1845. Shaftesbury felt that all he had to show for his efforts was the Colliery Act of 1842 and even this encountered resistance in its implementation.
[37] SHA/PD/4, 27 October 1845.

career; it was then, they argue in their biography, that Shaftesbury became absorbed in philanthropic work, 'turning him from a politician striving to serve his Christian conscience into a monk or missionary who remained in politics with less than half his mind'.[38] But he did not retire; as soon as he had thoughts of doing so, he felt spurred on to persevere. He was, he wrote, 'ashamed' of the idea that he might abandon public life: 'I have perhaps chosen ill for my honour and happiness in this world: but have I so for the happiness of others?'[39] And although he did devote considerable attention while out of parliament to two movements, the Labourers' Friend Society[40] and the Ragged School Union,[41] the Hammonds seem rather premature in their judgment that this was the point of withdrawal from an active political life. Shaftesbury felt that if he did not return to the House of Commons, his 'means of usefulness', as he put it, would be greatly curtailed;[42] and certainly after his return to the House in 1847 he took up various characteristic causes: in 1848, the question of public health,[43] on which, indeed, he became a frequent speaker on his appointment in that year to the General Board of Health;[44] a project, also in 1848, for government funds to pro-

[38] J., L. and B. Hammond, *Lord Shaftesbury* (4th edn., 1936, reprinted 1969), p. 124.

[39] SHA/PD/4, 27 October 1845.

[40] Founded in the early 1830s by the Bishop of Bath and Wells to provide allotments for rural labourers, the Society was taken over in 1844 by a group of which Shaftesbury was a prominent member. It aimed to provide model dwellings for the poor and blocks of model lodging houses were built in London under its auspices. It later changed its name to the Society for Improving the Condition of the Labouring Classes.

[41] Founded in 1844 by a small group of London Sunday School teachers engaged in running 'ragged schools' which were designed to reach children who were destitute or who 'from their poverty or ragged condition (were) prevented from attending any other place of religious instruction'. (Hodder, volume I, p. 481). The primary purpose of the schools was to inculcate evangelical Christianity, but they also offered elementary education and various social and recreational facilities. The Union, of which Shaftesbury became president in November 1844, was intended to give permanence to existing ragged schools and to promote new ones throughout the Metropolis. In 1870, it possessed 192 school buildings, in which it conducted 137 Sunday schools, 186 day schools and 192 evening schools, with average attendances of 31,835, 22,883 and 8,748 respectively. (*Ragged School Union Magazine*, 1871, p. 124.) The Education Act of 1870 resulted in a running down of the schools and some of their buildings were sold to the new board schools (see below, p. 181). Other towns and cities also ran ragged schools, some of these being conducted rather differently from the Ragged School Union's schools. (See D. Owen, *English Philanthropy 1660–1960* (Cambridge, Mass., 1965), pp. 150–51.)

[42] SHA/PD/4, 14 July 1847.

[43] Hansard, *Parl. Debates*, 3rd ser., xcviii, 779–87. Shaftesbury had taken considerable interest in the question of public health for many years. He was involved in the formation of the Health of Towns Association in 1844 and was chairman of the London Association.

[44] One of Shaftesbury's principal duties as a commissioner at the Board of Health was to steer its business through parliament. On such occasions, he was often assisted by briefs from Chadwick, with whom he established a close and harmonious relationship (R. A. Lewis, *Edwin Chadwick and the Public Health Movement* (1952), pp. 183, 185).

vide for the voluntary emigration of ragged school pupils;[45] in 1849, a proposal to subdivide densely populated parishes into more manageable units;[46] in 1850, attempts to safeguard the ten hour day, achieved in 1847 during his absence from parliament, but since evaded;[47] and also in 1850, a motion, backed, he claimed, by petitions with more than 700,000 signatures to stop Sunday labour in the Post Office.[48] As in the past, his efforts met with varied fortunes;[49] and indeed, his acquiescence in a ten and a half hour day in factories earned him severe displeasure and criticism in the Ten Hour Movement.[50] Nevertheless, Shaftesbury's

Shaftesbury also took an active part in the Board's work 'in the field', especially during the Cholera Epidemic of 1848–9 (*ibid.*, pp. 208 ff, and see also S. E. Finer, *The Life and Times of Sir Edwin Chadwick* (1952), pp. 344–53). He remained at the Board until its dissolution in 1854. He had several disputes with Lord Seymour who was appointed president of the Board over his head in 1850; on that occasion, indeed, he tendered his resignation but was persuaded to withdraw it. In common with Chadwick, Shaftesbury was often infuriated by Seymour's lack of interest or, on occasion, obstructiveness as president. (R. A. Lewis, *op. cit.*, pp. 238 ff.)

[45] Hansard, *Parl. Debates*, 3rd ser., xcix, 429 ff.   [46] *Ibid.*, ciii, 11 ff.

[47] The Factory Act of 1847 provided that from May 1848, no person under eighteen and no woman should work for more than ten hours a day or fifty-eight hours a week. (Monday–Friday, ten hours; Saturday, eight hours). The act was, however, evaded by the adoption of a shift or relay system which split up the hours so that those who were restricted to a ten hour working day had to be available for work for a considerably longer period. The Ten Hour Movement revived to condemn the relay system and on his return to parliament, Shaftesbury was under pressure to introduce a measure to ban it and thereby safeguard the ten hour day. He took steps to carry this out in March and April 1850 (*ibid.*, cix, 883 ff., cx, 1058 ff.) but found considerable difficulty in ensuring an effective limitation; and when the government showed itself willing to accept a compromise measure, Shaftesbury thought it desirable to agree to it (*ibid.*, cx, 1431). This established a normal working day between 6 a.m. and 6 p.m. (Monday to Friday) and 6 a.m. and 2 p.m. (Saturday). No relays might be worked, but allowing one and a half hours for meals on weekdays and half an hour on Saturdays, the working weekday was extended to ten and a half hours (but shortened to seven and a half on a Saturday) and the working week was extended to sixty hours. By an omission, children, between the ages of eight and thirteen, whose hours remained regulated by the 1844 Act to six and a half a day (see footnote 25), were not protected by the 1850 Act, and were not brought within its scope until 1853. (See M. W. Thomas, *op. cit.*, pp. 290 ff for a full examination of the position between 1847 and 1853.)

[48] Hansard, *Parl. Debates*, 3rd ser., cxi, 466 ff.

[49] A Government grant was made in 1848 to assist emigration, but when Shaftesbury raised the matter again in 1849 (*ibid.*, cvii, 897 ff), no second grant was made and the emigration scheme had to be financed privately. Over the division of parishes, a commission was appointed to examine Shaftesbury's proposal and under church building acts, the division of large parishes into smaller ones went forward after 1850, but with rather meagre results (K. S. Inglis, *Churches and the Working Classes in Victorian England* (1963), pp. 27 ff). The motion over Sunday labour in the Post Office was carried in a small house against the wishes of the Government and for a period, Sunday deliveries and collections were abandoned. The Government, however, rescinded part of the measure and allowed one delivery and one collection on Sunday (O. Chadwick, *The Victorian Church* (1966), Part I, pp. 459–60).

[50] It had been suspected by some elements of the Ten Hour Movement that Shaftesbury would accept a compromise measure and when he did, they were quick to denounce him as a traitor to the cause. Shaftesbury realized that his acceptance of

last years in the House of Commons were still marked by a considerable range of paternalistic and evangelical endeavour.

A more decisive step in Shaftesbury's career came in 1851, on his father's death. The inheritance of the estate involved heavy demands on his time; and if he had often been discouraged by his experiences in the Commons, promotion to the Lords marked his entry to a sphere where he felt altogether ill at ease. It is true that the settlement of the factory question in 1850 removed a long standing preoccupation; and the improvement in the country's economic and social conditions in the 1850s gave less scope for his great speeches of the '40s. Nevertheless, he entered the Upper House determined, as he wrote, 'to show its activity and power in the institution of social improvements',[51] and he assured their Lordships that the people looked to them for the redress of many of their grievances.[52] But he found the ambience of the Lords quite unhelpful and unsympathetic. The Upper House, he felt, was completely remote from the centre of political life; he might as well 'be removed to the Pampas or Timbuctoo: know nothing, see nothing, hear nothing'.[53] And he could find little response to his schemes: 'a Statue Gallery could not have been so silent,' he commented on one occasion, 'for it would have echoed; not a word in support. . . .'[54] Further, he became increasingly conscious of hostility towards him and all his works. 'Every day,' he wrote in 1854, 'makes me see how many there are who secretly hate me and many more who, tho' they hate not my personal self, hate everything that I proposed.'[55] Again, in 1860 after an unsympathetic hearing, he noted his impression that the peers 'treated me as a Gracchus, or a Tribune, speaking on behalf of the People and loathed me and showed their loathing accordingly'.[56]

From the 1850s there was, therefore, a certain, although by no means complete, withdrawal from an active parliamentary life. Certainly now, honours and office were, he felt, out of the question. In 1852, there were rumours that he might be offered the chancellorship of Oxford University on the death of Wellington. He commented that there would be 'candidates enough'; he would rather retain those places for which there are *no* candidates', like the Chairs of the Ragged Union and the Field Lane Refuge.[57] This, he felt, was his province: 'I am called to this,

ten and a half hours would cause him considerable unpopularity and he was saddened by the abuse which he suffered; but he felt that nothing better could be achieved and that the extra two hours spread through the week 'could take nothing of consequence from the operatives' (SHA/PD/5, 9 May 1850).

[51] SHA/PD/6, 23 August 1853.   [52] Hansard, *Parl. Debates*, 3rd ser., cxxv, 407–8.
[53] SHA/PD/6, 7 July 1851.   [54] SHA/PD/7, 1 May 1860.
[55] SHA/PD/6, 27 May 1854.   [56] SHA/PD/7, 1 May 1860.
[57] One of the original ragged schools in London was at Field Lane in Saffron Hill. Refuges were run by some schools, in certain cases for casual vagrants, in others for the support and education of young persons.

and not to any political or social honours.'[58] Despite such self-depreciation, he was, in fact, offered the Garter in 1853 by Aberdeen, but he refused it, partly on the grounds of the expense involved, but also because he wished to remain, and be seen to remain, 'altogether independent'.[59] It is true that between 1855 and 1865, during the political ascendancy of Palmerston, Shaftesbury felt 'near the fountain-head of all information',[60] and his influence on Church appointments was considerable.[61] Moreover, he accepted the Garter from Palmerston in 1861. But when office was broached in 1855, he expressed severe misgivings; its acceptance, he told Palmerston, would involve 'so large a surrender of many important occupations . . . that I should make up my mind with great reluctance to enter on a new career'.[62] Further, the influence which he had on Palmerston owed much to the family relationship between the two men, a fact which also goes some way to explain his acceptance of the Garter.[63] The last offer of office made to Shaftesbury was in 1866 by Derby; again it was refused and again mainly on the grounds that he would have to withdraw from many pursuits which, he felt, seemed to increase rather than diminish as he grew older.[64]

Such activities cost Shaftesbury an immense amount of work and effort. 'Letters and Chairs,' he wrote in 1852, 'eat me up; I never refresh my mind with new stores, always speaking, never reading or thinking.'[65] And in 1857: 'time, as usual, chopped "as small as herbs for the pot" and not a moment of leisure.'[66] And there was, indeed, little slackening of the pace with the passing of the years. In a week's visit to Glasgow in 1871, Shaftesbury carried out a strenuous programme of engagements. It included an address to factory workers on Glasgow Green, visits to churches and missions in the poorer parts of the city,[67] an address to a public meeting held under the auspices of the Glasgow Working Men's Sabbath Protection Association,[68] attendance at a meeting organized by the Glasgow Young Men's Christian Association[69]

[58] SHA/PD/6, 24 September 1852.　　[59] Hodder, volume II, p. 476.
[60] SHA/PD/8, 30 October 1865.　　[61] Hodder, volume III, p. 191 ff.
[62] *Ibid.*, volume II, p. 492.
[63] SHA/PD/7, 19 May 1862. Palmerston also smoothed the way by ensuring that Shaftesbury did not pay the fees.
[64] Hodder, volume III, p. 211.　　[65] SHA/PD/5, 8 July 1848.
[66] SHA/PD/7, 16 June 1857.
[67] Shaftesbury had a very long association with such societies as the London City Mission, founded in 1835, and the Church Pastoral Aid Society, founded in 1836, which had a special concern for evangelical work in such areas of towns and cities.
[68] Shaftesbury was president of the Working Men's Lord's Day Rest Association from 1870 until his death in 1885. I am grateful for this information to Mr H. J. W. Legerton, General Secretary of the Lord's Day Observance Society, an organization in which Shaftesbury also took a keen interest as chairman of its metropolitan committee.
[69] Founded in 1841, although a similar organization, the Young Men's Society for Religious Improvement had been in existence in Glasgow since 1824. These were local

and other religious organizations for youth, a conference on such varied topics as Bible and Tract Circulation,[70] Dwellings and Lodging Houses for the Working Classes, Night Asylums for the Homeless and Industrial Schools.[71] The week ended with a visit to the Clyde Industrial Training Ship, *Cumberland*, on the Gareloch.[72] It was, he said, several days of 'intense work and speechifying'[73] and in the extent to which the programme reflected his long-standing interests and activities, it was almost a microcosm of his life and work. A fuller impression of this may be derived from the number of societies which sent deputations to Shaftesbury's Memorial Service in Westminster Abbey in 1885; these run to almost four pages of double columns in Edwin Hodder's biography.[74]

In all Shaftesbury's comments about his isolation and exclusion from official public life, there was certainly an element of rather over-dramatized self-martyrdom. A man of often sombre mood, he tended to be unduly self-pitying and sensitive to criticism: and equally, he yearned for praise and appreciation. He was, moreover, apt to overlook the fact that his activities brought him immense fame and no little

associations, as was the London YMCA which was founded in 1844 and of which Shaftesbury was President from 1851–85. In 1851, the members of the London YMCA took advantage of the Great Exhibition to make their work known to young men visiting the Exhibition from abroad and this resulted in the formation of YMCAs in various parts of the world. In 1855, the first World Conference of YMCAs was held. In 1882, a national organization of YMCAs in England, Ireland and Wales was formed; Scotland had, and still has, its own National Council. (I am grateful for this information to Mr G. Ronald Howe of the National Council of YMCAs.) The Glasgow Association was instituted for the purpose of promoting the intellectual, moral and religious improvement of young men, a purpose which had much in common with that of other Associations.

[70] Shaftesbury became president of the British and Foreign Bible Society in 1851 and retained this office until his death. The Society was founded in 1804: its object was the 'circulation of the Holy Scriptures without note or comment' throughout the world. With the aid of various auxiliary bodies which contributed to its funds, the Society became a very wealthy and extensive organization. By 1825, with its auxiliaries, it had spent over £1,000,000 and distributed 4,500,000 Bibles in a variety of languages. (D. Owen, *op. cit.*, p. 128.)

[71] Many of the ragged schools ran industrial classes to train their pupils in the elements of certain trades.

[72] Shaftesbury was closely associated with a plan to set up a training ship for homeless boys in London and this was done in 1866 when the Government made the *Chichester* available for such purposes. Later, the *Aretheusa* was also granted.

[73] SHA/PD/9, 1 September 1871.

[74] The societies might, indeed, be divided into the two heads of 'paternalistic' and 'evangelical'. Thus under the first, there were deputations from Industrial Schools, National Refuges and Training Ships and the Factory Workers of Bradford (time tended to efface memories of the 'betrayal' of 1851); under the second, deputations from numerous societies concerned with home and foreign missions, the YMCA, and the Lord's Day Observance Society. In many cases, however, such as the great number of deputations from ragged schools, paternalism and evangelicalism were both combined.

respect. Aberdeen's offer of the Garter in 1854 was to mark his admiration of Shaftesbury's 'unwearied exertions in the cause of humanity and social improvement';[75] and while in Glasgow in 1871, Shaftesbury was given the freedom of the city on the grounds of his 'long continued and valuable services in the promotion of all measures having as their object the amelioration of the great body of the people and their intellectual and religious progress'.[76] Again, not all of Shaftesbury's work was unofficial; he did, after all, spend a lifetime in the administration of the lunacy laws and six extremely active years at the General Board of Health. Further, in his social life, he was by no means without aristocratic friends and he made a regular practice of visiting their country houses. Shaftesbury's estimation of how men regarded him is not, therefore, always the most complete or reliable of evidence; and he was neither a total outsider nor outcast. His commitment to paternalism, moreover, was designed essentially to 'afford protection', as he put it, 'to those helpless individuals who could not protect themselves';[77] it stopped well short of any interference with the contract between master and man over such matters as wages. Here again, his position was not wholly eccentric.

Nevertheless, even allowing all such considerations, there was some substance to his feeling of alienation. If men were often prepared to admire him for his efforts, this was by no means always the case; he certainly had to suffer indifference, criticism and abuse. And there were few tangible rewards. The last occasion on which he held office was in 1835 and official recognitions of his efforts were rather sparse and rather late; he was not given the freedom of London, the scene of so many of his labours, until the year before his death. His administrative work was extremely important, but it received little publicity, few thanks and no salary. And if his efforts at social improvement did not grossly offend the canons of conventional economic wisdom, they certainly went further than many contemporaries thought desirable. It is, therefore, understandable that he could, on occasion, feel that all who had any regard for him were 'in the poorer or inferior walks of life',[78] and that for favour and acceptance, he had to go to the back slums of Shoreditch or Westminster.[79] That the common people received him gladly was, indeed, a great consolation to him and, he felt, his source of strength. He said that he would rather be president of the Ragged School Union than of the Royal Academy,[80] and that his 'power to do good and to

[75] Hodder, volume II, p. 474.
[76] *Speeches of the Earl of Shaftesbury in Glasgow* (Glasgow, 1871), p. 6.
[77] Hansard, *Parl. Debates*, 3rd ser., xv, 392.
[78] SHA/PD/4, 30 October 1845.   [79] SHA/PD/6, 7 August 1852.
[80] Quoted by J. Wesley Bready, *Lord Shaftesbury and Social-Industrial Progress* (1926), p. 74.

force the Government to do good, depends on the belief that people
entertain of my possessing the love and confidence of the masses'.[81] It
was appropriate that at his death, Westminster Abbey should have been
thronged with representatives of his societies and that of his eight pall
bearers, not one was a titled man or a great public figure.[82] Shaftesbury
had felt more at home at the annual May meetings of his societies than
in the House of Lords; he had found the people more receptive and
respectful than the politicians, the masses than the classes.

It would, however, be entirely false to conclude from this that
Shaftesbury was hostile to an hierarchical structure of society; the truth
is, in fact, quite the reverse. He had an acute sense of rank: 'distinction
of order,' he wrote, 'is of God's own appointment'.[83] His paternalism
and evangelicalism combined, however, to ensure that it was always the
responsibilities of rank which he emphasized. Thus in 1844, he wrote:
'We must have . . . a just estimate of rank and property, not as matters
of personal enjoyment and display, but as gifts of God, bringing with
them serious responsibilities and involving a fearful account.'[84] And
although he was primarily concerned with the benefit and blessing
which the discharge of these responsibilities would confer on the individual body and soul, Shaftesbury did not lose sight of the advantages
which would thus accrue to the existing political and social order. In his
various schemes, Shaftesbury followed out Southey's remark of 1832[85]
that the rich must, in their own interests, look to the state of the poor.
Thus he saw the factory question as, in part, political, for 'it would
decide whether tens of thousands should be left in discontent, aye, and
just discontent.'[86] Further if the essential purpose of the ragged schools
was to preach the gospel in dark places, the work which those schools
carried out was bound to have immense benefit in a more secular sense.
Poor children would be submitted to moral discipline;[87] they would be
prevented from growing up as paupers or thieves and from thus becoming a burden on the country's resources or a threat to its property.
Again, the attempt to stop Sunday posts sprang mainly from the
'religious obligation of the day'; but it would also show that the upper

[81] SHA/PD/8, 12 October 1867.
[82] All were officials of Societies with which Shaftesbury had been associated: the
British and Foreign Bible Society and the Shoeblacks' Brigades (an offshoot of the
ragged schools, organized in 1851 to clean the shoes of the crowds at the Great
Exhibition); the Religious Tract Society and King Edward Industrial Schools; the
YMCA; the Costermongers' Mission (with which Shaftesbury became associated in
1868); the Ragged School Union; the National Refuge and Training Ships; the
George Yard Ragged School; the London City Mission. (Hodder, volume III, p. 525).
Again, paternalism and evangelicalism were amply represented.
[83] SHA/PD/2, 20 May 1841.   [84] SHA/PD/3, 21 November 1844.
[85] See above, p. 161.   [86] Quoted by Hodder, volume I, p. 154.
[87] *Ragged School Union Magazine* (1852), p. 103.

and leisured classes cared about the welfare of those who were less fortunate: 'If relaxation was necessary for those who lived in great measure of ease,' Shaftesbury told the House, 'how requisite it must be for those sons of toil who laboured from morning to night.'[88] Further, the subdivision of parishes would, he felt, be a 'glorious winding-up' of his schemes for social improvement.[89] It would enable the clergy to get to know the needs of their people: it would enhance the prestige and authority of the Church and allow it to 'conservatise' the Kingdom.[90] And if only all this redeeming and reconciling work were attempted, rewards would surely follow. Shaftesbury was convinced that there was a 'strong tendency to respect rank',[91] and he saw the people as loyal and deferential if shown sympathy and consideration. When on a factory tour in 1841, he wrote:

What a sin it is to be *ignorant* of the sterling value and merit of these poor men! A few words of kindness are as effectual with them as a force of fifty thousand soldiers on a French population. Never have I met with such respect and affection as on this journey. I see and feel the truth of Oastler's observation, 'they are neither infidels nor Jacobins; they love Monarchy and they love religion.'[92]

The trouble was, however, that in the state of society as Shaftesbury saw it, the temptations to become infidels and Jacobins were in full force: the encouragement to love Monarchy and religion were non-existent. Thus in all his approaches to the people, Shaftesbury was at pains to set this right. His speeches at great meetings were never designed to stir the people up against their natural rulers; rather they were in the nature of homilies and sermons. In 1846, on the eve of the achievement of the ten hour day, he exhorted a factory meeting at Oldham 'solemnly to use aright the blessing . . . God would give them; and turn it to his honour in the moral improvement of themselves and their children'.[93] Later in the same year, he wrote of his methods:

Surely it is a novel form of agitation to abstain from excitement and appeal: to adopt rebuke, exhortation and counsel to the people whom you address! But such thank God, is the plan I have pursued; and it will prosper I trow. My desire has been to raise the moral character and feelings of the working classes; and this end can be effected only

[88] Hansard, *Parl. Debates*, 3rd ser., cxi, 472–3.
[89] SHA/PD/5, 22 February 1849.　　　　　[90] *Ibid.*, 1 March 1849.
[91] SHA/PD/2, 20 May 1841.
[92] *Ibid.*, 6 August 1841. For a consideration of Oastler's views, which had much in common with Shaftesbury's in these respects, see C. Driver, *op. cit.*, pp. 424 ff.
[93] SHA/PD/4, 6 March 1846.

by instructing them of their real dignity as immortal beings and treating them as such.[94]

Further, despite his disapproval of avaricious mill owners, Shaftesbury did not seek to engender class hostilities. When the Ten Hour Day was achieved in 1847, he wrote to the short time committees warning against any 'language of triumph, as though we had defeated an enemy'.

Let us be very thankful [he continued] that the struggle is over, and that we can once more combine, not merely the interests, but also the feelings, of employer and employed, in a mutual understanding for the comfort and benefit of each other, and for the welfare of the whole community.[95]

Shaftesbury's harshest comments were reserved for movements and individuals who proposed to divide the community into warring classes, to agitate for the advancement of any one class and to undermine respect for authority and religion. The Anti-Corn Law League earned his severe displeasure: 'the language of the League,' he wrote, 'is become the tongue of extreme Democracy and modified Infidelity; it is not possible that scurrility against individuals or classes can have any deeper venom or fuller swing.'[96] Cobden was always a target for criticism: on his death, Shaftesbury wrote that 'his policy in respect of English institutions was ultra-democratic, ultra-jacobinical, and, I suspect, ultra-infidel'.[97] And although he had sympathy for the sufferings on which Chartism fed, he had none for the Chartist remedy. His prescription for improvement was for parliament to 'assume the proper function of law, protect those for whom neither wealth, nor station, nor age have raised a bulwark against tyranny'.[98] And if paternalism was one remedy,[99] evangelicalism was the other. Churches must be built and ministers of religion sent forth to 'sow wheat among the tares'. This would 'give content instead of bitterness, engraft obedience on rebellion, raise purity from corruption, and life from the dead'.[100] Far then, from having any

[94] SHA/PD/4, 17 March 1846.
[95] Quoted by Hodder, volume II, pp. 195–6.
[96] SHA/PD/4, 18 December 1845.
[97] SHA/PD/7, 4 April 1865.
[98] Hodder, volume I, p. 323.
[99] In 1848, Shaftesbury expended an immense amount of energy in arranging for Prince Albert to address the Labourers Friend Society and was much gratified by the result: 'Aye, truly,' he wrote, 'this is the way to stifle Chartism . . . rank, leisure, station are gifts of God, for which men must give an account. Here is a full proof, a glowing instance, the aristocracy, after a long separation, are re-approaching the people; and the people the aristocracy. Oh Cobden, Bright and all that dismal crew, you will be crushed in the friendly collision.' (SHA/PD/5, 20 May 1848.)
[100] Hodder, volume I, pp. 323–4.

sympathy for radical movements which sought to advance class interests, Shaftesbury hoped by his efforts to outflank them.

Despite his sense of estrangement from the classes, Shaftesbury thus never saw himself as a tribune of the people nor as a 'Jacobin'.[101] He once said that he did not consider himself as the champion of the factory operatives but as their friend.[102] It is, of course, true that he appealed frequently to the Legislature on behalf of the rights of the people; but it was with their rights as 'immortal beings' that he was concerned, not with their rights, political, social or economic as members of any class. His plea was that the Legislature should make it possible for the working classes 'to walk erect in newness of life, to enter on the enjoyment of their inherited freedom and avail themselves (if they will accept them) of the opportunities of virtue, of morality and religion'.[103] If he indulged in agitation, it was directed at the aristocracy to make them realize and act upon their obligations and responsibilities. In 1867, he wrote that his 'whole life (had) been spent in endeavouring to build up the moral, social, political, and religious estimation of the Aristocracy',[104] and that he hoped by his career to do 'some little good to his "class" and keep it steady in general estimation'.[105] If he spoke harshly of his 'class', it was not because of any hostility to it as such; rather it was because it was neglecting its duty and was even blind to the best prospects for its own survival. These feelings certainly entered into his quarrels with the Tory party. 'All Peel's affinities', he wrote, 'are towards wealth and capital . . . (to him) cotton is everything, man nothing!'[106] Peel was casting away his 'patrimony . . . the especial protection of the working classes'[107] and he was thus driving them into the arms of the Chartists; Peel's refusals, he wrote, 'create an appetite for O'Connor's offers'.[108] And more generally, Shaftesbury felt a constant sense of regret and disappointment that so few members of his own class were prepared to follow that 'example to his order' of which his monument in Piccadilly Circus so aptly speaks. The ragged schools were 'too low for the rich and dignified: I get little sympathy and less money'.[109] And in 1850, he lamented:

> I began in the hope that many of the aristocracy would first follow and then succeed me. Not one is to be found; a few at my request, put their hands to the plough, but they looked back and return not to the furrows.[110]

[101] Melbourne, perhaps not altogether seriously, once referred to Shaftesbury as 'the greatest Jacobin in (Her) Majesty's Dominions'. (Hodder, volume I, pp. 420–21.)

[102] Hansard, *Parl. Debates*, 3rd ser., cxi, 832–3. [103] *Ibid.*, lxiii, 1352.

[104] SHA/PD/8, 1 October 1867. [105] *Ibid.*, 23 October 1867.

[106] SHA/PD/2, 24 February 1842. [107] SHA/PD/3, 23 March 1844.

[108] SHA/PD/2, 18 August 1842. [109] SHA/PD/5, 21 March 1848.

[110] SHA/PD/6, 26 December 1850.

There were occasions, however, when Shaftesbury felt that his efforts with the masses had not been in vain. He approved of the conduct of the factory workers. In 1845, he wrote:

No violence of language or action, no threats, no expressions of vengeance, no bitter accusations, no unhealable wounds. This was . . . a bright example to the whole world of the mode in which a people should demand, and will obtain, their inalienable rights.[111]

Further, he felt that his efforts to secure Ten Hours and its achievement in 1847 stood the country in good stead the following year. He thanked God that in 1848 the operatives of Lancashire and Yorkshire 'suffering as they are, remain perfectly tranquil' and he attributed this to 'sympathy and generous legislation'.[112] And if, in his view, factory reform helped to save the day in 1848, so too did ragged schools. In 1849, he told the Annual Meeting of the Ragged School Union that he did not scruple to say that

. . . the existence of these institutions, aided by frequent visitations— by the constant expressions of sympathy—by the increased intercourse of the poorer with the wealthier classes—mainly contributed in the past year to keep the metropolis in peace, while the whole world . . . was in the throes of convulsion.[113]

Paternalism might and should have been more widely practised; but it had played its part. And so too had evangelicalism. In 1849, Shaftesbury told the House of Commons that during a recent visit to Paris he had found it universally agreed that the religious habits of the people had enabled England to stand erect during the disturbances of 1848. 'Nothing was more true,' Shaftesbury commented, 'than that religion . . . saved this country.'[114]

During the last twenty years of his life, however, Shaftesbury became more and more convinced that the causes to which he had devoted his attention were being steadily undermined. He saw the beginning of the end as he contemplated the passing of the Second Reform Act of 1867. He did, it is true, acknowledge the presence of an 'expansive force among the people', encouraged by social improvements which made them dissatisfied with their institutions,[115] and he was prepared to admit that a measure of parliamentary reform was inevitable. But the 1867 Act went far beyond what he thought was desirable in allowing the people

111 SHA/PD/4, 17 October 1845.
112 SHA/PD/5, 21 March 1848.
113 *Ragged School Union Magazine* (1849), p. 109.
114 Hansard, *Parl. Debates*, 3rd ser., cx, 468.
115 *Ibid.*, clxxxviii, 1926.

political power; it would 'lift . . . the whole residuum of society to the level of the honest, thrifty, working man', and would throw 'the franchise broadcast over the heads of men who will accept it, but who will misuse it.'[116] And it would mean the end of his paternalistic schemes. Thus he wrote that he had

> . . . long entertained a fond belief that, while making the welfare, physical, temporal and spiritual, of the working classes my primary object, a secondary one might be obtained in the contentment of the people; the repression of Democracy, and the maintenance of our ancient Institutions. It is now manifest that my aspirations will be fruitless. Democracy will be established by the present Conservative Government . . . thus I am dispirited. I have now partially (non nobis Domine) gained the first; I have totally failed of the second and I see nothing before me but Darkness, gloominess and speedy extinction.[117]

With the passing of the years, the gloom only thickened. Since the masses now had political power, they had no need of his paternalistic efforts. Thus in 1880, he wrote: 'The great mass of the people are no longer in need of Friends and Champions: they can and they do, defend themselves.'[118] And if their increased political power put them in the position of patrons rather than clients, there were many in the field ready to win their patronage: all those 'New Men', as he put it, whom the people liked better than the old:

> . . . the old men [he wrote] only undertook to lead them to the profession and enjoyment, of their physical, social and moral rights; the New Men promise them far more; they promise them to aid them to a stronger hold on the Capitalists; a more equitable distribution of electoral power; a larger share in the government of the country. Such Counsellors, Advisers, Friends, Representatives, must, of course, have the preference. . . .[119]

The people were thus beyond the reach of paternalism; and they were, Shaftesbury felt, also increasingly beyond the scope of evangelical religion and its concern for the individual person. As State intervention increased, an impersonal secularism was winning the day. Thus Shaftesbury bemoaned and resented the fact that his role as an authority on many social questions was being taken over by others, who had a different outlook:

[116] *Ibid.*, 1919.
[118] SHA/PD/11, 16 October 1880.
[117] SHA/PD/8, 2 March 1867.
[119] *Ibid.*

My course [he wrote] has ever been tainted, in the estimation of not a few, by the intermixture of Religion. It was endured so long as there was no other. But now the Secularists have entered the field of Philanthropy (the dreadful word) and their favour is great with the Public and the Press.[120]

This was particularly true in the field of education, where, indeed, Shaftesbury did his utmost to defeat the Secularists over the terms of the Education Act of 1870.[121] He stressed the particular need for religious teaching when such a wide extension of the franchise had so recently been carried through:

Is this a time [he asked] to take from the mass of the population, in whom all power will henceforward reside, that principle of internal self-control . . . which alone can constitute the honour and stability of democracy? Is this a time to take from the mass of the people the checks and restraints of religion?[122]

He realized that a national system of education was inevitable; but he also felt that it must

. . . eliminate all religion, and freeze up the flow of genuine, simple, evangelical, life. The moment these children become the object of state care, they will cease to be objects of private compassion . . . when ten thousand are taught to read, not one hundred will be taught to know that there is a God! The heart of England will become a great Iceberg.[123]

Shaftesbury took some comfort from the fact that religious teaching was not to be barred from the new system, even if it was not to be distinctive of any particular denomination;[124] but he took the view that such teaching would be 'hardly worthwhile to mention . . . as conducing in any way to a Christian life'.[125] He urged the Ragged School Union that if its schools subsisted under the new system, it 'must give them more and more of a religious character . . . [and] endeavour to catch the children

[120] SHA/PD/10, 6 January 1872.
[121] Shaftesbury was very active in the demonstrations of the National Education Union, founded in November 1869, to maintain the denominational system in the face of the efforts of the National Education League, which campaigned for unsectarian education.
[122] Hodder, volume III, p. 265.   [123] SHA/PD/9, 17 March 1869.
[124] This was in accordance with the amendment proposed by W. F. Cowper-Temple and known as the 'Cowper-Temple clause'. (J. Murphy, *The Education Act, 1870, Text and Commentary* (1972), pp. 61–2.)
[125] *Ragged School Union Magazine* (1871), p. 129.

when they come out of the secular furnaces and bring them under the influence of the Gospel'.[126] But, in fact, as Shaftesbury had foreseen, ever fewer ragged schools did survive as the newly created board schools made them increasingly redundant. Shaftesbury realized that this would abridge his labours; but, as he put it, it also broke his heart.[127] And if the people were no longer to be exposed to the saving truths of the Gospel, they would be subjected to sinister and pernicious influences such as those perpetuated by the press, the object of which was to 'make life trivial, easy, full of mirth and levity, eager on the present, reckless of the future. . . .'[128] In 1868, Shaftesbury reflected on the saying which he had heard twenty years earlier that religion had saved England; 'the sentiment,' he wrote, 'is now effete; it will save us no more'.[129] And all that happened thereafter confirmed him in this view. Having never really had the classes with him, he was fast losing the masses. Despite all discouragement he did, it is true, soldier on to the end, striving to 'elevate the Residuum . . . by the forcing pump of the Gospel'.[130] And there were occasions when he felt heartened, as on his visit to Glasgow in 1871, with the evidence which it presented of missionary enterprise, Christian work among the young and Sunday observance. But he saw the tasks of such bulwarks against secularism as increasingly difficult in an alien and hostile world; and he saw himself as ever more isolated, like 'an ancient, weather-beaten rock with the sea receding from it'.[131] The tinge of sadness and melancholy always present in Shaftesbury's life came into full prominence at the end.

Shaftesbury's career was one of many paradoxes. Some were, perhaps, inherent in his paternalism and evangelicalism. He worked for the physical and spiritual advancement and fulfilment of the people; yet at the same time to restrain their political aspirations. Again, his efforts at social improvement clearly implied the involvement of the State for their effective implementation; yet the intervention of the State could not fully promote that religious and moral development of the individual which was so essential to Shaftesbury's approach. There were, too, paradoxes more personal to himself. As one who seemed destined for a successful political career, he held office for a total of less than three years, the last occasion being fifty years before his death. His pursuits took him outside the political and social world of his inheritance and birth; yet he never lost the instincts of that world and those pursuits were, in his view, best calculated to promote its survival. And there were anomalies of temperament: his commitment to a life of service and sacrifice and yet a very considerable measure of ambition and thirst for

[126] *Ibid.*, p. 130.
[127] SHA/PD/10, 9 January 1872.
[128] SHA/PD/9, 27 August 1869.
[129] SHA/PD/8, 16 February 1868.
[130] *Ibid.*, 19 November 1868.
[131] *Ibid.*, 18 January 1867.

recognition; a rather morbid introspection and self-questioning and yet an almost total absorption in public life. But what was certain and consistent throughout more than fifty years was his resolute refusal to be wearied in well doing; and despite all limitations of outlook and personality, this led to a career of public service unique in the nineteenth century in its length and in the variety of its endeavour. It must surely count to Shaftesbury for righteousness that a life which could have been shaped by all his advantages of birth and social standing was instead based on his belief that from those to whom much is given, much will be required. His was a trust well kept.

Further Reading

The standard biography of Shaftesbury remains Edwin Hodder, *The Life and Work of the Seventh Earl of Shaftesbury, K.G.* (3 volumes, 1886–7). Although essentially a work of pious respect, it is thorough and comprehensive in content and its quotations from Shaftesbury's Diary, despite certain minor errors in dating, are full and accurate. J. L. and B. Hammond, *Lord Shaftesbury* (first edn., 1923) is based largely on Hodder's three volumes, but it is more penetrating in its judgments. It tends, however, to be more a history of the times than of the man and, in particular, a social history. J. Wesley Bready, *Lord Shaftesbury and Social–Industrial Progress* (1926) is to some degree a response to what the author regarded as the unfair and unsympathetic interpretation of the Hammonds, although the Hammonds in their fourth edition (1936, reprinted 1969) deny that their approach was lacking in admiration for Shaftesbury. J. Wesley Bready's study has much interesting material, but it is over-defensive and protective. G. F. A. Best, *Shaftesbury* (1964) is an examination of the main themes of Shaftesbury's life rather than a formal biography, but it includes material not used by earlier writers. Written with considerable zest and vigour, it is fresh and stimulating in its approach, and although not uncritical of Shaftesbury, is prepared to give credit where credit is due.

8

Edward Baines

Derek Fraser

Edward Baines Junior (1800–1890) was the second son of Edward Baines (1774–1848), the proprietor of the *Leeds Mercury* which was the leading provincial reform newspaper of the early nineteenth century and which by 1833 had the largest circulation of any journal outside London. Unlike his elder brother, Matthew Talbot Baines who used a successful legal career to launch into politics,[1] the young Edward followed his father into journalism. At the age of fifteen he joined the *Mercury*, in his early twenties he was joint editor and when his father became MP for Leeds in 1834 he assumed full control, running the paper until his own parliamentary duties in the 1860s forced him to share responsibility with his younger brother Frederick. It was through the *Leeds Mercury* that the Baines family first built up a local influence and eventually achieved national notice.[2] The power base of Baines Junior's long career was thus a journalistic rather than an industrial empire.

Baines junior occupied a key role in the politics of Leeds in the 1830s, acting as secretary of the well known organization the Leeds Association[3] and, as befitted a devout independent, leading the non-conformist campaign against Church rates. It was his extreme dissenting viewpoint which earned Baines a national reputation when in 1843 he accumulated a mountain of statistics to oppose Graham's factory education proposals. From 1847 he was sharing with Edward Miall the leadership

[1] M. T. Baines (1799–1860) attended Trinity College, Cambridge, and was called to the Bar in 1825, becoming a QC in 1841. He was recorder of Hull from 1837 to 1847 and then sat as MP for Hull from 1847 to 1852 and for Leeds from 1852 to 1859. He was President of the Poor Law Board from 1849 to 1855 (except for the short lived Conservative ministry in 1852) and sat in Palmerston's cabinet as Chancellor of the Duchy of Lancaster from 1855 to 1858.

[2] The exposure in the *Leeds Mercury* of the notorious Oliver the Spy in 1817 was the Baines family's greatest journalistic scoop and led to the quotation of the *Mercury* in Parliament.

[3] The Leeds Association was launched by Baines senior in 1830 to organize Leeds liberal politics and it operated mainly behind the scenes to galvanize activity. Baines junior was prominent in the Reform Registration Society which succeeded the Association in 1835.

of the dissenting movement and was widely acknowledged as the great oracle of voluntaryism.

Matthew Talbot Baines did not share these extreme views and indeed he became an Anglican but Baines was still proud to see his brother as MP for his native town of Leeds between 1852 and 1859. Baines himself succeeded his brother and continued to sit for the town until 1874, so that for twenty-nine out of the forty years from 1834 Leeds was represented in parliament by a Baines. It was a remarkable political dynasty based upon the influence of the press. As an MP Edward Baines Junior echoed his father's prominent support of dissenting causes and in addition pressed strongly for moderate parliamentary reform, introducing his own proposals in 1861 and 1864. In the event it was this moderation which lost him his seat in 1874.[4] His political career was finally crowned with a knighthood in 1880.

Baines as editor of the *Leeds Mercury* was well placed to act as spokesman for the readership which sustained his paper. The *Mercury* spoke the language, espoused the cause and extolled the virtues of the middle class, 'the pride and stay of England and the bulwark of its liberties'.[5] Baines had unquestioning confidence in middle class values and attitudes for he believed 'never in any country beneath the sun was an order of men more estimable and valuable, more praised and praiseworthy than the middle class of society in England'.[6] Hence he regarded the economic achievement of the English middle class as justification for their claim to political leadership since they were 'the most virtuous the most attached to well regulated liberty, the most interested in freedom of trade and therefore the best depositaries of political power'.[7] His well known biography of his father, *The Life of Edward Baines* (1851), is not simply a filial tribute but a guide book to middle class morality, an example to the young of a virtuous life. Baines senior, like the tramping artisan, had walked from Preston to Leeds in search of work with, as Oastler put it, 'all his sins and all his "wardrobe" on him'.[8] Yet within forty years he was in parliament and within sixty his eldest son was sitting in the Cabinet. Here was social amelioration and individual self help personified in the career of one provincial middle class Englishmen.

For all his support of the middle class claim to political advancement

[4] See J. Vincent, *The Formation of the Liberal Party* (1966), pp. 124–6, for Baines's explanation of his defeat.

[5] *Leeds Mercury*, 12 December 1840.

[6] Quoted by D. Read, *Press and People* (1961), p. 119.

[7] *Leeds Mercury*, 24 September 1842.

[8] R. Oastler, *Letter to a Runaway M.P.* (Leeds, 1836), p. 3. This event in Baines's life became something of significance in local affairs, taken as evidence of his unfitness to lead by his opponents and of his industry and self-reliance by his supporters.

the younger Baines was no radical. He had none of that anti-aristocratic sentiment which characterized Cobden and Bright. Indeed Cobden wrote of him that unlike others 'who have democratic principles at heart *Baines is aristocratic*' and that 'apart from his polemics . . . he is not liberal'.[9] A valuable insight into Baines's political morality is unconsciously given when, paraphrasing his father's attitude to the 1832 Reform Act, he explains his own views on political change. 1832 had been

> one of those peaceful constitutional victories which are the glory of England,—victories, the fruit of extending knowledge,—in which even the defeated party is not without the merit of concession,—which speak a national sense of justice,—which do not outrage our older laws and institutions,—and which contrast so happily with revolutions of violence and blood, where everything ancient is overthrown, and nothing remains venerable or sacred in the eyes of the people.[10]

The Bainesite ideals were always those of the archetypal middle class Whig—constitutional progress matching the steady march of social improvement, periodic adjustment *within* England's traditional political system and moderate reform of government rather than its overthrow. His celebrated cry of 'Three Groans for the Queen' in the midst of the Reform Bill crisis was an indiscreet aberration of youth.

The essential constitutionalism and caution which were so characteristic of Baines were nevertheless moulded in a fifty year political career of extra-parliamentary agitation. Three things drew him inexorably into pressure group politics in the mid-nineteenth century. First, family background, career, and personality made him a natural propagandist. Edward Baines senior had been one of the key figures in the transformation of the provincial press from the eighteenth century news sheet into the nineteenth century propagandist journal.[11] Baines, father and son, made the *Leeds Mercury* a real organ of opinion which deliberately sought to lead and convert. The paper grew from about 20,000 words per issue to some 120,000 in four decades and over the same period its circulation grew over twelve fold from 700 to 800 in 1801 to between 9000 and 10,000 in the 1840s. With a readership mainly in the West Riding but also much further afield the *Mercury* was a prominent opinion forming agent and the younger Baines had the necessary industry and logic to fill its crowded pages with closely argued editorials. Using the family belief in the motto 'knowledge is strength' Baines used his pen to

[9] Cobden to Bright, 26 December 1848, B.M. Add. MSS. 43649, f. 123; *idem.*, 22 December 1848, *loc. cit.*, f. 107.
[10] E. Baines, *The Life of Edward Baines* (1851), p. 161.
[11] D. Read, *op. cit.* 74–9.

disseminate political knowledge as widely as possible. Through his father he inherited influence: the 'Bainesocracy' based that influence upon the power of argument.

Second, Baines was closely involved with the achievement of the aspirations of that public opinion which the *Mercury* sought both to lead and to reflect. The content of, and priority within the political reform programme varied, but there always existed a stock of objectives to which Baines' journalistic talents were committed—parliamentary and municipal reform, retrenchment, the abolition of slavery, the removal of Church rates and the disestablishment of the Church of England, university reform, free trade, and commercial reform. These and other issues of the moment were seen by Baines as intellectually justifiable truths requiring practical expression and it was in order to see these materialize in the real world that Baines was so often involved in political agitation.

The third thing which drew Baines into such fields was his faith in organization. One of the distinctive marks of urban society was in his view that citizens were 'accustomed to associate and organize themselves for a great variety of public objects'.[12] The closely knit paternal structure of rural society made such organizations unnecessary because of 'that natural connection together which exists among the tenants at will of a large landowner, by means of the steward, by means of the landowner himself'.[13] Organization for common political objectives was the means by which urban society could itself cohere and discover its own identity. The organized political movement thus became the means of establishing the values of the new society and supplanting those of the old.[14] It was organization by which 'the influence of the press and of public opinion will be substituted for the traditional influences of landlordism or of feudalism'.[15]

Inherited polemical skills, a programme of political aspirations and an appreciation of the values of organization thus made a popular politician of a natural Whig. In many ways the agitational career so launched was like a giant political sandwich with free trade and suffrage reform as the outer slices of bread and Dissenting Voluntaryism as the real meat. It was the exaggeration of this one strand in the new middle class interest which became the distinctive badge of Edward Baines.

It was very natural that one so wedded to the interests of industrial society should put a high priority upon free trade. The entry of Baines

---

[12] *Leeds Mercury*, 12 December 1840.   [13] *Ibid.*, 27 January 1838.
[14] Cf. *Leeds Times*, 3 January 1846, 'public opinion is now the chief governing power of Great Britain': it went on to argue that only through union and the pooling of resources in political associations could such power be effectively exercised.
[15] *Leeds Mercury*, 2 June 1849.

upon the local political stage was on the occasion of an Anti-Corn Law
meeting in 1825 and his elder brother commented '*my* public life will be
commenced under the auspices of a name already made honourable by
the talents of two generations of the family'.[16] Free trade was for Baines
the natural corollary of an economic philosophy based upon the free
market and competition of classical economics. Baines saw as one of
his tasks in conducting a newspaper that of disseminating the ideas of
such modern writers as Malthus and Ricardo and he had a profound
belief in

> the clear and acknowledged right which every merchant has to the free
> exercise of his talents industry and capital in any way he may think
> best, unless when that individual freedom may be incompatible with
> the general welfare.[17]

His well known defence of machinery[18] marked him as a doctrinaire and
theoretical supporter of the free market system, which earned him the
persistent enmity of working class leaders for many years. It was extremely significant that he cited as one of his reasons for opposing universal suffrage the short sighted views on commercial policy of most
working men 'advocating restrictions in industry and exchange under
the idea of protection, opposing machinery and all improvement, calling
for a minimum of wages, condemning competition etc.'[19]

This ideological deference to classical economics did not extend to the
social sphere. Baines, for all the denigration of Oastler and Sadler, supported factory legislation for children, though not for adults who were
free agents. Though he viewed the 1834 Poor Law as a great tribute to
political economy he thought it obvious that 'outdoor relief cannot be
refused in these districts owing to the fluctuations in the amount of
employment'.[20] In the public health and environment field he was an
embryonic collectivist, wishing social utilities to be publicly controlled
and financed by taxation.[21] He was not at all opposed to State action in
social affairs *per se* though he was desperately fearful of bureaucratic

[16] M. T. Baines to E. Baines Junior, 4 April 1825, Baines Papers (Leeds City
Archives), 11/3; cf. *Leeds Mercury*, 19 March 1825.
[17] *Leeds Mercury*, 13 February 1830.
[18] *An Address to the Unemployed Workmen of Yorkshire and Lancashire* . . . (1826).
[19] *Leeds Mercury*, 24 September 1842.
[20] *Ibid.*, 4 February 1837.
[21] He was a persistent critic of municipal intransigence on the grounds of economy
and supported strong measures of environmental control. On the water question, for
instance, he strongly favoured a municipal scheme as against those who wished to
leave water supply to the market forces of joint stock companies. For further details
see D. Fraser, 'The Politics of Leeds Water', *Publications of the Thoresby Society*, volume
LIII (1970), pp. 50–70.

centralized control, preferring power to be dispersed in local self-government.[22] This theme was also prominent in his suspicion of state education with its connotations of bureaucratic dictatorship.

Baines was also unwilling to translate free competition into the political sphere and, as we shall see, did not desire that confrontation between aristocracy and middle class which some free-traders relished. This was not initially obvious for he perceptively identified the crucial role the industrial north would have in the struggle to push Corn Law repeal through an unwilling parliament. He wrote of Lancashire and Yorkshire, 'it is to the loud and persevering expression of public opinion from their towns and villages that we are to look for any important influence on the legislature.'[23] The role of these industrial counties crystallized once the Anti-Corn Law League was launched. Manchester looked to Baines to set the wheels of activity in motion for the *Leeds Mercury* gave him a strategic importance.

The League campaign began well in Leeds and Baines was a regular delegate to conferences in Manchester and London.[24] Many local free traders, however, soon deserted the League for household suffrage,[25] and Cobden complained to Smiles, 'I wish the Leeds ACL men had held on to the question for a year or two more'.[26] A revival of activity in 1841 was hardly more encouraging since his natural Whiggish inclinations induced Baines to support Russell's fixed duty and to promote a campaign for free trade generally. The former move received short shrift from Cobden who chastised Baines, 'we have done our duty in eschewing Chartism—Toryism—Household Suffrageism—and now we are determined to resist ministerialism'. The latter suggestion was tantamount to 'a virtual secession from our League'.[27]

However, when the League fund raising schemes were launched Baines was returned to favour, again because of the *Mercury*. He was under no illusions about his own demagogic abilities and urged Cobden to come over and communicate 'to us a little of your own fire'.[28] When the £50,000 appeal produced a disappointing response Cobden commiserated with Baines, 'we are obliged to you for the energetic appeals in your paper. It is not your fault if the Leeds people do not contribute all

[22] This came out strongly in the years 1847 and 1848 when government proposals for public health legislation were under discussion. He was a strong advocate of the line popularized by J. Toulmin Smith in *Centralisation or Representation* (1848).
[23] *Leeds Mercury*, 14 January 1837.
[24] *Ibid.*, 19 January, 9 February 1839; 22 February 1840; 3 April, 13 November 1841; 28 January, 6 May 1843.
[25] See below, p. 203.
[26] T. Mackay (ed.), *The Autobiography of Samuel Smiles* (1905), p. 98.
[27] Cobden to Baines, 4 January 1841, Correspondence of Sir Edward Baines (Leeds City Archives), no. 25; Smiles, *Autobiography*, p. 99.
[28] Baines to Cobden, 27 October 1842, B.M. Add. MSS. 43664 f. 135.

that we would wish to the Fund.'[29] The 'energetic appeals' in the *Mercury* continued and became part of the League's propaganda output. Baines's letters to Russell in 1843 were reprinted as a pamphlet and the League ordered a quarter of a million copies for circulation. In the following year similar if smaller scale interest was shown in his letters to Harewood.[30] Baines was playing a part in that education of opinion which was fundamental to the League's strategy, for, as Cobden explained, 'our primary object is to work the printing press—not upon productions of our own, but in producing the *essence* of authoritative writers'.[31]

Thus far, with minor altercations, Baines and the Manchester men had seen eye to eye on the best mode of organizing the League. The all important shift in emphasis on to registration and manufacture of votes was to expose a fundamental divergence of view both on the legitimate functions of a pressure group and its ultimate aspirations. While the League acknowledged that most counties were beyond the pale of free trade influence, Manchester eyes nevertheless focused on the industrial counties which were within reach. In 1844 Cobden addressed Baines on this subject:

What are you doing in the West Riding county matter? S. Lancashire, the West Riding and Middlesex may and must be won. . . . I suggest that a portion of the League fund could not be better expended than in a judicious attention to your important district.[32]

While acknowledging in the summer of 1844 the desirability of an alliance between urban free traders and Whig county squires, Cobden was in the autumn in favour of a separate League organization based on the towns. He was prepared to throw down the gauntlet and challenge the sincerity of free trade aristocrats like Earl Fitzwilliam. He told Baines that 'unless the Whig squires will join the towns heartily you would be better without their half-hearted fellowship', and urged him 'you must set up for yourselves as free traders'.[33]

Three factors underpinned Baines's implacable opposition to such a course. First, on a purely personal level there was a close contact between his family and the county gentry. Ever since Baines senior had

[29] Cobden to Baines, 17 December 1842, *idem.*, f. 136.
[30] *Leeds Mercury*, 25 February, 4 March 1843, 2, 9, 16, 30 March, 6 April 1844; Baines to Wilson, 10 March 1843, Wilson Papers (Manchester Reference Library); Wilson to Baines, 11 March 1843, 6 April 1844, Correspondence of Sir Edward Baines nos. 80, 81.
[31] Cobden to Baines, 25 October 1842, B.M. Add. MSS. 43664, f. 132.
[32] Cobden to Baines, 24 June 1844, *idem.*, f. 153.
[33] Cobden to Baines, 19 October 1844, 22 March 1845, *idem.*, ff. 166, 186.

pledged his paper's support for Lord Milton in the great county election of 1807[34] the Baines's were *persona grata* at Wentworth Woodhouse, the Fitzwilliam seat. Even though the imposition of Brougham in 1830[35] ruffled a few county feathers, Baines senior retained good relations in the county. Lord Morpeth, later Earl of Carlisle, could write from Castle Howard that Baines Senior had been 'one of the foster fathers of my public life'.[36] Baines Junior could not lightly throw aside his father's contacts and he reminded Cobden, 'there is the strongest attachment and the deepest respect felt for Lord Fitzwilliam himself and we must on no account separate from him'.[37]

Second, the very nature of the West Riding with its mixture of urban and rural interests encouraged the maintenance of an alliance between town and county. The West Riding, like England as a whole, was by no means dominated by industry. Leeds, Sheffield, Bradford, Halifax, and Huddersfield were bursting into a regional network which still revolved around such places as Wentworth Woodhouse, Castle Howard, and Harewood House. Landed gentlemen, many of whom owned industrial interests, were becoming increasingly aware of 'how much the activity of manufacturers and the enterprise of trade contribute to the welfare of the proprietors and cultivators of the soil'.[38] Such a situation promoted ideas of compromise between industrial and landed interests rather than dominance by one over the other.

Much of West Riding politics in the mid-nineteenth century involved the search for a stable basis for such an alliance of compromise.[39] It brought county representation into sharp focus as urban Liberals sought to make elections reflect the balance of commercial and landed interests in the Riding. The election of the Leeds flax-spinner John Marshall in 1826 was the first recognition of urban aspirations while Brougham's success in 1830 was a sign of strident urban self-consciousness in West Riding affairs. A quiescent period followed largely because of the enfranchisement of the boroughs in 1832 and easy Whig success in the county but Tory resurgence in the later 1830s forced Whig squires to look to the register and hence involve urban activists in county political

[34] Reputedly one of the costliest elections ever fought in which Lord Milton of Wentworth House defeated Lascelles of Harewood House. Wilberforce was at the head of the poll.

[35] Brougham was suggested by Baines senior and was launched before the county Whigs could prevent it, see Norman Gash, 'Brougham and the Yorkshire Election of 1830', *Proc. Leeds Phil. & Lit. Soc.* (1956), pp. 19–35.

[36] Morpeth to Baines, 6 August 1848, Correspondence Sir E. Baines, No. 18.

[37] Baines to Cobden, 12 November 1844, B.M. Add. MSS. 43664, f. 175.

[38] Draft Address of Earl Fitzwillim *c.* 1841, Wentworth Woodhouse MSS. (Sheffield Public Library), G5.

[39] Cf. F. M. L. Thompson, 'Whigs and Liberals in the West Riding 1830–1860', *E.H.R.*, vol. LXXIV (1959), pp. 214–39.

organization. In times of tension Earl Fitzwilliam might wish to preserve gentry influence even by coalescing with landed Tories, or extreme dissenters might seek to assert urban dominance by imposing their sectarian views on the Riding. Yet cool heads always saw the need for compromise for as one commented 'I do not like party divisions to run by classes and not by principles: all the aristocracy and landed gentry on one side, the democracy and town people on the other. . . .'[40] Among the gentry Sir Charles Wood, later first Viscount Halifax, consistently saw the necessity of preserving 'good understanding between country gentlemen and the towns' and took into national politics that sense of compromise which had been nurtured by the West Riding.[41] The towns produced Baines who felt that political pressure groups had to run parallel with and not counter to the social structure. Ironically the cause of an eventual split, Baines nevertheless saw that the free trade question could combine the two interests and later wrote to Wood, 'I earnestly hope the Whig gentry and the town Liberals will cordially unite . . . to return two free traders.'[42]

Baines was thirdly temperamentally out of sympathy with that anti-aristocratic feeling which underlay so much of the League's case, that, in the words of one of the lecturers, the anti-Corn Law struggle was really one 'between the aristocracy and the nation—between 30,000 landowners and 26,000,000 men'.[43] Some were perceptive enough to see that the Manchester question represented a desire to supplant aristocratic control of executive government, as a Halifax manufacturer later explained;

> The Cobden and Bright party are striving for power. Their object is to form a middle class administration in contradistinction to the aristocratic element which has hitherto predominated in the government of the country.[44]

Baines did not go all the way with Cobden on this question, since his whole outlook was tempered by that constitutional Whiggism which desired an alliance between conflicting interests. Here was an opportunity for Baines to apply one of his basic beliefs:

[40] J. G. Marshall to Earl Fitzwilliam, 29 November 1848, Wentworth Woodhouse MSS., G.7(d), Marshall went on to warn Fitzwilliam not to over react to insubordination from urban activists, 'Those who are their natural leaders on such occasions should have much patience and forbearance and be very slow to forget or disown their long cherished traditional principles.'

[41] C. Wood to 6th Earl Fitzwilliam (n.d.), Hickleton MSS. (Garrowby), A4/40. Wood was prominent in the attempts to reconcile different sections of the Whig party and to avoid divisions over Liberal party strategy.

[42] Baines to Wood, 26 February 1851, *loc. cit.*, A4/160.

[43] *Leeds Mercury*, 22 December 1838.

[44] E. Akroyd to Sir Charles Wood, 1 March 1852, Hickleton MSS., A4/135.

The principle of *preservation* is quite as important in the institutions of a country as the principle of *improvement*. Monarchy and aristocracy tend naturally to *preserve* and democracy to *improve*. The *former* it is true have too little love for improvement but it is also true that the *latter* has too little regard to preservation. A combination of both produces the happiest results.[45]

Essentially the League demanded middle class social and political *pre-eminence*: Baines the great middle class champion in fact wanted *partnership*.

Hence the strategic implications of whether the League should subsidize and build on the existing West Riding organization or launch its own separate association took on for Baines enormous significance. The tactics of a pressure group called into question its role. If social harmony and political stability were to prevail then it seemed to Baines that the traditional political system had to be coaxed into admitting the legitimacy of middle class aspirations for a share of power. A head-on clash between entrepreneur and aristocrat could only exacerbate social tensions and threaten the fabric of the English constitution. Peel's desire to use Corn Law repeal as a means of avoiding the collision of great social interests was thus nearer in spirit to Baines than to Cobden.

It was true that the West Riding Reform Association[46] was deficient of funds and enthusiasm, though both revived at the first sniff of a League invasion. Fitzwilliam agreed to finance renewed activity and added revealingly, 'indeed I shall do so *con amore* if the alternative be a registration by the League—this wd. be destructive of everything'.[47] Baines acted as Fitzwilliam's mouthpiece and would have no truck with Cobden's separatist tendencies.

Lord Fitzwilliam thinks that the Free Trade cause in the West Riding would be endangered by any acknowledged connexion with the League . . . my decided opinion is that we ought to take no course that would alienate these powerful and respected Liberals. To do so would split not only the Liberals but also the Free Traders into shivers . . . it would not therefore be prudent in my opinion to set up a new Regis-

[45] *Leeds Mercury*, 28 January 1837.
[46] The Association was launched in 1837, with J. A. Ikin a Leeds solicitor as its first secretary as a straightforward registration society. When Ikin became Town Clerk of Leeds in 1843 he was succeeded as secretary by Edward Newman, Fitzwilliam's Barnsley solicitor. The association was persistently short of money especially after the demoralizing Whig defeat in 1841, when the Tories won both West Riding seats.
[47] Earl Fitzwilliam to Sir C. Wood, 22 July 1844, Hickleton MSS., A4/36; cf. T. W. Tottie to Fitzwilliam, 19 July 1844, Wood to Fitzwilliam, 25 July 1844, Wentworth Woodhouse MSS., G11.

tration machinery but rather do all that is practicable within the present committees ... all this may be done without coming into conflict with the Whigs.[48]

Beneath registration technicalities lay a divergent view of the ideal mid-Victorian world.

The League did in the event invade the West Riding, though under the nominal aegis of traditional county influence, and it was perhaps a triumph for Baines that the full extent of the League takeover was not immediately apparent. It was Baines who visited Castle Howard to invite Morpeth to a great League demonstration at the end of 1845; to Baines that he wrote his letter accepting total and immediate repeal; and it was Baines who read to an excited audience Morpeth's letter of conversion.[49] Morpeth's uncontested return as MP for the West Riding in the by-election of 1846 (caused by the elevation to the peerage of the sitting member Stuart Wortley on the death of his father Lord Wharncliffe) has been strangely ignored by historians. It was in fact the League's greatest victory, for Morpeth's invincibility rested on the League registration campaign although his name and background conformed with Bainesite views on social leadership in the Riding. In truth there could be no quarrel with Cobden's view that had he taken Fitzwilliam's advice to keep his nose out of the Riding then 'Lord Morpeth might still have been rusticating at Castle Howard'.[50] The West Riding was indeed being 'unresistingly scourged by Manchester moneybags' and 'trampled upon by supercilious and ambitious cotton Lords'.[51]

It was ironic that the alliance in the West Riding between urban Liberals and county Whigs was in the end shattered by Baines himself, doubly so in view of his father's efforts to build bridges between smoky towns and country estates. Whig-liberalism was plunged into fissiparous dispute by dissenting voluntaryism, which on education became an exaggerated case study of justice to nonconformists. The middle classes whom Cobden wished to lead into the political kingdom were mostly, though not wholly, dissenters in religion, a connection movingly illustrated by the great Anti-Corn Law conference of dissenting ministers in 1841.[52] Achievement in economic policy or political reform would

[48] Baines to Cobden, 12 November 1844, B.M. Add. MSS. 43664, f. 175.

[49] Morpeth to Baines, 24 November 1845, Correspondence Sir E. Baines, No. 15; Baines to Wilson, 27 November 1845, Wilson Papers; *Leeds Mercury*, 29 November 1845; Morpeth to Sir C. Wood, 30 November 1845, Hickleton MSS., A4/37.

[50] Cobden to Parkes, 16 February 1846(?), B.M. Add. MSS. 43664, f. 5.

[51] *Leeds Intelligencer*, 24 January 1846.

[52] A. Prentice, *History of the Anti-Corn Law League* (1853), volume I, p. 230; N. McCord, *The Anti-Corn Law League* (1958), pp. 104–7. For details of dissenting grievances, see D. Thompson, 'The Liberation Society', p. 211 f.

always be undermined by the galling personal injustice under which dissenters laboured. Proscription from local office on the grounds of nonconformity finally disappeared in the 1830s, a decade which also saw civil registration, while earlier tithes had often been commuted locally. There remained the patent inequity of Church rates, the difficulties over university education, bishops in the House of Lords, and in short the privileged position of a state Church. The dissenting movement to disestablish the Church of England was a blow aimed at the root of religious inequality.

The cause of justice to dissenters was a matter of conscience. Though it did involve an assault upon the pocket it was mainly an affront to dignity. In such matters of principle there was less room for the manoeuvre of compromise and on questions affecting the religious conscience of dissent Baines almost invariably took the ideological rather than the pragmatic line. Hence on Church rates Baines started from an uncompromising position,

> We demand freedom of conscience and we deny the right of any government or any Church to exact by the civil power one sixpence for the support of worship in any form which he who pays the money does not approve.[53]

Such views account for a great deal of Baines's political activity in the 1830s. He was prominent in organizing the chapels which were the local components in the anti-Church rate movement. He was even more active in launching petitions and originating public meetings which were regular features of Leeds politics in these years. More than this Baines continued his father's work in using the local political system to relieve dissenters of the financial burdens of Church rates.[54] In the 1820s Baines senior had opened up parochial administration to public scrutiny and from the later 1820s Liberal church wardens favouring economies in expenditure were elected. Baines Junior took over the leadership of the parish dissenting movement, and it was he who proposed the Liberal list at the annual churchwardens elections.[55] From 1836 these were all dissenters who refused even to levy Church rates so that Leeds dissenters were relieved of paying what they regarded as an unjust imposition.

---

[53] *Leeds Mercury*, 1 January 1842. In general, see D. Thompson, 'The Liberation Society', p. 212, below.

[54] Cf. D. Fraser, 'The Leeds Churchwardens 1828–1848', *Publications of the Thoresby Society*, LIII (1970), pp. 1–22.

[55] Cf. his remarks *Leeds Mercury*, 24 December 1841 on being pilloried for defending Church rates, he had, he said, 'taken the most decided stand against the system and has (by the request of successive yearly meetings of the Liberals . . .) . . . moved the Liberal Church wardens at the Vestries'.

Many towns such as Birmingham and Nottingham also stopped paying Church rates and this tended to transfer attention to the position of the State Church itself. In the later 1840s there were thriving local societies belonging to the Anti-State Church Association which Baines strongly supported. Again his activity centred on the Chapels and on public meetings. Again too he adopted an uncompromising line urging total disestablishment. The same single minded doctrinaire purity characterized his attitude to Sabbatarianism. He refused to acknowledge any practical benefits (even such as working class self-improvement) which might accrue from relaxation of strict observance of Sunday's laws of conduct. His opposition to Sunday opening pushed the Leeds Zoological Gardens into disintegration and he was later involved in vociferous opposition to Sunday opening of the Crystal Palace.[56] A rare exception to this high principled refusal to compromise was his willingness to tolerate a Church rate in order to provide extra burial grounds for Leeds. For once practical considerations (the health hazards of putrid corpses) overcame Baines' idelogical opposition to the State Church.[57]

Perhaps something of the same pragmatism characterized Baines's early views on education for in 1834 he expressed the hope for 'a proper application of the voluntary principle to a system of national education, aided by the nurturing hand of an enlightened and paternal government'.[58] However by the early '40s he had arrived at the unbending voluntaryism which he was to promote for a quarter of a century. His educational dogma originated in a faith in universal education. Unlike those who feared that education might disturb the social equilibrium Baines held firmly that only through education 'can we have a wise, a temperate, a sober, a right thinking, a well informed and virtuous population'.[59] Social disturbance was judged to be the result of deficient education and so when Chartists broke up a nonconformist meeting it merely proved 'the need there is of a scriptural education for the working classes'.[60] Deficiency of provision did not suggest to Baines the need for State education. Since one of the main purposes of education was to inculcate the spirit of self-reliance and independence the system itself had to be voluntary and free from State control. Only thus could liberty be maintained, for in State education was the threat of the indoctrination of subservience by an obedient educational bureaucracy. Finally

[56] *Leeds Mercury*, 21 August 1841, 12 February 1853, 24 June 1854; *A Correspondence between Edward Baines . . . and B. Oliveira . . . on the Sunday Opening of the Crystal Palace* (1854).

[57] On this occasion (1841–2) he preferred a Church rate to doing nothing about Leeds' overcrowded burial grounds, see Fraser, 'Leeds Churchwardens', pp. 16–17.

[58] *Leeds Mercury*, 18 October 1834.   [59] *Ibid.*, 27 January 1838.

[60] *Ibid.*, 14 September 1839.

since all education was at heart moral education and all morals derived from religion, then religion itself had to be the basis of all elementary education. As Baines explained in 1846, 'religion is incomparably the most powerful as well as the holiest ally of education' and years later he was still convinced that the exclusion of religion was 'a violation of our duty to God and man, and the elimination from the schools of the most precious element of education'.[61]

From this complex syllogism Baines derived a universal truth of stunning simplicity—the State had no right to educate. His mild flirtation with State aid in the 1830s was soon terminated by Graham's Factory Education Bill of 1843 which convinced him that state education was a mere appendage to Anglican supremacy. It was in the massive outburst of dissenting opposition to this bill that Baines first acquired some national recognition. The *Leeds Mercury* was the vehicle for some of the most virulent criticism of the proposals and their implications. Furthermore much of Baines's outpouring achieved wide circulation through separate publication in pamphlets.[62] As with the Anti-Corn Law League Baines took on the role of provider of propaganda, the essence of which was that northern middle class dissenting voluntaryism had no need of subvention or assistance from a paternal Anglican State. His massive accumulation of statistical evidence satisfied him that 'there is no educational want that may not be supplied by the voluntary efforts of the people themselves'.[63]

1843 witnessed the polarization of opinion on education the consequences of which were clear enough to Ashley:

'Combined education' must never again be attempted—it is an impossibility and worthless if possible . . . let us have our own schools, our Catechism, our Liturgy, our Articles, our Homilies, our faith, our own teaching of God's Word.[64]

It was in such an atmosphere that sectarian extremism could flower and whereas in 1843 Baines was an able lieutenant, still a second to the national figure of Edward Miall, by 1847 he had achieved national

[61] *Ibid.*, 5 September 1846; Baines to Reverend W. Arthur, 6 March 1874, *Baines Papers*, 16/19.

[62] See especially *Letter to the Right Honourable Lord Wharncliffe*, *The Manufacturing Districts Vindicated*, and *The Social, Educational and Religious State of the Manufacturing Districts*.

[63] *Life of Baines*, p. 315. Much of the Baines case rested on the Sunday schools and Samuel Smiles commented drily that the figures were meaningless 'unless it be imagined that two or three hours spent on one day in the week in a Sunday school constitutes a sufficient education for the rising generation', *Leeds Times*, 16 September 1843.

[64] Ashley to Graham, 28 March 1843, quoted by J. T. Ward and J. H. Treble, 'Religion and Education in 1843 . . .', *Journal of Ecclesiastical History*, volume xx (1969), p. 109.

pre-eminence. This Miall acknowledged when he remarked 'somebody from Leeds came up to London to call upon all true hearted nonconformists to assert a great principle', a view echoed by a dissenting journal which explained that 'the attention of the kingdom was directed to Leeds as having taken the lead in opposition to the educational policy of the government'.[65]

The oracle of extremism was most vociferous when there were signs that some were in fact prepared to compromise, for Unitarians and some Catholics and Wesleyans were prepared to accept that voluntary provision of schools would never meet the need.[66] Above all there was some movement within Anglicanism, symbolized by the moderate and conciliatory proposals from W. F. Hook, the High Church vicar of Leeds.[67] Well before national attention was fully roused Baines from the summer of 1846 filled the pages of the *Mercury* with the dogmas of voluntaryism and almost single handedly made education the great question of the day. On the morrow of Tory fragmentation over Corn Law repeal Whig Liberalism in Yorkshire found itself threatened by Bainesite voluntaryism.

Baines embarked on a wide ranging campaign 'to show that it is not in the province of government to train the minds of the people'.[68] He addressed letters to government ministers, to hostile critics and to misguided journals;[69] he organized meetings and petitions; he roused the chapels which sent him as a delegate to London to lobby parliament;[70] he piously warned the nation.[71] The 500 delegates and half a million petitioners were inadequately reflected in the passage of ministerial proposals in April 1847 by 372 votes to 47.[72] This was not so much the

[65] *Leeds Mercury*, 30 October 1847, *Eclectic Review*, volume XXII, September 1847, p. 367; cf. *Leeds Intelligencer*, 19 October 1850, Leeds was 'the very focus of the most violent and unscrupulous opposition to national education, the seat of the great oracle of voluntaryism'.

[66] Cf. G. I. T. Machin, 'The Maynooth Grant, the Dissenters and Disestablishment 1845–1847', *E.H.R.*, volume LXXII (1967), pp. 61–85.

[67] W. F. Hook, *On the Means of Rendering More Efficient the Education of the People, Letter to the Bishop of St. David's* (1846); cf. W. R. W. Stephens, *The Life and Letters of Walter Farquhar Hook* (1880), volume II, pp. 205–12.

[68] *Leeds Mercury*, 2 January 1847.

[69] *Ibid.*, 25 July 1846 to 17 October 1846, twelve letters to the Prime Minister, published as *Letters to the Right Hon. Lord John Russell* (1846); *ibid.*, 19 September 1846, letters to William Ewart and Robert Vaughan, 12 December 1846, to the editor of *The Patriot*; *ibid.*, 24 October 1846 to the *Westminster Review*, 7 November 1846 to the *British Quarterly*; *ibid.*, 13 February 1847 to Lord Lansdowne, published as *A Letter to the Most Noble Marquis of Lansdowne* (1847).

[70] Baines organized the meeting at East Parade Congregational Chapel which elected delegates to travel to London; he was prominent at a meeting attended by 15,000 which sent the main Leeds anti-state education petition; he himself was in London lobbying parliament when the measures finally passed. See *Leeds Mercury*, 20 February, 20 March, 17 April 1847.

[71] *Leeds Mercury*, 27 February 1847, *An Alarm to the Nation* (1847).

[72] Machin, *op. cit.*, p. 77.

work of a single pressure group as that of a concerted *ad hoc* organization based on the chapels and geared to the defeat of a specific measure. Baines's activity took on the characteristics of a pressure group but did not limit itself to the normal field of extra-parliamentary agitation. The pressure group sharpened the cutting edge of the nonconformist attack which made full use of the whole political system.

His use of parochial institutions to combat Church rates has been mentioned. In the midst of the education dispute he sought to add municipal weight to his attack and injected voluntaryism into Leeds Town Council. It was a minor victory for Baines that a bitterly divided council registered a narrow majority in favour of voluntaryism.[73] Above all voluntaryism was made the sole criterion for parliamentary election as Yorkshire delegates, demoralized by their parliamentary reverse, once more assembled at East Parade Chapel in Leeds and vowed for vengeance on their betrayers.[74] In pursuit of ideological purity Baines recognized the clash with 'my personal feelings, my party attachments and my old political connexions' but he found himself under 'an imperious sense of public duty'.[75] The same public duty was laid upon all dissenters who were solemnly instructed by the Anti-State Church Association on

> the duty of employing the franchise entrusted to them by divine Providence in indication of those ecclesiastical principles which constitute the sole basis of religious freedom and equality.[76]

In short, dissenting agitation was prepared to utilize the full potential of the political system and not restrict itself to the tools of the pressure group.

The Bainesite 'education crotchet' became the shibboleth of the West Riding and voluntaryists became known everywhere as 'the Baines party'. The attempt to force voluntaryism on to the county electorate, what was called 'the fire from Leeds',[77] sacrificed Whig–Liberal seats at Leeds and Halifax in 1847 and in the Riding in 1848.[78] Baines put prin-

[73] *Leeds Mercury*, 3, 10 April 1847. The council rejected a State education petition by 31 votes to 27.
[74] *Ibid.*, 8 May 1847.   [75] *Ibid.*, 13 February 1847.
[76] *Nonconformist Elector*, 23 July 1847.
[77] J. Parker to Sir C. Wood, 31 July 1847, Hickleton MSS. A4/52. Other phrases used by contemporaries included the Baines mania/frenzy/nonsense.
[78] In Leeds in 1847 Joseph Sturge was nominated by the Baines party who refused to combine with the mainstream liberals and their candidate J. G. Marshall. A liberal–Tory coalition between Marshall and William Beckett, the sitting Tory member, kept Sturge out. Similarly in Halifax Charles Wood joined Edwards to keep out the Radical-voluntary partnership of Ernest Jones and Edward Miall. In 1848 the Bainesite nominee was Sir Culling Eardley Eardley whose extreme voluntaryism was too much for the Whig liberals and the Tory E. B. Denison was returned largely on Whig abstentions or transfers.

ciple before political expediency and was prepared to risk party unity to purge his conscience. Indeed some dissenters were willing to build a new political grouping upon voluntaryism:

> The Anti-State Church principle—the principle of religious freedom and equality has in it sufficient vitality, energy and aptitude to the times to become the germ of a new party.[79]

Paradoxically, devotion to one principle could involve compromise on others and Baines was able to reconcile his persistent opposition to Joseph Sturge's radicalism[80] with total commitment to Sturge's voluntaryism. Baines was honest enough to admit the difficulty when urging Sturge to stand at Leeds in 1847.

> I have differed from you sometimes especially on the subject of complete suffrage, which I do not think expedient in the present state of society . . . but I most heartily concur with you on the great questions now before the public as to the severance of Church and State and the repudiation of Government interference in Education.[81]

God moved men in strange ways and in pursuit of religious and moral truth Baines the Whig took on the guise of Sturge the radical.

The promotion of sectarianism at the expense of party unity earned Baines the contumely of former allies and he had need of the self-administered morale boosting reminder, 'I must not shrink from the steadfast and zealous maintenance of my principles because I am in a minority'.[82] None was more critical than Cobden who could not understand the insistence on 'the narrow platform of voluntaryism'.[83] It seemed to him almost laughable that Baines, having upset the country gentry, still hankered after the old aristocratic alliance.

> . . . the League had alienated the heads of the aristocratic Whigs from the mass of the Liberals . . . the union between the *Mercury* politicians and the Whig aristocracy is at an end. Why will Baines still cherish the delusion that there is a party to which Lord Fitzwilliam and he

[79] *Nonconformist*, 9 June 1847.
[80] From the time Sturge deserted the Leage for Complete Suffrage Baines had pilloried him. Indeed in 1842 Baines had complained that Sturge lacked 'that soundness of judgment or that mental capacity which should entitle his opinions to much deference . . . Mr. Sturge's high moral character is no guarantee whatever for the soundness of his opinions.' *Leeds Mercury*, 24 September 1842.
[81] Baines to Sturge, 22 May 1847, B.M. Add. MSS. 43845, f. 34.
[82] Lines written by Edward Baines on his fiftieth birthday, 28 May 1850, Correspondence Sir E. Baines.
[83] Cobden to Bright, 25 August 1848, B.M. Add. MSS. 43649, f. 73.

belong? Our friend may write as courteously as he pleases to spare the nerves of the Yorkshire aristocracy, but the latter regard him with his voluntaryism as quite as dangerous a character as myself.[84]

Cobden had no regrets over the defection of the Whig gentry but he never forgave Baines for splitting the middle class liberals, the only people who could really dispute aristocratic control in counties such as the West Riding.

The tension between Cobden and Baines epitomized the rivalry between Manchester and Leeds. Leeds largely because of Baines was the great seat of voluntaryism, while Manchester perhaps because of its essential practicality[85] gave birth to a number of prominent movements which accepted some form of state aid, the Lancashire Public School Association in 1847, the Manchester and Salford committee on Education in 1851, and the Manchester Education Aid Society in 1864. The mutual mistrust came to a head over the Crimean War, an issue not unrelated to the moral stance Baines had taken. Baines's jingoistic support of the war seemed a blatant betrayal of principle to Cobden, since as early as 1830 the young editor had asserted that the main aim of free trade was international peace.[86] Furthermore, Baines had supported Sturge, one of the best known pacifists of his day, and Cobden was amazed by 'the elasticity of conscience on some things which men of fanatical tempers on others can exhibit'.[87] Baines justified his conduct on the grounds of Russian aggression and neatly turned the argument by using the example of Russian despotism to support the case for voluntaryism. He also employed the view which was to be thrown into the face of unilateral disarmers a century later:

I would follow you through evil report and good report in the noble scheme you put forth for a general reduction of armaments if I saw the least hope of its being generally adopted. But do we not see that whilst the governments of Western Europe were diminishing their armies and fleets Russia was devoting her whole strength to accumulate an overwhelming fleet and army.[88]

As early as 1848 Cobden asserted that 'the principle of State education is virtually settled both here and in all civilized countries'[89] but

[84] Cobden to Bright, 1 November 1848, *loc. cit.*, f. 85.

[85] Cf. Professor Vincent's perceptive reference to the 'great capacity for getting to the bottom of social issues and sparing no pains which characterized the League generation at its best.' *Op. cit.*, p. xxviii.

[86] E. Baines Junior, *The Moral Influence of Free Trade* (Leeds), 1830.

[87] Cobden to Bright, 4 November 1855, B.M. Add. MSS. 43650, f. 153.

[88] Baines to Cobden, 19 January 1856, B.M. Add. MSS. 43664, ff. 217–18.

[89] Cobden to Baines, 28 December 1848, *idem.*, f. 205.

Baines marched through the mid-Victorian period with the banner of voluntaryism flying, cutting down the State education enemy wherever it appeared. Baines saw no inconsistency between mainstream middle class social philosophy and voluntaryism. Voluntaryism was simply a means of introducing free trade into education, since 'freedom and competition will give the same social stimulus to improvement in our schools as they have done in our manufactures, our husbandry, our shipping and our commerce'.[90] Voluntary education was an expression of Smilesian self-help which was threatened by Russell's 1856 proposals for local rate aided schools. Baines wrote,

> I believe that civil and religious freedom depends upon this self relying action of the people and that the more the people are taught to depend upon the Government, the feebler become their virtue and their love of liberty.[91]

Baines was still using the political system to advance the voluntary cause and his anti-State education influence was partly responsible for the withdrawal of W. E. Forster in the 1857 Leeds election and once more the surrender of one seat to the Tories.

Baines was himself elected to parliament in 1859 and this marked a watershed in his career. His propaganda was now intra-mural rather than extra-parliamentary in emphasis and he was never able to ride the two horses as effectively as Cobden had done in the 1840s. Pressure groups which had been successful, such as the anti-slavery movement, had used influence inside parliament but had also maintained close links between the House of Commons and the grass roots of the movement. Aware of this Baines still found it difficult to provide in the 1860s. Moreover he could see at first hand the reality of increased State aid in the education estimates, evidence despite Lowe and the Newcastle Commission of self-sustained bureaucratic growth. Baines knew of the difficulties of the Congregational Union which true to its principle had refused state aid. Despite raising nearly £200,000 in its first twelve years[92] it could not compete with denominational schools which drew funds from voluntary and State sources.

His membership of the Taunton Commission[93] was the precursor of

---

[90] E. Baines, *Education Best Promoted by Perfect Freedom Not State Endowments* (1854), p. 45.

[91] E. Baines, *National Education, Remarks on the Speech and Plan of Lord John Russell* (1856), p. 4.

[92] *Ibid.*, p. 32. Baines had been instrumental in launching the Congregational Union in 1843 to promote voluntary education within the Independent/Congregational communities.

[93] The Schools Enquiry Commission under Lord Taunton reported in 1868 after having examined endowed and proprietary secondary schools. Of greatest significance here was its proposal to bring secondary education under close state supervision.

his conversion and his announcement in 1867 of his abandonment of voluntaryism was itself a precursor of the Taunton Commission's report. In October 1867 he reminded the Congregational Union that the dissenting press had deserted voluntaryism and that even the great Miall had 'declared that as a practical politician he must bow to forces which he cannot withstand'.[94] The same practicality characterized Baines's announcement to the doyen of State education, Kay Shuttleworth:

> I confess to a strong distrust of government action and a passionate love for voluntary action and self reliance. But though the passion still rules, I now acknowledge that it was allowed too absolute sway and as a practical man I am compelled to abandon the purely voluntary system. . . .[95]

At last in 1867 Baines allowed pragmatism to compromise with ideology. He would not travel as far as secular schools, refusing to accept 'a system which must exclude religion from the schools and sever them from the religious communities'.[96] But for the moment Baines had lifted the proscriptive ban on State education—the battle over what kind of State education it should be remained to be fought out in the new school boards. As ever sectarian pressure groups played the system.

Baines's reluctant renunciation of voluntaryism was accompanied in October 1867 by his reluctant acceptance of household suffrage. There were in fact many links between the education and suffrage questions. The Reform Act made State education inevitable not because of Lowe's apocryphal 'we must educate our masters' but because it generated the political will. Baines had opposed State education 'but the people *would have it* and with Household Suffrage they became irresistible'.[97] While at this overt political level education depended on the suffrage, in a much subtler way extension of the suffrage was dependent on the spread of education. Baines never believed in a philosophy of natural rights which conferred the entitlement to the suffrage upon all citizens,[98] but rather saw the vote as a privilege to be earned by respectability. Hence Baines conceived that the level of the suffrage ought to vary directly with the level of education.[99]

[94] *National Education Address of Edward Baines* . . . 11 October 1867, p. 8.
[95] Baines to Kay Shuttleworth, 19 October 1867, *Baines Papers*, 23/11.
[96] *Ibid.*
[97] Baines to Reverend W. Arthur, 6 March 1874, *Baines Papers*, 16/19.
[98] 'We deny that any man rich or poor has any natural right to the franchise', *Leeds Mercury*, 13 October 1838.
[99] 'We hold that the franchise should be gradually extended as the humbler classes grow in information and improve in their moral and social condition', *Leeds Mercury*, 21 November 1840.

One of the major motivations which stimulated middle class patronage of voluntary educational agencies such as mechanics institutes or Sunday schools was the desire to use education as a means of social control. Such agencies were avenues for the transmission of respectable values and attitudes to the working class. Baines viewed the working class as being under middle class tutelage, for there existed

> A kind of spiritual superintendence on the part of sixty thousand teachers, generally taken from the middle class, over three hundred and sixty thousand scholars, generally from the working class. . . . Sunday Schools establish a bond of the greatest importance between the two classes of society.[100]

As working men came to reflect more and more a middle class image so Baines became more sympathetic to an extension of the suffrage. It was the Lovett rather than the O'Connor line which moved Baines. Once more political agitation had to serve the interests of social harmony and stability.

Baines and his father had never had any doubts about the justice of reform demands before 1832, for it seemed self-evident that respectable, wealthy, independent, and important interests were unrepresented. The Bainesite view of the passage of the 1832 Reform Act has been quoted and it seemed to the two editors that such a legitimate and satisfactory change could hardly be repeated in the near future. The severity of the depression of the later 1830s coupled with apparent Whig intransigence on the Corn Laws convinced some of the Leeds middle class free-traders that an extension of the suffrage was vital. Hamer Stansfeld and George Goodman, large scale cloth merchants, J. G. Marshall head of the largest flax-spinning firm in Europe, and Samuel Smiles the doctor turned journalist launched the so-called 'Leeds New Move' in 1840 in an attempt to combine middle and working class reformers.[101] It was an anticipation of the Complete Suffrage Union. The defection of so many important middle class free-traders on his doorstep forced Baines to explain himself at some length. He was in no doubt that the middle classes were rightful possessors of the urban franchise for they were 'the best depositories of political power'.[102]

[100] *Leeds Mercury*, 17 June 1843. A slightly amended version which referred to 66,000 teachers and 400,000 pupils appeared in E. Baines Junior, *The Social Educational and Religious State of the Manufacturing Districts* (1843), pp. 24–5. Cf. Baines on middle class lecturers addressing working men on entomology 'with the view of elevating their moral feelings and enabling them to assume a higher place in the respect of society in general'.
[101] *Leeds Times*, 1 August; 5 September 1840. See A. Wilson, 'The Suffrage Movement', p. 83, above.
[102] *Leeds Mercury*, 24 September 1842.

We do not believe there is in the world a community so virtuous so religious and so sober minded as the middle classes of England . . . for a safe, intelligent and independent constituency the substance and staple must be found in the middle classes.[103]

Household suffrage in 1840 would undoubtedly swamp a middle class independent electorate with uneducated masses. Demos threatened the social and political order. In an interesting echo of the Tory versus Whig debate in 1831–2, Baines believed that the extension of the suffrage would bring nearer that revolution which the reformers hoped to avoid by concession.[104] All Baines's other arguments were mere debating points compared to his fundamental fears about the disastrous social and political upheaval which would inevitably follow a transition to democracy.

Baines retained this hostility to suffrage reform for some years. In 1848 however Hume detected a change in the Bainesite outlook, which appeared now to favour 'another Reform Bill as a means of satisfying the just claims of millions of our countrymen'.[105] Hume held out the prospect of Baines using his influence to reconcile all the industrial classes and the conscious assumption of this role dated from January 1852 when Baines participated in joint middle and working class reform meetings.[106] From then on Baines, in pursuit of social and political harmony, was a parliamentary reformer.

Two discoveries underlay the conversion of Baines on the suffrage question. The first was a growing awareness that the working classes, certainly the upper echelons of the skilled artisans, were not revolutionary. The educational process paid dividends as responsible, sober, diligent citizens seemed to be emerging out of the Chartist whirlpool with its tinges of spoliation. He commented in 1864 on the great improvements since 1832 'in education, in habits of reading, in political knowledge, in habits of association for mutual improvement and insurance, in temperance, in providence and in attendance upon public worship'.[107] Underlying this no doubt was increased affluence and Baines himself had commented in 1850,

. . . it seems by no means impossible that the whole of the working

[103] *Ibid.*, 5 December 1840, reprinted as E. Baines Junior, *Household Suffrage and Equal Electoral Districts* . . . (Leeds, 1841).
[104] *Leeds Mercury*, 21 November; 5, 12, 19, 26 December 1840; 2, 9 January 1841.
[105] Hume to Baines, 22 April 1848, Correspondences Sir E. Baines, no. 47. Baines supported Hume's 'Little Charter' movement, see *Leeds Mercury*, 8, 15 April, 6 May 1848.
[106] *Leeds Mercury*, 10, 24 January 1852.
[107] Hansard, 11 May 1864, 3rd ser., CLXXV, column 293.

classes should be raised above the dread of poverty—that all should be comfortable, all educated, all well fed, well clothed, well lodged.[108]

Mid-victorian prosperity allowed working class self-help and respectability to flower and the accumulation of property made working men, in Smiles's phrase, 'steady sober and diligent. It weans them from revolutionary notions and makes them conservative.'[109] Baines thus concluded that the respectable artisan could safely be entrusted with the vote. The risks of 1839–42 had disappeared with the *embourgeoisement* of the English working class.[110]

The second of Baines's discoveries was that an extension of the suffrage would not swamp a middle class electorate *per se*. Baines, like every other mid-Victorian reformer, had to familiarize himself with the minutiae of rates and rents, because some mathematical formula had to be found to identify the respectable artisan with an entitlement to the vote. Moderate liberal reformers like Baines latched upon a £6 franchise which would still leave two thirds of the male population without the vote, according to his often quoted estimate of 1864. More important was his calculation that even with such an extension 'the upper and middle class would still constitute two thirds of the voters in the boroughs'.[111] Earlier he had hoped to persuade the traditional aristocratic system to admit the middle classes into partnership: now he assumed that the new rulers (the upper and middle class) could safely *absorb* the 'labour aristocracy'. Conviction dictated that the middle class should not dominate the old society: strategy dictated that the working class should not dominate the new.

The natural compromizing Whig found himself in the ideal milieu as the moderate reformer, thus strengthening the English constitution by periodic adjustments to reflect social change.[112] If this agitation was to achieve its aim of strengthening the links between a bourgeois working

---

[108] *Leeds Mercury*, 14 September 1850.

[109] Quoted by S. J. Price, *Building Societies Their Origins and History* (1958), p. 140.

[110] While commenting on the spread of land ownership Baines remarked on 'the greater stability which will be given to the social fabric, for it is an unquestioned axiom in politics that the strength of the social fabric will be in direct proportion to the number of those who have a share in its accumulated wealth, and most of all when that share is in the soil itself.' *Leeds Mercury*, 2 June 1849.

[111] *Extension of the Franchise, Speech of Edward Baines on . . . the Borough Franchise Bill* (1864), p. 11. The *Baines Papers* contain numerous calculations about rents/rates/voting, etc. and it is likely that the origin of this statement is to be found in item 27 where he computed that in Leeds a £6 franchise would produce an electorate of 10,759 of whom he estimated 3,552 as working class, hence two-thirds as middle class or above.

[112] In his view the great strength of the English constitution was that it was 'susceptible of continual improvement and adaptation to the circumstances of the people', *Leeds Mercury*, 24 September 1842.

class and the Bainesite middle class then it was essential to avoid divisive
extremism which might destroy the alliance. Baines thus used the old
family stratagem of agreeing on general principles rather than allowing
disagreements on details. His brother was preaching to the converted
when he advised on reform meetings, 'for the sake of giving unanimity
and real effect the best thing would be to pass a resolution in favour of a
substantial and large extension of the suffrage without specifying any
particular extension.'[113] This was exactly the ploy used by Baines Senior
to maintain Whig–Radical unity before 1832.

Once in parliament Baines was well placed to reflect the radical
liberalism which was strongly based in Leeds and his patronage was
sought and given to the Leeds Working Men's Parliamentary Reform
Association launched in 1860.[114] His whole strategy was based upon
retaining the support and pursuing the interests of those he characterized as 'readers, thinkers, members of Mechanics Institutions, teachers
in Sunday Schools and enrolled in clubs of mutual insurance or as
depositors in Savings Banks'.[115] Indeed it was partly to establish grass
roots support for the emerging Liberal party that Baines clung to reform.
He judged it important to redeem the pledge in the early '60s that some
reform would be granted by parliament and he was thinking here of
both potential and actual electors. He reminded Locke King the gentry
radical in 1863

> The Liberal party is so distinctly pledged to the carrying of a Reform
> Bill that I don't know how the members will again meet their consti-
> tuents if they cannot show that they have done their best to attain that
> object ... it will be thought that there is no longer a distinction
> between *soi-disant* Reformers and Tories. Confidence in public men
> will be grievously shaken and the Reform party will be much dis-
> united.[116]

An extension of the suffrage was seen by Baines as a *sine qua non* of a
real liberal party and at the same time such a party had to have a dissenting orientation for Baines regarded himself rather as the national
conscience of nonconformity. Indeed mid-Victorian liberalism was
critically different from the Whiggism of Grey and Melbourne in its
commitment to the cause of justice to dissenters for which Baines and his

[113] M. T. Baines to E. Baines, 18 December 1858, *Baines Papers*, 11/12.
[114] Address of Leeds Working Men's Parliamentary Reform Association, *Baines Papers*, 26/17; William Hickes to Baines, 3 September 1860, *idem.*, 26/19; *Leeds Mercury*, 13 December 1860.
[115] E. Baines, *Position of the Question of Parliamentary Reform* (Leeds, 1864), *Baines Papers*, 26/13.
[116] Baines to Locke King, 28 December 1863, *Baines Papers*, 27.

father had struggled for decades. This was dear to Baines's heart as was Gladstonian finance since he had announced years earlier, 'we consider all taxes evils and every remission as a blessing'.[117] These obvious *Liberal* viewpoints were however couched in a persistent deference to the traditional Whiggism imbibed in his youth. It was if the stock of the Whigs of 1832 was almost inexhaustible. Unlike Cobden and Bright, Baines had no wish to rock the Palmerstonian boat and so he became identified as a Whig apologist.

Hence for Baines suffrage reform was seen as a means of strengthening the English constitution which it would do so long as reform was moderate, i.e. so long as reform did really strengthen and not threaten the fabric of society and constitution. Because of this Baines had to face the ambivalent situation of proposing reform in the 1860s that was too extreme for parliament yet too moderate to inspire public support. He realized that he was struggling against middle class conservatism, that in Leeds 'very few indeed of the Liberal voters favour an extension of the suffrage'.[118] He acknowledged the moderation of his own 1865 proposals and wrote, 'the Bill is so limited as not in the slightest degree to warrant the fears of democracy which Lowe Horsman and Elcho conjure up'.[119] He was in a cleft stick for a really extensive bill would have been intrinsically counter productive—it would not be safe and would swamp middle class voters.

Never sharing Bright's desire to use an extended suffrage to supplant the aristocracy Baines was committed to a moderate fabianism which could not ignite enthusiasm and which hardly earned him his recent description of a 'thorough going Radical'.[120] Cobden as ever saw through Baines:

> I have little confidence in the Leeds Liberals or the Yorkshire politicians generally . . . nothing but registered manhood suffrage would induce the masses to agitate . . . Baines' plan will not excite any sympathy from the working class and in my opinion nothing will be done until the excluded classes demand in loud tones their rights. *Then* if *they* call for household suffrage the Lords will pass a substantial measure to escape something worse. But nothing will be got by *cooing* and I look on what is coming from Leeds as little better than child's play.[121]

Such child's play did not arouse support and as Cobden had predicted reform did not come until the occasion of 'a great crisis, some shock to

[117] *Leeds Mercury*, 2 November 1836.
[118] F. Baines to E. Baines, 7 April 1865, *Baines Papers*, 4.
[119] E. Baines to A. Ritchie, 12 May 1865, *Baines Papers*, 16/15.
[120] F. B. Smith, *The Making of the Second Reform Bill* (1866), p. 51.
[121] Cobden to Bright, 4 February 1865, B.M. Add. MSS. 43652, ff. 218–20.

move the world and everything will be conceded by our cowardly ruling class to panic fear'.[122]

The tide flowing from Hyde Park which carried Bright forward in fact swamped and capsized Baines. His plans had always been conditioned by a desire to legislate while working class calm existed lest popular excitement should result in a more extensive reform that could be safely contemplated.[123] In the crucial 1866–7 period Bainesite moderation was discarded as his leadership became redundant. His celebrated absence from a giant Reform League demonstration earned him the censure of former allies who now wished to throw him over.[124]

Once again Baines had to marry social theory with political expediency. Since persistence with moderate reformist ideas in the face of imminent radical achievement could only drive him into an Adullamite wilderness, Baines swam with the tide with self conscious reluctance. In April 1867 he appeared at a reform meeting with radicals and by October his presence at a Reform League banquet signified his acquiescence.[125] Like Disraeli his fears over this leap in the dark were somewhat allayed by his observation of English society:

> . . . so long as human nature and the structure of society remain what they are so long we need not fear that Parliament will ever be composed of low class men, or fail to contain the foremost men in the kingdom.[126]

So long as the middle class accepted that 'while the possession of property confers privileges it also imposes duties', so long as they did not 'shrink from the duties and responsibilities which rank and station and honourable place bring with them',[127] then social harmony and political stability would persist. In such social peace the basic middle class virtues of religion, sobriety, industry, and self reliance could spread their benevolent influence and it was to make England a haven of such middle

---

[122] Quoted by D. Read, *Cobden and Bright* (1967), p. 159.

[123] Cf. his notes for speech (prob. 1860s), *Baines Papers*, 27. The point was made in Hansard, 11 May 1864, 3rd ser., CLXXV, column 287.

[124] *Leeds Mercury*, 22 August, 9 October 1866; cf. Smith, *op. cit.*, p. 141. Radicals had always regarded Baines's proposals as merely a first step and from the mid-1860s Baines began to lose control in the West Riding to more extreme men such as R. M. Carter, the self-made Leeds coal merchant. When he refused to throw in his lot with the Reform League Carter and his allies wished to dispense with Baines's leadership altogether.

[125] *Leeds Mercury*, 24 April, 16 October 1867.

[126] Baines to Ritchie, 12 May 1865, *Baines Papers*, 16/15. Cf. Hansard, *loc. cit.*, Column 286.

[127] *Leeds Mercury*, 21 December 1839, 21 October 1848. Cf. Hamer Stansfeld, 'the legitimate influence of property can never be done away with especially if it performs its duties as well as it exacts its rights', *Leeds Mercury*, 19 December 1840.

class attitudes that much of the political career of Edward Baines was dedicated.[128]

Further Reading

The best starting point for a study of Edward Baines is his own writing and much is revealed in the biography of his father, *The Life of Edward Baines* (1851, new edition and introduction by D. Fraser, Brighton, 1974). Of his pamphlets only *The Social, Educational and Religious State of the Manufacturing Districts* has received a modern reprint (London 1971) but those mentioned in the footnotes are well worth searching out. There has been a brief modern study—J. R. Lowerson, 'The Political Career of Sir Edward Baines' (unpublished M.A. thesis, Leeds 1965)—but this did not make use of all the extant Baines papers. Another researcher has some perceptive things to say about Baines's social theory, R. J. Morris, 'Organisation & Aims of the Principal Secular Voluntary Organisations of the Leeds Middle Class 1830–1851' (unpublished D.Phil. thesis, Oxford 1970). The family newspaper is well handled in D. Read, *Press and People* (1961) and the Leeds background may be gleaned from A. S. Turbeville and F. Beckwith, 'Leeds and Parliamentary Reform', *Publications of the Thoresby Society* XLI (1954), from the studies in township politics by D. Fraser in *idem*. LIII (1970), and from the same author's 'The Fruits of Reform: Leeds Politics in the 1830s', *Northern History* VII (1972). For the history of Dissent see R. G. Cowherd, *The Politics Of English Dissent* (1959) and D. M. Thompson, *Nonconformity in the Nineteenth Century* (1972). The latter gives no special treatment to Baines but he figures more prominently in G. I. T. Machin, 'The Maynooth Grant, the Dissenters and Disestablishment 1845–1847', *E.H.R.* LXXII (1967). He also receives passing treatment in two standard works on the factory question, C. Driver, *Tory Radical: The Life Of Richard Oastler* (1946) and J. T. Ward, *The Factory Movement* (1961). For mid-Victorian politics see J. R. Vincent, *The Formation of the Liberal Party* (1966), F. B. Smith, *The Making of the Second Reform Bill* (1966) and R. Harrison, *Before The Socialists* (1967).

[128] Baines's political career did not of course end with the second Reform Act for he sat in parliament until 1874 and was locally active into the 1880s. He was even more identified as an elder statesman of the Whig school but continued to promote dissenting causes especially those involving religious teaching.

9

The Liberation Society
1844-1868[1]

David M. Thompson

In 1841 the Reverend Edward Miall left the Congregational chapel in Leicester of which he was the minister, and came to London to found the *Nonconformist*. The first issue was published on 14 April. With its coming, radical dissent had found its first public platform; for the paper was committed to work for the separation of Church and State, which Miall saw as the only way to solve the problems of dissent. Three years later the Anti-State Church Association was founded to further this same object and this society, by a change of name in 1853, became the Society for the Liberation of Religion from State Patronage and Control, always popularly known as the Liberation Society. It became one of the best-organized nineteenth century pressure groups, and although it is an exaggeration to say that 'its history as a modern propagandist organization is absolutely unique' (the words of one of its protagonists, C. S. Miall), Professor Vincent has more recently called it 'the epitome of rational agitation' and has described its role in mobilizing militant dissent behind the new Liberal party.[2] Yet the Liberation Society never achieved its main object—the disestablishment and disendowment of the Church of England—and its success in obtaining its preferred solutions in its other campaigns is questionable. Professor Gash goes so far as to say that disestablishment was 'a millstone round the neck of Dissenting political activity'.[3] Where then does the significance of the Society lie? The answer to this question sheds light on both the potential

[1] I wish to thank the Reverend G. A. D. Mann, secretary of the Free Church Federal Council, and the Reverend H. A. Jacquet, secretary of the London Dissenting Ministers, for permission to consult documents belonging to them, and the staff of Dr Williams's Library and the Greater London Record Office for their courtesy and helpfulness during the research for this paper.
[2] H. S. Skeats and C. S. Miall, *History of the Free Churches of England, 1688-1891* (London, 1891), p. 533; J. Vincent, *The Formation of the Liberal Party, 1857-1868* (London, 1966), p. 68.
[3] Norman Gash, *Reaction and Reconstruction in English Politics* (Oxford, 1965), p. 107.

and the limitations of any political pressure group in the period between the first two Reform Acts.

Dissenting politics in the later 1830s were in confusion.[4] The agitation against the Test and Corporation Acts in 1827–8 had been conducted by a combination of forces[5] and this pattern had been followed with more limited success after 1833 when a united committee representing various nonconformist groups had campaigned for the redress of dissenting grievances. The principal grievances were exclusion from the universities of Oxford and Cambridge, the obligation to pay Church rates (for the upkeep of the parish church), the legal requirement of a certificate of baptism by an Anglican clergyman, the fact that dissenters could only be buried in parish churchyards with an Anglican form of service and the fact that the only legal marriages were those performed in parish churches. Only Quakers were exempt from some of these requirements. Some success came in 1836 with legislation on Marriages, General Registration, Tithes, and a charter for London University, but attempts to remedy the Church rate grievance in 1834 and 1837 were unsatisfactory and unsuccessful. In 1836 also the old dissenting coalition was broken up by the split between unitarian and trinitarian dissenters, as a result of the legal battles in various parts of the country over the right of unitarians to hold property acquired by them at a time when they were still orthodox in belief. Quite apart from the disastrous effect this controversy had on the relations between Unitarians and other dissenters,[6] it also had political consequences: for the Unitarians had provided the political leadership for dissent. They, and not the radicals, had the ear of the Whig politicians; and they were not interested in the disestablishment crusade which radical dissenters were now beginning to contemplate.

Radical dissent was represented by such groups as the Society for Promoting Ecclesiastical Knowledge, formed in London in 1829 to publish information about the history and principles of dissent, and the Church Rate Abolition Society, which held its inaugural meeting at the City of London Tavern on 19 October 1836 and declared that nothing less than total abolition of Church rates would be acceptable to

[4] The history of this period is in 'The Proceedings and Position of Dissenters', *Eclectic Review* (1839), pp. 1–40; J. Stoughton, *History of Religion in England*, viii (London, 1901), pp. 10–15, 114–20; Skeats and Miall, *op. cit.*, pp. 471–91; Gash, *op. cit.*, pp. 63–89; W. G. Addison, *Religious Equality in Modern England* (London, 1944), pp. 60–86; R. G. Cowherd, *The Politics of English Dissent* (New York, 1956), pp. 84–96; W. R. Ward, *Religion and Society in England, 1790–1850* (London, 1972), pp. 177–205.

[5] See R. W. Davis, 'The Strategy of "Dissent" in the Repeal Campaign, 1820–1828', *Journal of Modern History* (1966), pp. 374–93.

[6] B. L. Manning, *The Protestant Dissenting Deputies* (Cambridge, 1952), pp. 53–93.

dissenters.[7] In February 1837 some 320 delegates from local Church Rate Abolition Societies, Independent, and Baptist Churches gathered in London to discuss Church rates, and the Reverends Edward Miall and J. P. Mursell of Leicester were among them. Another local expression of radical dissent was the number of voluntary Church societies, which spread into England from Scotland after 1834. These societies had first been formed in Glasgow, Edinburgh, and other Scottish towns during the Scottish voluntary Church controversy which had been sparked off in 1830 by a sermon attacking the establishment principle. The cause in England was assisted by the presence of Congregational ministers from Scotland in the northern towns.[8] But Church rates were not abolished; dissenters failed to secure candidates favourable to themselves in the 1837 General Election; and their frustration was further increased in 1839 when the Church of England secured significant concessions for itself in the government's education scheme. Edward Baines senior did his best in parliament to fight the dissenters' battle: he raised the case of Thorogood (imprisoned for non-payment of Church rates in Chelmsford) in the House of Commons; he supported Duncombe's motion for a Church Rates Bill in 1840, and with others stopped Sir Robert Inglis's move to secure a government grant for Anglican church extension.[9] But for those fighting Church rates locally the parliamentary approach seemed inadequate, and this was the context in which the *Nonconformist* was founded. Miall in his editorials mercilessly attacked not only the establishment, but also those dissenting ministers whom he regarded as having been too timid in their approach to the matter. To work only for the redress of grievances, he said, was superficial.[10] Miall also embraced radical politics. Because of the dissenting failure to win substantial representation in the reformed House of Commons, he argued that a precondition of success was a further reform of the franchise. Thus the *Nonconformist* also supported the Complete Suffrage Union, led by Joseph Sturge, and provided regular space in its columns for news of the Union's activities. Like the Union therefore, the *Nonconformist* attempted to keep the Chartists and the Anti-Corn Law League together, and Miall was one of the speakers at the conference

[7] Not 29 October, as stated in Skeats and Miall, *op. cit.*, p. 484. Notes of Minutes of the Church Rate Abolition Society are in the possession of the Free Church Federal Council, and have now been deposited in the Greater London Record Office. I owe this reference to Mr D. W. Bebbington.

[8] W. R. Ward, *op. cit.*, pp. 194–5. The original sermon was preached by the Reverend Andrew Marshall of the United Secession Church, who attended the Anti-State Church Conference in 1844: *Nonconformist*, 1 May 1844, pp. 285–6.

[9] *Edward Baines, A Memoir by his son* (London, 1851), pp. 254, 261–2. The strictures of Skeats (Skeats and Miall, *op. cit.*, p. 492) are rather unfair.

[10] A. Miall, *Life of Edward Miall* (London, 1884), pp. 37–40. Several of Miall's early editorials were published as *The Nonconformist's Sketch Book* (London, 1842).

in Birmingham in April 1842 when all shades of reforming opinion were represented.[11]

The influence of the *Nonconformist* should not, however, be exaggerated, for its radicalism by no means appealed to all dissenters. The economic depression and the fear of Chartism made the radical programme seem risky to many, especially in London. A more cautious political line was represented by the Religious Freedom Society, formed in 1839 on the initiative of Josiah Conder, a Congregational journalist who was editor of the *Patriot* (and until 1837 the *Eclectic Review*). Conder opposed the extreme tone of the Ecclesiastical Knowledge Society, and sought the support of liberal anglicans, such as Charles Lushington who became the society's chairman. Others eschewed political action altogether and formed the Evangelical Voluntary Church Association and were later involved in the formation of the Evangelical Alliance in 1843–5: such men were the Reverend John Angell James of Birmingham and Dr Robert Vaughan who, whilst not supporting establishment themselves, refused to press this view on others.[12] The new denominational sense reflected in the formation of the Congregational and Baptist Unions in 1831–3, which had been an element in the split with the unitarians, also fostered a greater concern with religious than with political activity.[13] Dissent was thus split all ways, and the accession of Peel's government in 1841 heightened the gloom. It was not until 1843 that dissenting forces could be reunited.

Two events made this possible. One was the Disruption of the Church of Scotland. The issues behind the Disruption are complex[14] but in the eyes of nonconformists there was only one: the 470 ministers who withdrew from the Church of Scotland in May 1843 were standing up for the spiritual rights of the Church against the interference of the State. The adherence of the Free Church of Scotland to the establishment principle was glossed over in England and attention was concentrated upon their success in raising £1¼ million for stipends, building over 600 churches and setting up schools and colleges in the next ten years: this was hailed as proof of the success of voluntaryism. The other event was the controversy over the education clauses of Sir James Graham's Factories Bill which coincided with the climax of events in Scotland. The Church of England was to be given a favoured position in the

[11] H. U. Faulkner, *Chartism and the Churches* (New York, 1916), pp. 22–3, 34–5, 97–9, 119–20; Cowherd, *op. cit.*, pp. 112–16; Gash, *op. cit.*, p. 75. For the C.S.U., see A. Wilson, 'The Suffrage Movement', p. 84 f., above.

[12] Cowherd, *op. cit.*, pp. 158–9; Ward, *op. cit.*, pp. 193–4.

[13] Ward, *op. cit.*, pp. 196–201; Addison, *op. cit.*, pp. 82–5; I. G. Jones, 'The Liberation Society and Welsh Politics, 1844–1868', *Welsh History Review* (1961), pp. 199–202.

[14] There is a good account in A. B. Erickson, 'The Non-Intrusion Controversy in Scotland, 1832–1843', *Church History* (1942), pp. 302–25.

factory schools which Graham proposed. His suggestions were accepted by Lord John Russell for the Whig opposition, but were opposed by dissenters throughout the country, roused by the *Patriot* and the *Nonconformist*. An unprecedently large number of petitions poured into Parliament, and Graham was forced to withdraw the education clauses.[15] The result was a remarkable triumph for dissenting extra-parliamentary pressure, and indicated that there were limits beyond which government support for the Established Church could not go. The significance of these two events was enhanced by the fact that in both cases the Wesleyan Conference (representing the largest single nonconformist denomination) took the same line as other nonconformists. But this did not mean that the Wesleyans had abandoned their generally conservative posture in politics, and without their support the other nonconformists were to discover that their position was much weaker.

The question which faced nonconformists in the summer of 1843 was how they could build upon their triumph. Miall's suggestion was for a a convention—'a representation of the whole dissenting community, freely chosen, meeting for a limited time, and then returning to their constituents'.[16] This was similar to the Convention summoned by the united committee in London in May 1834 to discuss dissenting grievances and the gathering of February 1837 to discuss Church rates. The Anti-State Church Conference, which met in London from 30 April to 2 May 1844, was the fulfilment of Miall's dream. But it is important not to assume that it therefore represented a complete victory for radical dissent of the kind Miall favoured. To do so is to fall into the trap of identifying the Liberation Society too closely with Miall himself, and to ignore the fact that the history of the society is one of a steady move from the extreme to the middle ground. Indeed the success of the society depended upon this being so.

The initiative for the Anti-State Church Conference was certainly radical. It came from the ministers in Leicester, led by Miall's old friend, the Reverend J. P. Mursell.[17] Seventy-six dissenting ministers in the Midlands signed a memorial to the secretaries of the dissenting bodies in London asking them to call a convention of dissenters from all parts of the country to consider the next steps. But the response of the Dissenting Deputies (lay representatives of the London dissenting

15 Addison, *op. cit.*, pp. 87–9; Gash, *op. cit.*, pp. 86–91; F. Adams, *History of the Elementary School Contest in England* (London, 1882), pp. 118–31. The petitions attracted one and three quarter million signatures.

16 *Nonconformist*, 17 May 1843, p. 360.

17 *Nonconformist*, 29 May 1844, p. 398. Whether Miall suggested this to Mursell is not clear: in the *Nonconformist*, 20 September 1843, p. 641, Miall wrote that the first step had been taken by others, but of course his idea had been public for several months.

Churches) and of the London dissenting ministers was lukewarm. Three meetings of the London dissenting ministers were held between 3 October and 5 December which failed to reach agreement.[18] If London had been prepared to give a lead, it seems clear that provincial dissent would have followed.[19] But by December it was too late. On 7 December 1843 a meeting was held in the Town Hall, Leicester for dissenting ministers and laymen in the Midlands. Also present were Edward Miall, Dr Cox, and Dr Price from London. The last two, both Baptist ministers, had taken a leading part in radical London dissent since the formation of the Ecclesiastical Knowledge Society, and Price was editor of the *Eclectic Review*, which had supported the idea of a Convention. Cox was unanimously called to the chair and stressed the importance of securing the co-operation of all. The meeting resolved to convene a conference of delegates 'representing all persons in these realms who repudiate the principle of a religious Establishment, and who are of opinion that this is a suitable method of commencing a serious movement against it'.[20] A list of 120 names for a provisional committee was drawn up and Cox agreed to act as Secretary. The three London men were appointed a sub-committee to set the provisional committee going. The good spirit of the meeting removed Cox's former doubts about the Convention idea.[21]

At this point, however, London recovered some of its lost ground. A group of radical ministers asked Miall to suspend publication of any report of the Leicester meeting for a fortnight, which he agreed to do. Meanwhile they held a meeting at which they decided not to wait any longer for their more conservative brethren and agreed to co-operate with the Midland ministers. The *Patriot* now announced its support for the Convention.[22] Most of the members of the provisional committee nominated at Leicester accepted nomination, and this committee proceeded to elect by post an executive committee of twenty-one to organize the conference. All but eight of those elected came from London.[23] The executive committee issued an address signed by Cox explaining the conference. It was a skilful reconciliation of the differences: the object of the conference was 'to act upon the conscience and

[18] Manning, *op. cit.*, pp. 391–2; *Minutes of the London Dissenting Ministers* (Dr Williams's Library), pp. 200–209. The Minutes carefully do not give the text of the resolutions under discussion, but it seems clear from the group proposing them and from the subsequent reference to religious liberty that the Anti-State Church Convention was under discussion.

[19] A meeting of Liverpool dissenters agreed to support a London movement on 20 November: *Nonconformist*, 22 November 1843, pp. 785–6.

[20] J. Waddington, *Congregational History: continuation to 1850* (London, 1878), pp. 568–9. Waddington mistakes the date.

[21] *Nonconformist*, 27 December 1843, pp. 865–6.

[22] The *Nonconformist*, 3 January 1844, p. 2.   [23] *Ibid.*, 7 February 1844, p. 77.

the heart of the dissenting community ... and the adoption of such a plan of organization as may secure unity of action without endangering freedom'; only when the time was ripe would the question be agitated inside and outside parliament, though it was hoped that the time would be soon.[24] This arrangement of emphases, was characteristic of the more moderate East London Religious Liberty Society whose joint secretary was J. Carvell Williams (later to be secretary of the Liberation Society) and which numbered 1,000 members by November 1843.[25] Miall's supporters in London were grouped in the smaller Metropolitan Anti-State Church Association. The move back to the moderate ground had begun.

The Conference of some 700 delegates, elected by congregations, public meetings or dissenting colleges, met at the Crown and Anchor Hotel, London, from 30 April to 2 May 1844. The only general representative body in England to send delegates was the Baptist Union, and there were only three ministers from leading London Congregational churches present. It is not true, however, that most of the delegates came from the Midlands: about one hundred did, but there were about ninety from London too.[26] The latter were mainly laymen, whilst the former included many ministers. There were several from Scotland, and also representatives of the Friends and the Unitarians. Complete Suffrage Union leaders like Sturge and Crawford (MP for Rochdale) were also there as delegates, though Feargus O'Connor and Percy Bunting (son of the Wesleyan leader, the Reverend Jabez Bunting) were both expelled for not having proper credentials.[27] The Conference heard a series of papers on various aspects of the establishment principle and resolved to set up a society to be called 'The British Anti-State Church Association'. Its constitution was similar to that of the Anti-Corn Law League with a Council of 500 and an executive committee of fifty. A full conference would be held every three years.[28] Dr Cox, Edward Miall, and Mr J. C. Hare (of the *Patriot*) were appointed secretaries, thus representing the various strands (ministerial and lay, radical and moderate) which supported the movement.

[24] *Ibid.*, 28 February 1844, p. 125; part quoted in Miall, *Life of Miall*, p. 93.

[25] The *Nonconformist*, 29 November 1843, p. 802. The East London Religious Liberty Society and its more extreme rival are described in A. H. Welch, *John Carvell Williams: the Nonconformist Watchdog* (unpublished Kansas Ph.D. thesis, 1968), pp. 9–16. There is a copy of this thesis in the Greater London Record Office.

[26] Stoughton, *op. cit.*, p. 272, is misleading when he says 'the greater proportion' or delegates came from the Midlands, and he has been copied by others, e.g. Addison, *op. cit.*, p. 91.

[27] *Nonconformist*, 6 May 1844, p. 302. This was a special issue reporting the Conference.

[28] The constitution is in *The Proceedings of the First Anti-State Church Conference, 1844* (London, 1844), pp. 149–54, and the *Nonconformist*, 15 May 1844, pp. 349–50. Cf. N. McCord, *The Anti-Corn Law League* (London, 1958), p. 164.

The Conference did not discuss politics and a suggestion that a petition be sent to parliament was withdrawn. This did not ease the suspicions of conservative dissenters like Vaughan, who launched the *British Quarterly Review* because he regarded the *Eclectic* under Price as having 'thrown itself into the hands of an extreme section of our body'.[29] Nor did the Conference involve many of the Unitarian whigs, though one or two were there. Methodists too were generally sparsely represented. But the Conference did succeed in bringing together various strands of moderate and radical dissent, and in particular united those such as Miall, who wanted an aggressive political movement, with those such as Cox, who preferred a defensive political stance. The origins of the Society thus help to explain the variations in its policy, the nature of its support, and the tensions these produced.

Article XV of the Society's constitution indicated the range of activities it contemplated.[30] The first four classes were concerned with education—the publication of tracts, employment of lecturers, assistance to local groups and general stimulation of interest; the next two envisaged work for the election of suitable Members of Parliament and support of them in parliament by petitions and memorials; clause 7 affirmed the desire to remove the question from party feeling and place it on religious grounds; and clause 8 committed the society to work for enactment of laws to secure religious liberty. However non-political the atmosphere of the 1844 Conference was, therefore, the way was left wide open for direct political action; and Miall's concept of education was as much concerned with the development of political consciousness as it was with a religious appeal to conscience. It was not easy in the early days to build up a national organization. The Act against Political Corresponding Societies of 1794 made provincial associations in correspondence with a central executive illegal, so the executive committee copied the Anti-Corn Law League and suggested the appointment of registrars in each district to receive subscriptions, keep a membership book and give advice on suitable lecturers and meetings for their district.[31] In some areas local committees were formed. Neither method was particularly successful financially, and in 1858–9 district agents paid out of central funds were appointed with rather more

[29] Quoted in Waddington, *op. cit.*, p. 575. For articles attacking and defending see *Congregational Magazine* (1844), pp. 392–4, and the *Eclectic Review* (1844), xvi, pp. 724–41.
[30] This article is reproduced in the *Eclectic Review* (1844), pp. 737–8, and in D. M. Thompson, *Nonconformity in the Nineteenth Century* (London, 1972), pp. 125–6. It is not in the extracts from the constitution quoted in H. J. Hanham, *The Nineteenth Century Constitution* (Cambridge, 1969), p. 430.
[31] *Nonconformist*, 14 August 1844, p. 588. Cf. McCord, *op. cit.*, p. 134.

success.[32] There were also sometimes difficulties in hiring rooms for meetings and in 1850 the railway bookstalls refused to sell the Society's publications.[33]

In the early years when the Society was finding its feet the publication of tracts and the organization of lecture tours were its main activities. Much time was spent by the literary subcommittee in sponsoring and examining publications. Efforts were also made to use the press. In 1854 the parliamentary committee agreed to spend up to five guineas on securing 'seven or eight very well written letters to be inserted in *The Times*, to place the Dissenters well with the non-dissenting political public'.[34] In 1855 the Society started its own magazine, *The Liberator*, which appeared monthly, and in 1860 H. S. Skeats (Miall's son-in-law) was appointed to act as a kind of research secretary for the Society.[35] This kind of activity remained vital even when the Society was more heavily committed to parliamentary and electoral action. In 1861 when the Society's bill to abolish Church rates was defeated in the Commons for the first time in five years, a massive programme of a hundred lectures and public meetings was organized, and special efforts were made to cultivate the support of the local liberal press. 'It is by incessant iteration that a new idea has to be hammered into the public mind,' reported a special subcommittee at this time, and they suggested 'No State favouritism' and 'No Monopoly' as suitable slogans.[36] The bicentenary of the Great Ejectment in 1862 was also seen as an opportunity to spread the Society's principles, though it took no formal part in the organization of the celebrations.[37] Again in 1865 it was decided to distribute free copies of *The Liberator* much more widely, including the public reading rooms of Mechanics' Institutes and other institutions.[38]

Tracts and lectures, however, needed a focus; and this was usually found in current parliamentary business. An example of the early methods used by the society is the (abortive) Irish Church agitation of 1850. The episode began in January when Miall reported to the executive committee that J. A. Roebuck (MP for Sheffield) intended to pro-

[32] *Liberation Society Executive Committee Minutes* (in Greater London Record Office), ii (A/LIB/2), m. 363, 29 October 1858; m. 986, 23 September 1859; m. 998, 11 November 1859.

[33] Miall, *Life of Miall*, p. 97; *Executive Minutes*, i (A/LIB/1), m. 334, 12 December 1850; m. 399, 20 February 1851.

[34] *Parliamentary Committee Minutes* (A/LIB/13), m. 19, 23 May 1854.

[35] W. H. Mackintosh, *Disestablishment and Liberation* (London, 1972), pp. 50–52; Welch, *op. cit.*, pp. 26–8, 104–5; *Executive Minutes*, ii, m. 1128, 30 November 1860; m. 1133, 21 December 1860.

[36] *Executive Minutes*, ii, m. 1206, 27 September 1861; m. 1229, 15 November 1861.

[37] *Nonconformist*, 8 May 1862, p. 386; Skeats and Miall, *op. cit.*, pp. 569–75; Mackintosh, *op. cit.*, p. 131.

[38] Welch, *op. cit.*, pp. 119–20.

pose a motion in the coming session on the Irish Church and was prepared to do so on the principles of the Association. A subcommittee was appointed to draft a motion and to recommend appropriate action. The proposals it made were typical of all the Society's agitations: resolutions of the executive committee on the matter were published in the press; local committees and registrars were circularized so that they might organize public meetings, local petitions to parliament, and memorials to MPs; an address to the public was published; forms of petition were prepared; and a public meeting in London was to be held to launch the agitation. Unfortunately Roebuck did not propose his motion until after Easter and so the programme of meetings was curtailed. Then the House was counted out before Roebuck's motion was reached.[39] Despite, or indeed because of, its unsatisfactory conclusion the episode is a good example of the Society's work. Experiences such as this stimulated the society to improve its organization. At the same time a closer relationship developed with nonconformist MPs who had been more firmly attached to the Whigs, such as Edward Baines the younger. Such a rapprochement had seemed possible in 1847 at the time of the controversy over Lord John Russell's new education scheme. Miall in the *Nonconformist* had supported the Central Nonconformist Committee formed on 26 Febrary 1847, of which Dr Robert Vaughan and Edward Baines were leading members. At a public meeting in Exeter Hall, London, with John Bright in the chair on 15 April, Miall and Baines spoke on the same platform for the first time; but Baines who had hitherto stood aloof from the Anti-State Church Association stressed his difference from Miall by pointing out that he was a life-long Whig.[40] When the government's scheme went through at the end of April, Miall expressed the hope that the forthcoming triennial conference of the ASCA would unite Dissent, but Baines did not attend.[41] After the electoral success of 1853, however, which produced nearly forty 'religious liberty' MPs, Baines and Miall moved closer together. The triennial conference of that year adopted Baines's suggestion for a new name for the society, which implied a wider programme than disestablishment. At the same conference Miall, who had become MP for Rochdale at the election, read a paper suggesting more direct links between the Society and parliament. As a result, a parliamentary subcommittee was set up in January 1854 and an electoral subcommittee

[39] *Executive Minutes*, i, m. 13, 10 January 1850; m. 27, 24 January 1850; m. 69, 7 March 1850; m. 158, 22 May 1850; m. 163, 29 May 1850.

[40] *Nonconformist*, 3 March 1847, p. 132; 16 April 1847, pp. 249–51; cf. *Eclectic Review* (1847), xxi pp. 108, 528–9, 635–55. For Baines, see D. Fraser, 'Edward Baines', above.

[41] *Nonconformist*, 28 April 1847, p. 269. Baines did not attend the 1850 Triennial Conference either.

in March 1855.[42] The result was a considerable shift in the emphasis of
the Society's activities and a much more systematic programme of
agitation.

The tasks of the parliamentary committee were to keep a careful
watch on parliamentary business, to develop contacts with friendly
MPs, and to decide on priorities among the questions the society wished
to pursue in parliament. Its chairman was Dr C. J. Foster, a Baptist who
lectured in law at University College, London. The least spectacular
part of its work was the examination of legislation to see whether it
would adversely affect dissenters. Often the bills concerned were local,
such as the Stoke Newington Church Bill of 1854 which was defeated
without a division because it was opposed by other Church interests as
well; but sometimes they were broader in scope, such as the Union of
Benefices Bill of 1860 which was only passed after most of the amendments sought by the committee had been accepted.[43] The larger questions required joint action with other groups, such as the agitation
against the religious profession clause in the 1861 Census which was
undertaken by a committee representing the society, the Dissenting
Deputies, and the Baptist, Independent, Unitarian, and Wesleyan
bodies. Another task was to support MPs who campaigned on issues in
which the society was interested. An early example was the support
given to James Heywood in his efforts to amend the Oxford and Cambridge University Bills of 1854 and 1856 so as to admit dissenters to
university degrees. Resolutions on the subject were advertised in nine-
teen newspapers and petition forms were circulated. In three months
391 petitions with 27,530 signatures were sent into parliament. Paying
tribute in 1865 to the Society's help, Heywood said that it was done very
quietly through the penny post.[44] The Society was also prepared to back
different sides in pursuing this policy: it supported Fagan's Roman
Catholic campaign against Ministers' Money in Ireland (a tax to support the Established Church) and also Spooner's protestant campaign
against the government grant to Maynooth.[45] Finally, the parliamentary committee initiated legislation of its own through sympathetic

[42] *Nonconformist*, 9 November 1853, pp. 902–5, 908; *Executive Minutes*, ii, m. 75,
23 January 1854; m. 329, 2 March 1855. Miall's paper, rather than the Religious
Census Report or the Crimean War (as suggested by Vincent, *op. cit.*, pp. 70–71)
seems to me to be the turning-point in the Society's activities, and was probably
stimulated by his own parliamentary experience.

[43] *Parliamentary Committee Minutes* (A/LIB/13), m. 11, 7 March 1854; m. 13, 13
March 1854; 25 June 1860; 9 July 1860; 26 September 1860. One of the amendments
limited its application to London.

[44] *Parliamentary Committee Minutes*, m. 5, 27 February 1854; m. 8, 7 March 1854;
8 June 1854; *Nonconformist*, 4 May 1865, p. 345.

[45] *Nonconformist*, 8 May 1856, p. 312, where Foster defended the policy publicly;
Parliamentary Committee Minutes, 16 February 1857.

members. The best example of this is the agitation over Church rates, for which the Society became largely responsible after 1853. The motion to introduce a bill was first carried in 1854; it got as far as a second reading in 1856 and completed all stages in the House of Commons in 1858 only to fail in the House of Lords. In 1861, 1862, and 1863, however, the bill lost its House of Commons majority and its sponsor, Sir John Trelawny, resigned further charge of it.[46] Another example, which shows that certain members of parliament were not merely agents of the society, is the Burials Bill of 1859. In January Foster was asked to prepare a bill authorizing interments by dissenting ministers in unconsecrated ground and to consult with Mr Massey, MP, over its introduction. Massey's response was that the draft contained too drastic a departure from the principles of the recent Burial Acts for him to introduce it, but he was prepared to introduce a bill to remedy the practical grievances complained of. The committee therefore prepared a new bill but Massey then had to withdraw because of a parliamentary appointment. The committee found another sponsor, but had to accept further amendments from him. By this time it was the end of the session—a good illustration of the hazards of parliamentary activity.[47]

Effective parliamentary action required careful organization and consideration of tactics. One of the keys to the Society's success was the 'whipping' system which it developed. From its inception the parliamentary committee sent circular letters to MPs on matters of importance. A good example is that of 22 May 1854 on Church rates, which read:

> Sir, You are earnestly requested to be in your place tomorrow at Four o'Clock to support Sir w. CLAY's Motion (first in the paper) for leave to bring in a Bill for the total abolition of Church-Rates. Being on a Tuesday, you are aware that it is not the duty of Government to make or keep a House.[48]

The first use of the word 'whip' comes in 1857 and Foster, as chairman, was still issuing whips in 1859. Sir Charles Douglas for a number of years acted as the society's whip on religious liberty issues, and for the Church Rates Bill in 1861 he was joined by Mr Dillwyn and Mr Hardcastle.[49] In 1860 Mr Hadfield requested a whip for his Offices

[46] *Parliamentary Committee Minutes*, 13 May 1863.

[47] *Parliamentary Committee Minutes*, m. 7, 19 January 1859; m. 34, 2 March 1859; mm. 38–40, 9 March 1859; m. 43, 25 March 1859; m. 58, 14 June 1859; m. 67, 15 July 1859; mm. 73–4, 2 August 1859.

[48] Loose copy in *Parliamentary Committee Minutes*, opposite p. 19.

[49] *Parliamentary Committee Minutes*, 16 February 1857, 19 February 1859, 8 February 1861.

Qualification Bill.[50] But whipping was only the end of the process. Division lists were analysed to see whether it was possible to secure a majority, as in 1854 over Church rates when a canvass revealed that the Bill could be read a second time against government and opposition.[51] Sometimes private memorializing of MPs might be more effective than general petitioning, as in 1860 when railway timetables were carefully examined to work out itineraries for committee members to visit the maximum number of MPs.[52] Again, parliamentary timing was important. In 1863 the committee went for an early second reading of their Church Rates Bill and asked their MPs to come up to London early.[53] Or a snap division might be tried, as with the success on the second reading of Hadfield's Offices Qualification Bill in 1863.[54] The committee also had to judge the best moment for calling in pressure from outside, and Sir John Trelawny paid tribute to the work done outside the House of Commons by men such as Foster in 1858 when the Church Rates Bill passed through all its Commons stages for the first time.[55]

Parliamentary work, however effective, was only half the battle, even if it was the half which required more continuous effort. The other half was electoral action. Systematic attempts by dissenters to influence elections can be traced back at least to the committee formed on 26 November 1834, which heard reports on likely candidates and constituencies.[56] In 1847 also, following the government's education cheme, a Dissenters' parliamentary committee had been formed and dissenters were asked to vote for only those candidates whose views on the state Church question were satisfactory. The campaign was hardly successful, but some comfort was drawn from the fact that many Whig candidates were elected only with Peelite support and that some impact had been made without registration or any other preparation.[57] After the experience of 1847 the Society was more cautious in its approach. In 1850 Miall had been due to read a paper on electoral action at the Triennial Conference, but not having time to prepare it moved a resolution instead. He was very careful to avoid any suggestion that the Society was seeking to dictate to people how they should vote.[58] At the 1852 election the executive committee was advised not to ask for Anti-

---

[50] *Ibid.*, m. 87, 4 February 1860.   [51] *Ibid.*, 8 June 1854.
[52] *Ibid.*, 21 and 27 December 1860.   [53] *Ibid.*, 30 January 1863.
[54] *Ibid.*, 3 March 1863.   [55] *Executive Minutes*, ii, m. 827, 25 June 1858.
[56] Note from the minutes of these meetings are in the possession of the Free Church Federal Council, now deposited in the London County Record Office. I owe this reference to Mr D. W. Bebbington.
[57] *Eclectic Review* (1847), xxi, pp. 635–55; xxii, pp. 1–19, pp. 103–24, pp. 354–82; Addison, *op. cit.*, p. 93; Cowherd, *op. cit.*, pp. 162–3; Gash, *op. cit.*, pp. 100–103.
[58] *Nonconformist*, 3 May 1850, p. 349. Cf. *Executive Minutes*, i, m. 18, 17 January 1850; m. 123, 25 April 1850.

State Church pledges because the issues were expected to be parliamentary reform and free trade. A circular was issued to electors suggesting questions that candidates might be asked, but no pledges were sought. Thirty-eight Dissenters were returned at the election, and the executive was told that most of them were identified with the Society and they represented some of the largest constituencies in the country. Miall was returned for Rochdale.[59]

In 1855 Samuel Morley, who had been chairman of the Dissenters' committee in 1847, became chairman of the Society's electoral sub-committee. One of its first tasks was to send out circulars to eleven county constituencies urging that an effort should be made to increase the number of religious liberty voters: agents were promised a fee of one shilling for each dissenting vote added to the register in the constituencies concerned. It was estimated that the cost of this would be from £70 to £100.[60] For the 1857 election much more elaborate arrangements were made: addresses were circulated, a statement of the subjects on which the Society would take action in the next parliament was provided, and a special election fund was established. Reports on the voting of MPs in the previous session were sent to the constituencies in large numbers and candidates were interviewed on their attitude to religious liberty questions. After the election the committee reported the winning of at least twenty seats but the loss of at least nine. Two of the gains were in places circularized in 1856. The nine losses included such friends as Miall, Clay, Heywood, and Pellatt.[61] How much influence the Society actually had is far from clear—*The Liberator* itself was not sure—but the executive committee was convinced of the value of the electoral committee's work and at its next meeting Dr Foster read a paper urging more systematic efforts at electoral registration.[62]

Early in 1859 Morley and Pryce, the Society's travelling organizer who was secretary of the electoral committee, resigned in order to concentrate on their work for the parliamentary reform committee,[63] and Foster and Carvell Williams were appointed to transact the business of the new electoral committee. Foster was to introduce candidates to constituencies and Williams was in charge of general action in the constituencies. The committee sat daily during the election: 5,000

[59] *Executive Minutes*, i, m. 707, 12 February 1852; m. 825, 26 June 1852; m. 940, 25 November 1852.

[60] *Executive Minutes*, ii, m. 604, 30 June 1856. The counties were Bedfordshire, Cambridgeshire, E. Norfolk, E. and W. Suffolk, N. Essex, E. Somerset, W. Gloucestershire, N. Wiltshire, and N. and S. Northumberland.

[61] *Ibid.*, m. 682, 9 March 1857; m. 685, 23 March 1857; m. 687, 6 April 1857.

[62] Vincent, *op. cit.*, pp. 72–3; Welch, *op. cit.*, pp. 77–8; *Executive Minutes*, ii, m. 695, 13 April 1857; m. 704, 20 April 1857.

[63] *Executive Minutes*, ii, m. 898, 19 January 1859; m. 925, 14 March 1859. Mackintosh (*op. cit.*, p. 60) completely confuses this.

copies of a circular to friends and an address to electors were distributed, together with an analysis of MPs' voting. The committee exerted its influence in favour of friendly candidates and suggested suitable nominees, but they transacted less of this business than in 1857, partly because there were fewer changes and partly because of the exertions of the parliamentary reform committee and the Ballot Society. They regretted that they had been unable to find an opening for Miall. Unfortunately the report of the committee is blank in the Executive's minutes.[64]

After the defeat of the Church Rate Bill in 1861, electoral policy again became tougher. It was decided that the parliamentary committee should act as the electoral committee, paying special attention to Wales. The shift in emphasis was indicated by Foster's resumption of his practice at the Bar as a common law and parliamentary counsel.[65] The Society's friends in the Oxfordshire, Lincoln, and Grimsby by-elections in January 1862 were urged to withhold support from candidates who declined to support the abolition of Church rates.[66] In the summer of 1863 Foster resigned as chairman of the parliamentary committee in order to emigrate to New Zealand, but it was decided not to fill the vacancy and instead to adopt a defensive parliamentary policy. All effort was concentrated on electoral action and in November a special conference was held in London. Morley moved a resolution expressing the conviction

> that the friends of Religious Equality have . . . less inducement than at any former period to subordinate to traditional party claims the serious responsibilities imposed on them by their conscientious convictions and . . . that the exercise of the parliamentary franchise with a primary view to obtain the recognition of their principles by the Legislature will not affect injuriously a single question of policy in which the country at large is interested.

But this delicately phrased warning was not enough for the more extreme spirits, and Alfred Illingworth of Bradford moved another resolution asking the executive to prevail on its supporters to back up their demands by threatening to withhold their votes.[67] This policy was sup-

[64] *Executive Minutes*, ii, m. 937, 25 March 1859; m. 944, 8 April 1859; m. 946, 27 April 1859; m. 948, 13 May 1859.

[65] *Ibid.*, m. 1217, 18 October 1861; m. 1224, 1 November 1861. See also Jones, *op. cit.*, pp. 215–22; P. M. H. Bell, *Disestablishment in Ireland and Wales* (London, 1969), pp. 20–21.

[66] *Executive Minutes*, iii (A/LIB/3), m. 13, 17 January 1862.

[67] *Parliamentary Committee Minutes*, memo, p. 135; Welch, *op. cit.*, pp. 139–40; *Nonconformist*, 18 November 1863, p. 919; 16 December 1863, p. 1005.

ported by similar conferences in Manchester and Bristol. In 1864 surveys were made of every constituency and the voting of MPs for the last thirty years; the information for electors was revised and a special agent, J. M. Hare, was appointed to visit the constituencies and consult with the leading friends of the Society and other liberal electors. It was decided to concentrate on thirty-three boroughs where there was the possibility of influencing the election mainly by making lukewarm supporters more active.[68] In the first six months of 1865 the Society was engaged in strenuous activity trying to secure favourable candidates in a number of seats, and they were successful in many places. This was as important as winning contested elections, and perhaps more so.

After the 1865 General Election the electoral committee reported triumphantly. As well as those places where they secured favourable candidates, they claimed success in six constituencies where negligent Liberals were defeated by Tories, the moral influence of which they felt to be of a wholesome kind.[69] They claimed that all but eight or ten of the Liberals were in favour of the total abolition of Church rates (though the minority included Gladstone and Roundell Palmer), and they observed that the Liberals who had lost seats belonged mainly to the old Whig party, whilst those who had gained them were advanced Liberals. Two of the executive committee and fifteen other subscribers were returned and the total number of nonconformists elected was about eighty-seven. But they regretted the failure to secure seats for Miall and Henry Richard, and Sir Charles Douglas's failure at Banbury. Eight hundred thousand bills and tracts had been circulated, and 1,500 copies of MPs' votes; perhaps not surprisingly therefore religious equality had been a more prominent issue in the election. But most important of all, they concluded from the result that the tough electoral policy, far from weakening the Liberals, had actually made them stronger—a conclusion which was to be fatal over the education question in 1874.[70] By contrast the 1868 election was an anti-climax. The Irish Church was the dominant issue, but as this was Gladstone's policy there was no need to seek pledges. Although the electoral fund only raised £700 instead of the target of £2,000, the electoral committee reported success with a Liberal majority of 114. Four members of the executive were returned (including Henry Richard) but Morley resigned after a well-publicized

[68] *Parliamentary Committee Minutes*, 13 January 1864; 3 February 1864; 17 February 1864; 30 September 1864; 21 October 1864; 10 November 1864. These were Andover, Ashburton, Aylesbury, Bath, Beverley, Birkenhead, Blackburn, Boston, Bridgnorth, Bury, Chester, Clitheroe, Cockermouth, Colchester, Denbigh, Dover, Esher, Frome, Grimsby, Halifax, Haverfordwest, Lichfield, Lincoln, Macclesfield, Marlborough, Northallerton, Portsmouth, St Ives, Salisbury, Stafford, Stoke-on-Trent, Stroud and Wareham.
[69] Lichfield, Wareham, Northallerton, E. Norfolk, W. Norfolk and Dover.
[70] *Executive Minutes*, iii, m. 563, 21 July 1865.

and controversial exchange in Bristol. Twenty supporters of the Society and a number of other nonconformists were elected, but three others were defeated and eleven others, including Miall, failed to secure seats. The total cost of the year's agitation, mainly on the Irish Church, was £3,145.[71] Whatever we may conclude about the Liberation Society's responsibility for Liberal success in 1865 and 1868, there is no doubt that they put in a considerable amount of work, especially in Wales.[72]

It was in Wales too that the Society's relationship to the local Liberal party organization was most direct, for there its work led to the foundation of registration societies.[73] Elsewhere it is more difficult to generalize because of the widely varying patterns of local political organization. In the boroughs the Society was only one group among several on the Liberal side, and its efforts seem to have been directed less at registration than at securing a favourable nomination through the efforts of the Society's friends among the leading Liberal supporters. Part of the value of Hare's visits to the borough constituencies in 1864–5 lay in the information he obtained about the precise weight and character of the leaders of the Liberal party in them.[74] In the county seats the electoral committee stimulated the creation of new freehold votes and the registration of those already qualified, and its direct access to dissenting chapels enabled it to do this without necessarily having to form registration societies. The strength of Dissent in the countryside and small market towns and the absence of the competing organizations which existed in the larger towns made these the ideal areas for the Society's influence. Here too its national organization provided a most effective advantage. Eleven county seats were considered in detail by the parliamentary committee in June 1865, and in five of them victories were secured in the election.[75] But it has to be remembered that, except in Wales where the religious issue could be presented as an overriding one, the Society was concerned to win support for particular measures rather than a political party as such: and the loss of Pryce and Morley to the parliamentary reform campaign in 1859 indicates the ever present danger of fragmentation in single-issue politics. It was after 1868 rather than before that the Society came to tie its fortunes directly to the

[71] *Parliamentary Committee Minutes*, 10 June 1868, 2 December 1868; *Executive Minutes*, iv (A/LIB/4), m. 202, 4 December 1868; E. Hodder, *Life of Samuel Morley* (London, 1887), p. 276 ff.

[72] Bell, *op. cit.*, pp. 107–9.

[73] Vincent, *op. cit.*, p. 71; Jones, *op. cit.*, pp. 221–3.

[74] *Executive Minutes*, iii, 21 July 1865; *Parliamentary Committee Minutes*, 1864–5, *passim*.

[75] They were N. Essex, S. Essex,* N. Hants,* N. Herts, W. Kent, N. Shropshire,* S. Shropshire, N. Warwickshire,* N. Wilts, S. Wilts, N. Yorks.* (Asterisks indicate the seats which were won.)

Liberal party as a political organization. It is also possible that the decline of nonconformist influence in local Liberal parties owed much to their being completely swamped in the large borough electorates after 1867: and they may have lost more by the merging of small boroughs in county constituencies after 1885 than they gained by the enfranchisement of the rural labourer.

Who then were the people who supported the Liberation Society? The Society always stressed that it was not an exclusively nonconformist body, though its constitution acknowledged a special mission to professed nonconformists.[76] But in 1853 it declined to unite with the Dissenting Deputies because it could not narrow its basis,[77] and in its parliamentary agitation it depended on the support of liberal anglicans like Lushington, Trelawny, and others. Nevertheless the Society was always a predominantly nonconformist enterprise, and within nonconformity it drew its main support from the old dissent. Baptists too seem to have been more solidly behind it than Congregationalists: Miall was a Congregationalist, as was Carvell Williams, but the conservative dissenters who held aloof were mainly Congregationalists too; whilst J. P. Mursell of Leicester, who pushed Miall on in 1840–41 was a Baptist, as were Cox, Price, and Foster. Baptist churches and associations also seem to have been more ready to send delegates to the triennial conferences.[78] There was some support from Free Methodists—Robert Eckett sat on the executive committee for a time—and the *Wesleyan Chronicle* hoped that Wesleyan laymen might involve themselves in the Anti-State Church Conference in 1844.[79] A special attempt was made in 1860 to secure the support of those methodists who opposed Church rates. There had been a reaction in the Wesleyan Conference of 1860, led by the Reverend W. M. Punshon, against the conservative evidence given by the Reverend G. Osborn and Percy Bunting to the House of Lords select committee on Church rates in 1859, and the Society appointed a special agent for three months to cultivate methodist support.[80] Generally, however, methodists were not prominent in the Society, an important weakness as they were the largest bloc in nonconformity.

The Society also seems to have been, at least in its early days, more successful among the young than the old. Young men's associations had

[76] *Constitution*, article XV, clause 3.
[77] *Executive Minutes*, i, m. 933, 17 March 1853; m. 947, 23 March 1853; the *Nonconformist*, 23 February 1853, pp. 154–5.
[78] For the radicalism of Baptists, see Faulkner, *op. cit.*, pp. 100–102.
[79] *Nonconformist*, 3 January 1844, p. 2.
[80] *Executive Minutes*, ii, m. 1228, 15 November 1861; *Gladstone Papers*, B.M. Add. MSS. 44754, ff. 145–57; Vincent, *op. cit.*, p. 70. Interestingly Punshon's protest in 1860 is not mentioned in F. W. Macdonald, *Life of W. M. Punshon* (London, 1888).

been established in conjunction with voluntary Church societies in the 1830s and it was the Young Men's Committee against the Factories Bill in London which formed the Metropolitan Anti-State Church Association in 1843.[81] Miall himself was only thirty-two when he came to London to start the *Nonconformist* in 1841. Support for the proposed Anti-State-Church Conference was received from the students at Homerton College, Glasgow Congregational College, Western College, Exeter, and Pontypool College; and it is significant that the Conference made provision for the representation of dissenting colleges. The Metropolitan Collegiate Association, representing the London theological students, passed resolutions supporting the Conference on 9 February 1844 with six dissentients in a meeting of about sixty, and a considerable number of students attended the meeting of the Metropolitan Anti-State Church Association to elect representatives on 20 March.[82] Homerton and Highbury Colleges demanded that their students should withdraw from the Association and the *Nonconformist* noted bitterly that no such action was taken when they protested at the Factories Bill. Dr Pye Smith prevented serious action being taken against the Homerton students, but at the Glasgow Congregational Academy nine students were expelled for political activities.[83] This appeal to youth was not lost. Mr Kingsley, the Society's travelling agent, reported on the enthusiasm in Manchester in 1853:

> Very large body of young men employed in the various warehouses & severally connected with the Chapels, Sunday Schools & other educational institutions of the Town, who are ready & most anxious to give their help in any way in their power.[84]

Miall also expressed his faith in the Sunday school teachers, whom he regarded as the very salt of nonconforming society and contrasted unfavourably with the prestige-loving dissenting participants in municipal politics and the ministers who came into contact mostly with these better off persons.[85] As late as 1867 the executive committee arranged a conference of young men in London, showing that it had not forgotten the importance of the group. The support of the young in the 1840s may

[81] Skeats and Miall, *op. cit.*, p. 477; *Nonconformist*, 9 August 1843, p. 546.

[82] *Nonconformist*, 13 December 1843, p. 833; 3 January 1844, p. 2; 24 January 1844, p. 46; 31 January 1844, p. 61; 27 March 1844, p. 189. The Glasgow letter was signed by Alexander Hannay, later Secretary of the Congregational Union.

[83] *Nonconformist*, 3 April 1844, p. 205; 7 August 1844, p. 558; J. Medway, *Memoir of John Pye Smith* (London, 1853), pp. 471–2.

[84] *Executive Minutes*, i, m. 925, 10 March 1853.

[85] *Nonconformist*, 25 October 1843, p. 721; 6 December 1843, p. 817. The conflict between ministers and Sunday School teachers, especially in Methodism, is one of the themes in Ward, *op. cit.*

explain the 'growth' of the Society's influence in the 1850s and 1860s, just as the enthusiasm of the young of those decades for other causes might explain its 'decline'.

Miall also hoped to appeal to the 'serious poor', but the evidence here is scanty and difficult to assess. The report on the financial recovery of 1860 noted that £400 of the increase in giving (about 80 per cent) was in subscriptions of under a guinea, so that a majority of the 1,500 new subscribers must have been in this category. The same was true of Welsh support for the Society.[86] But the great financial support came from the few: £8,000 of the special fund in the 1860s came from 133 people; and in the early 1870s the Society was making rather vain efforts to increase its working class support.[87] It is interesting that the first three district agents appointed in 1858 to cover Yorkshire, Somerset, and Gloucestershire, and the eastern counties were the proprietor of a temperance hotel, a Quaker grocer, and a travelling agent for a building society.[88]

Further light on the nature of the Society's support comes from an examination of its geographical spread (see Appendix at the end of this chapter). A report on the financial position of the Society in 1850 showed that seventy-one towns had efficient registrars or local committees: the majority of these were in the south and did not include any of the large industrial towns other than Birmingham and Sheffield.[89] In another 110 towns subscriptions were received in various ways, but it was thought that they could be doubled by an efficient canvass: again these were mainly in the south. No subscriptions were received from 133 towns: nearly a quarter of these were in the north, a higher proportion of northern towns than in the first two groups. Finally twenty-one towns had been canvassed but required further canvassing: nearly two thirds of these were in the north and the group included all the largest towns in the country apart from Liverpool.[90] Too much emphasis should not be placed on one survey early in the Society's history, but it does indicate that the Society's strength lay in provincial market towns in the south and midlands rather than in the northern industrial towns. The constituencies where the Society claimed electoral successes in 1857 and

[86] *Executive Minutes*, ii, m. 1099, 3 August 1860; Jones, *op. cit.*, p. 206.

[87] S. M. Ingham, 'The Disestablishment Movement in England, 1868–74', *Journal of Religious History* (1964), pp. 47–51; 56–7.

[88] *Executive Minutes*, ii, m. 863, 29 October 1858.

[89] Nearly two-thirds of these towns had a population of less than 10,000. The largest were Birmingham, Sheffield, Bolton, Leicester, Plymouth, Derby, York, Dudley, Stroud, Southampton, Halifax, Ipswich, Chatham, Oxford, Cambridge, Worcester, Northampton, Bilston and Reading. See Appendix 1.

[90] *Executive Minutes*, i, m. 188, 27 June 1850. Analysis is complicated by the fact that some towns appear in more than one category, but this does not unduly distort the overall picture.

1865 were also more often small boroughs or counties than the large industrial boroughs.[91] This has to be set against the fact that small market towns vastly outnumbered northern industrial towns, a disproportion reflected in the distribution of parliamentary seats; but it is nevertheless clear that the Society's strength did not lie primarily in the new industrial centres, and this reflects the distribution of dissent nationally. As Professor Vincent has shown, the importance of the industrial areas lay in the fact that they provided the largest sums of money. In 1860 Lancashire and Yorkshire contributed £572 and £385 respectively to the Society: the next largest amounts were £254 from Gloucestershire and £128 from Essex.[92] Only in Wales, which contributed very little before the early 1860s, was the Society stronger in industrial areas than elsewhere.[93] Thus the goegraphical and the social evidence shows that the Society's Radicalism did not come from the industrial working classes.

The Liberation Society had to live with three kinds of internal tension: between London and the provinces; between its long-term and its short-term aims; and between religion and politics. The first two affected several pressure groups of that type; the last was peculiar to the Society because of the nature of its agitation.

The Liberation Society has often been represented as a triumph for the provinces over London. This was the contemporary view. Miall in 1843 was suspicious of any suggestion that a London-based society should take the lead and argued for a representative conference on these grounds.[94] When the conference was held, Dr Thomas Price, editor of the *Eclectic Review*, spoke forcefully in the same vein: the reason that some had held aloof, he said, was that

> there were now taken out of the hands of individuals or cliques whether in London, in Manchester, in Birmingham, or in Liverpool, the control and management of dissenting matters. (Cheers.) They were now placing their affairs where they ought to be, in the hands of the dissenting body itself. (Renewed Cheers.) Previously, [he continued], conferences were organized by London wire-pullers.[95]

But, unlike the Anti-Corn Law League which was also suspicious of London, the Anti-State Church Association made London its head-

[91] *Ibid.*, ii, m. 687, 6 April 1857; iii, m. 563, 21 July 1865.
[92] Vincent, *op, cit.*, p. 69. The number of places from which subscriptions were received went up from 400 to 517 after the financial reforms of 1858–9: *Executive Minutes*, ii, m. 1099, 3 August 1860.
[93] Jones, *op. cit.*, pp. 204–6.
[94] *Nonconformist*, 22 November 1843, pp. 785–6, 787–8, 792.
[95] *Nonconformist*, 6 May 1844, p. 311.

quarters.[96] Provincial dissent wanted London to take the lead, and the Leicester ministers sent their memorial to the London dissenting bodies before they acted on their own. Nor did the constitution effectively protect provincial interests. The representative conference met triennially and the Council annually: the executive committee was inevitably dominated by London because that was where it met. Only a fraction of the executive committee of fifty regularly attended meetings—the average attendance was six or seven. Miall said, when challenged on this point at the 1856 Triennial Conference, that country members were always consulted on matters of importance even though they attended meetings only occasionally: but an examination of the Minutes does not suggest that policy decisions were ever changed as a result of this.[97] When the Dissenting Deputies, who set up their parliamentary committee at about the same time as the Liberation Society, rejected a suggestion for constant communication, they added that free communication between the two would be useful, 'the Dissenting Deputies as representing Metropolis, [the] Society the Provinces': the Liberation Society was not flattered by the suggestion.[98] By this time Miall has to be counted as a Londoner, but in any case he was not the regular attender at executive meetings that his son suggested: John Carvell Williams for all his Welsh ancestry was also effectively a Londoner and he rarely missed a meeting of the executive. By 1865 he was clearly the master-mind of the society. Miall and Williams were also responsible for closer co-operation with the Deputies in the 1860s, when Williams was a Deputy himself.[99] Obviously the executive was sensitive to provincial opinion, particularly because the Society's work depended on provincial financial support; and occasionally provincial pressure forced the executive's hand, as at the London Conference on electoral action in 1863, with Illingworth's bolder resolution. But generally London provided the lead and the provinces were content to follow.

This is also brought out by looking at the tension which existed between the Society's long-term and short-term aims. The long-term aim of the Society was the disestablishment and disendowment of the State Churches in England and Wales, Ireland, and Scotland. In Miall's view this differentiated it from those groups which simply wished to tackle specific grievances. Yet Edward Baines, MP, congratulated the 1859 Triennial Conference for attacking practical grievances with practical measures. At the same conference a country speaker who asked the executive to bring the question of Church and State before the legislature

[96] McCord, *op. cit.*, pp. 40–54.
[97] *Nonconformist*, 8 May 1856, p. 312.
[98] *Executive Minutes*, ii, m. 181, 9 June 1854; Manning, *op. cit.*, pp. 278–9.
[99] Welch, *op. cit.*, p. 25; cf. Miall, *Life of Miall*, p. 96; *Executive Minutes*, iii, m. 575, 15 September 1865; Manning, *op. cit.*, pp. 394–5.

at an early time was told by Dr Foster that this would throw the question back three or four years, and Miall appealed to the Conference to trust the executive![100] So much for London wire-pullers. The fact was that the issues which really rallied support for the Society were the practical grievances. The danger which faced the Society in the late 1860s was that as grievances were settled the ultimate issue became more remote not closer at hand. It also became clear that the stress on disestablishment could actually lose the support of some in parliament who would admit that dissenters had legitimate grievances. This seems to have been one result of the cross-examination of Foster and Morley by the House of Lords select committee on Church rates in 1859, when they were persuaded to 'admit' that they viewed the abolition of Church rates as a step to disestablishment.[101] Disraeli, who had always opposed the suggestions of some Conservative Churchmen for a Church rates compromise, then played the 'Church in danger' card in his Amersham speech (December 1860) and the Society lost its anti-Church rates majority in the Commons.[102] Yet another set of pressures prevented the Society from adopting a pure grievance approach and trying to settle for the best compromise they could get. In 1856 the Society supported government amendments falling short of total abolition and were criticised at the Triennial Conference for this: Miall defended the action by saying that they were not an anti-Church rate society.[103] Again in 1860 the parliamentary committee advised the executive to stick to a policy of unconditional abolition, and this was accepted, lest the campaign in the country be weakened by doubts.[104] In the end, of course, success only came on the Church rates issue by the acceptance of a compromise. It seemed that practical success depended on moderating the demands of the Society's supporters in the country.

The third tension was rather different: was the Society religious or political? Those who opposed its formation said it was too political: 'many of us are opposed to a confederation, half religious and half political, entitled the Anti-Church and (*sic*) State Conference', wrote John Angell James of Birmingham, whilst John Blackburn in the *Congregational Magazine* condemned it because it wished 'to employ worldly influence for the advancement of Christian objects, and to use

[100] *Nonconformist*, 9 June 1859, pp. 449–51. The same point was raised in 1865: *Nonconformist*, 4 May 1865, 348–9.

[101] *Parliamentary Papers:* H. C. 1859 (2), v, pp. 100–101, 185–202.

[102] W. F. Monypenny and G. E. Buckle, *Life of Benjamin Disraeli* (Revised edn., London, 1929), ii, pp. 87–8, 90–91. The Speech was actually delivered at Prestwood: I owe this information to Mr. C. J. Howard.

[103] *Executive Minutes*, ii, m. 531, 19 March 1856; m. 607, 3 July 1856; *Nonconformist*, 8 May 1856, pp. 310–11.

[104] *Parliamentary Committee Minutes*, 15 October 1860; *Executive Minutes*, ii, m. 1113, 19 October 1860.

Christian Churches for the promotion of political objects'. It was thus open to the same objections as the State Church itself.[105] It should be stressed that these men did not believe in establishment, but they thought that the spiritual truth of this position could only be demonstrated by spiritual witness.[106] Moreover the Evangelical Alliance, which James fostered, was prepared to take a political stance on certain matters, especially 'No Popery' issues. In 1845 the Anti-State Church group retired from the Anti-Maynooth Conference because they felt the 'No Popery' objection too shallow: only a consistent stand on all establishments would do.[107] It is, in fact, very difficult to see any fundamental difference between evangelical politics and liberationist politics, just as there is little real difference between what critics called 'political dissent' and what might now be called the 'political anglicanism' of someone like Disraeli. What is important is that contemporaries thought there was a difference. Miall always made it clear that his grounds for belief in disestablishment were ultimately religious, but the Liberation Society, whilst not abandoning this position, gradually moved in practice to a more political emphasis. This was apparent from the change of constitution in 1853, when the declaratory principle of 1844 was deleted with the explicit purpose of opening the society as wide as possible.[108] It was not until 1874, when John Morley and one or two other agnostic politicians became active in the Society, that it ever really attracted any non-religious people. Morley believed that the society had to recognize that it must be political, and this may be why the Reverend R. W. Dale, who always admired Miall, found that the presence of some Liberationists 'made it impossible to discuss a great religious question on religious principles'.[109] But Dale was more of a theologian than any of his Free Church contemporaries and this remark probably applies more to the later period than the earlier. The Society has been criticized for being too religious: certainly the overwhelming majority of its members were always nonconformist, but it remains an open question as to whether religion or politics was uppermost in their minds.

Finally, how successful was the Liberation Society? Much depends on the criterion of success adopted. It did succeed in building up a significant organization and financial structure. Though they always moaned about their debt, they raised significantly higher sums than comparable

[105] Stoughton, *op. cit.*, p. 273; *Congregational Magazine* (1844), p. 394.
[106] Stoughton, *op. cit.*, pp. 119–20.
[107] Skeats and Miall, *op. cit.*, pp. 503–5; Cowherd, *op. cit.*, pp. 159–60. E. R. Norman, 'The Maynooth Question of 1845'; *Irish Historical Studies*, xv (1966–7), pp. 430–36.
[108] *Nonconformist*, 9 November 1853, pp. 902–5.
[109] Welch, *op. cit.*, pp. 205–12; Ingham, *op. cit.*, pp. 55–6; A. W. W. Dale, *Life of R. W. Dale* (London, 1905), pp. 378, 386–7.

organizations.[110] Their organization certainly won the respect of their opponents.[111] But in the attainment of their policy objectives they were less successful. At the Triennial Conference of 1865, Miall claimed four achievements.[112] Only one of these was actually complete—the defeat of the attempt to extend the establishment to the colonies. The others were all, he suggested, accepted in principle. One was the granting of equal and unrestricted civil and political rights to all nonconformists. This was virtually completed in the next three years with the Qualification for Offices Act, 1866, the Dublin Professorships Act, the Transubstantiation Declaration Act, and the Offices and Oaths Act, 1867, and the abolition of University Tests followed in 1871. Another principle was the end of taxation for religious purposes. The most obvious example of this, of course, was Church rates. Compulsory Church rates were abolished in 1868 when Gladstone carried his bill against the government. But in the general thanks and congratulations afterwards only Sir Charles Douglas hinted gently that the outcome fell short of the Society's stated policy of entire and unconditional abolition.[113] Gladstone himself hoped that voluntary Church rates would survive in the countryside with little change, and the fact that he was mistaken should not be allowed to obscure his crucial role in the final stage.[114] Despite its majority in the Commons the Liberation Society realized that it would be difficult to get total abolition through the Lords: they were therefore in a weak position to negotiate with Gladstone, even though they were unhappy with his compromise, and may even have expected it to fail as previous attempts had done. Gladstone's position was strengthened by the fact that he knew that a majority of nonconformists supported his compromise: he was in touch with moderate Congregationalists and Wesleyans.[115] His remark in a letter to the Society afterwards that he appreciated the 'loyal and considerate' conduct of the Abolitionists is more subtle than it might appear.[116] The extent to which the Society could claim success is ambiguous. Even more is

[110] Vincent, *op. cit.*, pp. 69–70; H. J. Hanham, *Elections and Party Management* (London, 1959), pp. 140, 413–19. The Society's debt was never less than £600 p.a. and sometimes as high as £1,600 in the later 1850s: *Executive Minutes*, ii, m. 973, 15 July 1859.

[111] *Executive Minutes*, ii, m. 1206, 27 September 1861; Bell, *op. cit.*, pp. 18–19; R. Masheder, *Dissent and Democracy* (London, 1864).

[112] *Nonconformist*, 4 May 1865, pp. 342–3.

[113] *Executive Minutes*, iv (A/LIB/4), m. 156, 7 August 1868; m. 165, 11 September 1868.

[114] *Gladstone Papers*, B.M. Add. MSS. 44411, f. 5.

[115] *Executive Minutes*, iv, m. 20, 24 January 1868; m. 56, 20 March 1868; *Parliamentary Committee Minutes*, 7 February 1868, 6 March 1868; *Gladstone Papers*, B.M. Add. MSS. 44188, ff. 31, 68; 44410, f. 110; 44754, ff. 145–57. Williams's account of the settlement in Skeats and Miall, *op. cit.*, pp. 595–7, is interesting in this context.

[116] *Executive Minutes*, iv, m. 165, 11 September 1868.

this the case with Miall's final claim—that the right of the people to deal with ecclesiastical establishments and the national property appropriated to their support was increasingly recognized. The Church of England never was disestablished, and the Society played a secondary role in Irish disestablishment. In 1865, whilst suggesting a bold parliamentary policy, Miall said that Irish disestablishment was not something for the Society to initiate, but should be supported if introduced by others; and the executive did not decide on a general campaign until July 1867.[117] Here too Gladstone's decision was crucial; here again he had the support of more nonconformists than just the Liberationists; and when drafting his bill he kept the society at arm's length.[118] The Society's main achievement probably lay in persuading the catholics to accept disendowment rather than insisting on concurrent endowment.[119]

This analysis makes it clear that the major successes of the Society were achieved in co-operation with others. To suggest that ultimate success was due to the participation of one group alone is therefore misleading.[120] The Liberation Society had two things to contribute to these joint efforts: its leadership and its national organization. Its leaders may well have been more important as individuals in nonconformist politics than as representatives of the Society: Edward Miall through the *Nonconformist* and John Carvell Williams through his tireless organizing capacity, to name but two. The joint committee on the 1861 Census passed a special vote of thanks to Williams, but did not publish it for fear that the public would identify the committee too closely with the Liberation Society.[121] The organization of the Society, though Skeats and Miall may have exaggerated its democratic character, was based on a clearly identifiable constituency in the dissenting chapels and organizations, and may have given a voice to lay dissenting opinion that did not emerge so clearly through the parallel Baptist and Congregational unions.[122] The realization that the Society had to work with others, led Williams to believe that it could only be successful if it co-operated with the Liberals from within, a policy which, as Vincent points out, won a number of concessions but left dissenters further than ever from their theoretical objective.[123] Attempts to blackmail the Liberals in order to get more, with the exception of 1865, only misfired. The fact that the Radicals coalesced with the Whigs to form the

[117] *Parliamentary Committee Minutes*, 15 November 1865; *Executive Minutes*, iii, 24 July 1867; E. R. Norman, *The Catholic Church and Ireland in the Age of Rebellion* (London, 1965), pp. 177–81; 325–30.
[118] Bell, *op. cit.*, pp. 107–8, 115.   [119] Norman, *op. cit.*, p. 325.
[120] Manning, *op. cit.*, pp. 183–95, does not mention the Liberation Society in his account of the Church rates agitation.
[121] *Parliamentary Committee Minutes*, 16 July 1860.
[122] Skeats and Miall, *op. cit.*, pp. 533–4.
[123] Welch, *op. cit.*, pp. 159–66, 175; Vincent, *op. cit.*, p. 76.

new Liberal party deprived nonconformists of the possibility of playing one off against the other, and they never stood to gain anything from Conservatives.

> They were formidable in agitation; they were effective in obstruction. . . . What they could not do was to formulate and impose a policy of their own.[124]

Professor Gash's verdict on the dissenters of the 1830s and 1840s holds good for the Liberation Society in the next two decades. They were able to agitate and obstruct, as over the 1861 Census and Church rates. They made the Church rates issue a major parliamentary question: 547 MPs voted in the division on the second reading of the Abolition Bill in March 1861.[125] They made the Irish Church an issue in England.[126] But they were not able to ensure that their policy was adopted. Like the Anti-Corn Law League, they had to see others take the final decisions.[127] But who does deserve the credit: the person who takes the decision, or those who make it necessary for a decision to be taken? Perhaps there is yet some truth in the words of Edward Miall:

> Though comparatively unknown, the supporters of the Liberation Society are the Ironsides of modern times who are content to gain victories for religious freedom, the laurels of which will be gathered by other hands.[128]

Further Reading

Nearly all the published material available for following up the story of the Liberation Society has been referred to in the footnotes. The recently published history of the Society, *Disestablishment and Liberation* by W. H. Mackintosh (London, 1972) provides a narrative but lacks any critical analysis. A. H. Welch's unpublished Ph.D. thesis, *John Carvell Williams: The Nonconformist Watchdog* (Kansas, 1968) is much better, though less comprehensive. The most penetrating analysis in print is I. G. Jones, 'The Liberation Society and Welsh Politics, 1844–1868', *Welsh History Review*, i, 1961, to which may be added the cameo in J. Vincent, *The Formation of the Liberal Party* (London, 1966), pp. 65–76. H. S. Skeats & C. S. Miall, *History of the Free Churches of England, 1688–1891* (London, 1891), pp. 470–612, provide a favourable treatment, not

[124] Gash, *op. cit.*, p. 107.
[125] *Executive Minutes*, ii, m. 1149, 8 March 1861.
[126] See the tribute by O'Neill Daunt: Norman, *op. cit.*, p. 325.
[127] Cf. McCord, *op. cit.*, p. 208.
[128] *Nonconformist*, 7 May 1868, p. 433.

always accurate in detail, by two members of the Society. W. G. Addison, *Religious Equality in Modern England* (London, 1944), pp. 78–144, gives a general history of dissenters' battles in the period. The most detailed political treatment of the beginning of the period is in N. Gash, *Reaction and Reconstruction in English Politics* (Oxford, 1965), pp. 60–118, which may be supplemented by R. G. Cowherd, *The Politics of English Dissent* (New York, 1956), especially chapter 10. On the later period there is useful material in S. M. Ingham, 'The Disestablishment Movement in England, 1868–74', *Journal of Religious History*, iii, 1964; P. M. H. Bell, *Disestablishment in Ireland and Wales* (London, 1969), pp. 17–21; and H. J. Hanham, *Elections and Party Management* (London, 1959), pp. 117–24, 170–79.

Appendix—*Towns listed as having active local committees or registrars in 1850 with population in 1851*

Birmingham (Warwicks)	232,841	Margate (Kent)	9,107
Sheffield (Yorks)	135,310	Leek (Staffs)	8,877
Bolton (Lancs)	61,171	Brentford (Middx)	8,870
Leicester (Leics)	60,584	Darwen (Lancs)	7,020
Plymouth (Devon)	52,221	St Albans (Herts)	7,000
Derby (Derbys)	40,609	Newbury (Berks)	6,574
York (Yorks)	40,359	Rugby (Warwicks)	6,317
Dudley (Worcs)	37,962	Kingston (Surrey)	6,279
Stroud (Gloucs)	36,535	Alnwick (Northbland)	6,231
Southampton (Hants)	35,305	Dartford (Kent)	5,763
Halifax (Yorks)	33,582	Bishop's Stortford (Herts)	5,280
Ipswich (Suffolk)	32,914	Leominster (Herefs)	5,214
Chatham (Kent)	28,424	Kettering (Northants)	5,125
Oxford (Oxfs)	27,843	Dewsbury (Yorks)	5,033
Cambridge (Cambs)	27,815	Walthamstow (Essex)	4,959
Worcester (Worcs)	27,528	Tonbridge (Kent)	4,539
Northampton (Northants)	26,657	Dunstable (Beds)	3,589
Bilston (Staffs)	23,527	Farnham (Surrey)	3,515
Reading (Berks)	21,456	Dorking (Surrey)	3,490
Gloucester (Gloucs)	17,572	Coggeshall (Essex)	3,484
Boston (Lincs)	17,518	Newmarket (Suffolk)	3,356
Leamington (Warwicks)	15,692	Braintree (Essex)	2,836
Taunton (Somerset)	14,176	Hemel Hempstead (Herts)	2,727
Barnsley (Yorks)	13,437	Blandford (Dorset)	2,504
Scarborough (Yorks)	12,915	Lutterworth (Leics)	2,446
Ramsgate (Kent)	11,838	Long Buckby (Northants)	2,341
Darlington (Durham)	11,228	Market Harborough (Leics)	2,325
Wisbech (Cambs)	10,594	Royston (Herts)	2,061
Stockton (Durham)	9,808	Stoney Stratford (Bucks)	1,757
Poole (Dorset)	9,255	Staplehurst (Kent)	1,660

Appendix—*cont.*

Kelvedon (Essex)	1,633	Bugbrook (Northants)	860
Billericay (Essex)	1,533	Bramfield (Suffolk)	740
Southminster (Essex)	1,482	Aldwincle (Northants)	540
Coleford (Somerset)	1,372	Kington (Herefs)	229
Brill (Bucks)	1,311	Nailsworth (Gloucs)	No figure
Clipstone (Northants)	865		given

Population is taken from the borough tables wherever possible. Using the groupings of counties followed in the Census, 38 of the above places are in the southern counties, south Midlands and eastern counties; 17 are in the north and west Midlands; 11 are in Yorkshire, the north-west and northern counties; and 5 are in the south-west.

10

David Urquhart and the Foreign Affairs Committees

Richard Shannon

Urquhart and the Urquhartites have been unusually problematical for historians who, as a trade, tend to be excessively non-plussed by a phenomenon which initially presents the difficulty of deciding whether or not it is to be taken seriously. Urquhart can never be scrubbed up and made presentable for any intellectually respectable contemporary taste. Yet he impressed Marx,[1] King William IV, and Palmerston himself, as well as high officials in the Foreign Office. The electors of Stafford were proud to send Urquhart to the House of Commons as a Tory in 1847. That the central cause of his crusade, the impeachment of Lord Palmerston as a Russian agent who conducted Britain's affairs, including the Crimean War, under Russian supervision, with the flower of the political establishment more or less in collusion with him, that this cause gained sufficient credence to float some kind or degree of popular agitation, is a phenomenon of illuminating potential. Most by far of the attention paid to Urquhart has related to the affairs of the Near East. He is also of minor interest to historians of Chartism, for it was among Chartists in 1839 and 1840 that Urquhart first conceived the idea of harnessing the well meant but misdirected energies of radical working men to the service of his own crusade. But more needs to be known about Urquhart's doctrines, and the nature of their appeal to a significant segment of popular opinion in the middle years of the nineteenth century. Above all, a more comprehensive view is needed of the relationship of the response to Urquhart's appeal to the general theme of popular dissent, especially in the era when the Chartist movement was disintegrating and alternative modes of dissident expression were seeking a voice.

[1] H. M. Hyndman, with characteristic tactlessness, went out of his way to express amazement at the extent to which Marx swallowed Urquhart's fantastic theories about Russian evil and Turkish virtue 'with a lack of direct investigation that surprised me in a man of so critical a mind'. H. M. Hyndman, *The Record of an Adventurous Life* (1911), p. 274. For Marx's curious relationship with Urquhart see Robert Payne, *The Unknown Karl Marx* (1972), pp. 144-5.

The quirkiness of Urquhart's beliefs had much to do with the quirkiness of his upbringing. He was born in 1805 at Cromarty, the younger son by a second marriage of David Urquhart, titular head of the clan Urquhart of Cromarty. His father died when he was a child and his mother exposed him in turn to French Catholicism at Sorèze, to a violent dose of Calvinism at Geneva at the age of fifteen, followed by another dose of Catholicism in Spain. His education was wholly irregular and without discipline. Being constantly in delicate health, he was coddled and indulged. Moreover, his mother, herself well-connected, impressed upon Urquhart the importance of being an Urquhart of that Ilk; patrician hauteur remained the most prominent single ingredient of Urquhart's character. His patrimony was modest but sufficient for a gentlemanly existence. He was a Tory of the cradle. In 1827 his mother's connection with Jeremy Bentham and through him with John Bowring and the London Greek committee took Urquhart off on a Byronic quest in the service of Greek liberty, which was quickly displaced by a more permanent enthusiasm for Turkey and the Turks. His mother also had valuable interest with Sir Herbert Taylor, from 1830 secretary to King William IV, and this led to Urquhart's being preferred to semi-official and then official diplomatic status at Constantinople.

There Urquhart's all-consuming Turcophile obsession began to take on strong paranoid Russophobe overtones. The Russians were at this time completing their suppression of the Polish insurrection, to the intense indignation of radical opinion in Britain. The Russians also, in 1833, concluded with the Turks the Treaty of Unkiar Eskelessi, giving Russia what was generally thought to be a dangerous ascendancy in Constantinople. Urquhart's characteristically megalomaniac and indiscreet attempts to assume the direction of British policy in the Near East and if possible to embroil Britain in war with Russia led in 1837 to his dismissal as an embarrassing nuisance. Urquhart easily persuaded himself that he had been discharged by Palmerston at the instance of St Petersburg; and thus began the delusion which thereafter inflamed his Russophobia that Russian gold and influence penetrated the very heart of British policy.

Everything about Urquhart's early circumstances conduced to make him a pattern of confidently dogmatic and obsessive self-centredness. His companions in Greece noted that his conversation had a 'peculiar' quality and that he frequently 'talked mysteriously'. In 1835 Urquhart wrote: 'I cannot help feeling amazed myself at my singular destiny.'[2] He was early established as a ripe character, of extraordinary magnetism.

The Turkish bath campaign was the best known of his peculiar

[2] M. H. Jenks, 'The Activities and Influence of David Urquhart, 1833–1856' (London University unpublished Ph.D. thesis, 1964), pp. 6, 96.

public activities. His argument was that Turkish society avoided all the evils evident in European and especially British society by the practice of communal bathing. In the West, only the rich had taken to cleanliness; and thus class antipathy and weakened social morale resulted. Turkish baths would remove unhealthy class distrust, as well as suppressing drunkeness, comforting the poor, and making for a healthier population. Urquhart himself was involved in a project to establish a bath in Jermyn Street.[3] Less well known but even more revealing was his abomination of the western custom of the 'offensive manual act' of handshaking. He regarded it as a vulgarity and a sign of corruption and autocratically forbade his committee members to shake hands.[4] Such crankiness reflects accurately enough the general character of Urquhart's intellectual 'system'. The quirks were perfectly logical and coherent, once their premises were conceded. The same is true of his doctrines, which indeed were a coherent 'system', logically dependent on certain premises, and involving in fact a considerable degree of psychological insight.

Urquhart's fundamental premise was the concept of the Law. Essentially this was a doctrine of natural religion, whereby men instinctively teach themselves to be just and virtuous, combined with a version of a Rousseauistic general will, a rationalist vision of the oneness and accessibility of Truth. For Urquhart, the laws of nature as applied to government—that is, international law—were exactly as 'natural' and 'true' as Newton's law of gravitation. The Law is in the breast of every man. There is no need of special holy books to discover it.

> My grounds are these: that each individual, however humble, however lowly, however incapable he may be, it matters not—gentle or simple, learned or ignorant, high or low, retaining or recovering in his own breast the sense of law, is a power available for resisting and repelling, extirpating and punishing and cutting off evil from the land.[5]

[3] See D. Urquhart, *The Turkish Bath, with a view to its Introduction into the British Dominions* (1856). Unless otherwise indicated, all references to publications henceforth are to be attributed to Urquhart. His 'Hammam' was destroyed in the 'blitz' on London during the Second World War.

[4] The terror Urquhart could inspire is clear from a letter from T. W. Fenton, a woollen manufacturer, writing in 1874, 'Then again at parting from you . . . at Keighley you gave me a lecture [for offering you my hand] which I shall not easily forget.' Fenton to Urquhart, 8 August 1874. Urquhart MSS., Balliol College Library, Box G. I am grateful to Mr E. V. Quinn, Librarian of Balliol, for his help in making the *Urquhart Papers* available to me. Undoubtedly the finest moment of the Urquhartite doctrine on handshaking occurred in 1873 when a foreign affairs committee delegation to the French Assembly at Versailles politely but firmly declined the proffered hand of its president, the Duc d'Audiffret-Pasquier (*A Day with One of the Committees by A. G. Stapleton, Esq. Also Politeness as an Element of Power* (1875), p. 5).

[5] *The Right of Search* (1862), pp. 28–9.

All men have the capacity to be right, and hence the duty. Why then are they not? Because they are blinded by 'self-love', they prefer *seeming* right to *being* right. Only when such self-love is dead and men are convinced of their boundless and bottomless ignorance, can 'a real conversion or a new birth' occur in which they will find their true selves, selves capable of obtaining the truth uncontaminated by the 'modern spirit and public opinion'.[6]

Thus, Urquhart taught, his method led naturally and irresistibly to an ultimate conviction of certainty, which was the central attribute of the newly found, or rather 'recovered', self. The self expresses its recovery not only in word but in deed. So, not to shake hands was, for Urquhart, a permanent kind of symbolic testimony of rightness, an assertion of will, the external and visible sign of the Urquhartite state of grace. One of Urquhart's converts from Chartism, Richard Hart, put his finger on the crucial psychological effect of the Urquhartite assertion of certainty: 'If you are not right, your words are so ridiculously false that a child could expose them. If you are right, these are the only words worth listening to.'[7]

It followed, for Urquhart, that there could be no distinction between public and private morality. The essence of public righteousness was the subordination of the regal and executive power to the judiciary, particularly so in matters of peace and war, thus allowing government, as in Turkey, to be carried on the basis of 'a few simple maxims, capable of adjustment and application to every variety of local circumstance'.[8] This was still the case in a more local example, the Channel Islands where, 'like our ancestors, they have no idea of an obligation that they have not accepted, or consequently of a political law they have not desired'.[9]

Englishmen had lost their own happy general will when, with the coming of William of Orange, popular rights had been usurped by executive authority. The need was to restore local corporations, the shire mote, courts leet and courts baron. The cabinet, which was an illegitimate encroaching body, must be extinguished and the privy council resume its full rights and powers. High officials should be rendered directly responsible to the people by reintroducing impeachment. In his early days, Urquhart had looked to parliament to do this; but later he realized that parliament itself was a mere 'bastard imposition', which interposed itself to destroy popular organization and extinguish the council of the King. Hence all questions of parliamentary

[6] G. Robinson, *David Urquhart* (1920), pp. 27–8.
[7] *A Day with One of the Committees*, pp. 5–6.
[8] *Recent Events in the East* (1854), p. 201.
[9] *The Channel Islands. Norman Laws and Modern Practice* (1844), p. 8.

reform were nonsense, a complete misdirection and waste of the radical energies of the people.[10]

Faction was the fruit of parliament and cabinet, the fraudulent means whereby secret collusion between ostensibly opposed politicians was disguised from the people. Urquhart was nowhere more eloquent than in his picture of the 'sickening sight' of 'party broils', and on the need for a united national policy.[11] He was equally clear that the diplomatic corps must be disbanded. Only consuls were needed. Above all, 'SECRECY', that 'monster of diplomacy', must be abandoned.[12]

Secret diplomacy had done greatest damage in that most solemn act of state, war. War was almost a religious act, Urquhart considered, a trial of justice, a punishment of crime just as in the Old Bailey, and the same rules of evidence prevailed. The underlying law of nations is a universal moral law and every nation's government must conform to it. A corrupt state fights an immoral war: an unjust war turns a nation into brigands and bandits. Urquhart's foreign affairs committees were established at the time of the Crimean War 'in order to work for the restoration of the Law of Nations'.[13]

Urquhart did not spare criticism of the behaviour of his countrymen, whom he believed had frequently offended the law of nations. They had lusted for conquest in India, China, Afghanistan. They had behaved treacherously towards the French in 1840. In 1860 Urquhart preached to them at the height of the French invasion panic:

> They have attempted to govern the world. They have coveted the territories of others. They taught themselves to call them virtues. Hence they do not see the finger of God in the penalty which now overtakes them. To redeem themselves in the eyes of mankind, they must cease to do evil and also learn to do well. They can escape the penalty only by repentence and reparation. Each man in England must be convicted of guilt, for England to regain a hold on existence.[14]

Although vigorously hostile to all Cobdenite criticism of the old colonial empire, Urquhart was extremely sensitive to British policy against

[10] Newcastle Foreign Affairs Committee, *Limitation of the Supply of Grain. Constitutional Remedies. Evidence of Mr Urquhart before the Above Committee* (1855), p. 25.
[11] *An Appeal against Faction in Respect of the Concurrence of the Present and Late Administrations, to Prevent the House of Commons from Performing its Highest Duties* (1843).
[12] *Recent Events in the East*, p. 48.
[13] *Mr Urquhart on the Italian War* (1859), pp. 6–9; *Appeal against Both Factions and their Leaders* (1880). Urquhart pointed admiringly to the Laws of Mohammed on Peace and War. Muslims cannot draw the sword without a 'judicial decision pronounced against the enemy'. See *The Four Wars of the French Revolution* (1874), pp. 44–5.
[14] *The Invasion of England* (1860), p. 3.

Asian peoples, especially the Afghans and the Chinese. And a similar respect for non-European peoples comes out strongly in the affair of Governor Eyre of Jamaica in 1865.[15]

Urquhart therefore required a certain frame of mind from his followers: their conviction of guilt and sense of sin, healthy fear, and the recovery of self through purgation and self-examination; to this he added his 'system' of dialectic: the sacredness of verbal precision as the foundation of all intellectual honesty; and the need for a thorough study of the 'march of events', not in 'volumes which are called history, but by the aid of official documents, of journals, and especially of contemporary pamphlets'.[16]

> Now what is to be done for a people . . . that is always wrong—that is as certain to be in error as it is to speak, and to cut its own throat as to act? You cannot send a nation to a nursery, but you may send it to school: it has got to learn, and in your case, to unlearn—that is, to study. It has to drop leaders, and take to public documents, and to give up newspapers for the book of laws. . . . I say to you read the Blue Books; study the Blue Books; come to us, who are engaged in their perusal and in their study. . . . Come to us, and study with us to be honest; for unless we can make honest men in the land, how shall we have an honest minister?[17]

The religious strain in all this is readily apparent. The potentiality of truth and justice existed in an actuality and omnipresence of sin. But, as one doubter put it, 'It has been concluded that your warnings are useless because you see Russia everywhere. . . . I and everyone would see Russia somewhere, if you would be content with the modesty of such an assent!' Urquhart replied that unless there was any countervailing action in a formed righteousness, then sin must be everywhere if it was anywhere. In his later despairing days Urquhart inclined to the doctrine of the necessary temporary triumph of Antichrist, who is to found his empire in modern Babylon (Russia, naturally) before being destroyed by the Second Advent.[18]

[15] *Free Press*, April 1866, p. 46; see also *Appeal against Faction*, pp. 49–51, where he tried to get a parliamentary inquiry into the Afghan war, an attempt supported by Roebuck and seventy-five MPs.

[16] *Four Wars of the French Revolution*, p. 39. Urquhart himself first came to public notoriety in 1835–6 when he published confidential Russian papers in his *Portfolio*; and the first great parliamentary fuss he engineered was about the alleged dishonesties and evasions of the Afghan Blue Books. (See G. J. Alder, 'The "Garbled" Blue Books of 1839—Myth or Reality?', *Historical Journal*, 1972.) Together they gave him his taste for documentary revelation.

[17] *Mr Urquhart on the Italian War*, pp. 16–17, 29–30.

[18] *Russia, if not Everywhere, Nowhere. A Correspondence* (1867), pp. 1–3; *Conscience in Respect to Public Affairs. A Correspondence* (1867), p. 9.

Urquhart never made it precisely clear why Russia had become the monstrous force which he depicted, the very personification of evil. Russia was intolerant, a persecuting power, restrictive and prohibitive in character, constantly aggressive and expansive. Her laws were bureaucratic, illiberal, and centralist. Above all, religion, instead of being a vital moral force, was extinguished in the service of statecraft. In reality, Russia was a power in decline, unlike Turkey which was rejuvenating, and which, had it been left alone, would easily have defeated Russia in the Crimean War. The French and British invasion of the Crimea was quite deliberately arranged by Russia to divert attention from her real ambitions and vulnerability, which was in the Caucasus, where the brave Circassians, betrayed by Palmerston, were being butchered and subjugated.[19]

Russia had her agents in every cabinet: Napoleon III was, just as much as Palmerston, a creature of Russia. 'How does Russia succeed? Russia only works by instruments. . . . The danger of the world proceeds solely from the sentence "The days of impeachment are gone by".'[20] This 'gigantic means of attack and this extensive organization' secured for Russia a 'complete ascendancy' in 'the councils of England herself, and our diplomacy and influence rendered null, except in furtherance of projects of our enemy'.[21] This theme Urquhart pursued relentlessly: how Russia plotted to corner the grain supply of Europe; how she schemed to deprive Britain of her maritime ascendancy; how Russia embroiled the states of Europe in the Italian war of 1859; how she promoted the Civil War in the United States, and the Indian Mutiny. On the question of Sicilian sulphur in 1840, Urquhart moved out into direct accusations of Palmerston: 'Let the man who does not see TREASON in these acts endeavor otherwise to account for them.'[22]

Palmerston's immediate reaction to the charges of treason was to embark on legal proceedings from which he was wisely dissuaded. It took him many years to inure himself to the ceaseless barrage of Urquhart's malice and vituperation. Palmerston was in good treasonable company. Sir Robert Peel, by rejecting Urquhart's demand for a parliamentary enquiry into the Afghan war, revealed himself as a Russian agent, as was *The Times* and Prince Albert himself, who

[19] *Recent Events in the East*, pp. 20–21, 307–11; *Mr Urquhart on the Italian War*, pp. 28–9; *The Circassian War. As Bearing on the Polish Insurrection* (1863), pp. 14–18.

[20] *Right of Search*, p. 86.

[21] *Foreign Policy and Commerce* (1838), p. 3.

[22] *The Sulphur Monopoly* (1840), p. 8. Urquhart kicked up sufficient fuss that the French Prime Minister, Thiers, thought it expedient to receive Urquhart and a delegation in Paris, but quickly assessed him as a crank, 'received coldly' Urquhart's 'statement regarding the ignorance of Public Men in France'; and when next observed, 'was sound asleep!' (A. J. P. Taylor, *The Trouble Makers* (1957), p. 48).

in turn subverted the Queen to Palmerston's treasonable purposes.[23]

Two examples illustrate Urquhart's paranoid logic. First, the inner mystery of the Schleswig-Holstein question, which baffled European statesmen in the 1850s and 1860s: the 'heir general' to the Danish duchies, Urquhart pointed out, was the line of Holstein-Gottorp, or none other than the Czar Nicholas. Russia is the 'heir' to both the Sound and the Bosphorous. Q.E.D.[24] Second, the Italian war of 1859: the inner mystery, revealed to Urquhart, was that the Savoy King was King of Sardinia 'because' he was King of Cyprus and Jerusalem. Cyprus and Jerusalem both belonged to the Ottoman Porte. Russia sought to get this inheritance. 'Now you see the connexion of Russia with the affairs of Italy.' Q.E.D.[25]

This exegetical method, which appears grotesque to a later generation, would have been perfectly familiar to Urquhart's contemporaries who freely searched Holy Writ for illumination as to the significance of current events. In this context Urquhart is properly to be seen as a somewhat unorthodox practitioner of the commonest Victorian *genre* of political literature. Much in Urquhart's doctrines echoed stock radical notions of the time: the historical 'wrong turning' since the seventeenth century; the need to revive local agencies of government; the general conspiracy of the establishment against the people. But what appealed also was Urquhart's profound and pervasive religiosity, and especially the way religious attitudes, themes, sentiments, frames of reference, could be turned from conventional preoccupations and applied to a grand moral regeneration of politics. This had its more narrowly sectarian appeal: Urquhart offered initiation into an inner fraternity of the elect, the few virtuous men who would redeem Sodom; he offered the secrets of wisdom, veiled from the unregenerate mass of mankind. In an age when 'free thought' had become for the first time a vehicle of popular radical politics under such men as Holyoake and Bradlaugh, the instinct for 'natural' religion still remained strong. The essence of Urquhart's public role was that of ministry; his call was to vocation. In an era of Sankey and Moody revivalism, one clergyman revealed his appreciation of this when he wrote: 'I believe your object is to work a moral and religious Revolution in the minds of the present generation which is much to be admired.'[26] Modern historians have compared his

---

[23] *An Appeal against Faction*, p. 18; *Recent Events in the East*, pp. 22, 39–40; *The Queen and the Premier. A Statement of their Struggle and its Results* (1857), p. 9.

[24] *Denmark and the Duchies* (1852), p. 1.

[25] *Mr Urquhart on the Italian War*, pp. 25–6.

[26] Walter Irvine (incumbent of All Saints, Newcastle), to Stobart, 11 November 1858. Urquhart MSS. G. Likewise, Hewart E. Rolland, one of Urquhart's most faithful Newcastle disciples, praised a recent Urquhart speech as having 'now firmly established religion in its real sense as the basis of the movement' (Rolland to Urquhart, 29 December [1858], *ibid.*).

foreign affairs committees to the Union of Democratic control in 1914, or to a successful WEA class. A more apt twentieth century analogy might be Moral Rearmament.

How was he to raise the nation from its lethargy, pierce the 'means of disguise and concealment' and detect and punish the 'enemies within'? Urquhart's certainty about the sureness of his grounds did not permit him to entertain doubts about the possibilities of this. 'The day will come,' he announced in the *Morning Herald* in August 1854, 'when it will be wondered at that I could have been doubted.'[27] Again: 'Amongst a generation so despicable as this, what may not be done? To manage one fool is not a difficult task, how easy must it be to manage twenty-seven millions of fools.'[28] Parliamentary action and political reform as a means to that end were of course ruled out; 'Parliament, the Nation, the Crown were equally powerless and ignored by those who really managed.'[29]

When in 1831 the bewildered 'Patriot King' William IV asked of young Urquhart 'What is to be done?', Urquhart answered that six clerks should be seconded to study diplomacy. Why six of them? Because fewer than this and they would 'assuredly become traitors' and succumb to 'the wiles, the pressure and temptation of foreign influence'.[30] This was the origin of Urquhart's concept of an organization of many such small groups under his central guidance and direction which would permeate the national consciousness. The nature of the training would emphasize verbal precision as the foundation of scientific exactness. Diplomacy, Urquhart always insisted, 'was a science that could only be acquired and practised as all other sciences'.[31] This was the key to the foreign affairs committees.

When Urquhart returned from Constantinople in 1838, sore and discomfited, his first move was to appeal to those interests which shared most directly his own concern with the relation of trade to diplomacy. Protective tariffs in Russia had led to a decline of the Russian trade in its established British centres, Glasgow and Newcastle. Their merchants, manufacturers, and bankers listened sympathetically to Urquhart's denunciations of the 'haughty contempt of British statesmen for commerce' and to his insistence that trade with Turkey was an appropriate alternative.[32]

Already Urquhart was building up a group of disciples around him.

[27] Jenks, p. 321.
[28] *Mr Urquhart on the Italian War*, pp. 15–16.
[29] *Limitation of the Supply of Grain*, p. 25.
[30] *Mr Urquhart on the Italian War*, pp. 16–17.
[31] *Ibid.*, p. 19.
[32] *Foreign Policy and Commerce*, pp. 10–11.

There were the inevitable military men of eccentric leanings, Major Hodgson Cardogan, a faithful chief of staff until warned off by embarrassed Tory party managers, and Colonel Pringle Taylor. Above all, he captured William Cargill, a Newcastle business man, who contemplated starting an Urquhartite newspaper, and who wrote to Monteith, a Glasgow merchant, on the prospect of a great meeting at South Shields, in a very rictus of fanaticism:

> I promise you—and I never made a promise of this sort before—that what I shall bring out at that meeting will strike *like a thunderbolt* on *the country*! Yes—Durham & Londonderry-ridden as this accursed town and neighbourhood is—powerful, & universal, & constant as their damnable efforts in the work of poisoning, are—stupid & ignorant as the public is—actively opposed as all my efforts are by my own friends, relations & *partners*, when they *dare*—every means both by friends and foes silently made use of to turn me away from the whole thing—and with an overwhelming load of private business on my shoulders—notwithstanding all this, by God, I will not let my country die *quietly* if it were to depend on any denunciations from me![33]

It was Monteith in May 1840 who organized a petition in Glasgow signed by 20,000 names urging parliament to investigate Palmerston's anti-French policy in the Near East. Monteith appears also to have formed committees to investigate the charges against Palmerston.[34]

Urquhart himself at this time indulged in the apocalyptic mood: 'A nation slumbers thus over a Tomb; its very awakening, if we could do it, would make one tremble.' The nation's fate could 'be lost by our deficiencies', or 'saved by our own energy & decision'.[35] His apocalypticism had much to do with his intervention in the attempted Chartist insurrections of late 1839 and early 1840 which he claimed he personally foiled. He was convinced that the Russians had penetrated the Chartist movement and perverted it to their own fell purposes. Beniowski, 'a *Polish Jew*', was the chief Russian agent, according to Urquhart, who persuaded the Chartist shoemaker, William Cardo, and Thomas Doubleday, editor of the Chartist *Northern Liberator*, of this Russian plot. From April 1840, the *Liberator* for its last six months of publication, supported Urquhart's accusations against Palmerston.[36] Urquhart proceeded to alert the forces of authority, in the form of

[33] Cargill to Monteith, 29 April 1840. Urquhart MSS. G.
[34] Jenks, p. 214.
[35] Urquhart to Pringle Taylor, 19 December 1839. Urquhart MSS. E (copy).
[36] J. H. Gleason, *The Genesis of Russophobia in Great Britain* (1950) p. 262.

General Lord Anglesey (it was clearly pointless appealing directly to a government already riddled with treason: as Colonel Pringle Taylor put it bluntly to Lord Normanby, the Home Secretary, 'I cannot prevail upon myself to think that the Russian agent is unknown to some of the Government').[37] The veteran Chartist Thomas Frost thought Urquhart's intelligence was probably quite accurate; but his claim to a decisive role in events was megalomaniac.[38]

His disciples set up a National Subscription to Urquhart for effecting 'a complete alteration . . . in the minds of leading Chartists',[39] and they split off sections of Chartists in Newcastle, Carlisle, and Glasgow. Efforts were concentrated on leading individuals, such as Charles Attwood, brother of Thomas Attwood, the Birmingham radical. One of the most interesting of their catches was Robert Lowery.

Lowery was a leading Chartist in Newcastle in the 1830s, prominent in the Chartist Convention and among the 'physical force' faction. Between 1839 and 1842 he underwent at the hands of Urquhart and his movement a 'conversion experience' comparable to that of evangelical religion. He went on to associate with the Quaker philanthropist Joseph Sturge and the temperance movement.[40] In 1840 Lowery met Urquhart himself, who opened up 'a wider and clearer view'. Urquhart 'did not look at mere *forms* of government, but at the principles and spirit developed in its *action*'. Lowery hitherto had devoted himself to political reform but Urquhart taught him that 'all law was dead unless its spirit was in the people'. Lowery concluded that 'his power of attaching men of different classes and opinions to his views was amazing; minds discordant on other subjects became one'.[41]

Another rewarding convert was Collet Dobson Collet, an early secretary of the People's Charter Union, of whom Holyoake said he 'never knew any one more discerning than he in choosing a public cause, or in promoting it with greater plenitude of resource'. His capture by Urquhart 'is the greatest mystery of conversion I have known'.[42]

Nonetheless, Urquhart failed to bring over the Chartist movement as a whole, for he was vociferously opposed by G. J. Harney and in any

---

[37] Pringle Taylor to someone as informant to Lord Anglesey, 22 September 1839, *ibid*. Pringle Taylor to Normanby, 11 November 1839, *ibid*. (Copies).

[38] T. Frost, *Forty Years' Recollections, Literary and Political* (1880), p. 108.

[39] Urquhart MSS., National Subscription.

[40] See B. Harrison and P. Hollis, 'Chartism, Liberalism and the Life of Robert Lowery', *English Historical Review* (1967).

[41] 'Passages in the Life of a Temperance Lecturer', *Weekly Record*, 14 March 1857. This autobiography is shortly to be reprinted by B. Harrison and P. Hollis.

[42] G. J. Holyoake, *Bygones Worth Remembering* (n.d.), II, pp. 267–9. Holyoake reports that Bright would offer Collet his hand which Collet would refuse saying 'he could not take the hand of a man who knew Lord Palmerston was an imposter and ought to know he was a traitor, and still maintained political relations with him'.

case after 1841 the Near Eastern crisis passed and Palmerston went out of office with the coming of Peel to power. Urquhart was not to regain his standing until the resurgence of working class radicalism at the end of the 1840s. In the meanwhile he became MP for Stafford in 1847: the House emptied when he rose to speak, and he soon became a butt of *Punch*.[43] He ceased to attend the Commons regularly after 1849 and did not stand for re-election in 1852. The educated classes were hopelessly corrupt, the nation was 'perishing through Faction'. Only those 'excluded from the privileges of the State' were 'exempt from defilement'. The movement must be directed towards 'the more simple and unperverted' working men.[44]

Urquhart's rather equivocal situation, as a strong anti-radical seeking alliance with the forces of the working classes on the basis of a mutual condemnation of the corrupt establishment, caused him constant embarrassment. Nothing made him more indignant than charges that he was 'raising the democracy':

They would have a Revolution—I point to the Law. They would head an excited mob on the untried paths of political convulsion—I would lead an indignant and instructed people back to the old ways of the Constitution. . . . No one has set his face as I have done, or so raised hand and voice, against popular delusions and popular agitation. I have gone forth single-handed among the towns of England against the Chartist insurrection, and subdued it. . . . I have professed myself a Tory in the purest sense of the word—a Tory of the times of Anne.[45]

With the Chartist revival in 1848, Urquhart won new supporters: James Grant, editor of the London *Morning Advertiser* (second only to *The Times* in circulation), and George Crawshay, a Gateshead ironmaster who provided finance for Urquhart's new twopenny weekly paper, *The Free Press*, launched in 1855 with C. D. Collet as editor.[46]

The foreign affairs committees movement proper was inaugurated as Turkish and Russian relations deteriorated towards the point of war in 1853. Urquhart went on a major speaking tour; the first of the committees was established in Newcastle in October 1854 by Crawshay and Attwood. In the autumn of 1854, Urquhart called a special conference at Manchester following which he put sixty of his postulants for ordina-

43 Jenks, p. 271.
44 *Address of the Men of Birmingham to the People of England* (1855), p. 4.
45 *Recent Events in the East*, pp. 268–9.
46 Published 1855–65; continued as *The Diplomatic Review*, 1866–77. For interesting details see C. D. Collet, *History of the Taxes on Knowledge* (1899), II, pp. 57–61. Collet stayed with the paper until 1877.

tion through an intensive three month training as missionaries, at the same time maintaining their families at his own expense.[47]

Meanwhile the Crimean War deteriorated. Palmerston replaced the discredited Aberdeen in February 1855; the scandals and mismanagement of the winter still reverberated in the report of the Roebuck Committee; hopes of a great western crusade to liberate Poland were dashed. On 14 August 1855 Urquhart held a conference of his Association for the Study of National and International Affairs at Birmingham. Some seven to eight thousand were present. The Conference unanimously adopted the findings of the Birmingham foreign affairs committee, that 'our danger is derived from the *direct power* of Russia, only in so far as her designs have been aided by positive collusion upon the part of the Ministerial Servants of the British Crown'. Of these, Palmerston was the most guilty.[48]

By now there were some sixty-eight committees in existence, mainly in the north of England in areas where Chartism was strong and where Urquhart had correspondingly devoted most of his efforts. He had chosen Birmingham for his headquarters in 1855 envisaging a second 'Convention of the Industrious Classes'. His new assistants [49] were mostly business men or artisans in a small way, dependent on subsidies from Urquhart for their expenses, and often in difficulties from having to neglect their affairs. Such were Thomas Johnson of Newcastle, who set up the Birmingham committee, and John Johnson, John Shallcross, and William Peplow (an ex-Chartist) of Stafford, and George Stobart and Hewart Rolland of Newcastle. Another ex-Chartist of note was Richard Hart, who by February 1856 was reporting from Newcastle: 'The Chartists have come over in a body and have made up their minds

[47] Robinson, *Urquhart*, p. 125. Urquhart described his indoctrination thus: 'During that time we had many public meetings, and made excursions to the neighbouring towns, but the object of bringing together these men, these keen and stirring spirits of the working class was study. They were divided into sections and their studies were directed by those who had already worked with me. They assembled at ten in the morning, and all passed through the same course of lectures on the Law of Nations and the Constitution of England. Then they were divided into separate branches of those studies. . . . The hours of work were from ten in the morning till one o'clock for dinner. They resumed work at two and went on till seven, when they stopped for tea. At eight o'clock all met in the same room, and I discussed with them for never less than two hours the subjects on which they had been at work during the day. These men, grave, diligent, enthusiastic, were a sight worth seeing.' (G. Robinson, *Some Account of David Urquhart* (1921), pp. 8–9.)

[48] *Address of the Men of Birmingham*, pp. 1–8.

[49] For the committees, see the *List of Addresses of the Foreign Affairs Committees*, probably 1855, Urquhart MSS. G. One of his staunchest assistants was his wife, whom he married in September 1854. She was Harriet Fortescue, sister of Lord Clermont and of the politician Chichester Fortescue, who took pains to check whether Urquhart had ever been 'in confinement' for lunacy. See O. W. Hewett, *Strawberry Fair. A biography of Frances, Countess Waldegrave, 1821–1879* (1956), and *. . . and Mr Fortescue* (1958), p. 70.

to go for impeachment and agitate the country. We are warming fast.'[50] But official Chartism held Urquhart at bay, considering him a tool of the ruling class especially promoted to sabotage their movement. Karl Marx, who fully shared Urquhart's hatred of Palmerston and Russia but who also wished to cultivate the Chartists in the direction of scientific socialism, had much ado keeping a foot in both camps. He noted in April 1856 that 'bitter controversy' prevailed 'between the Chartists and the Urquhartists' in Newcastle, London, Birmingham, and 'several other places'.[51]

But if Urquhart failed to win a popular feeling, what was the size of the popular response he did elicit? Newspaper reports are unreliable, as they range from the dismissal by the 'quality' press to the inflation by Urquhart's supporters. Committees were often transient, and often exposed to permeation by others. At their height they may have numbered 150, with some 2,000 or 3,000 working class supporters.[52] Much also depended on current events, and whether Urquhart could turn them to account. The Indian mutiny of 1857 undoubtedly stimulated a somewhat flagging agitation and W. Green reported to Urquhart in September 1857 in Ashton: 'The people appeared to take great interest in the proceedings and when the meeting was concluded assembled in groups to discuss the various topics that had been advanced.' A few nights later they had an audience of 300 and sold fifty-six *Free Presses* to 'an attentive audience'. Other reports speak of six to seven thousand at Pudsey in August 1857, 500 at Gloucester on the Chinese war in November 1858, 200 at Walsall in October 1855.[53] But even in the early days, constant pressure was needed to keep small committees from disintegrating. Kidderminster committee had no more than eight active members, though Johnson strengthened them with a few more books

[50] Hart to Urquhart, 5 February 1856. Urquhart MSS. G. According to Urquhart, Hart approached him at a torchlight parade in Stafford in 1853 to say: 'For three hundred years no man of your class has come among men of my class . . . save to gain votes, or popularity; that is to cheat and befool them.' How did Hart recognize Urquhart's genuineness? 'You do not shake hands' (*A Day with One of the Committees*, pp. 5–6).

[51] H. Collins and C. Abramsky, *Karl Marx and the British Labour Movement* (1965), p. 10. J. Saville, *Ernest Jones; Chartist* (1952), pp. 239–40.

[52] Robinson, *Urquhart*, pp. 169–70.

[53] Taylor notes that Urquhart's 'enthusiastic audience' at Preston 'consisted of twenty secularists and one Swedenborgian'. (*Trouble Makers*, p. 47.) See correspondence in Urquhart MSS. G.: Hart to Urquhart, 26 September 1855; Johnson to Mrs Urquhart, 6 September 1855; Green to Urquhart, 2 September 1857. Hart was particularly optimistic, reporting a 'great meeting' at Worcester of two thousand in September 1855, and at Birmingham compared with the Administrative Reformers, who 'did just nothing', they were doing 'very well'. See also Jenks, p. 333.

and pamphlets. Dewsbury committee numbered eleven, and that was considered one of the stronger ones.[54] William Hilton, secretary of the Bolton committee, reported in March 1862: 'Our Committee still continues its usual weekly meetings. Average attendance about 4 in number. During the last few weeks we have had special meetings on Sunday evenings to go through the Blue Book "Affairs of Syria 1860–61" which was presented to us by L. Col. Gray Edy, a portly vol. of 517 pages which we have not completed.'[55]

Nor did their efforts at lobbying politicians and notabilities appear more fruitful. Unwary MPs being polite could certainly find themselves entangled in endless correspondence,[56] but wary MPs dealt with their deputations decisively. Johnson of Newcastle reported that when they tried to nobble Octavius Duncombe, Conservative MP for the North Riding, they were told ' "You are imposing on the working men", whom he said "were great fools for sending us".'[57]

But while it is not easy to establish with any precision the quantity of support for Urquhart's movement, it is possible to build up an impression of the quality of life of a committee: its characteristics, techniques, and above all its difficulties. John T. Harlow, of Small Heath, Birmingham, is a revealing case of an Urquhartite: an earnest, rather parsonical mind in search of a mission in life. He had 'walked many miles and spent many hours' attempting to establish a foreign affairs committee in 1859, though so far only two persons were 'pledged'. 'Meanwhile,' Harlow continued, 'I shall continue to beat up the neighbourhood in search of likely men.'

Harlow returned thanks for a copy of Urquhart's *Familiar Words*,[58] which had something of the status of a bible among members of the movement. It laid down Urquhart's doctrine on the need for absolute precision in the use of words. Harlow dilated on the sacred theme: to think correctly upon any subject it was necessary to 'ascend beyond mere words'—which were 'at best but imperfect representations of the things themselves'. Harlow had to keep a strict watch upon himself to prevent 'unmeaning words slipping inadvertently into my speech'. Words must always have 'definite meanings'.

Harlow tried to obtain members by 'reasoning with men as to their beliefs', and especially their political beliefs. But this was not easy:

[54] Cooke to Urquhart, 22 August 1855, Urquhart MSS. G (Kidderminster); J. Cockburn and A. Robinson to Urquhart, 29 April 1857, *ibid.* (Dewsbury).
[55] Hilton to F. Johnson, March 1862, *ibid.*
[56] E.g. George Dixon of Birmingham, entangled with the 'Price Street Mutual Improvement Society'. See *The Privy Council the only Check on the Executive* (1872).
[57] T. Johnson to Urquhart, 19 June 1856. Urquhart MSS. G. Duncombe took care to have a witness present.
[58] *Familiar Words, as Affecting the Character of Englishmen and the Fate of England* (1855); Part II: *Familiar Words, as Affecting the Conduct of England in 1855* (1855).

However successful I may be in convincing them that they are in error, totally wrong in particular instances; yet there are so many of these instances, each of which they insist upon treating as separate and distinct from the others, that it seems at times an endless, almost hopeless task, thoroughly to shake a man's confidence in himself so as to get him to begin anew the building up of the edifice of his convictions.

In his perplexity Harlow confessed that 'I can scarcely say that I have succeeded perfectly entirely with any one man, though I have laboured hard and long with several', because such men believed as true those things uttered by the greatest number of people they considered 'respect-worthy'. Harlow concluded with a request for a loan of books to help him; he is short of money.[59]

Possibly somewhat less untypical than Harlow's refined and literary turn of mind, was the near illiteracy of Daniel Walton, secretary of the Farsley committee:

Mr Urquhart, Sir, We are glad that an oppertunity is offer'd us, by such influencial men as you and your colleagues, has will give us an insight into our Home and Foreign Policy there is an inquirey into those things with the working class and we think this a fine oppertunity as those things are put into our hands gratuitous and we heartily give you our thanks [*sic*].[60]

One of Urquhart's most important itinerant missionaries, Thomas Johnson of Newcastle, in June 1855 described his efforts to engage an 'incumbent' and his flock, reading the war news from the Crimea, and his failure. He tramped from public house to commercial hotel in search of likely conversational prospects: again in vain. He disclosed plans to infiltrate a 'ward administrative reform' meeting where he proposed to put a motion to stop the war which would gain support.[61] Joseph Baron of Bolton in 1859 similarly proposed to attend a Reform meeting: 'I intend to ask Questions if there is any chance of doing so with advantage. At all events I will present every person present with a copy of the F. Press supplements for we have about 50 left.' At the reform meeting, the speaker, Robert Cooper of Manchester, was pressed on the question of ministerial responsibility—to Law or merely to public opinion? And what guarantees would there be that a reformed parliament would reduce taxation? Could taxation in any case ever be other than unjust

[59] J. T. Harlow to John Shallcross, 16 January 1859, Urquhart MSS., G.
[60] Walton to Urquhart, 1857, *ibid*.
[61] T. Johnson to Urquhart, 11 June 1855, *ibid*.

if levied indirectly? Cooper in reply referred to his knowing 'what school the young men who put the above questions belong to'; he honoured them for their patient study and earnestness of character; but they were wrong to deny that parliamentary reform was the vital issue.[62]

Reports were sometimes more formal and brisk. George Stobart reported from Tyneside:

> Our Committee during the last month have had *eight* ordinary meet-ings—besides, in some numbers attending a district Conference in Sunderland . . . to consider the address to the *Crown*—for the restora-tion of the functions of the Privy Council—which was adopted.

A 'useful conversation' followed on the Afghan papers and Indian affairs.[63]

Urquhart was constantly approached as an oracle. Typically, the Birmingham committee asked him to reveal 'the name of the Heir to the Throne of Denmark, who was induced to give up his claim upon the promise of the Throne of the *"Principalities"*, with some few particulars; that they may be used at a towns meeting on Wednesday next at the Town Hall'.[64] One zealot in Dundee, David Scott, manager of the local branch of the Electric and International Telegraph Company, pro-posed to buy the whole of Urquhart's works, including back numbers of the *Free Press*, 'to complete my Conversion to political truth'.[65]

Correspondence with him was invariably respectful and often grovel-lingly humble. One of the rare cases of Urquhart's being answered back reveals a significant degree of working class resentment at middle class patronage. The committees were very sensitive to Chartist charges of 'pecuniary recompense', the subsidies that Urquhart provided to give his people the means to leave off work from time to time and devote themselves to study. But in turn Urquhart demanded results. Michael Rafferty wrote from the Birmingham home and foreign affairs com-mittee, when Urquhart accused them of internal 'squabbling':

> We do not disparage what you have done for us, your efforts for our improvement we appreciate, your labour to impress us with a know-ledge of our duties we applaud; for the books and documents, from which we learned much we thank you and for your own elucidations we are grateful. But Sir for the 'means' which sets us free from the pressure of hourly toil, recoils about us and glaringly stamps us as

[62] J. T. Baron to C. D. Collet, 8 May 1859, *ibid.*
[63] G. Stobart to ? Urquhart, 24 August 1857, *ibid.*
[64] Hawkins to Urquhart, 22 March 1857, *ibid.*
[65] Scott to ? Urquhart, 19 November 1860, *ibid.*

subsidised Working men, of which the majority of our Committee is formed, and poor as we are and though perhaps we may be consigned to incessant bodily labour, yet we would rather have remained ignorant of ministerial treachery, and the wiles of diplomacy, together with Russian aggression and Turkish subjection, Danish succession and Austrian duplicity, than be branded as subsidists. Better by far had you contented yourself with giving us instruction after our hours of labour, than caused us to abstain from our usual occupation and thereby left us open to the charge of paid tools bribed agents and hired politicians. You will perhaps say, 'You should have seen that at the time'. But how could we when judicial blindness obscured our eyes, and occult propositions darkened our view.[66]

But though the committee obviously disliked the financial dependence and possibly the intellectual dependence of their position, there is no suggestion that it would be appropriate to repudiate Urquhart's doctrine.

More generally, Urquhart's authority was sustained by the climate of moral righteousness which invested the movement. Much of the inner life of the committees evidently had to do with mutual improvement, emphasizing moral as well as intellectual progress. Crawshay, the Newcastle chairman, wrote in 1856 to a worried Urquhartite pamphleteer advising him to blend religion and politics.

> . . . I am not surprised to hear of the falling off. I think you assume too much knowledge in your readers, and write about *collusion* with Russia as if *they had* the key to the events *you* have—you must assume on their part ignorance & put yourself in their position. Unless you can be yourself and your reader at the same time you will certainly fail.
>
> The most easy mode of reaching them is by taking up matters from the point of view of *character* alone & doing this frequently. If there were *no Russia* our acts are not the less wicked.

The author should constantly stress themes of guilt and punishment: 'moral iniquity of acts of Govt.'; 'complicity of a people'; 'the vengeance sure to follow'. These were 'themes magnificent in themselves & to which any reader with moral sense can be attracted'.

Then: 'That the vengeance sure to come must come from some definite

---

[66] Rafferty to Urquhart, 16 June 1856, *ibid.* Likewise, when the Kidderminster committee squabbled, evidently on class lines, Noah Cooke wrote to Urquhart, that he would withdraw, and form 'a subcommittee of working men only' (Cooke to Urquhart, 22 August 1855, *ibid.*).

quarter & that quarter Russia is the next step. Russia's mode of action must of course be kept before your readers—but it is *subtle* not easily understood.' And finally: 'We can only be saved by the influence of one man—but you must not forget—*you are a bridge* between him and the rest.'[67]

These were problems of technique common to most movements of propaganda. More peculiar problems attached to Urquhart's more idiosyncratic requirements, especially the dialectical style and the precision of words and logic. George Stobart, of the Newcastle and Sunderland committee, reported in high glee to Collet in June 1859 of a trip to London where he fell into conversation with a Unitarian minister, one Matthews:

I cannot find time to tell you one half of what was said suffice it to say that I never felt so strongly before the superiority of the method we have been taught by Mr U. to pursue in dealing with men and I felt conscious that I had made an impression on his mind that would not soon be effaced.[68]

But what armed the able was often beyond the reach of more puzzled followers. Thomas Woodruff, a factory operative of North Shields, wrote, rather sadly, that though he had tried the dialectical method on several occasions, he had 'always failed . . . I don't think I have the ability or capacity of applying the result of a series of questions in order to expose my neighbour's ignorance'. Even were he 'perfect' however, 'what effect would it have on the great Leviathan of deception, cunning and knavery of the Government? Would it in the least change their acts? I doubt it! Nay I almost despair.'[69]

By 1861 indeed what hope could Urquhart have himself of making a serious impact on the political scene? Woodruff added to his letter that at North Shields there was 'no Committee here now, all are gone, & I doubt of ever being able to find any stable minds to form one'. By 1860 William Crowther of Rostwick could report to J. Johnson of finding 'lost' committees, out of touch with any central organization, rather like bewildered castaways on desert islands. He found one such in Dewsbury, another in Ellend, who would be glad to receive any instructions they could get.[70] For without adequate and expensive supervision, lacking leisure, and lacking self-generated finance, most committees were quickly out of their depth. The pitifully meagre scale of financial

---

[67] Crawshay, 13 September 1856, *ibid.*
[68] Stobart to Collet, 15 June 1859, *ibid.*
[69] Woodruff to Urquhart, 19 February 1861, *ibid.*
[70] Crowther to Johnson, 2 July 1860, *ibid.*

operation comes out in Daniel Walton's letter to Collet in 1857: 'You sent us two small works and you stated that if we sent the worth of them in postage stamps they could be considered as our own. I have got a little money and shall send it to you in stamps and afterwards we will send you something more. . . .' The Brighouse committee could only afford two copies of the *Free Press*, and in 1866 Collet had to turn it into a shilling quarterly, the *Diplomatic Review*.[71]

The pathetic case of R. W. Richardson of South Shields shows the movement near its last gasp in 1867. Richardson tried to raise money for the cause:

> . . . the means I chosed were (having failed to induce my Master to raise my wages which being only 18/- per week were *hardly* enough for my family, and certainly did not leave anything for other purposes) to ask him, as he employed a horse and cart occasionally, to give me that work to do, and when granted if he would lend me money to buy a horse and cart with, this he also granted me but at Bank interest, *viz 10 per cent.* . . .

Richardson was soon in great difficulty. He had borrowed £16, much of which were still outstanding to his Master, and this after having sold off the horse. His liabilities were over £20, and he stood to lose his house, which he and his poor wife had struggled twenty-one years to make. With his 'mind in extreme distress', Richardson could not study foreign affairs and resist the 'dangerous' people crying out for reform. And yet 'I know there may be and are more able men under your instructions, but there are none who will more reasoultly stand out against the difficulty of labour amongst my fellow men than your humble servant.'[72] Such was the power of Urquhart's magnetism.

Even when supervision was available, members could still be out of their depth. John Wilson of the Cononley committee wrote in March 1858 to one of the organizers at Manchester:

> You complain that we do not 'write oftener'. You will excuse me, when we tell you, that we are so bewildered that we scarce know what to write, or where to begin. Some of us knew not but that we were, to some extent, knowing chaps before we entered on this great enquiry; but we find that all our previous knowledge has been of a very superficial character. . . .

[71] Walton to Collett, November 1857, *ibid*. As Urquhart himself had perhaps less than £600 a year, and was occasionally in difficulty with hotel bills, he was in no position to help. His expenditure on his sixty ordinands at Manchester must have been a very heavy burden on him.

[72] Richardson to Urquhart, 5 April 1867, *ibid*.

They had had to give up the Turkish Treaty because to understand that they needed to understand the Treaty of Adrianople, the Treaty of Warsaw, the Treaty of Vienna, and so on *ad infinitum*. However, they laboured on.[73]

Urquhart had failed to sustain the initial impetus of 1855, and when he called his conference in Manchester in 1860, he could count on some eighteen committees still surviving.[74] He himself retired almost permanently to his Savoyard chalet in 1864, though he returned to England in 1867 to conduct a tour of his committees to gather support for his forthcoming appeal to the Pope and the Vatican Council. Urquhart came back for one final tour of the committees in 1874 when a last Conference of the Association was held at Keighley. His last, posthumous, publication in 1878 paid tribute to 'the handful of men who still remain in England capable of exercising a sane judgment on public affairs'.[75] The final spasm of the committees came with the Near Eastern crisis of 1875–80. David Rule at the head of a still vigorous Newcastle committee agitated for the impeachment of Disraeli as a betrayer of Turkey to Russia.[76]

Urquhart denied that his movement had 'failed' because it had not achieved its general object of social permeation and mass conversion to belief in his doctrines, or because it had not achieved any specific objective such as repudiating the Declaration of Paris or restoring the privy council. He relied, naturally, on negative assertion. The foreign affairs committees, according to him, had 'broken down and stopped all the political, social, atheistical, and revolutionary agitations that have been attempted in England, either by sporadic infection or foreign design'. These 'planned but arrested catastrophes' included 'three European wars'.[77]

This invulnerability he purchased at a high price. In the last analysis his whole appeal to the public depended upon his claim that he could demonstrate the existence of accessible truth, and that in his system of logic he provided an infallible means of access to it by removing obstacles set up in men's hearts and minds by the moral and intellectual corruption of the times. Urquhart aimed to change fundamentally the bearings of thought and action of an entire generation.

In one sense Urquhart asked too much: the bathos unavoidable in

[73] Wilson to J. Johnson, 28 March 1858, *ibid.*
[74] Those who signed the Newcastle petition on the Afghan papers in 1860 were Newcastle, Manchester, Keighley, Park (Sheffield), Armley, Winchester, Leeds, Bolton-le-Moors, St Pancras, Marylebone, Cononley, Idle, South Shields, Stockport, Manchester Gaythorne, Rastrick, Morley, Staleybridge.
[75] *The Two Affghan Wars* (1878), p. 1.
[76] R. T. Shannon, *Gladstone and the Bulgarian Agitation, 1876* (1963), p. 237.
[77] *A Day with One of the Committees*, p. 7.

detecting an interior corruption in the form of Lord Palmerston and an exterior corruption in the form of Russia. But in another sense he asked too little: that the remedy was a simple replacement of cabinet government by a privy council tempered by impeachment. Urquhart in this way stretched a credibility gap between himself and his intended public who were unable to connect convincingly for themselves and for others such an enormity of evil with such a facility of virtue.

This meant that Urquhart entirely neglected the central ground of politics. This is the second, and doubtless much more important lesson of his failure. A successful 'Pressure from Without' concentrates its energies on a socially plausible relationship between cause and effect. The evils of drink, of church establishments, of corn laws, of unreformed parliaments, of subjugated womenhood, of illiteracy, and the virtues which would assumably flow from the suppression of such evils, have clearly this kind of plausible relationship. Popular politics of this style must be concrete and 'visible': a land without drunkenness, votes for all. On this test, Urquhart failed completely. In trying to convert Chartism to his purposes, he was trying to translate a movement with an intensely concrete and 'visible' programme on to a plane of moral metaphysics. It was far from being merely a case of working class suspicions of the 'Tory' Urquhart; it was much more the case of one appealing for a popular following in a foreign and untranslatable tongue.

Further Reading

Most attention paid to Urquhart has related to the affairs of the Near East. See G. H. Bolsover, 'David Urquhart and the Eastern Question, 1833-7. A Study in Publicity and Diplomacy', *Journal of Modern History*, VIII (1936); C. Webster, 'Urquhart, Ponsonby, and Palmerston', *English Historical Review*, LXII (1947); Margaret H. Jenks, 'The Activities and Influence of David Urquhart, 1833-56, with special reference to the affairs of the Near East' (London University unpublished Ph.D. thesis, 1964). There is also much on Urquhart in J. H. Gleason, *The Genesis of Russophobia in Great Britain* (1950). The only biography devoted to him is the hagiography by Gertrude Robinson: *David Urquhart. Some Chapters in the Life of a Victorian Knight-Errant of Justice and Liberty* (1920).

The need now is to explore Urquhartism as a phenomenon in its own right. Three historians have given a lead in this direction. A. J. P. Taylor's *The Trouble Makers* (1957) p. 47, interprets Urquhart's Association for the Study of National and International Affairs as the 'first forerunner' of the Union for Democratic Control of 1914; Asa Briggs suggests that the foreign affairs committees of the West Riding could assume the character of a 'prototype of a highly successful and intelligent WEA tutorial class' (Asa Briggs, 'David Urquhart and the West Riding Foreign Affairs Committees', *Bradford Antiquary*, N.S., Part 39 (1958), pp. 206–7). John Salt in his 'Local Manifestations of the Urquhartite Movement', *International Review of Social History*, XIII (1968), p. 365, sees the committees as manifesting the claims of ordinary people against the bureaucratic structures of the modern state.

I I

The Administrative Reform Association, 1855–1857

Olive Anderson

Unlike most organized nineteenth century pressure groups, the Administrative Reform Association was the result, and not the cause, of an agitation. Only one closely comparable case springs to mind—that of the Eastern Question Association formed in December 1876. Like that Association, the Administrative Reform Association was preceded by several months of spontaneous public agitation in response to humiliating and tragic events in the Near East, during which an exceptionally varied cross-section of society was aroused. Like that Association, it soon suffered the likeliest fate for an organization founded in such circumstances: it was never judged on its own terms. The hero of that earlier movement, Layard of Nineveh, was universally assumed to be its mouthpiece, although he had no official standing in the Association whatsoever, and its sober official declarations of policy were either disregarded, or dismissed as misrepresentations of what the Association really stood for. Nor indeed was this altogether unjustified, for the Association at the beginning was an exceptionally heterogeneous movement, with two conflicting styles of leadership, and many contrasts in social and political tone between its members and sympathizers; and its cautious executive officers were quite out-classed in platform oratory by those who sought to make it a continuation of popular agitation. For such a divided and derivative movement the only chance of success was to catch what was left of the original tide of enthusiastic agitation, and make the most of that; but this the Association entirely failed to do. Yet to dismiss it as simply one of the most abortive parts of the whole abortive Crimean crisis in English affairs, would certainly be quite wrong. For the Association did not fade away when the Crimean crisis ended; instead, it became what its original chairman, that philanthropic tycoon Samuel Morley, had always wanted it to be—an organization for the diffusion of political knowledge, whose immediate efforts were concentrated upon securing legislation making it obligatory for all junior clerks in government offices to be recruited by examination. For ten months from August 1855 it pursued these limited goals in the most non-inflammatory way, until early in June 1856 it underwent a third metamorphosis, when its leadership passed to the veteran radical MP, 'Tear 'em' Roebuck. Its goal became the more challenging one of bringing the public service up to the fabled standards of private enterprise, and its tactics and organization were drastically altered to concentrate upon electoral manipulation. The Association was still thus preoccupied in March 1857, when Palmerston, having been defeated on the Chinese war, dissolved parliament and won a landslide victory. The havoc included, apparently, the demise of the Association.

In its time the Administrative Reform Association thus played many parts. To study its history, in fact, is to study each of the three main types of 'pressure from without' characteristic of the first period of pressure politics in Britain, the period which begins with the spread of the Yorkshire movement during the American War of Independence, and ends with the rise of national party organizations and associations based on economic function in the last quarter of the nineteenth century. In the first place, the Administrative Reform Association is an example of *expressive* pressure (to use the terminology adopted by Henry Jephson in his classic work on *The Platform* in 1892), that is, pressure which claimed to express deep-seated and widespread public feeling on some great issue. In the last resort, such pressure could only be effective either through intimidation (whether based upon social fear of 'revolution', or individual fear of loss of reputation, office or property), or through a successful appeal to doctrines of popular sovereignty. Secondly, the Association is also an example of *deliberative* and *didactic* pressure, exerted through rational analysis of a specific alleged evil and the diffusion of the case for a particular remedy. This kind of pressure derived its force from confidence that rational argument could swiftly alter the views and behaviour of men, members and ministers, and was particularly often used in the 1850s and 1860s, when such confidence was very widespread indeed. Finally, it is an example of *controlling* pressure, intended to ensure that between elections, Members continuously reacted to the flow of events in a manner acceptable to those to whom they owed their election. This kind of pressure could succeed only to the extent that convention, inclination or apparent electoral necessity induced a Member to behave like a delegate rather than a representative—a state of affairs which was also becoming distinctly more common in the '50s and '60s than it had been in the '30s. As it happens, the history of the Administrative Reform Association is much more obscure in its second and third phases than in its first, 'expressive' phase. What follows will therefore inevitably be a comparatively poor illustration of the deliberative and didactic, and controlling kinds of pressure from without. This is a pity, since different kinds of pressure tended to have not only different goals and tactics, but also different social and geographical bases, and different kinds of relationships with the flow of events, both political and non-political. Enough can be said, however, about all three phases of this protean Association to show something of the importance of such matters in the history of 'pressure from without'.

Perhaps the most surprising thing about the history of the Administrative Reform Association is that it was launched as late in 1855 as 5 May. As early as the beginning of December 1854 public disappointment about the way the Crimean war was going was beginning to make the great towns seem ripe for agitation to expert eyes;[1] on 23 December W. H. Russell's famous despatches began to appear in *The Times*. When parliament reassembled on 29 January 1855, it immediately voted for a committee of inquiry and thus precipitated the resignation of Aberdeen's coalition government. There followed three shameful weeks of ministerial crisis, from which Palmerston emerged as the head of a very Whiggish government—only to lose public sympathy by two jaunty major speeches which made him seem another Nero rather than a second Pitt. Meanwhile, inside and outside the House Henry Layard —the public's favourite Asiatic expert and the lion of literary institutes and Sunday schools as much as of society drawing rooms[2]—was attacking the conduct of the war in precisely the melodramatic style which Palmerston and the governing classes abhorred, but which exactly met the public's sense of crisis. When it is also remembered how passionately the public had supported the war, how confident they had been of quick victory and how often they were told by the press that official shortcomings alone had deprived them of it, the marvel is not that public meetings proliferated in the second half of February, but that they did not proliferate sooner. From this point onwards, it was only a matter of time before an association of some kind was formed to urge the remedy propounded at these gatherings, namely the elimination of inefficiency throughout the public service. For very many years after 1846 the legend of the triumphant Anti-Corn Law League ensured that any

[1] Hughenden MSS., Bxx/98, G. A. Hamilton to Disraeli, 6 December 1854. (I owe my thanks to the National Trust for permission to use these papers.) Some aspects of the Crimean crisis mentioned here are discussed in parts I and II of my book, *A Liberal State at War. English Politics and Economics during the Crimean War* (1967).

[2] Layard's *Nineveh and its Remains* caused a great sensation in 1849, and a popular abridged version was published in 1851. He was returned for Aylesbury in 1852 and given the freedom of the City of London in 1853, when his *Nineveh and Babylon* was also published. A recent biography is G. Waterfield, *Layard of Nineveh* (1963).

group with a cause or an interest to promote, inevitably thought of copying that magical model—although after the Chartist *débâcle* they fought shy of national petitions and conventions.

In this case, an association was in the field from the end of February which successfully avoided being tarred with the Chartist brush, but failed completely to emulate the League. The National and Constitutional Association, as it was called—and its title well suggests its anti-Chartist, semi-Urquhartite flavour—was a thoroughly unimpressive, petty bourgeois affair, under the patronage of two minor radical MPs, Apsley Pellatt and J. P. Murrough.[3] Not surprisingly, by the end of March bigger and very different fish were stirring the waters. Among them were Charles Dickens and the journalists of his circle,[4] and at their centre a small group of City 'merchant princes,' the busiest and noisiest of whom was William Shaw Lindsay, a conceited, ambitious, devious Scottish shipowner and radical MP, who by denouncing the transport service was trying in a small way to play much the same game as Layard, and making an even worse mess of it. Layard himself seems to have been too busy as a popular hero to do more than inspire these exertions. All through April word circulated that a great City association was being formed on Anti-Corn Law lines, to take up 'in a discreet and legitimate way' the question of the hour—'administrative reform'.[5] (By this, it is essential to remember, was meant something far wider than the civil service reform which we should understand by that phrase.) Yet not until 5 May did the much-trumpeted meeting at last take place in the London Tavern, with an overflow in the Guildhall, and then it hardly came up to expectations. The audience (estimated at 5,000) was solid but undistinguished, and the platform all too accurate a match; Layard was absent (probably from malaria), and none of the twelve MPs on the platform was of any real importance either inside or

[3] *Morning Advertiser*, 23 and 27 February, 17 and 31 March, 3 and 27 April 1855. This association can be pretty accurately placed socially and politically from its membership cards available at a shilling from many public houses, and the fact that its promoter was the *Morning Advertiser*, the licensed victuallers' official journal, which under James Grant was then successfully providing political pabulum exactly to their customers' palate—a distinctive blend of well-matured Cobbett and Urquhart, with a dash of Crystal Palace style modernity.

[4] Dickens's all-pervasive anti-establishment radicalism would have secured his sympathy in any case, but it seems to have been a meeting with Layard at Miss Burdett-Coutts' which inspired him to personal exertions (G. Hogarth and M. Dickens (eds.), *The Letters of Charles Dickens* (1882), i, p. 390.)

[5] On 10 April Dickens was agreeing to look over a set of resolutions Layard had prepared for a great meeting on 24 April (*Layard Papers*, B.M. Add. MSS. 38947/16); on 12 April Lindsay with characteristic pretentiousness warned the First Lord of the Admiralty for the ear of the Cabinet alone that his efforts were about to produce an unparalleled City demonstration (*Halifax Papers*, B.M. Add. MSS. 49555/17); and by 29 April a lesser light, J. G. Frith, was confiding to Layard that 'several Thousand Pounds' had been promised (B.M. Add. MSS. 38983/263).

outside the House. After the inevitable Chartist take-over bid had been foiled (in circumstances which made a bitter enemy of Ernest Jones), and some speeches distinctly 'lacking in electricity' had been heard, the resolutions so often passed at public meetings during the last three months were passed again, followed by another establishing an administrative reform association and nominating a committee. Twenty-five gentlemen subscribed £100 on the spot (following the fashion set by the League), a total subscription of £6,010 was announced, and the meeting broke up after receiving a report of the much livelier proceedings in the Guildhall. There, a rider had been passed in favour of an extension of the suffrage, and the business ended with 'three cheers for Mr Layard'.[6] Clearly the occasion had not been a failure; but neither had it been a great success.

The Association had missed the flood-tide of public excitement by many weeks, and in the next few weeks it was to miss the ebb-tide too. It did so above all because of its almost symbiotic relationship with Layard's parliamentary strategy. A week before the City meeting, Layard in his role as parliamentary mouthpiece of the Crimean blunders agitation had given notice of his intention to move a set of resolutions in the House virtually identical with those repeatedly passed at public meetings since February 1855, and again at the founding of the Association—resolutions which attributed national discredit and disaster to 'the manner in which merit and efficiency have been sacrificed, in public appointments, to party and family influences, and to a blind adherence to routine'. In a very real sense the immediate purpose of both the Administrative Reform Association and of the local meetings which followed its founding was to organize support for these resolutions of Layard's, that is, to exercise expressive, intimidating 'pressure from without' on one particular debate in the House. Layard's motion was intended to be the second great popular triumph in parliament of the war (the first having been Roebuck's successful motion for a select committee to inquire into the condition of the army besieging Sebastopol), and from it, great things were expected.[7] This inter-dependence was

[6] The more select audience in the London Tavern cheered the Queen, the Emperor and 'the independent M.P.s'. The meeting was widely reported (see especially the *Daily News*, some of whose owners and staff were directly involved, and *The Times*, 7 and 8 May 1855 and for the Chartist point of view, *People's Paper*, 12 May 1855). There are some further details in Viscountess Enfield (ed.), *Leaves from the Diary of Henry Greville* (2nd series, 1884), p. 215. For a list of the MPs present, see below, p. 287.

[7] The high hopes entertained of Layard's motion are well illustrated by Samuel Laing's letter to Morley of 19 May, asking whether the committee of the Association thought the independent Liberals (among whom Laing was a leading spirit) should vote for it, even if the Palmerston government was brought down thereby, and whether, if asked, they should support any subsequent Tory government (E. Hodder, *Life of Samuel Morley* (1887), p. 123). Layard saw the purpose of the City meeting

disastrous. Layard's attack inside the House was delayed, diverted, and finally humiliatingly defeated, partly by some well-timed government concessions which were quite enough to satisfy the average Member, and by his own blunders and follies; but above all by the success of Derby and Disraeli in stealing as much of Layard's thunder as was likely to detonate with any effect inside parliament. The prolonged delay before his resolutions came on was enough in itself to ruin his parliamentary chances and to dissipate outdoor pressure in his support. First arranged for 14 May, then postponed until 24 May because the Conservatives had staged a major debate along closely similar lines in the Lords on that very day, then postponed again to make way for the great debate on Disraeli's motion censuring the conduct of the way which lasted from 24 May until 8 June, it was not until 15 June that Layard's resolutions were debated at last. By then practically their every word seemed grotesquely out of date. In those six or seven weeks not only the parliamentary situation, but the domestic and military and international ones had changed profoundly. In any case, his annihilation in the division lobbies was certain from the moment when the Conservatives decided to put forward an amendment which would attract the votes of parliamentary 'administrative reformers' and of their own men, while still being acceptable to the government. Predictably, on 18 June his motion was defeated by 359 votes to 46 amid loud laughter.[8]

This prolonged delay not only completed Layard's parliamentary ruin, but dissipated the effect of outdoor pressure in his support. For by far the greater number of local 'administrative reform' meetings had been held between 15 and 22 May, when his motion was still down for 24 May. These meetings requested local Members to support Layard's resolutions, passed similar resolutions themselves, and petitioned parliament in his support; only comparatively rarely did they establish local

quite simply as 'to support me' (B.M. Add. MSS. 38944/35). For the wording of his motion, see Hansard, *Parliamentary Debates*, 3rd series, 138/2079.

[8] Layard's motion had been put down before 27 April (Palmerston to the Queen, 27 Apl., 1855, R.A. A24/49). (I have to acknowledge the gracious permission of H.M. the Queen to cite documents from the Royal Archives, Windsor Castle.) For its checkered history, see Hansard, 138/359, 2040–2133, 2154–2225, 139/679; Palmerston to the Queen, 20 May and 14 June 1855, R.A., A24/59, 73; G. A. Hamilton, to Disraeli, n.d., Hughenden MSS., Bxx/98; J. L. Ricardo to the 3rd Earl Grey, 18 June 1855, Howick MSS. (I owe my thanks to the Department of Palaeography and Diplomatic of the University of Durham for permission to examine these papers); Viscountess Enfield, *op. cit.*, p. 218. Layard's defeat did not mean that the House was hostile to administrative reform, as supposed by M. Wright, *Treasury Control of the Civil Service 1854–1874* (1969), p. 64; indeed, the opposite was rather the case (cf. e.g., Palmerston to Clarendon, 26 May 1855, Bodleian MSS., Clarendon deposit c. 31, f. 228 (I owe my thanks to the Earl of Clarendon for permission to use these papers), and below, p. 285, n. 45).

committees to co-operate with the City Administrative Reform Association. In other words, they had been geared to the exercise of pressure on one specific parliamentary debate, and the postponement of that debate for nearly a month necessarily deprived them of their effect. When the debate finally came on, in greatly altered circumstances, there could be no repetition of such pressure, semi-spontaneous as it had been. Only the City Association itself was able to time its meetings so that they did immediately precede the long-awaited debate; hence its inactivity after 5 May, and its frenzied efforts from 13 June, when it held the first of a projected series of spectacular meetings in Drury Lane theatre. On that night, thirty-two MPs were secured for the stage, and Layard ('Henry Dauntless') made the speech of the evening, supported by 'Le Père Noble' and 'the Funny Man' (Morley and Lindsay). Dickens was the star of the second meeting, held on 27 June in the hope of getting up steam again after Layard's parliamentary defeat. This time there were only nine MPs on the platform. If it was difficult to control semi-spontaneous popular pressure closely enough to influence one specific parliamentary debate, it was even more difficult artificially to create popular pressure for a vague, abstract and distant goal in an atmosphere of anti-climax. The third Drury Lane meeting was cancelled, and in July meetings everywhere came to an abrupt end. Layard and Dickens retreated to the continent, sadly disgusted by their disappointments.[9]

Nevertheless, the Administrative Reform Association survived, as its comparatively pedestrian official leadership steered it into narrower and safer channels. At the first business meeting on 8 August, when a mere hundred or so subscribers turned up, the officers and leading members of the committee succeeded in defeating the militants who wanted a general radical programme, and securing the adoption of their own carefully worked out plans for concentrating upon the furtherance of the recruitment of junior government clerks by examination.[10] In reality this development was far less of a *coup* than it seemed to many contemporary outsiders. Indeed, it was precisely the fact that the official

[9] The two Drury Lane meetings were very widely reported, e.g. *Daily News* and *The Times*, 14 and 28 June 1855. Dickens's speech (published as a twopenny pamphlet) is reprinted in K. J. Fielding (ed.), *The Speeches of Charles Dickens* (Oxford, 1960), p. 200. Thackeray drafted a speech for the cancelled meeting planned for 11 July (G. N. Ray (ed.), *The Letters and Private Papers of William Makepeace Thackeray*, iii (1946), pp. 678—84). For Layard's intense depression, see B.M. Add. MSS. 38944/38 42. Dickens consoled himself with writing *Little Dorritt* and the pleasures of Paris (J. Forster, *Life of Charles Dickens* (1872—4), iii, p. 123; Hogarth and Dickens, I, p. 406).

[10] The press reports (e.g. *The Times* and *Morning Advertiser*, 9 August 1855) should be supplemented by Administrative Reform Association, Official Paper no. 6, Report of the General Committee adopted at a meeting of subscribers held at the London Tavern, 8 August 1855.

leadership had always possessed a quite different conception of the Association from that entertained by the public and promoted by its leading orators, which had finally ensured its failure earlier that summer. While Dickens, for example, was exclaiming that the 'great, first, strong necessity is to rouse the people up', and Layard and Lindsay were making practical efforts to do so in the way which was indeed essential if 'expressive' popular pressure was to be built up,[11] the official tone and conduct of the Association remained inhibitingly restrained. No systematic promotion of provincial branches or lobbying of Members or Ministers was attempted; the subscription was kept too high for there to be any possibility of a mass membership; only two mass meetings were held; and the publications upon which official efforts were concentrated were extremely slow in appearing, extremely badly written, and incongruously narrow and technical in scope.[12] From the beginning the Association's organization and tactics were all too firmly controlled not by its platform stars and activists, but by its sober officials, and above all by its chairman and treasurer, Samuel Morley and John Ingram Travers.

Both Morley and Travers were City 'princes', congregationalists and political reformers by upbringing and conviction, and heads of large and still famous firms. Travers was fresh from his successful chairmanship of the City Committee for the Reform of the Customs, on which the Administrative Reform Association was partly modelled.[13] Nevertheless Morley was clearly the more important of the two, and very far indeed from being a mere figure-head chosen to impart an aura of earnestness and business success. Since 1843, three concerns had increasingly drawn that imperious man into politics; first, a concern to promote education; secondly, a concern to increase parliamentary sympathy towards nonconformity and hence to promote not only the return of nonconformist MPs but the independence of MPs in general; and thirdly, a concern for increased departmental efficiency. All three concerns would be furthered by 'administrative reform' as he understood it; hence his activity in promoting the Association, and subsequent

[11] For Dickens's view, see Hogarth and Dickens, i, p. 399 and B.M. Add. MSS. 38947/16; for examples of Layard's and Lindsay's activities, B.M. Add. MSS. 38983/399 and *Daily News*, 17 May 1855.

[12] Contemporary criticism of all this abounded, and not only in the Palmerstonian and extreme radical press (e.g. *Lloyds Weekly News*, 3 June; *The Press*, 16 June; *Leader*, 28 July; *Morning Advertiser*, 10 August 1855). See especially 'H.B.', *Administrative Reformers—What have they done?* (1855).

[13] The overlap in personnel, tactics and outlook between the two Committees is marked, e.g. the *Final Report of the City Customs Reform Committee*, 13 June 1854, p. 13, criticized the Northcote–Trevelyan report along the same lines as the Administrative Reform Association. Like several of his colleagues Travers was a keen supporter of commercial education (Joseph Travers and Sons, *Chronicles of Cannon Street* (1957), p. 26).

chairmanship of it. From the beginning Morley was thinking in terms of deliberative and didactic pressure, and he was strongly encouraged in this by a revived connection with that confirmed propagandist and manipulator, Edwin Chadwick, to whom he had fed information in 1854 for his memorandum in response to the Northcote–Trevelyan enquiry. Chadwick at this time was unemployed, and restlessly trying to get his own cures for the country's administrative troubles adopted by assiduously exploiting his old political contacts, as well as by pamphleteering. In May 1855 Morley allowed him to become, anonymously, the Association's official writer, and Chadwick duly put together its first three pamphlets, and made himself something of an *éminence grise* to the committee.[14]

By the autumn, however, while still continuing their discreetly didactic approach, the committee were also trying to meet their critics' charges that their pamphlets were unreadable, their proposals vague and their organization exclusive. Chadwick was dropped as their writer. A detailed programme of immediate reforms was embodied in a petition to parliament published in October, which gave pride of place to a bill to oblige all junior clerkships to be filled by examination. The committee became elective, the membership subscription was lowered to a shilling, and a couple of earnest pamphlets published, clearly aimed at ambitious youths, their parents, teachers and mechanics' institutes, and committing the Association to the view that open competition would promote 'middle class' education and social harmony.[15] But this was almost the whole extent of their endeavours. Only, apparently, in Southwark—always the stronghold of the Association—was the routine step taken of organizing a meeting to get up a petition to parliament in favour of the junior clerkships bill, and to request the two local MPs to support it (both were in fact prominent in the Association). A meeting

[14] Morley at this time was not himself politically ambitious. Hodder, *op. cit.*, conveys his character well; see especially pp. 79, 97, 181, 488. For Chadwick's relations with Morley and the Association, see *Chadwick Papers*, University College, London, Morley to Chadwick, 1 July 1854, 28 August 1855, Chadwick to Travers, 28 June 1855, and Chadwick to Sir Charles Shaw, 16 July 1855. (I owe my thanks to the Librarian of University College, London, for permission to consult these papers.) Chadwick's authorship of Official Papers, nos. 2–4, is well discussed in R. A. Lewis, 'Edwin Chadwick and the administrative reform movement, 1854–56'. *Birmingham University Journal*, ii, 1949–50, pp. 190–200. For Chadwick's allied activities in 1855, see S. Finer, *The Life and Times of Sir Edwin Chadwick* (1952), pp. 483–7.

[15] See Official Papers, nos. 8–11. The Association's bill attracted some attention and encouraged Disraeli to work on one of his own, since administrative reform around Christmas 1855 seemed a coming question (G. Buckle, *Life of Benjamin Disraeli*, iv (1916), pp. 35–6). A different note was struck in Official Paper no. 7 which printed the voting record of MPs throughout the session on issues connected with administrative reform, and was thus a harbinger of the approach to be developed under Roebuck.

in January to demand an inquiry into the loss of Kars, and another in March 1856 with a more general purpose, were both conspicuous failures.[16] From the beginning of 1856 Morley was acknowledging that the Association had been inefficient, and the disappointing defeat of Goderich's promising motion for open competition on 24 April may have been the last straw. Whatever the reasons, early in June 1856 Morley publicly declared that the tactics hitherto followed had failed, and handed over the chairmanship to that very different character, John Arthur Roebuck.

Vehement, opinionated, a born attacker who detested the rigidity and exclusiveness of English politics and society, and a born independent who was never a party man; a utilitarian politician, moreover, who since 1832 had made the House of Commons his chief battleground (he considered his poor health unfitted him for outdoor agitation)—it was not to be expected for a moment that Roebuck would be content with the quiet, increasingly schoolmasterly tactics so congenial to his predecessor. Roebuck's primary concern was to attack aristocratic supremacy inside and outside the Commons, and he soon began to beat the rousing drum of class again. Moreover, he had always been convinced that the key to political success lay not in trying to influence public opinion, but in getting power inside the House of Commons itself, by forming 'an efficient parliamentary party'. To this end, in June 1856 he completely changed the executive organization of the Association, creating four honorary Secretaryships: Financial (still held by Travers), General (to which he appointed his old henchman John Revans in place of the City actuary Samuel Brown), and much more novel and significant, Corresponding (held by Morley) and Statistical (held by John Peter Gassiot).[17] It was the Corresponding Department whose role Roebuck chiefly stressed, with its plan to open a ledger of constituencies, with 'alphabetical entries of all information which has power in an election there'. Morley was the natural man to be asked to preside over this, for since 1847 he had been chairman of the dissenters' parliamentary committee, formed to exploit dissenting urban voting strength in precisely this way, and regarded as having been highly successful in the previous general election. His new department now duly opened a book 'containing every post-town in the kingdom', and circulated known sympathizers and contacts in each town, asking for the name of local people likely to give practical help; each name was

[16] *The Times*, 11 and 28 January, 26 March 1856.

[17] For Roebuck's circular to the members of the Administrative Reform Association explaining his plans see *Daily News*, 7 June 1856. For his career as a whole R. A. Leader (ed.), *Life and Letters of John Arthur Roebuck* (1897) remains indispensable. A. Briggs, *Victorian People* (1954), chapter 3, provides a study of him during the Crimean war.

then entered in the ledger, 'under his post-town'.[18] By the later 1850s
these were almost classic methods of attempting to mobilize electoral
pressure in order to secure some leverage in parliament. In a quite
different radical vein, John Gassiot set about giving the Association's
information-collecting activities an altered significance, by pains-
takingly compiling, not information about comparative methods of
recruitment and so on in the Chadwickian–Morley style, but statistics
about the behaviour of MPs in the division lobbies.[19] Through publishing the parliamentary record of every member, the Association hoped
to induce electors to call absentees and voters in the wrong lobby to
account and exact precise pledges in the future; and by opening its data
for public inspection, it hoped to prevent such members from escaping
retribution by switching to a new constituency where their misdeeds
were unknown. Gassiot's Statistical Department thus explicitly aspired
to become an instrument for the exertion of a controlling pressure from
without upon the House. Time, however—as well as much else—was
not on the Association's side. The proofs of Gassiot's fourth analysis are
dated 18 March 1857; on 20 March, Palmerston dissolved the House
after his defeat on the Chinese war. No detailed study of that election
has yet been attempted, but it is clear enough that the Association's new
tactics were utterly powerless to check the massive return of Palmers-
tonians to the House. That the Association disappeared after this radical
electoral rout cannot be categorically stated; but at least no trace of it
has been found after this blow, and it is consequently here that narrative
must end, and analysis begin.

In any analysis of a pressure group, certain essential questions need to
be asked; who supported it and why? How did it function and legitimate
itself and with what effect? It is particularly desirable that all these
questions should be answered many times with regard to pressure group
activity in Britain between about the 1820s and the 1870s, since only
when this has been done can the causes and consequences of the transformation which occurred during these years in the status of pressure
from without be properly assessed. For in these fifty years or so, such
pressure came to be regarded not as clearly unconstitutional but as
evidence of health in the body politic, a demonstration of the flowering

[18] Encouraging extracts from the replies received were published by the Association
(probably in late February) under the title, *Public Opinion on Administrative Reform*
(1857).
[19] J. P. Gassiot, *Four Letters to J. A. Roebuck Esq.* (1856–7). He claimed to have
a record of how each MP had voted in all the 198 divisions of the 1856 session. Like
several other members of the Association, Gassiot combined business with scientific
writing and experiments (he was an FRS as well as a partner in Martinez, Gassiot
and Co., the wine merchants). He had already worked with Travers on the City
Committee on Customs Reform.

of active citizenship, and not of a perverted disregard for social order. Here, clearly, is another manifestation of those deep changes in the prevailing vision of man, society, and politics which certainly occurred between the beginning and the end of the nineteenth century in England, but whose pace, mechanism, and wider significance remain largely unsettled. Unfortunately as far as the Administrative Reform Association is concerned, it is only with regard to its early heyday that the questions which it is so necessary to ask can be answered at all fully, and it is consequently to this phase of its history that the analysis which follows relates.

Who then supported the Administrative Reform Association? Its social base was an unusual combination, for its hard core consisted of City merchants, brokers, wholesalers, agents and bankers on the one hand, and London professional men on the other. Some of the latter were indeed habitual joiners of political pressure groups, but the City was notoriously hard to move politically. Yet a study of the printed subscription list proves to the hilt that these were the people who joined it, and that moreover the City men were often solidly wealthy and the professional men successful in the many-sided early Victorian way (there was indeed some overlap between the two groups). It was certainly not a dissenting or evangelical stronghold, although it attracted some support from political nonconformists and (strange bedfellows) Christian socialists. Unlike many other secular pressure groups, it was joined by few doctors.[20] The City Administrative Reform Association was thus an organization distinctly outside the artisan tradition of London radicalism, and one which attracted many people who had hitherto kept clear of 'pressure from without'. Yet if one turns to its branch associations and the outer ring of sympathizers who attended meetings to urge 'administrative reform', an instructively different picture emerges. With regard to branch associations as opposed to meetings, indeed, the most striking thing is their rarity. Outside London

---

[20] A printed subscription list and statement of the Association's objects is bound up at the end of the British Museum's set of the Official Papers, nos. 1–7. There were 1,076 subscribers down to 31 August 1855. Nearly one-fifth of the names are those of firms, many of them readily identifiable from the *London Post Office Directory* for 1855. They include such famous names as Samuel Courtauld and the de Rothschild brothers. 'Men of letters' include Dickens, Thackeray, Johnstoun Neale, W. J. Fox, A. B. Richards, John Forster, Matthew Higgins, John Wade and Edward Miall; scientists, Charles Babbage and Jacob Bell; architects, William Tite and James Bell; W. C. Macready the actor, Lowes Dickinson the pre-Raphaelite portrait painter. Men with a foot in both worlds include Samuel Brown and William Newmarch (City actuaries and statisticians), Apsley Pellatt, artistic glass manufacturer and a prominent member of the Institute of Civil Engineers; Francis Bennoch, minor poet and partner in Bennoch and Twentyman, silk agents; J. P. Gassiot, wine merchant, FRS and writer on electricity; and McGregor Laird, African explorer and merchant. On all these men, see the *Dictionary of National Biography*.

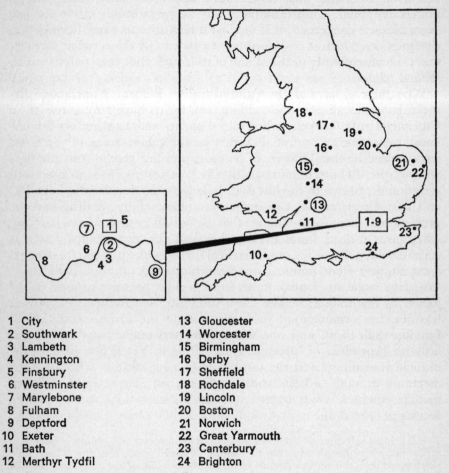

1 City	13 Gloucester
2 Southwark	14 Worcester
3 Lambeth	15 Birmingham
4 Kennington	16 Derby
5 Finsbury	17 Sheffield
6 Westminster	18 Rochdale
7 Marylebone	19 Lincoln
8 Fulham	20 Boston
9 Deptford	21 Norwich
10 Exeter	22 Great Yarmouth
11 Bath	23 Canterbury
12 Merthyr Tydfil	24 Brighton

(Branches were formed in the places circled)

Figure 1 Location of meetings and branches connected with the Administration Reform Association (where Southwark, Marylebone, and Deptford quickly formed associations), only four or five branches are known to have been set up—in Norwich, Gloucester, Birmingham, possibly Boston, and (belatedly) Glasgow. As an organization, the Administrative Reform Association remained predominantly a London affair, whose keenest support, ironically enough, came from that rowdy metropolitan radicalism which most of its City members deprecated and held apart from. Numerous meetings were indeed held in the provinces, but their audiences were far less homogeneous than the London ones. Their geographical distribution alone suggests what dissimilar kinds of protest they expressed: the traditional, anti-government 'country' feeling of historical provincial cities like Exeter and Lincoln, and the 'middling-class' ratepayer radicalism of Bath and Great Yarmouth, as well as the rather cranky, quasi-millennial radicalism of the West Midlands small master belt and the advanced class-conscious radicalism of Rochdale and Merthyr Tydfil; yet, interestingly, not the mercantile, manufacturing, nonconformist radicalism of Manchester, Liverpool, and the West Riding, in all of which there was too little support for meetings to be held. Press reports emphasized how often these provincial meetings attracted not only the liberal and radical regulars, but men who were normally not politically active at all, and a sprinkling of Tory country gentry, notables, and working men. Their speakers often eschewed the London language both of modern progress and of advanced radicalism, and relied heavily upon the lowest common denominator of popular political oratory in the mid-1850s—the traditional rhetoric of the ancient constitution, whose balance had been upset, and must be restored by popular action. Altogether, it is clear that in the provinces though not in London, the meetings associated with 'administrative reform' came close to being what the Association officially aspired to be and what its metropolitan supporters denounced—a national, and not a class or party movement.[21]

Analysis of the parliamentary base of the Association shows that socially and politically it was very similar to its base outside the House. Thirty-nine MPs formally supported the Association in May and June 1855, in the sense that they sat on its platforms, or (although this was much more rare) subscribed to it or held some sort of office. Big business

[21] The second half of this paragraph is based on the reports in the London press. *The Spectator* alludes to a branch at Boston on 19 May 1855, but none is mentioned in the full reports of the town's meeting held there on 16 May reprinted from the local press. The Glasgow branch was formed on 3 November, and all the others between 15 and 24 May. Both Liverpool and Manchester had been active in the agitation which preceded the Association; for the difficulties encountered in mid-May, see *The Times*, 18 and 19 May 1855 (Liverpool and Manchester), and B.M. Add. MSS. 38983/399 (West Riding).

and the professions, especially literature and journalism, were even more heavily represented among these MPs than in the Association's subscribing membership as a whole. Politically, most of them were advanced liberals simply jumping on to the progressive bandwagon of the moment, supporters in varying degrees of such shibboleths as an extension of the franchise, shorter parliaments, the ballot, and the abolition of religious endowments. Among their number were some of the 'independent Liberal party', led by Samuel Laing and closely associated with the activities of Morley's dissenters' parliamentary committee; and eight members of the Independent Irish party. Any movement to weaken the power of the ties of place, party and connection obviously had a strong claim to any independent party's support. Finally there were four Conservatives and two 'Old Whigs', with very miscellaneous reforming interests. None of the thirty-nine seems to have acted from a direct desire to curry favour with his constituents; rather, they gave the Association more or less perfunctory support because it seemed to fit in with their political stance and social outlook. Indeed, apart from the metropolitan MPs only four of them represented places where there was local activity sympathetic to the Association. There are thus scant grounds indeed for seeing 'controlling' pressure at work here.[22]

It ought to be added however that the Association notoriously attracted disappointed parliamentary candidates with no money, family, or party influence to push them on, since its theme of fitness alone as the pathway to parliament and office made it seem a promising launching-pad, especially in the early summer of 1855 when 'administrative reform' could be a good electioneering cry. The Association thus acquired an unsavoury reputation for being the stepping-stone of adventurers.[23] This reputation stuck to it all the more because its showiest orators, Layard, Lindsay, and Admiral Napier, were clearly all frustrated men trying to further their ambitions by cultivating

[22] A list of the MPs concerned will be found on p. 288, below. Only six of them were not committed to parliamentary reform of some sort. J. H. Whyte, *The Irish Independent Party, 1850–59* (1958), e.g. p. 45, shows how the contemporary desire for place was that party's chief problem. It is no accident that the strongest independent among them, J. F. Maguire, was also the one who took the most prominent part in the Association's proceedings.

[23] William Tite's was the case which contemporaries never forgot. While deputy chairman of the Association, Tite captured Bath at the end of May 1855 on an administrative reform platform, having unsuccessfully contested Barnstaple the previous August. Other aspiring candidates active in the Association were Admiral Sir Charles Napier (returned for Southwark, an Association stronghold, in November 1855), Torrens McCullogh (defeated at Great Yarmouth in 1852, but returned in 1857, and the Association's 'delegate' there in May 1855), Jacob Bell, Secretary of the Marylebone branch (defeated at Marylebone in 1854), and Sergeant Stephen Gaselee (defeated at Portsmouth in March 1855).

'outdoors'.[24] A final odour of political insincerity came when the Association failed officially to repudiate the early exploitation of the movement by the Conservative party's activists, who were obviously manoeuvring thereby to attract votes in parliament and improve their image in the towns.[25] The bohemian, flamboyantly anti-establishment tone of Dickens and his friends thus simply completed the clouding over of that atmosphere of earnestness and solidity which had impressed contemporaries at the very beginning.

Socially and politically, then, once the various outer rings of adherents, sympathizers, and exploiters are taken into account and not only the hard core of subscribers, the Association is revealed as having very mixed sources of support indeed. It is consequently all the less surprising that its objects prove to have been likewise extremely diverse. Even the wording of its official programme—'to secure the recognition of the principles of fit men in fit places, promotion by merit, a free career open to talent, and the application to all departments of the Military, Naval, Diplomatic and Civil services of the country of those principles of common sense which the practical experience of private affairs suggests as essential to avert failure and ensure success'—is enough to show that the view is misleading which sees it as a pressure group for the implementation of the Northcote-Trevelyan report.[26]

Analysis of its leaders' speeches and correspondence together with contemporary comment, establishes beyond any doubt that its watchwords were fitness and responsibility, its bogeys party and nepotism, and its prime remedy independence from the fetters of party and personal connections. Its loudest call was to the electorate: if they would only choose their representatives from merit alone, and then refrain from asking them for favours, they would set off a chain reaction which would transform the calibre of the men in public life and the relationships between those who exercised electoral, legislative, executive, and administrative functions, right to the very top. Clearly if the Association

[24] Layard was extremely bitter at not getting the Under-Secretaryship for War in February, the offer of which Palmerston had to withdraw under royal and Cabinet pressure—'the only place in the Government except a Cabinet Office which I could have accepted without losing my excellent position and forfeiting my reputation' (B.M. Add. MSS. 38944/34). For Lindsay and Napier, see p. 288, n. 44, below.

[25] The committee was anxious to preserve its all-party line. Thackeray, however, intended to say at the meeting planned for 11 July, 'we don't want Godpapa's [Disraeli's] party to manage for us' (Ray, *op. cit.*, iii, p. 678). To be fair, Disraeli had been pushing administrative reform long before the Association came on the scene.

[26] A fuller discussion of the Association's programme will be found in my article, 'The Janus face of mid-nineteenth century English radicalism: the Administrative Reform Association of 1855', *Victorian Studies*, March 1965, pp. 231–42, to whose editorial board I owe my thanks for permission to use again some of the material used there.

was attempting to implement anything, it was Carlyle's *Downing Street Letters* rather than the Northcote-Trevelyan report.[27] Its true political antecedents are to be found primarily in mid-nineteenth century discontent with the practical inefficiency and social narrowness of government, exacerbated between 1846 and 1859 by the confusion of parties, the instability of ministries, and the legislative inefficiency of parliament. In reality the Association is quite as much part of the history of changing concepts of ministerial responsibility and party government, and of schemes for dealing with electoral corruption and private bill legislation, as it is part of the history of civil service reform.[28] Indeed in this first phase, very few of its supporters seem to have favoured recruitment by competitive examination, and none recruitment by competitive *literary* examination. Nor is this surprising, for in 1855 competitive examinations were still a new and controversial device. Those who condemned them as promoting pedantry and creating fresh barriers for the humbler classes to surmount, had many sympathizers inside the Association's circle. To them, not 'rules and regulations' but fit choosers were what was needed to secure fit men; reformers should resist the 'sophistries and pedantries of the Trevelyan school', and remember that what was wanted was men who were 'the types of the day and of the spirit of the age', not 'men of learning and brilliant talents'.[29] Even those in the Association who did support recruitment by examination (and, as has been explained, they dominated the Association in its second phase), had in mind a directly vocational, qualifying examination to establish professional fitness on the model of the examinations

[27] See especially Morley's speeches, reported in *The Times*, 7 May, 14 and 28 June 1855, and Travers's, *ibid.*, 7 May 1855. Contemporaries often assumed (wrongly) that Carlyle supported the Association. Intelligent comment frequently regarded the movement as primarily one for parliamentary and ministerial, not civil service reform, and emphasized its hostility to the principles of party government (cf. *Fraser's Magazine*, li (1855), pp. 607–26; *The Spectator*, 12 May 1855; Hansard, 138/527, 2119).

[28] The manifesto which Layard drafted for the Association late in June 1855 ranged widely over questions of governmental personnel and machinery, and especially legislative–executive relations and the machinery for dealing with private bills and election petitions. Only two of its twenty-two clauses deal with recruitment by open competitive examination, and this was to be 'in a prescribed course of subjects, *not of books*, and excluding the dead languages' (B.M. Add. MSS. 39053/7–8). Many of these clauses reappear in the Association's 'Petition to the House of Commons', published as Official Paper no. 9. Election petitions were a particularly topical problem, since after the 1852 election their number suddenly doubled (see the table in N. Gash, *Politics in the Age of Peel* (1953), p. 431).

[29] This is the usual editorial line of the *Daily News* (which was then almost the Association's organ), see 16 May and 13 June 1855, 25 April 1856; and cf. Ayrton at the meeting of 8 August, *The Times*, 9 August 1855. Layard was so evasive on this point in the House, that Northcote criticized him for not proposing recruitment by open competition, although Gladstone (rightly) understood that he had done so (Hansard, 138/2105).

then being introduced, for example, for doctors and solicitors, and not the competitive, mandarin, 'generalist' ideal of Macaulay.[30]

As for the underlying hopes and fears which the Association drew upon, the best evidence of their diversity is perhaps the diversity of the styles of rhetoric used by its supporters. Three main clusters of political and social ideals can be identified. The first was associated predominantly with the City Association itself, with its successful businessmen confident that that largest of all enterprises, government, should be run like their own, and its climbing professional men who condemned amateurs in the public service as vigorously as they did amateur interlopers in their own fields of expertise.[31] For both, their support of the Association reflected impatience with the successful resistance of the old regime, and a vision, not of an egalitarian society nor of a democratic state, but of a mobile and pragmatic society served by an efficient, workmanlike government,[32] with personal merit as the determinant of status in each. Secondly, there were the very different hopes and fears characteristic of the outer ring, especially in the provinces. Inspired chiefly by injured national pride, the instinctive need for a scapegoat, and a dogged determination that Britain should retrieve her reputation in Europe, they called for 'the right man in the right place' so that 'England, old England, shall be herself again'.[33] Popular nationalism was the force at work here, reinforced at the edges by idealistic, Coleridgean nationalism of the kind expressed by the Christian socialists, with its vision of an organic society and a government based on ideals of responsibility and reverence for all men.[34] Lastly, the

[30] Cf. Official Paper no. 6; Tite, Hansard, 139/739, and Jacob Bell, reported in *The Times*, 26 March 1856. (Bell had entered parliament in 1847 with the object of introducing a Bill to regulate the qualifications of pharmacists, according to DNB; and he was not the only member of the Association active in furthering professional tests.)

[31] Good illustrations of this confidence that public administration ought to model itself upon business administration are provided by W. S. Lindsay's pamphlet, *A Confirmation of Admiralty Mismanagement* (1855) and his speech at Norwich reported in *The Times*, 17 May 1855. Some of the 'men of letters and science' concerned with the Association had been fighting the control of aristocratic patrons over the scientific and literary societies for years. In these very months Dickens and Forster were manoeuvring to get control of the Royal Literary Fund entirely into the hands of literary and scientific men, and as long ago as 1830 Babbage had started a fierce dispute by ascribing the low state of science in England to the dominance of noblemen, army officers, clergymen and lawyers in the Royal Society.

[32] The promotion of practical social reforms (water supply, burials and so on) and the application of science to public administration were quite often predicted as likely consequences of securing practical men in government (e.g. Tite, *The Times*, 7 May, and the petition of the inhabitants of Derby, *ibid.*, 17 May 1855).

[33] For illustrations see the speeches of Layard at Liverpool (*The Times*, 23 April, Lindsay at Norwich and W. Matthews at Birmingham (*Daily News*, 17 and 22 May 1855)).

[34] Cf. F. D. Maurice, *Administrative Reform and its connexion with Working Men's Colleges* (1855); C. Kingsley to Chadwick, 31 August 1855, *Chadwick Papers*. This par-

Association drew upon the exceedingly heterogeneous cluster of feelings and ideas associated with political radicalism. True, despite a promising start, it failed to tame the Chartists and to bring the new proletarian, anti-capitalist radicalism under its umbrella.[35] But it drew very heavily and successfully upon the traditional rhetoric of 'old corruption', which with its denunciation of borough-mongering, fiscal exploitation, 'secret influences' and monopolies of every kind, expressed ancient political and social assumptions and ideals which could still bridge that gulf between 'the middle and working classes' which contemporaries often feared the Association would widen.[36] Less happily, the Association also attracted —and disappointed—many advanced Liberals and radicals for whom an extended suffrage and the ballot were the only way to a better world; and it was this strand of strictly electoral radicalism which grew stronger among the Association's activists as its wartime national aura faded, although to the end organic parliamentary reform was kept out of its official programme.[37]

Extreme variety of base and purpose, then, is an outstanding characteristic of the Association in its first phase. It is probable that this heterogenity partly explains why the legitimacy of the Association's activities was so calmly debated by contemporaries. Undoubtedly this was due even more to the diversion of attention throughout 1855 to the question of newspaper pressure from without, and above all to the debilitating atmosphere of anti-climax which soon surrounded the Association. But at the beginning, the distinctive features of its tone and tactics were also of some importance. From the outset, the official leadership strove to dissociate it from 'agitation', and on the whole

ticular kind of nationalism, however, was of more importance in diffusing support for administrative reform generally in the earlier 1850s, than in the Association itself. (It is the chief key to Goderich's actions and association with Layard in 1855.)

[35] The Association's intermediary, James Acland, that incorrigibly violent veteran of the campaigns against the newspaper stamp duties and the corn laws, probably went beyond his brief in promising that Jones should second a resolution at the Guildhall meeting and have a place on the committee (*People's Paper*, 5 and 12 May; *Daily News*, 31 May 1855). At any rate, none of these promises were kept, and Jones embarked upon a strenuous campaign in the *People's Paper* to encourage Chartists to wreck administrative reform meetings everywhere. Only in the London area however were they really successful.

[36] A striking example is W. Torrens McCullogh's very well-received speech at Norwich (17 May 1855, *Daily News*).

[37] Resolutions were passed to the effect that parliamentary reform was the necessary preliminary to administrative reform at meetings in Finsbury, Southwark, Lambeth and West Brompton (*Daily News*, 23, 25, 30 May, 7 June 1855). T. Duncombe, Sir J. Shelley and G. F. Muntz were among the radical MPs dissatisfied with the Association on this score. In the autumn of 1855 the committee went so far as to send to its subscribers James Acland's strident *Parliamentary Incongruities and Electoral Anomalies*, but 'solely as a collection of important facts for the consideration of the electors; the Association is not to be considered pledged to its opinions or political tendencies' (title-page).

succeeded, thanks to its ticket meetings, guinea subscription, General Committee composed of subscribers of £50 or more, and the high average age as well as income of its supporters. Like so many other early Victorian reformers, they pinned their faith upon the sheer power of knowledge to convince and activate. True, in May and June 1855 these didactic tactics were challenged by the aggressive demagoguery and strident personalities favoured by Dickens, Layard, and their ilk, but this was counter-balanced by the indisputably legitimate style of action which prevailed in the provinces. Most of the provincial meetings in these months were neither ticket meetings nor strictly speaking public meetings, but were held in response to a requisition to the mayor signed by all shades of local opinion for a 'town's meeting' in the town hall under his chairmanship. They were thus organized within the historic framework of the local community, in a manner apparently fairly rare in mid-nineteenth century agitations, but indisputably impressive.[38] All things considered, it is not surprising that contemporaries blamed the Association more often for ineffectiveness than for unconstitutional violence.

Even so, in its brief heyday its doings seemed disturbing enough to prompt the rehearsal of the two commonest mid-nineteenth century defences of pressure from without: that it was a source of social stability, and that it was necessary for political progress. When popular feeling was aroused, the first argument ran, agitation was a safety-valve which prevented the worse evil of disorder; Catholic emancipation, parliamentary reform and free trade, the second maintained, all proved that large reforms would only be yielded to agitation. Both these well-worn arguments defending pressure from without on practical grounds were pressed into service on behalf of the Association.[39] But unlike most contemporary pressure groups, the Association could also defend its activities on loftier constitutional grounds, and it was here that the keenest

[38] Town meetings were held in Birmingham, Boston, Brighton, Gloucester, Glasgow, Lincoln, Norwich, Sheffield; in Liverpool, the mayor refused the requisition. Their traditional purpose was either to send a petition to parliament, or to instruct the town's MPs, and if the latter were not present, they sent written apologies. In the same style, vestry meetings were held by requisition of the ratepayers in Marylebone and Westminster, duly presided over by the unsympathetic senior churchwarden (*Daily News*, 31 May and 29 June 1855), and on 25 March 1856 a meeting ostensibly of Westminster electors was presided over by the returning officer, the High Bailiff. Meetings convened by requisition had many advantages, both financial and intangible.

[39] For examples see editorial, *Daily News* 6 May, and Lindsay and Morley as reported in *The Times*, 17 May and 28 June 1855. In parliament the danger of allowing the conviction to grow that great evils could only be remedied by agitation, was stressed by Layard and the Conservatives exploiting the Association (Hansard, 138/470, 525, 2044, 2119). As a government spokesman retorted, underlying this argument was the assumption that parliament should lead public opinion and not vice versa, an assumption which went to the roots of constitutional debate (*ibid.*, 489).

debate took place. The 'national' aspect of its activities made it plausible for it to claim that the pressure it exerted was neither sectional nor 'interested', while the country's military and political situation could be held to prove the failure, almost the abdication, of the country's governors. After 1832 it was no longer pure Whiggery to maintain that provided it was 'wholesomely formed' and truly representative, public opinion had the right and indeed the duty to check and control parliament, to express the general mind when parliament failed to do so, and to correct the trustees of the people when they governed selfishly, and these were the high functions claimed for the Association in its heyday.[40] The debate on the early Administrative Reform Association, although neither a landmark nor a turning point, was thus a particularly wide-ranging one, and one which demonstrates once more how persistently in the mid-nineteenth century men clung to the old ideals of an organic society and a parliamentary polity, however altered their behaviour. Their novel political practices were defended, not by any resort to those concepts of pluralism and direct popular participation in government which would have been logically more appropriate, but by the deployment of traditional social and political concepts which harked back to Locke and the revolution of 1688, or most often of all by purely practical arguments from necessity alone.

But *was* the Administrative Reform Association defensible on practical grounds? How much did it accomplish in reality? Contemporaries judged it a clear failure, and quite rightly attributed this to the country's improved political and military situation and to the government's own activity in the field of administrative reform, as well as to the Association's faults in leadership, programme, and tactics.[41] Each of these three causes of failure was by no means peculiar to the Administrative Reform Association, and each is worth considering in the wider context of the general efficacy of 'pressure from without'. Expressive pressure could only be really effective when it could intimidate

[40] Layard told the banqueting notables of the Liverpool area that he was confident they would take their 'proper part in placing a check over those who govern you', and in Birmingham Thomas Attwood junior expounded an updated version of Locke: 'they were all shareholders in a great company, and (which was not a solitary case) they found that the managers and directors were using their influence and funds to promote their own interests. They had therefore been obliged to call a meeting of the shareholders and to take the business of the company into their own hands' (*The Times*, 23 April, 22 May 1855). Very often it was asserted that it was the duty of every individual to co-operate to secure responsibility and efficiency in government.

[41] See, e.g., the analyses in *The Times* 1 and 12 January 1856, *Saturday Review*, 1 December 1855, and *Leader*, 29 December 1855. The two faults potentially sympathetic men of affairs most often objected to, were its vaguely platitudinous programme and defective leadership. These, for example, deterred Sir Joseph Paxton (Chadwick to Travers, 28 June 1855, *Chadwick Papers*.)

those who held political power, and this it could only do with the aid of threatening external circumstances or a high degree of public unanimity and excitement. These were seldom forthcoming in this period in Britain. In this case, only in the spring of 1855, and chiefly before the Association was founded, did the conjuncture of events and public excitement combine to create the fear which might conceivably have had large results. During the summer of 1855 political and military circumstances quickly changed, and the patriotic war fever which had earlier contributed much to public indignation, accordingly tended only to restrain it. Quite different factors usually worked to emasculate didactic pressure. This type of pressure depended not on intimidation, but on rational conviction, and could hope to be effective only where comparatively narrow and concrete questions were involved. But again and again on such questions, didactic pressure groups found they had lost their thunder, as the substance of their demands was independently implemented by government. Contemporaries liked to suppose that this demonstrated the truth of the view that pressure from without was the great source of progress, but in reality such government action was predominantly independent, rather than a series of concessions. Significantly, the approach and underlying objectives, like the details and mode of execution of the measures taken by government, were often very different from those envisaged without doors.[42] British government in the mid-nineteenth century surely led the world in its faith in information and its zeal for social statistics and needed no amateur outside teachers (though indeed at the level of technical expertise, the distinction between 'within' and 'without' is often unreal). Government policies were affected by administrative and parliamentary considerations, and not directly by outside agitation. Thus each of the many measures of administrative reform taken in 1855 had a long parliamentary and administrative history of its own. The famous Order in Council of 21 May, for example, represented a compromise in a debate over recruitment to the civil service which had been going on for years, a compromise which was hammered out and accepted by Aberdeen's cabinet on 20 January 1855, which hung fire when Palmerston's less favourably disposed cabinet came in, but was finally hurriedly implemented as part of a whole series of *coups de théâtre* in May intended to defuse a parliamentary situation which threatened the survival of the Ministry.[43] In this long and many-sided process the Administrative

[42] For examples, see W. N. Calkins, 'A Victorian Free Trade Lobby: the Liverpool Financial Reform Association, 1848–1914', *Economic History Review*, 2nd series, xiii, 1960, pp. 90–104, and in a more familiar field, N. McCord, *The Anti-Corn Law League, 1838–46* (2nd edn., 1968), p. 203.
[43] An account of the Order in Council's antecedents will be found in E. Hughes, 'Civil service reform', *History*, xxvii, 1942, pp. 51–83. For the Aberdeen Cabinet's

Reform Association played only a small and indirect part, in so far as its disturbing early stages helped in a small way to create so strong a feeling inside parliament that action was necessary, that the parliamentary managers judged it wise to respond.

But this over-rated Order in Council apart, how far did the Association even indirectly promote the implementation of administrative reform? Did it in fact strengthen sympathy for such reform *per se* inside parliament? It may be said straight away that in this respect the Association seems to have done more harm than good. Its impact on parliament provides in fact a good example of another general factor which militated against the efficacy of persuasive as opposed to intimidatory pressure politics, namely, the persistent cultural gulf between 'within' and 'without'. However much the theory that parliament should express the general mind might triumph, in practice it remained impossible to rule parliament out of parliament. In so far as styles of leadership, rhetoric and tactics aroused enthusiasm outdoors, they were still, *ipso facto*, likely to disgust and antagonize the governing class. A motion phrased to appeal to the country, could be relied on to prove distasteful to parliament. Popular heroes, in short, were bound to be establishment cads or villains. Exceptions to this rule like Cobden and Shaftesbury were rare and precious birds indeed; and Layard was certainly not among their number, as he learnt with bitterness in the early summer of 1855.[44] As for the rank and file supporters of the Association in the House, advanced reformers, independent Irish, a handful of 'country' anti-government men, writers and business men as they were, they were unlikely to make much impact on their fellow Members.

decision, see J. B. Conacher, *The Aberdeen Coalition, 1852–55* (1968), p. 529, n. 3. Palmerston's letter to the Queen of 20 May 1855, R.A. A24/59, establishes that it was rushed through in anticipation of the debate on Layard's resolutions which was then expected to be held on 24 May. Among other tactically identical moves was Palmerston's sudden announcement on 11 May of the consolidation of the military departments and this too, as Derby said, was 'not in response to public opinion outside, but to the significant hint given by the Motion before the House' (Hansard, 138/453). Chadwick, too, when trying to reassure Morley that the Association had not been a failure, argued that it was 'the effect produced in the House of Commons by the Association' which had stirred the government to set up the Civil Service Commission (Chadwick to Morley, 19 June 1856, *Chadwick Papers*).

44 'Mr Lie-Hard' provoked the most intense indignation in the House by his personal attacks and refusal to retract when proved wrong (e.g. Hansard, 137/1872–97, 138/769–85), but equally intense admiration without doors for this 'fearlessness', as his in-letters show (B.M. Add. MSS. 38983). Lindsay, too, disgusted the House by his interminable and shuffling defence of his own firm against mismanagement or worse; but his denunciations of the transport service delighted popular feeling, all the more, in radical quarters, because the minister concerned was Sir James Graham, a radical villain because of his earlier record as Home Secretary. Admiral Napier, another Association orator, similarly, although the 'Hero of Acre' and another of Graham's martyrs outside, was despised and disliked inside the House for his melodramatic egoism.

Admittedly they were rather more assiduous in passing through the division lobbies than most, but their personal influence was negligible, and as parliamentary tacticians and speakers they were worse than useless. In any case, to conservatively-minded MPs the Association was damned beforehand as unconstitutional; to government supporters it was offensive because it gave expression to public criticism of Palmerston's relaxed style of handling the war crisis; while the open-minded were alienated by the vagueness of its proposals and the demagogic escapism of its rhetoric against 'the aristocracy'. Even to some of the radical MPs, its tactics seemed too misguided to be countenanced. The personal defects of its parliamentary supporters thus only aggravated an already bad image in the House. 'Outsiders', incapable of striking the right note, they made a politically distasteful organization seem an ungentlemanly dodge run by men on the make and supported by green-horns. It is not surprising that there were very many sincere administrative reformers in parliament who carefully kept clear of the Administrative Reform Association,[45] and a few (notably Vincent Scully) who deliberately tried to discredit its spokesmen there, to prevent them from doing any further damage to the cause.[46]

To emphasize the shortcomings of the Association, then—its inactivity, its delay in formulating any concrete programme and persistent preference for high-minded truisms, its badly written propaganda and the blunders and egoism of its leaders—is to explain its failure on altogether too superficial a level. To appreciate the extent to which it was bedevilled by its oscillation between different types of pressure is to go further towards understanding, but still not far enough. To be just, it is essential to recognize to what a very large extent the structure of society and politics in mid-nineteenth century Britain conspired to deprive

[45] Only eighteen of the 125 MPs who voted for (and nearly carried) Scully's motion for open competition on 10 July 1855 were supporters of the Administrative Reform Association. Fifteen of the latter voted in fewer than three of the eight divisions associated with administrative Reform in 1855, and only nine voted in six or more, a record which was equalled by five other MPs who kept clear of the Association (Goderich, Williams, Hadfield, Laslett, Kennedy). (It should be remembered, however, that absenteeism from the lobbies was extremely high in this parliament.) As the list on p. 288 below shows, none of the really influential proponents of administrative reform inside governing circles was connected with the Association. For some of their reasons, cf. Hansard, 138/2094, 2103. To judge from Hansard, the only speakers among the Association group, apart from Layard, Lindsay and, after October 1855, Napier, were Reed, Wise, Otway, Tite and Michell.

[46] Lindsay and Tite were easy targets (cf. Scully to Wood, 25 June 1855, B.M. Add. MSS. 49555/224; Goderich to Layard, 25 August 1855, B.M. Add. MSS. 38984/161; Hansard, 139/742; 'Jacob Omnium' (Matthew Higgins), *A Letter on Administrative Reform* (1855), pp. 6–7 and above, p. 276, n. 23. Russell in a gloomy diatribe to his father-in-law included a lament that 'Layard and Lindsay have done much harm by desecrating the good cause of administrative reform' (Russell to Minto, 22 July 1855, Public Record Office, *Russell Papers*, P.R.O., 30/22/12).

organized popular pressure groups of any sustained leverage upon the
sources of power. The tone of what was supposed to be public opinion
was indeed taken notice of much more seriously than at the beginning
of the century, thanks to changing ideas about both the actual and the
desirable relationship between parliament, electors and non-electors, as
well as to the existence of many more media for the expression of
opinion. But there could be little question of controlling MPs' behaviour
while the mainsprings of electoral behaviour were still so diverse and
undisciplined; and intimidatory, persuasive and didactic pressure, as
has already been shown, were equally unlikely often to succeed. In
reality, the very gulf which made pressure group activity seem so
necessary, served as a barrier against its impact. When such activity did
affect parliament or government, it did so deviously and erratically, and
often indeed harmed rather than helped the cause it was trying to promote. Administrative reform after 1855 went from strength to strength,
but not exactly in any of the ways the Administrative Reform Association had supported, and hardly at all because of any of its activities.

Yet it is its very failure which arguably at present constitutes a strong
reason for studying the Association, since it is only by ceasing to ignore
the multitude of obviously unsuccessful pressure groups that we can
arrive at a truer verdict on the significance of pressure politics in that
age. The vicissitudes of the Administrative Reform Association's two
years' history suggests that its significance was social and political rather
than administrative or parliamentary; and in this at least it may well
prove typical of the pressure groups of its time. With its heterogeneous
social base and purposes, its conflicting and shifting tactics and policies,
and its diverse claims to legitimacy, the Association demonstrates very
clearly how pressure group activity could bring together into one ram-
shackle, fluid alliance different social and political outlooks, varied
local traditions, conflicting hopes and fears. It could not remove these
differences and the conflicts they often involved; but it could give them
peaceful expression and prevent the building-up of self-contained social
enclaves and subcultures operating in dangerous isolation.[47] Thus mid-
nineteenth century pressure group activity did indeed act as a safety
valve, though rarely in the sense contemporaries supposed. It widened
the *de facto* political community and persuaded those 'without' that they
played a public role, despite the narrowness of the country's formal
political institutions; it accustomed them to view political activity as a
moral and rational activity to be undertaken by each individual for

---

[47] For an argument that the movements for temperance and Sunday observance
and against cruelty to animals diversified nineteenth-century class relationships and
thus shielded the social structure from violent change, see B. Harrison, 'Religion and
Recreation in 19th century England', *Past and Present*, xxxviii, 1967, pp. 98–125.

himself, side by side with other individuals, and not by communities or fixed interests alone; above all, it acted as a school for citizenship in an increasingly plural society. It was thus not the extent to which pressure group activity achieved its goals which made it important, but rather the activity itself, an activity which taught social and political lessons which the Gladstonian and post-Gladstonian eras showed to have been too thoroughly learnt to be quickly forgotten.

Further Reading

Historians have given the Administrative Reform Association only passing attention, and have unfortunately (though understandably) usually based their interpretations on its early Official Papers and the miscellaneous pamphlets on administrative reform often bound up with them. Some brief remarks will be found in A. Briggs, *The Age of Improvement* (1959), pp. 433–4, W. L. Burn, *The Age of Equipoise* (1964), pp. 143–4, and S. Maccoby, *English Radicalism, 1853–86* (1938), pp. 41–5. More detailed treatments of particular aspects will be found in the articles by R. A. Lewis and the present author cited above, p. 270, n. 14 and p. 277, n. 26. On the wider movement for administrative reform, as opposed to both civil service reform and the activities of the Administrative Reform Association and its supporters, nothing has yet been published.

Appendix—*List of Members of Parliament who formally supported the Administrative Reform Association in 1855*

(M = spoke or sat on the platform at the meetings held on i. May 5, ii. June 13, iii. June 27; S = subscriber; O = member of the committee or office holder.)

Alcock, T.	Surrey East	M ii
Bell, James	Guildford	M ii
Berkeley, F. H. F.	Bristol	M ii
Bowyer, G.	Dundalk	M ii
Brady, J.	Co. Leitrim	M i
Brand, H. B.	Lewes	M ii
Brown, H.	Tewkesbury	M i, S
Butler, C. S.	Tower Hamlets	M ii
Chambers, M.	Greenwich	S
Clay, Sir W.	Tower Hamlets	S
Currie, R.	Northampton	M ii, S, O
Duffy, C. G.	New Ross	M i
Dundas, G.	Linlithgowshire (Con.)	M ii
Follett, B. S.	Bridgwater (Con.)	M ii
Fox, W. J.	Oldham	S
French, F.	Roscommon	M i, ii

Appendix—*cont.*

Greene, J. E. J.	Kilkenny Co.	M ii
Jackson, W.	Newcastle-under-Lyme	M ii
Jones, D.	Carmarthenshire (Con.)	M ii
Lacon, Sir E. H. K.	Yarmouth (Con.)	M ii
Laing, S.	Wick	M i, O
Layard, A. H.	Aylesbury	M ii, iii
Lindsay, W. S.	Tynemouth	M i, ii, S, O
Maguire, J. F.	Dungarvan	M i, ii
Miall, E.	Rochdale	M ii
Michell, W.	Bodmin	M ii
Mowatt, F.	Cambridge borough	M iii
Murrough, J. P.	Bridport	M i, iii
Napier, Sir C.	Southwark (from Nov. 1855)	M ii
Oliveira, B.	Pontefract	M i, ii, O
Otway, A. J.	Stafford	M i, ii, iii
Pellatt, A.	Southwark	M ii, iii, S
Reed, J. H.	Abingdon	M i, ii, iii
Roche, E. B.	Cork Co. (until April 23, 1855)	M ii
Russell, F. C. H.	Bedfordshire	M ii
Scholefield, W.	Birmingham	M iii
Scobell, G. T.	Bath	M i
Swift, R.	County Sligo	M i, ii
Tite, W.	Bath (from June 6 1855)	M i, ii, iii, S, O
Wise, J. A.	Stafford	M iii, S

R. P. Collier, Colonel Freestun, Sir G. Goodman, Captain Kingscote and Colonel Watkins were apparently wrongly reported in the press as having been present at the meeting of 13 June (Hansard, 138/2079).

12

State Intervention and Moral Reform in nineteenth-century England

Brian Harrison

'In England,' said Lord Goring, 'a man who can't talk morality twice a week to a large, popular, immoral audience is quite over as a serious politician.' His comment highlights a neglected category of nineteenth century pressure group, and draws attention to aspects of nineteenth century legislation which administrative historians have so far by-passed. For in the areas of drunkenness, animal cruelty, vivisection, sexual immorality, and sabbath-breaking—the pattern and mood of state intervention contrasts significantly with the situation in the area of 'social' reform: that is, in public health, factory hours, poor law relief, and public education. The nineteenth century debate on State intervention cannot be fully understood unless the historian, like the Victorians themselves, discusses both moral and social reform together; for attitudes generated in the moral sphere carried over into the social. Yet this is something which has not so far been done by the leading analysts of nineteenth century government growth.[1]

Crusades for moral reform legislation also demand discussion because of their intrinsic importance. For much larger social groups were more directly affected by restrictions on recreation and by limitations on

[1] Quotation from Oscar Wilde, 'The Ideal Husband', in G. F. Maine (ed.), *Works* (London, 1949), p. 492; cf. J. Vincent, *Pollbooks. How Victorians Voted* (Cambridge, 1967), p. 50; J. Vincent, *The Formation of the Liberal Party, 1857–1868* (London, 1966), p. 79. I am most grateful to my colleague, C. C. W. Taylor, for clarifying the argument at several points in this article. The recent controversy over nineteenth century government growth largely takes the form of a commentary on A. V. Dicey, *Lectures on the Relation between Law and Public Opinion in England during the Nineteenth-Century* (1905). The major items in the controversy are O. Macdonagh, 'The Nineteenth-Century Revolution in Government: a Reappraisal', *Historical Journal*, 1958; H. Parris, 'The Nineteenth-Century Revolution in Government: A Reappraisal Reappraised', *Historical Journal*, 1960; D. Roberts, *Victorian Origins of the British Welfare State* (Yale, 1960); J. Hart, 'Nineteenth Century Social Reform: A Tory Interpretation of History', *Past and Present*, no. 31, July 1965.

drinking hours than by early nineteenth century legislation on factory hours or poor relief. Moral reform was at least as important as social reform in moulding the attitude of J. S. Mill and T. H. Green towards the State. The resourcefulness of the reformer and the passions of the pious were more actively engaged in the moral than in the social sphere. The conflict between religion and science was nowhere fiercer than in the controversy over vivisection after the early 1870s; and the clash between religion and popular culture was nowhere more bitter than when animal cruelty legislation was involved. The *causes célèbres* provoked by attempts at moral reform lie at the centre of nineteenth century local and national community life, and after the 1870s the temperance and anti-C.D. Acts movements came closer to the centre of nineteenth century inter-party conflict than social reform measures ever did. Three questions therefore seem worth asking about nineteenth century moral reform legislation: who were its advocates? How did they attempt to justify state intervention, and how do their activities relate to the growth of the modern administrative state?

Moral reformers, like social reformers, were never organized into a co-ordinated movement; but they shared many personalities, attitudes, and techniques. These connections can be clearly though crudely illustrated by arranging fourteen moral reform organizations in a circle, and by drawing a line between them whenever they share a prominent supporter or official during the randomly-selected year 1884. Figure 1 (see p. 319) probably understates the number of such connections. In relation to personalities, two points are immediately made clear. All the bodies analysed are connected indirectly, many directly; and there are many links between rival moral reform organizations operating in the same policy area. The institutional history of these bodies was riddled with disputes between reformers whose objectives were similar; yet—to judge from the temperance, humanitarian, and sexual purity segments of the circle—these schisms did not preclude strong personal linkages between warring institutions. At the local branch level, such links were no doubt even more frequent.

Figure 1 also clarifies some of the attitudes shared by moral reformers. The circle includes four additional reforming movements, whose linkages help to clarify moral reformers' standpoint on four other areas of contemporary debate. Firstly, poverty: the inclusion of the Charity Organization Society (COS) enables the figure to emphasize the crucial importance of moral factors in the Victorian diagnosis of poverty. The COS has links with eight of the fourteen moral reform organizations, links which would be stronger if the COS sample were not so predominantly metropolitan. Though not directly concerned with poverty, all fourteen of the moral reform organizations were indirectly concerned with it, and almost all incorporated the attack on poverty into their apologia. Nor were they, in their own eyes, preoccupied merely with the *symptoms* of poverty. All feared that material might outrun moral progress, and disliked the cruder types of popular recreation: the Sunday Closing movement's linkage of the temperance and sabbatarian movements is predictable, and Figure 1's triangular bond between the Royal Society for the Prevention of Cruelty to Animals (RSPCA), the Lord's Day Observance Society (LDOS) and the Central Association for Stopping the Sale of Intoxicating Liquors on Sundays (CASSILS) reflects a three-pronged assault which damaged many Victorian fairs, circuses, and festivals. The unitarian radical F. W. Newman (brother of the cardinal) and the radical humanitarian J. S. Buckingham were as active in defending animals as in launching prohibitionism: Lord Shaftesbury was as prominent in the sabbatarian and coffee-tavern movements as in the animals' crusade: and prohibitionists drew analogies between liquor prohibition and successful legislation against animal cruelty, duelling, and gambling.

By including the National Society for Women's Suffrage in Figure 1, we can show that a third concern of the moral reformers was to raise the social status of women. The figure would show this more clearly if temperance organizations other than the British Women's Temperance Association (BWTA) had assigned formal organizational roles to women. Temperance organizations saw themselves as championing female dignity against male selfishness, but unlike puritan and humanitarian organizations they did not allow their feminism to affect the composition of their own hierarchies. The links between feminism and moral reform are doubly confirmed, however, in the RSPCA, the Victoria Street Society (VSS), the purity organizations and the campaign against State-regulated prostitution, for these all sympathized with women and were partly managed by them. Indeed, Josephine Butler's campaign against the Contagious Diseases (CD) Acts is itself an important moment in feminist history. Of the fourteen organizations, only the LDOS lacked direct feminist connections.

One further common concern of the moral reformers was to uphold the dignity of the individual in an industrial and urban context. They all championed the rights of neglected groups—of women, drunkards, prostitutes, even animals. By including in the diagram two libertarian bodies—the Vigilance Association for the Defence of Personal Rights (VADPR) and the London Society for the Abolition of Compulsory Vaccination (LSACV)—we can see the moral reformers' close links with individualism and with attacks on the medical profession. P. A. Taylor told parliament in 1883 that compulsory vaccination was 'the most absolute invasion of the sacred right of the parent, of the right of individual liberty, at the bidding of medical supervision, that this country knows.'[2]

It is natural at this point to move from attitudes to techniques, because the moral reformers' defence of individual rights owed much to a campaign which pioneered many pressure group techniques—the anti-slave trade movement. Wilberforce and Clarkson had themselves been primarily motivated by disgust at the *moral* evils of slavery, and moral reformers looked back to Wilberforce for techniques and inspiration. Their campaigning attitutcs rcscmble his in four ways. Most moral reformers were relatively indifferent to theological and liturgical differences between denominations; although the Church of England Temperance Society (CETS) and LDOS were Anglican bodies, their links with dissenters through participation in moral reform movements were never negligible. Secondly, the moral reformers' campaigns were always based on voluntary work and the private subscription: the concept of the 'active citizen' was fundamental to them all. Thirdly, they all displayed anti-political tendencies which their leaders kept under varying degrees of restraint. Finally, in their style of argument—in striving to gain the moral advantage over their opponents, in posing as champions of the masses against the classes and as defenders of simple and often provincial idealism against official and often metropolitan sophistication and expertize—the moral reformers introduced nothing new.

But there were also strong similarities in pressure group technique. Victorian moral reformers admittedly pushed some of these skills further than their predecessors. The temperance and purity movements, for instance, carried the pledge-signing much further than the anti-slave trade movement; the Ladies' National Association (LNA), formed to combat the CD Acts, and the RSPCA gave women a more distinctive role than they had enjoyed in earlier movements; and, as we shall see later, the RSPCA financed inspectors to enforce its legislation. But moral reformers were as eager as the Anti-Corn Law League or the Liberation Society to utlilize the more familiar techniques—the petition, the subscription-list, the procession, the public meeting, the local branch, the reforming periodical, and the letter to the MP. Publicity of discussion was their means, influence with parliament and with religious groups their objective.

It is therefore not surprising to find some individuals appearing simultaneously in several moral reform organizations. W. S. Caine, the Liberal politician and temperance reformer, and Mrs Lucas, John Bright's feminist daughter, feature in six: Samuel Morley, the philan-

[2] 3 Hansard 280, c. 990, 19 June 1883.

thropist, and Thomas Burt, the miners' leader, in five: Lord Mount-
Temple, the evangelical leader, F. W. Newman and Lord Shaftesbury
in four: Queen Victoria and the radical Jacob Bright, brother of John,
in three.[3] But the links between moral reformers should not be drawn
too tight. Some were progressive, some were traditionalist: some were
Londoners, some provincials. The animals found advocates further up
society, the prohibitionists found supporters further down. Queen
Victoria could lend her name to the RSPCA and CETS, but she would
have abdicated rather than support the LNA's campaign against the
CD Acts. The fourteen moral reform organizations drew supporters
from all denominations, all political parties.

Who, then, were the moral reformers? They are perhaps best
analysed by intellectual outlook, political party, religious denomination,
and social class. Some moral reform legislators were influenced by the
'rationalist' humanitarian tradition. Bentham, J. S. Mill, and Edwin
Chadwick all supported the RSPCA: 'We have begun by attending to
the condition of slaves,' wrote Bentham: 'we shall finish by softening
that of all the animals which assist our labours or supply our wants'.
The United Kingdom Alliance (UKA), founded in 1853 to bank the
drink trade, also had its links with utilitarianism—in M. D. Hill, Lord
Brougham, and the Earl of Harrington. In its 1856 handbook, the
Alliance claimed that its views were 'in perfect accordance' with 'the
general principles of law laid down by BENTHAM', and cited his recommendation that strong drink should be banned in hot climates.

Moral reform movements provided opportunities for Benthamites to
co-operate with evangelicals. But whereas in social reform their co-
operation (as Dicey pointed out) involved breaking down restraints on
individual liberty, in moral reform it involved building up such
restraints and establishing, after the 1830s, apparently 'collectivist' precedents which Dicey saw as spreading only after 1865. And whereas
Dicey's social reform perspective emphasized similarities between
evangelicals and Benthamites, the study of moral reform legislation
highlights their important differences. For the Benthamites' progressive
and utilitarian outlook kept them out of the sabbatarian movement and
circumscribed their zeal for animals, whereas evangelicals were keen

---

[3] For these personalities, see J. Newton, *W. S. Caine, M.P. A Biography* (1907);
L. Stewart and J. A. Fowler, *Memoir of Margaret Bright Lucas. President of the British
Women's Temperance Association* (London, n.d.); E. Hodder, *Life of Samuel Morley*
(1888); Thomas Burt, *Autobiography* (1924); there is no adequate biography of Lord
Mount-Temple; I. G. Sieveking's *Memoir and Letters of Francis W. Newman* (1909) is
poor; E. Hodder, *Life and Work of the Seventh Earl of Shaftesbury* (3 volumes, 1886); for
Jacob Bright, see Mrs Jacob Bright (ed.), *Jacob Bright, M.P., Speeches 1869 to 1884*
(1885).

sabbatarians and flocked into the anti-vivisection movement with the aim of attacking science itself. Bentham never objected to vivisection on principle: he supported it when it had a 'determinate object, beneficial to mankind, accompanied with a fair prospect of the accomplishment of it'. Nor was it easy for Benthamites to participate in the more sectarian and emotional aspects of temperance work or in moral reform movements which obstructed public health legislation. In no moral reform movement were utilitarians as influential in moulding legislation as they were with factory, public health and poor law measures; this partly explains the major contrast between the patterns of state intervention in the moral and social spheres.[4]

Evangelicalism here, as in the factory movement, 'provided both the hard core of original leaders and their vocabulary'.[5] The moral reformers' peculiar strategy of imposing legal restraints on individual liberty without effectively extending governmental power could draw upon the evangelical's belief in the original sin of the citizen without exposing him to danger from the original sin of those in authority. In 1803, the evangelicals were prominent among the founders of the Vice Society—whose sabbatarian, temperance, humanitarian, and puritanical activities anticipate several of the moral reform movements under discussion. Evangelicals dominated the earliest (anti-spirits) phase of the temperance movement, and some returned to the movement after the late 1850s with the creation of the UKA, and the powerful CETS. They controlled the LDOS throughout the century; through T. F. Buxton they chaired the RSPCA's foundation meeting and, through William Wilberforce they were present on its earliest committee. The early Victorian RSPCA took care to advertise its Christian basis, but moral reform crusades later became less self-consciously religious in character. This enabled evangelicals to reunite with those who had formerly left the fold. The anti-vivisectionist movement, for instance, enabled Lord Shaftesbury to unite with the unitarian Frances Power Cobbe and the positivists J. H. Bridges and William Congreve, just as prohibitionism united the arch-evangelical Dean Close with Cardinal Manning, and with the unitarian F. W. Newman.

The evangelical connection combined with Tory protectionism, paternalism, and concern for public order—to ensure that moral reform always enjoyed a following within the Conservative party; the connection was reinforced in the late Victorian period when property

---

[4] Quotations from J. Bentham, 'Principles of Penal Law', in Bowring (ed.), *Works* (Edinburgh, 1843), I, p. 562; F. R. Lees, *Alliance Prize Essay* (2nd edn. London, 1857), pp. 20–21; J. Bentham, letter to the editor of the *Morning Chronicle*, printed in Bowring (ed.), *Works*, X, pp. 549–50. See also A. V. Dicey, *op. cit.*, pp. 64, 66, 399–400; D. Roberts, *op. cit.*, p. 318.

[5] J. T. Ward, *The Factory Movement, 1830–1855* (London, 1962), p. 418.

acquired an increased interest in promoting crusades which cut across class lines. Distaste for relaxations in the magistrates' control over drinking places, and therefore hostility to the rural beershops established by the free-trading Beer Act of 1830, gave the early temperance movement several Tory allies; traditionalism and concern for public order nourished mid-Victorian Tory support for Sunday closing; and although Conservatives were never more than a minority in the progressive, nonconformist, and largely urban prohibitionist movement, the growth of Anglican temperance in the 1860s and the accession of Liberal Unionists to the Conservative party in the 1880s prevented conservatism from ever aligning itself uncritically behind the drink interest. The LDOS, like the factory movement, displayed all the suspicion of railways and industrial innovation, all the distaste for city life, which many early Victorian Conservatives felt. The Society saw Sunday as a Christian and rural interlude of class harmony amidst the hectic rush of a materialistic, competitive, and urban society. Likewise the late Victorian RSPCA found more to admire in Lord Shaftesbury than in John Bright,[6] and moral reform legislators usually found their most persistent parliamentary enemies among radicals and political economists.

Moral reform, however, like social reform, cut across party allegiance. The prohibitionist and humanitarian movements were unlikely to attract the hard-drinking and traditionalist Tory who rode to hounds; for him, such movements were the weapons of urban meddlers who adopted a highminded pose while championing impracticable and self-interested legislation. Again, there were some Conservatives who feared that 'grandmotherly legislation' to promote morality might be taken as a precedent for State intervention of a more socialistic kind. A third group of Conservatives added numbers and noise to the two wealthier groups: the 'rough' element within the working class, led by publicans, sporting aristocrats, and army officers. A grumbling and potentially riotous Tory–radical popular distaste for meddlesome philanthropy, pious hypocrisy, and French spy-systems, was easily mobilized by T. S. Duncombe against animal cruelty legislation in the 1840s or by J. R. Stephens against licensing legislation in the 1870s, and the heart of many a Victorian moral reformer was chilled by the sound of hostile mobs singing 'Britons never shall be slaves'.[7]

---

[6] *Animal World*, 2 November 1885, pp. 168–9; 1 May 1889, p. 67. See also my 'Animals and the State in Nineteenth-Century England', *English Historical Review*, 1973.

[7] For this paragraph, see my 'Religion and Recreation in Nineteenth-Century England', *Past and Present*, December 1967, pp. 108–19, and my *Drink and the Victorians. The Temperance Question in England, 1815–1872* (London, 1971), pp. 267, 275–6, 391.

It is in fact the Liberal party which is the most closely associated with Victorian interventionism in the moral sphere—particularly in the sphere of temperance. The high moral purposes of their party made some late Victorian Liberals as cavalier in their attitude towards 'property in vice' as were many early Victorian Conservative social reformers in their attitude to the profit motive. Joseph Sturge had not been enthusiastic for giving £20 millions to the slaveholders in the 1830s, said the prohibitionist leader Wilfrid Lawson in 1868: the claims of dispossessed publicans were, he argued, no better. Liberal nonconformists were often impressed by the chapel's need for protection against recreational competition, and by the need to introduce into national legislation the 'religious socialism' of the local chapel and its strict supervision of moral conduct. The National Sunday League, which campaigned after the mid-1850s for more relaxed attitudes to Sunday leisure, often complained of obstruction from sabbatarian nonconformists inside the Liberal party.

Yet the Liberals, like the Tories, were divided on moral reform legislation. Anglican Liberals were suspicious of nonconformist sectarianism, and in opposing sabbatarian and temperance legislation found themselves in an often unfamiliar alliance with those radical nonconformists—like Miall, Edward Baines, and Henry Richard—who carried their voluntarist principles also into the sphere of moral reform. Nonconformists of the latter type argued that 'outward restraint does not regenerate the inward man', and shared J. S. Mill's view that 'the mental and the moral, like the muscular powers, are improved only by being used'.[8] So nonconformists remained divided on the sabbatarian and prohibitionist issues, and were never prominent in the RSPCA. Moral reform legislators therefore never captured the Liberal party's higher regions, though they always professed puzzlement at their failure. They remained a ginger-group on the left of the party, incapable even of uniting the radicals against the leadership, though occasionally able to attract Conservative allies. Yet the moral reformers' noise made up for their small numbers, and they gained disproportionate influence over Liberal party policy through their active involvement at the local branch level. The result was that these moral reform questions were extensively discussed in mid- and late-Victorian parliaments; ministers were sometimes even forced to act, though the outcome of their action rarely satisfied the zealots who had inspired it.

[8] Quotations from *Freeman*, 19 May 1871, p. 243; Beatrice Webb, *My Apprenticeship* (2nd edn., London, n.d.), p. 143; *Nonconformist*, 2 November 1853, p. 887; J. S. Mill, *Liberty* (Everyman edn., 1910), pp. 116–17. For Lawson, see *Alliance News*, 17 October. 1868, p. 331; cf. John Morley, in *Alliance News*, 12 December 1885, p. 805.

No simple tripartite social class model will explain the appeal of moral reform legislation. Admittedly these movements were run by a hard core of 'middling' nonconformists and evangelicals—aided by respectable and often self-interested householders living near cattle markets, drinking places, and recreation grounds. But they were never confronted by a united aristocracy; their anti-aristocratic tendencies were always blunted by support received from the sabbatarian Lord Shaftesbury, from the temperate Lord Stanhope, and from the humanitarian Lord Harrowby—not to mention the phalanx of humanitarian female aristocrats. The moral reformer was therefore limited merely to redefining the concept of what constituted a gentleman. 'The daily actions of every peer and peeress,' said J. S. Mill in 1840, 'are falling more and more under the yoke of *bourgeois* opinion.'[9]

Nor could the middle classes ever be united behind movements which assaulted many sceptical doctors and sporting servicemen, and which upheld the credit of commerce by attacking allegedly disreputable but potentially middle class trades such as slave-trading, drink-selling, pawnbroking, street-trading, brothel-keeping: particularly when J. S. Mill led so many of their more intelligent members against the moral reformers' methods, if not against their ultimate objectives. De Tocqueville cited American anti-drink legislation as an instance of the social tyranny one might expect from a democracy—to which J. S. Mill added a distaste for the narrowness of nonconformist culture. His *Liberty* therefore placed sabbatarian and temperance legislation at the head of its list of unjust interferences with individual freedom, and Mill refused to do more than subscribe to the RSPCA until the Society repressed the cruel sports of rich and poor alike. He subscribed to, and was repeatedly praised by, the anti-sabbatarian National Sunday League; and his frontal clash with the prohibitionists provoked them into launching a publicity campaign in the hope of winning over a hostile intelligentsia.[10] Middle class suspicions were nurtured in the 1870s by the anti-vivisectionist movement's assaults on the doctors: Sir William Gull told the 1876 royal commission that 'there might be very different legislation for the ignorant and the indifferent, as compared with the pursuers of science and the students of science'. Social tyranny seemed imminent to doctors confronted by an emotional and ignorant agitation which paraded its faith in publicity of discussion; and the notion that

[9] J. S. Mill, 'Democracy in America', *Edinburgh Review*, October, 1840, p. 67.
[10] A. de Tocqueville, *Democracy in America* (New York, 1960), I, pp. 217–18; J. S. Mill, *Liberty*, pp. 144–6. For Mill and the RSPCA, see the Society's Minute Book no. 11, pp. 80–82 (11 August 1868), *in situ*; cf. W. R. W. Stephens, *The Life and Letters of Edward A. Freeman* (London, 1895), I, p. 374.

298 *Pressure from Without*

physiologists should be 'licensed and regulated like publicans and prostitutes' seemed, to Sir John Simon in 1876, really offensive.[11]

Nor were the moral reformers confronted by a united working class. Even the elite among working men were divided: for those who shared the moral reformers' zeal for a rational Sunday and a sober and humane populace often shared Mill's and Miall's fears of social and religious tyranny. Holyoake, Hetherington, and Hartwell fall into this category; but the prohibitionist Lovett, the sabbatarian Broadhurst, and the tee-total Cassell counterbalance them, and in the moral reform diagram Thomas Burt features five times, Joseph Arch twice and Henry Broadhurst once. Burt was a vice-president of both the UKA and the National Association for the Repeal of the CD Acts (NARCDA). As for humbler working men, the raffish anti-sabbatarians are counter-balanced by the sabbatarian working men who relied on evangelicals to defend them against rapacious employers—just as the working class pub-goers were resisted by their deprived wives and by respectable working people who shared the prohibitionist movement's peculiar blend of anti-aristocratic and feminist moral idealism. The fact is that nineteenth century anti-bureaucratic campaigns for equality before the law could attract individuals from all social classes. The libertarian VADPR, which had many moral reform connections, included Joseph Arch on its committee for many years; its annual meeting in 1877 was addressed (admittedly somewhat equivocally) by that popular secularist leader G. J. Holyoake, and in 1885 by the ex-Chartist Benjamin Lucraft. It is surprising that attention has been directed only recently towards the intense suspicions of the State displayed by many nineteenth century working men.[12]

How did the moral reformers argue their case for State intervention? Their defence has three aspects: they emphasized the State's responsibilities towards morality: they evolved a positive concept of liberty: and they prescribed limits to the operation of the free market. Like J. S. Mill, they thought that 'one criterion of the goodness of a government' was 'the degree in which it tends to increase the sum of good qualities in the governed, collectively and individually'. But they questioned his applications of the idea that the individual should be 'amenable to society' only for the part of his conduct 'which concerns others'; for they were more conscious than he that modern urban society is a complex organism in which very few actions have consequences only for the

[11] R[oyal] C[ommission] on [the practice of subjecting live animals to] experiments for scientific purposes, P[arliamentary] P[apers], 1876 (C. 1397) XLI, QQ. 5842, 1491.
[12] See Henry Pelling's important 'The Working Class and the Origins of the Welfare State', in his *Popular Politics and Society in Late Victorian Britain* (London, 1968).

actor. They argued that sobriety or sabbath-observance could never prevail unless the State first modified the environment: 'so long . . . as men and women, like nine-pins, are so placed that one, in falling, probably spreads devastation all around, so long shall we continue to press . . . the urgent necessity of delivering our country from the liquor-traffic.'[13]

The sabbatarians claimed that the individual gained far more than he lost through sabbatarian legislation, which would at the very least ensure that Sundays introduced a 'moral cement' between 'the dislocated stones of our social fabric'. On Sundays, as on the fast-days which so many evangelicals advocated, the community would be united by the fact that all were taking their rest simultaneously: 'the laws regulate *common* time in manufactories, on the ground of humanity,' the LDOS argued in 1834, 'why may they not also regulate *sacred* time, for the benefit of the people?'[14] Likewise the RSPCA, by pursuing cruelty down mines and into slaughterhouses, and by its paternalist concern for educating the poor in humanitarianism, operated upon a notion of society far less atomistic than Mill's. In their 1856 handbook the prohibitionists emphasized the law's capacity for influencing social habits, and argued that the injunction 'lead us not into temptation' should be as much a guide to public policy as to individual conduct; prohibition was, like all moral reform legislation, 'the political reflex of the Lord's Prayer'. The prohibitionist reaction against Mill's libertarianism was quite self-conscious, and was the more self-confident for the fact that many prohibitionists had closely observed the impact of drink on family tragedies in the slums. Whereas Mill argued that drunkenness brought its own punishment, and that the spectacle of the drunkard's miseries provided in itself a moral lesson for society at large—prohibitionists saw drunkenness as 'a state of incapacity for every domestic, civil, and political duty' which brought misery upon wife and child.[15] They believed also that morality would hardly progress if such degrading sights were repeatedly advertised, and that no individual could be perfected in isolation from his fellows. To prohibitionists, Mill's views seemed utopian: his long-term objectives caused him to acquiesce in a level of suffering which, even in the short term, seemed to them intolerable.

[13] Quotations from J. S. Mill, *Representative Government* (Everyman edn., 1910), p. 193; *Liberty*, p. 73, see also pp. 136, 139–40. Final quotation from *Alliance Weekly News*, 7 May 1859, p. 781.

[14] Quotations from Hugh Stowell, in L[ord's] D[ay] O[bservance] S[ociety], *9th Annual Report, 1840*, p. 23, and from LDOS, *3rd Annual Report, 1834*, p. 17. See also Keith Thomas, *Religion and the Decline of Magic* (London, 1971), pp. 147, 622, and O. Anderson, 'The Reactions of Church and Dissent towards the Crimean War', *Journal of Ecclesiastical History*, October 1965, pp. 209, 216.

[15] Quotations from F. R. Lees (ed.), *Alliance Prize Essay*, p. 27; U[nited] K[ingdom] A[lliance], *No Case against the U.K.A. and the Permissive Bill* (n.d.), p. 71.

It is instructive to compare Mill's hostility to prohibition with his distaste for the CD Acts' compulsory registration, inspection, and treatment of suspected prostitutes. He felt that the prostitute should be assisted only *after* incurring the (infectious) consequence of her sin, for it was important to strengthen the willpower by never allowing sin to be separated from the risk of unpleasant consequences. 'You may draw a line between attacking evils when they occur', he said in 1871, 'in order to remedy them as far as we are able, and making arrangements beforehand which will enable the objectionable practices to be carried on without incurring the danger of the evil.'[16] The parallel between prohibition and State supervised prostitution is not of course exact: for the prohibitionists were not trying to minimize the consequences of drunkenness. But Mill's general outlook is the same in the two cases: the moral universe should be allowed to remain a self-acting system, and society should be arranged so as to give individuals the opportunity of displaying moral self-restraint. State intervention would weaken men's willpower as much by depriving them of drinking places as by providing men with clean prostitutes and women with safety in sin. It could do nothing which could not be better done by voluntary action, nor could there be any short cuts to moral progress.

The moral reformers were inevitably led into countering with a positive concept of liberty. Mill argued that the individual, as 'the person most interested in his own well-being', was likely to be the person best-informed on the subject, and should therefore as far as possible be left to look after himself. But the sabbatarians and prohibitionists applied in their respective spheres the exception which Mill himself allowed in the area of factory legislation. Sir Stafford Northcote was able to cite Mill on this parallel case in 1855, when arguing for restricting Sunday trading: in some areas, Northcote wrote, the law must interfere 'not to overrule the judgment of individuals respecting their own interest, but to give effect to that judgment, they being unable to give effect to it except by concert'. The moral reformer claimed that the State must intervene so as to enable the individual to exercise his choice in favour of a sober and godly life: otherwise the environment would be so moulded by drink-sellers and sabbath-breakers as to warp his decision. 'That ill deserves the Name of Confinement,' wrote Locke, 'which hedges us in only from Bogs and Precipices.'[17] Moral reformers knew

[16] R.C. on [the administration and operation of] the Contagious Diseases Act, *P.P.*, 1871 (c. 408) XIX, Q. 20,028; cf. *Nonconformist*, 14 December 1853, p. 1006.

[17] Quotations from J. S. Mill, *Liberty*, p. 133; A. Lang, *Life, Letters and Diaries of Sir Stafford Northcote* (London, 1890), I, p. 118; *John Locke, Two Treatises of Government* (P. Laslett (ed.), Cambridge, 1963), p. 323. See also *A Few Plain Facts respecting the Sunday Trading Bill. By a London Employer* (2nd edn., 1855), p. 3; W. J. Ashley (ed.), *J. S. Mill, Principles of Political Economy* (London, 1917), pp. 964–5.

that considerations of individual privacy would prevent them from obtaining in their sphere the degree of enforcement possible in the area of social reform. Even with factory hours, enforcement was at first possible only in the larger factories; with drinking, cruelty, sexual immorality, sabbath-breaking, and (according to G. H. Lewes, in his evidence to the 1876 royal commission) vivisection—real enforcement would require entry into every private home. Nor did moral reformers believe that morality could ever be displayed merely through responding to legislative coercion: their concern was simply to prevent the law from actually misleading the citizen as to his moral duties, and to ensure that the state should make it *possible* for him to make the right choice. Prohibitionists made much of Gladstone's statement that government should 'make it easy to do right and difficult to do wrong'. The LDOS insisted that sabbatarian legislation was protective, not coercive, and despised a political economy which assumed that the national interest could emerge from giving free rein to the pursuit of private profit.[18]

The moral reformers again diverged from Mill when they argued that many adults should be included with children and lunatics in his category of those who could not be expected to recognize their own interest. 'The uneducated man ... is after all but a child in the maturity of his physical powers', said an RSPCA speaker in 1846. All moral reformers saw law as the adult's equivalent of schooling. Mill described the artificial limitation of drinking facilities as 'suited only to a state of society in which the labouring classes are avowedly treated as children or savages', but the prohibitionist cited the prevalence of teetotal pledge-taking as evidence that many drinkers would really welcome prohibition; in the existing situation, however, drinkers were in effect prevented from promoting their own interest, even where they recognized it.[19] Our requirements of the individual are nowadays perhaps less rigorous than Mill's: our attitude to the role of the State is influenced by sociologists who inform us that no amount of exhortation can prevent a certain proportion of factory employees from injuring themselves on unfenced machinery, and by dieticians who acclimatize us to the idea that, in a complex urban society, government must clarify

[18] For Gladstone, see William Hoyle, *Our National Resources and How They Are Wasted* (cheap edn., 1871), p. 110; cf. T. H. Green, 'Liberal Legislation and Freedom of Contract', in R. L. Nettleship (ed.), *Works*, III, p. 374; Lord Macaulay, speech on the Ten Hours Bill, in *Life and Works* (Edinburgh edn., 1897), VIII, p. 368. For Lewes, see R. C. on ... experiments for scientific purposes, Q. 6334. For the LDOS see its *10th Annual Report, 1841*, p. 20; *12th Annual Report, 1843*, p. 16.
[19] Quotations from R[oyal] S[ociety] for the P[revention] of C[ruelty] to A[nimals], *20th Annual Report, 1846*, p. 20; J. S. Mill, *Liberty*, p. 156. See also 'Index' [G. Vasey], *Individual Liberty, Legal, Moral, and Licentious* (London, 1867), pp. 80, 84; J. T. Baylee, in S[elect] C[ommittee] of the H[ouse] of C[ommons] on Public Houses, *P.P.*, 1854 (367) XIV, Q. 235.

the act of choice for the individual by inspecting for adulteration and by educating in nutrition. Furthermore, psychologists now emphasize the irrational factors which affect an individual's choice. In Professor Hart's words, 'choices may be made or consent given without adequate reflection or appreciation of the consequences; or in pursuit of merely transitory desires; or in various predicaments when the judgment is likely to be clouded; or under inner psychological compulsion; or under pressure by others of a kind too subtle to be susceptible of proof in a law court.'[20]

A memorable episode in the moral reformer's shift towards a more positive view of liberty was the clash between the prohibitionists and Bishop Magee in 1872. 'If I must take my choice...,' the Bishop argued in the House of Lords, 'whether England should be free or sober, I declare ... that ... it would be better that England should be free than that England should be compulsorily sober. I would distinctly prefer freedom to sobriety, because with freedom we might in the end attain sobriety; but in the other alternative we should eventually lose both freedom and sobriety.' Magee was here accepting Mill's argument that moral progress could be attained only through individual moral self-cultivation; but the sharpness of prohibitionist rejoinders stemmed from their impatience with delay—from their recognition of how terrible would be the suffering under Mill's programme before any real progress could be made. Most prohibitionists also chose to misinterpret the Bishop, and to accuse him of championing freedom (whether drunken or sober) for its own sake; this led them into emphasizing qualitative factors in their attempts to define 'genuine' liberty. Their viewpoint entered the mainstream of late Victorian liberalism in 1873 at Oxford, with the confrontation between the prohibitionist T. H. Green and the libertarian W. V. Harcourt.[21]

Inevitably the moral reformers were drawn into outlining moral limitations to the free operation of the market; they were therefore vigorously opposed by all who drew crudely individualist conclusions from their reading of political economy, or who assumed that *laissez faire* principles applied universally. Here, as elsewhere, the moral reformers were preceded by the anti-slave trade movement: by the 1840s, humanitarians who wanted fiscal and naval harassment of the slave trade faced opposition from Cobden and Bright. On obscene literature and animal cruelty, the political economists could whip up an extensive popular following against the moral reformers. Joseph Hume in 1823

[20] H. L. A. Hart, *Law, Liberty and Morality* (London, 1963), pp. 32–3.
[21] Magee, in 3 Hansard 211, c. 86 (2 May 1872). The speech was much praised—see *Daily Telegraph*, 3 May 1872, p. 4; *Sheffield Daily Telegraph*, 6 May 1872, and my *Drink and the Victorians*, pp. 293—4. For 'genuine' liberty, see *Alliance News*, 11 May 1872, p. 355.

branded societies for the prosecution of vice as 'little better than conspiracies against the liberty of the subject' and contemptuously resisted animal cruelty legislation in all its early stages. In the long run, his failure was complete: for he could not prevent the RSPCA from cumulatively elaborating a whole complex of legal protection for animals.[22] His 1854 attacks on prohibition, as an attempt to do by law what should really be done by education, seem to us in retrospect rather less alien; but Roebuck's libertarian assault on Lord Campbell's 'preposterous' Obscene Publications Bill of 1857 could not prevent the moral reformers from applying to pornography the legislative methods used earlier against gambling. In the late Victorian period their legislation extended towards rooting out brothels, fraudulent registries, and obscene advertisements, and towards raising the age of consent. Through the National Vigilance Association (NVA), late Victorian moral reformers also altered magistrates' attitude to the enforcement of their laws.[23]

Against the sabbatarians, the free traders mounted an organized movement—the National Sunday League (founded in the mid-1850s) and the Sunday Society (founded in 1875). The LDOS despised 'that political economy which it is the disgrace of the present age to view as coincident with political morality', and saw itself as defending oppressed employees against rapacious employers. By contrast, the National Sunday League saw itself in 1875 as occupying 'the place towards Religious Liberty that the Anti-Corn Law League did towards true commerce'; its campaign for unrestricted recreational competition attracted free-traders as ardent as Roebuck, Holyoake, P. A. Taylor, J. S. Mill, Auberon Herbert, and Charles Bradlaugh. James Heywood, the Sunday Society's first president, had himself been an active Anti-Corn Law leaguer.[24]

In the area of drink, however, the opponents of moral reform legislation had less need to organize themselves into a distinct movement. The advocates of a 'free licensing' policy—which repudiated the idea that monopolies of local drink sales should be assigned to particular individuals—enjoyed powerful support from inside the early Victorian beer and wine traders, as well as from enthusiasts for free trade as such. And

[22] Quotation from L. Radzinowicz, *History of English Criminal Law*, III (London, 1956), p. 174; for Hume and the RSPCA see my 'Animals and the State', *loc. cit.*
[23] For Hume on prohibition, see *Alliance*, 29 July 1854, pp. 29–30; cf. Harriet Martineau, *Daily News*, 7 August 1855. For Roebuck, see 3 Hansard 147, c. 1475, 1477 (12 August 1857); contrast Samuel Smith, in *Vanguard*, July 1887, p. 51. For the NVA, see W. A. Coote (ed.), *A Romance of Philanthropy* (London, 1916), p. 228.
[24] Quotations from LDOS, *12th Annual Report, 1843*, p. 16; *Free Sunday Advocate*, February 1875, p. 142. For the LDOS and employers, see its *18th Annual Report, 1849*, p. 33; *7th Annual Report, 1838*, pp. 62–3.

although by the 1870s the temperance movement had helped to destroy free licensing as a guide to public policy, this in itself weakened the incentives for continuing the restrictionist alliance between temperance reformers and the monopolistic sections of the drink trade. By the 1880s, therefore, a powerful alliance between Conservatism and the drink industry was building up which made it still unnecessary to establish any distinct movement for upholding the individual's freedom to drink—though the Liberty and Property Defence League in the 1880s took up the cause of defending the publicans' and brewers' property against temperance attack.

Temperance reformers, like sabbatarians, emphasized the need to limit the application of free trade principles where they conflicted with considerations of national health and morality. In defending early Victorian ballast-weavers and coal-whippers against their publican employers, temperance reformers mobilized City philanthropists against doctrinaire free-traders. But when Gladstone recommended a public labour-exchange for the coal-whippers in 1843, he saw their plight as exceptional, and not as invalidating the general applicability of *laissez faire* principle. His persisting free trade zeal was amply demonstrated in 1860 when he opened out the wine trade, but by the 1870s temperance influences within the Liberal party were powerful enough to prevent him from pushing free trade any further. Restrictive policies were thus resumed much later here than in the sphere of social legislation and in some other spheres of moral reform. The temperance movement's counter-attack began in the early 1830s, when (with high Tory assistance) restrictions were imposed on the free trade in beer which had been instituted by the 1830 Beer Act. But the free licensing policy was not reversed until beerhouses were partially restored to magistrates' control in 1869—by temperance reformers, clergymen, and country magistrates acting in alliance. Prohibitionists always stressed that drink-sellers performed social as well as economic functions: the drink trade, said its champion Samuel Pope in 1856, 'does not respond to the ordinary laws of political economy. In it demand does *not* limit and regulate supply; supply *does* create and increase the demand.'[25]

Yet it would be wrong to portray the moral reform legislators as pioneers of Victorian collectivism. For their collectivism applied only to a very restricted area: it was regarded very much as a second-best to voluntary effort: and the machinery for its enforcement in no way resembled the bureaucratic machinery which enforced early Victorian

[25] Samuel Pope, letter to Lord Stanley, 26 September 1856, in *The Stanley-Pope Discussion* (Manchester, n.d.), unpaginated; cf. T. H. Green at Banbury, in *Alliance News*, 5 February 1881. For Gladstone, see 3 Hansard 71, c. 88 (1 August 1843).

social reform legislation. Increasing emphasis is now being placed on the pragmatism of the Victorians' response to social evils; Macaulay in 1846 emphasized that 'nothing can be more proper' than to apply in the same week *laissez faire* principles to the corn trade, and protection (through factory legislation) to morals and health. This pragmatism also characterized many moral reformers. Their enthusiasm for collectivist legislation was discriminating. 'It is . . . merely a question of that which would be most to the advantage of the public in general,' said Lord Robert Grosvenor in 1847, combating the libertarians in his campaign for the public control of London slaughterhouses. Prohibitionists and humanitarians were in fact vigorously anti-socialist, and many were ardent free traders in most spheres of life.[26]

Moral reformers resigned themselves to collectivist methods only after experimenting first with voluntary and individual reform. Moral reform movements had originally been created to supersede the need for State intervention. Only through voluntary association, said Wilberforce in 1787, could a free state give effect to George III's proclamation against vice: 'for thus only can those moral principles be guarded which of old were under the immediate protection of the Government'. Many early nineteenth century moral reformers felt that moral and religious advance would eventually reduce the role of the State. At first they saw legislation as temporary, and even as regrettable: as a means of creating the rational, self-respecting citizen whose prevalence would eventually enable the laws of political economy to operate humanely.[27]

Even after falling back on legislation, moral reformers did not cease to organize concurrent educational activity. Prosecution and education rivalled one another as priorities throughout the RSPCA's early history, and although legislation in defence of animals steadily extended after 1822, the Society increasingly emphasized educational methods. Indeed, the distinction between education and prosecution is perhaps, for that authoritarian age, somewhat unreal: for punishment was then seen as integral to education and for some humanitarians the government, by enforcing the law, acted as schoolmaster to the nation. Again, LDOS demands for legislation were preceded by several attempts at getting tradesmen to make voluntary Sunday closing agreements. Most prohibitionists had previously been members of the moral suasionist temperance movement, but this convinced them that 'the drink curse,' in T. H. Green's words, ' . . . is altogether too big a thing . . . to be dealt

[26] Quotations from Macaulay's speech on 22 May 1846, in *Works*, VIII, p. 376; Grosvenor, in SCHC on Smithfield Market, *P.P.*, 1847 (640) VIII, Q. 5826. See also W. C. Lubenow, *The Politics of Government Growth. Early Victorian Attitudes towards State Intervention, 1833–1848* (Newton Abbot, 1971), p. 84; H. Parris, *loc. cit.*, pp. 34–7.
[27] R. I. and S. Wilberforce, *Life of William Wilberforce* (London, 1838), I, pp. 131–2.

with by individual effort only'. Yet they did not see their movement as superseding the moral suasionist campaign for individual teetotalism; for they knew that a population unconvinced of the need for teetotalism would always find ways of getting round prohibition, through importing drink or manufacturing it at home. Most moral reformers recognized that legislation, in Bentham's words, could do no more than 'increase the efficacy of private ethics, by giving strength and direction to the influence of the moral sanction': it could only ensure that public conduct more closely resembled the conduct desired in private.[28] Unfortunately for the moral reformers however, society was so arranged that the poor were more dependent on public facilities than the rich; moral reform legislation could therefore easily be attacked as 'class legislation'.

During the coal-whippers' debate of 1843, Bowring saw the abstinence movement as a better cure for drunkenness than any public labour-exchange: 'instead of an act of Parliament,' he said, 'they should send the Apostle of Temperance [Father Mathew] among them. He was sorry to see the right hon. Gentleman [Gladstone] departing from the sound principles of political economy.' The earliest temperance reformers would probably have agreed with him; certainly English temperance reformers at an 1856 international congress regarded continental opponents of drunkenness as unduly eager for government aid, and prided themselves on the superiority of their own voluntarist methods.[29] Closer acquaintance with the problem in hand, however, impressed some temperance reformers with the need for combating environmental pressures; many therefore abandoned the political economist's voluntary methods which, in the ideal world, they would still have preferred. Further experience took some moral reformers out of moral reform crusading altogether, and into purely secular movements with more ambitious social programmes. This happened, for example, to many of the temperance reformers who joined the early labour movement; their evolution is well brought out by Hugh Price Hughes' response to W. T. Stead's revelations about London prostitution in 1885. These discoveries 'have shown us . . . that we cannot touch any point of this hideous vice . . . without also touching a thousand points in our ordinary life. . . . We have seen how the whole thing hangs together . . . and therefore we once more learn that it will be impossible

[28] Quotations from T. H. Green's speech at a conference of the Oxfordshire Band of Hope Union, *Alliance News*, 12 April 1879, p. 230; cf. *Alliance*, 19 May 1855, p. 364; H. Harrison (ed.), *J. Bentham, Principles of Morals and Legislation* (Oxford, 1948), p. 420. For prohibition/moral suasion, see my *Drink and the Victorians*, pp. 210–18.
[29] Bowring, 3 Hansard 71, c. 88 (1 August 1843); see also National Temperance League, *Annual Report, 1856*, p. 16; A. de Tocqueville, *Democracy in America*, II, pp. 117–18.

to do anything furthering morality by the law of the land without also touching the economical relations of society.'[30]

When it came to enforcing their legislation, moral reformers by no means abandoned their faith in voluntary bodies, or their dependence on the concept of the active citizen. They did not demand the appointment of public inspectors, and therefore in the area of moral reform Professor Macdonagh's dynamic of accelerating an increasingly complex bureaucratic involvement in legislation and enforcement never got under way. As we shall see, the moral reformers either provided their own machinery for enforcement: or they wanted enforcement entrusted to the local community: or they regarded the problem of enforcement with relative indifference.

Ruskin's famous expedition to repair the Hinksey road only carried to an extreme what was a characteristic of many Victorian reformers, whose appeals to the State were designed to assist voluntary effort rather than to supersede it. For moral reformers who brought legal cases, collected information or financed private systems of inspection, the mounting network of State intervention and the rising number of convictions testified to the vitality in England of individual enterprise, not to the increased power of the State. And far from concentrating power and knowledge in the State, these bodies were achieving Mill's objective of dispersing power and governmental experience. Of all the moral reformers under discussion, only the RSPCA—not surprisingly, the body which enjoyed links with fewest of the organizations in the moral reform circle—sought help from police and public inspectors. Even here the government evolved no expertise in the area: when the late Victorian Home Office wished for information on animals, it contacted John Colam, the Society's secretary. Furthermore, the RSPCA's enforcement policy went much further than the anti-slave trade movement's African Institution; it did more than merely keep government informed about lawbreaking—it built up its own inspection force. 'You are . . . the handmaid—the support—the carriers into effect of the acts of the legislature,' R. E. Broughton told its 1844 annual meeting. Its inspectors increased from 3 in 1837 to 120 in 1897: its convictions from 1,897 in the decade 1830–39 to 71,657 in 1890–99. 'In other countries the intervention of the State would be invoked,' said a supporter in 1870: 'and an organisation of public prosecutors and overseers would be established, but in England it was their pride to do these things themselves, and to trust to the State nothing they could accomplish by local efforts.'[31]

[30] Hughes, *Pall Mall Gazette*, 22 August 1885, p. 8.
[31] Broughton, in RSPCA, *18th Annual Report, 1844*, p. 37; Mr Laing, in *Animal World*, 1 February 1870, p. 96; cf. Lord Aberdare, in RSPCA, *68th Annual Report*, p. 145. Statistics from my 'Religion and Recreation', *loc. cit.*, p. 102.

When moral reform organizations did appoint inspectors, their role differed markedly from that of the government inspector who tackled social problems. Factory, public health, educational, and poor law inspection was conducted by educated and knowledgeable experts capable of extending and improving the law. Nowadays even voluntary bodies promote research into the problems they aim to solve. But with nineteenth century moral reform organizations—as with many Victorian charities—the legislative impetus came only from the moral indignation of the lay subscriber. Inspectors were merely his servants; lacking his social status, they could never hope to mould policy. Their role was law-enforcement, not research. The LDOS, lacking the RSPCA's wealth, could not even afford a full-scale inspectorate. Besides, the problem it attacked was so formidable that enforcement by private agency could hardly have been attempted; when the Reverend J. Bee Wright prompted sabbatarian prosecutions in London during 1871, he became so unpopular that he was soon forced to retire from the scene. The disadvantage of private systems for enforcing the law—such as those used against animal cruelty, or against employing climbing-boys—was that they seemed if anything more offensive to the delinquent than enforcement by the State; philanthropists were despised as busybodies and meddlers.

As for the temperance reformers, their failure to develop an inspectorate stems from the irrelevance of inspection to the problem they were tackling. For their aspirations were so extensive, their sympathy with the drunkard so great, and the evils of drunkenness were for them so patent—that mere inspection or investigation seemed superfluous; nor could they ever be concerned merely with prosecuting drunkards or with enforcing licensing legislation. Their movement had originated partly in a reaction against the Vice Society's prosecuting methods, and their eagerness to emancipate the State from dependence on a corrupt trade deterred them from supporting Bruce's 1871 scheme for a system of public-house inspectors. Temperance reformers (like the crusaders for sexual purity in the 1880s) sometimes created local vigilance groups to enforce the law, and the movement's very existence must have made drink-sellers more cautious; but the more energetic temperance reformers' main efforts were directed elsewhere.[32]

The prohibitionist movement was sceptical of existing licensing regu-

[32] For Bee Wright, see my 'Religion and Recreation', *loc. cit.*, pp. 109–10. For temperance vigilance groups, see *Leeds Temperance Herald*, 16 September 1837, p. 148; 30 September 1837, p. 156; S.C. of the House of Lords on Intemperance, Second Report, *P.P.*, 1877 (271) XI, QQ. 5240, 5322; P. T. Winskill, *The Temperance Movement and its Workers* (London, 1892), IV, p. 198. For vigilance groups in the purity movement, see White Cross League, *The Practical Working of the White Cross Movement* (1886), p. 28; W. A. Coote (ed.), *op. cit.*, pp. 28–9.

lations: in its founder's words, its aim was 'not to procure the enforcement of the present system, but to secure a better'. The study of prohibitionism, however, offers a second reason why moral reformers failed
to extend the functions and machinery of the State. In 1881, T. H.
Green pointed out that State intervention was often opposed 'by men
whose real objection is not to State interference but to centralization, to
the constant aggression of the central executive upon local authorities'.
J. S. Mill himself favoured public control of the water supply at the
local level. The prohibitionists saw their Permissive Bill, which would
have enabled a two-thirds ratepayer-majority to ban the drink trade
from a locality, as an official measure which could mobilize local pride
and democratic sentiment; from 1857 it was therefore substituted for
national prohibition (that is, for the 'Maine Law') as the main plank
of Alliance policy. They saw their measure as typical of modern legislative trends, and wanted the permissive principle applied elsewhere.
They feared the advance of centralized State power; indeed, in 1870
they wanted Westminster to 'cede its legislative power, in all difficult
and important internal and non-political questions, to the distributive
wisdom of the localities'.[33]

Other moral reformers were less explicit in their zeal for decentraliza-
tion, but implicitly favoured it in their practice. The RSPCA originated
in London, and sought to avoid blunders by centralizing its control over
inspectors and lawsuits: but it repeatedly tried to stimulate local initia-
tives, and normally refused to send inspectors to an area unless they
could be financed locally. Much of the impetus for moral reform in the
nineteenth century came, however, from the provinces; the anti-
vivisection, prohibitionist and purity movements, for instance, capital-
ized on Northerners' distaste for metropolitan corruption. W. T. Stead,
crusading in 1885 against London's clubland, relied upon 'the sober,
hard-working, intelligent men who in North and Central England
constitute the saving strength of our land'.[34] The LDOS was based on
London, but seems to have been provincial in a rather different way. It
was traditionalist and rural in outlook, and its opponents could never
establish themselves outside the large towns. Nineteenth century social
reform legislation also, of course, left much freedom of action to the
localities: but unlike legislation on moral reform, it simultaneously built
up considerable expertise at Whitehall.

[33] Quotations from SCHC on Public Houses, *P.P.*, 1854 (367) XIV, Q. 1967
(Nathaniel Card); T. H. Green, 'Liberal Legislation', p. 374; *Alliance News*, 22
January 1870, p. 28; cf. Lawson, 4 Hansard 145, c. 1069 (5 May 1905). See also
P. Schwartz, 'John Stuart Mill and Laissez Faire: London Water', *Economica*,
February 1966, pp. 71, 74.
[34] W. T. Stead, in *Pall Mall Gazette*, 11 July 1855, p. 1. For the RSPCA, see my
'Animals and the State', *loc. cit.*

The prominence of provincial zealots in some moral reform movements introduces a third reason why nineteenth century moral reformers can never feature in the collectivist pantheon: many were more eager for symbolic than for enforceable legislation. Yet it was enforcement, not mere legislation (Chadwick's measure of 1833, rather than the factory movement's proposals of 1832), which built up the modern administrative State. If there are contrasting nineteenth century patterns of State intervention in moral and social questions, this is not because of any fundamental contrast between the reformers' outlook in the two spheres; it is partly because in social reform the appointment of government inspectors—never (in the area of factory legislation, for instance) demanded by the extra-parliamentary reformers themselves—transformed the legislative climate. This is not to say that the moral reformers were insincere in their crusades. Indeed, one factor limiting their impact on social behaviour was that they were so intensely aware of the evil in question, yet so politically inexperienced, that free rein was given to the self-frustrating anti-political tendencies latent in all reforming movements. These tendencies are epitomized in the moral reformers' much-used slogan 'what is morally wrong cannot be politically right'. Peel firmly repudiated such arguments in the 1844 debate on the Ten Hours Bill; there were many things, he said, which he knew to be morally wrong, yet 'I tolerate them, because I am also convinced they are not within the sphere of legislation. However grave the offence against morality, the Legislature attempts to strike a balance, and see whether the attempt to interfere would not be more prejudicial than connivance.'[35]

The LDOS had much in common with evangelicals in the factory movement; throughout the nineteenth century, it was strangely indifferent to the problems involved in getting legislation enacted or enforced. In 1836, it claimed that it was not primarily aiming at legislation: that political support was 'valuable only as co-operating with those higher efforts which aim at influencing the heart and understanding by Christian appeals, Scriptural sanctions, and the testimonies of experience'. Its main concern was that the law should embody the undiluted principle of sabbath-observance, and it therefore gave little help to politicians who introduced actual measures in parliament. The Society only feebly supported Lord Robert Grosvenor, whose 1855 Sunday Trading Bill failed to recognize the divine authority of the sabbath; no doubt it shared Shaftesbury's view, expressed in his diary, that 'God does not own it'. The Society even treasured its unpopularity,

---

[35] Peel, 3 Hansard 74, cc. 1085–6 (13 May 1844). See also N. St. J. Stevas (ed.), *W. Bagehot, Works*, III (London, 1968), p. 123; *Gentleman's Magazine*, July 1809, p. 645.

as a sign that it was taking the highest possible ground; it never felt obliged to step down into the political marketplace. 'Better is it to have the laws of our Statute Book witnessing against sabbath desecration, even if their penalties should not be enforced,' it commented on Lord Chelmsford's measure of 1860, 'than to allow those laws to be superseded by an expediency that ignores the Divine Authority of the day.'[36]

The opponents of animal cruelty included many interventionists of this type, but the animals profited from the fact that shrewdly moderate RSPCA leaders, like John Colam, remained firmly in control. Richard Martin, campaigning for the earliest animal cruelty legislation in the 1820s; Auberon Herbert, crusading in 1872 for a broad but unenforceable protection of wild birds; uncompromising anti-vivisections of the 1880s, who repudiated the whole notion of licensing—these were individuals whose energies and ideas had to be harnessed but who could never be allowed to control the movement. For their political outlook was that of Mr Holt, who in 1876 regarded the anti-vivisection question 'as a moral question, and therefore one that does not admit of compromise'; in these circumstances, the very notion of public inquiry into the evil seemed offensive. As is revealed by the extraordinary exchanges between their secretary G. R. Jesse and the 1876 royal commission, the anti-vivisectionists despised it as heartily as the factory reformers had despised the royal commission of 1833.[37] Short term but tangible improvements could never come by this route; Colam therefore wisely encouraged the zealots into forming distinct organizations, and supported them only when it seemed prudent to do so.

A similar division of labour operated within the temperance movement. After the foundation of the UKA in 1853, temperance reformers anxious for modest, short term but tangible gains continued to operate the moral suasionist societies: whereas individuals inspired only by the vision of more dramatic, though distant, reforms became prohibitionists. The Alliance saw no halfway-house between free-trade and complete prohibition: a trade must either be right or wrong. It was not therefore eager to tighten up the licensing law—this would merely extend the powers of magistrates and government departments recruited from Londoners, Anglicans, and aristocrats: 'the extension of Government agency,' it pronounced in 1871, was 'a most dishonouring and dangerous

[36] Quotations from LDOS, *5th Annual Report, 1836*, p. 18; Shaftesbury quotation from my 'Sunday Trading Riots of 1855', *Historical Journal*, 1965, p. 240; LDOS, *29th Annual Report, 1860*, p. 12; cf. *30th Annual Report, 1861*, p. 13. See also LDOS *44th Annual Report, 1875*, p. 5; *68th Annual Report, 1899*, p. 21; *2nd Annual Report, 1833*, p. 24.
[37] Holt, 3 Hansard 231, c. 903 (9 August 1876). For Jesse, see R.C. on . . . experiments for scientific purposes, *P.P.*, 1876 (C. 1397) XLI, QQ. 5561, 6473, 6479, 6500, 6512.

tendency of our age.' It did not support schemes for municipal or State management, and did not want drunkenness eliminated through increasing drink taxes. Nor was it much concerned about the practical details of its Permissive Bill: law, like the Ten Commandments, should merely 'condemn every practice which has a tendency to affect injuriously the interests of the community'. It was more important for the law to set standards than directly to modify conduct.[38]

One powerful nineteenth century moral reform movement supported by prohibitionists, anti-vivisectionists, and by many of the moral reformers hitherto mentioned has not so far been discussed: the Ladies' National Association, Josephine Butler's campaign against the CD Acts. As a movement resisting the compulsory registration, inspection and medical treatment of women allegedly infected with venereal disease in garrison towns—it apparently differs markedly from moral reform movements which campaigned to extend the role of the state. Yet in the moral reform circle, the NARCDA is the one moral reform body which has connections with every other organization in the circle: furthermore, there is every reason to think that if the LNA had admitted men to membership, it too would have been tightly linked with most of the other organizations. On closer investigation, in fact, the LNA's attitude to the State resembles that of the other moral reform organizations so closely as to justify discussing it here as a way of summarizing the essentially libertarian and even anti-governmental features of so many nineteenth century moral reform organizations.

Josephine Butler, like other moral reformers, began with an extremely elevated concept of law. She saw her movement as 'a great school of principle', and insisted that the State should concern itself with morality; to deny this was 'the cardinal heresy of the Liberal party'. William Shaen, prominent in the NARCDA, claimed that 'the most powerful national schoolmaster is the Law of the Land'; if law ever conflicted with 'the Law of Conscience', national downfall would result.[39] This concern with what might be called the teaching element in legislation ensured—with Josephine Butler, as with so many moral reformers —that improvement could be expected only in the very long-term.

[38] Quotations from *Alliance News*, 7 January 1871, p. 8; Thomas Beggs, 'The Maine Law', in Viscount Ingestre (ed.), *Meliora, Second Series* (1853), p. 231; cf. Mrs Hubbard, of the Mothers' Union, on divorce legislation, in R.C. on Divorce, *P.P.*, 1912–13 (Cd. 6480), XIX, Q. 17,049.

[39] Quotations from Ladies' National Association, *15th Annual Report, 1884*, p. 73; *The Shield*, 3 December 1870, p. 316 (speech at Carlisle); William Shaen, *Suggestions on the Limits of Legitimate Legislation on the Subject of Prostitution* (British Committee for the Abolition of State Regulation of Vice in India, n.d., delivered 1877), p. 7. See also Josephine Butler's speech at Kirkdale, *The Shield*, 29 June 1872, p. 990.

Josephine Butler favoured the prosecution of pornographers and brothel-keepers and the raising of the age of consent; and after her movement's final triumph in 1886, some of her followers co-operated with the NVA in enforcing legislation of this type. Yet she combined this interventionism with a libertarian horror of officialism. She was deeply inspired by the anti-slavery movement, she opposed the protection of women through factory legislation, and she vigorously championed the liberties of the prostitute: 'the image of God may be marred,' she told the 1871 royal commission, 'but it never is wholly blotted out'.[40] For Mrs Butler, voluntary reclamation of the prostitute was the only alternative to prohibition; and partly because in this sphere prohibition was not enforceable, free-trade in vice must be allowed to prevail. Her objective was, however, that of the prohibitionist: both wished the State to enable the sinner to exercise a moral choice; both wanted the law to reflect Christian principle. Both repudiated the existing system—because State-regulated prostitution, drink taxes, and licensed drunkenness implicated the State (and therefore the innocent individual) in evil.

Again like other moral reformers, Mrs Butler believed in voluntary effort. Reclamation work among prostitutes had the double advantage of encouraging moral choice among the women and of facilitating moral effort amongst their reclaimers; furthermore, the persistence of venereal disease was an effective incentive to male purity. Unlike the CD Acts' supporters, she firmly subordinated considerations of public health to her concern for personal morality. She detested fashionable London doctors, and would certainly have echoed P. A. Taylor's anti-vaccinationist suspicions in 1883 of the 'small band of [medical] experts using their influence throughout the country' while public opinion was 'not exercised at all'. But here her movement diverged from the prohibitionists, and therefore attracted the support of J. S. Mill, because she seems to have shared Mill's belief in the existence of a self-acting moral universe, and had a livelier faith than the prohibitionists in what could be achieved solely by moral effort. The 1871 royal commission argued that unless venereal disease were curbed, innocent children might be infected through their parents; to this she replied that 'it is the law of nature that children should suffer for the sins of their parents, and I do not think that we can venture by legislative measures to interfere with that law, but that we may very much prevent the sufferings of infants by moral influences exercised on those who transmit to them

[40] Josephine Butler, in R.C. on ... the Contagious Diseases Act, *P.P.*, 1871 (C. 408) XIX, Q. 12,943; cf. her *Personal Reminiscences of a Great Crusade* (London, 1896), p. 387; and Church of England Purity Society, *A Central Church Society for Promoting Purity ... Meeting at Lambeth Palace, on 25th May 1883*, p. 37.

this evil.' The CD Acts, she wrote, necessitated 'the greatest crime of which earth can be witness', the 'depriving God's creatures of free-will, of choice and of responsibility'.[41]

The politician's objection to such a movement—as to the prohibitionist and sabbatarian movements—was that it offered no short-term and generally acceptable palliative for the evil in question. The royal commission doubted the potential of voluntary reclamation, but Josephine Butler was unconcerned: 'it only requires more voluntary agency, and a fuller measure of the true spirit of charity and justice, and the thing is done.' This outlook had no more in common with the essentially practical concerns of politicians, doctors, army officers, and administrators than did the views of so many other moral reformers at the time. Against the doctors' physiological and statistical arguments, Mrs Butler could offer only a principle. Yet this lent her movement a glorious simplicity which in 1883 and 1886 secured a reversal of government policy quite as dramatic as the mid-Victorian repudiation of free-trade in drink. It enabled her to repudiate the notion of publicly inquiring into a patent iniquity, and to feel no shame in confessing that 'of the operation of the Acts I neither can nor will speak, and I must decline to do so because I have no interest in the operation of the Acts. It is nothing to me whether they operate well or ill, but I will tell you what you wish to know as to my view of the principle of the Acts.' It was 'an absurdity, a mockery' thus to inquire into a moral question, and in her evidence she made no attempt to conciliate the commissioners.[42]

Josephine Butler's movement therefore closely resembles the sabbatarian, anti-vivisectionist, purity, and prohibitionist movements, and repressed tendencies within the RSPCA. It was perhaps more than an incidental contemporary benefit of such movements that they enabled the Clarksons of that world to distinguish 'the virtuous from the more vicious part of the community . . . the moral statesman from the wicked politician'. Reformers like Josephine Butler, Wilfred Lawson, F. W. Newman, and Frances Power Cobbe were thereby enabled to advertise their scorn for the art of the possible. 'Rulers require from time to time to be rebaptized in first principles,' Mrs Butler pronounced in 1870, 'and in that renewal to get rid of their theories of expediency, and state necessities, their slavery to precedent, and to deadly routine.'[43] To

[41] Quotations from 3 Hansard 280, c. 994 (19 June 1883), Taylor; R.C. on . . . the Contagious Diseases Act, *P.P.*, 1871 (C. 408) XIX, Q. 13,109; Fawcett Library, London, *Josephine Butler Papers*, Box 1 (Letter to the Members of the Ladies' National Association, August 1875). See also Dr Bell Taylor's and J. S. Mill's evidence to the Royal Commission, at Q.Q. 19,388 and 19,999, respectively.

[42] Quotations from *ibid.*, Q. 13,052, 12,863, 12,932; see also QQ. 12,856–8.

[43] Quotations from T. Clarkson, *History of the Rise, Progress, and Accomplishment of the Abolition of the African Slave Trade* (1839 edn., London), p. 613; *The Shield*, 28 March 1870, p. 27.

modern eyes, the nineteenth century politician is perhaps brought all the closer to Clarkson's 'virtuous . . . part of the community', by the very fact of his encountering such prickly reformers.

Where, then, does moral reform legislation stand in relation to the growth of the modern administrative State? Moral reform movements differ so markedly among themselves that only the broadest of generalizations can be attempted. Firstly, they all achieved some legislative successes, though never successes on the scale they desired. It was perhaps in the campaign against the CD Acts and in the RSPCA that outcome most nearly matched aspiration. The government was forced by Josephine Butler's movement to abandon the idea of extending the CD Acts in 1872, and the Acts were suspended in 1883 and repealed in 1886. As for the RSPCA, the steadily extending complex of its legislation in defence of animals has already been discussed. The antivivisectionists were less successful. In 1876, they succeeded in getting vivisection inspected, but only at the price of severely restricting the inspector's powers; Frances Power Cobbe, at the Victoria Street Society's 1884 annual meeting, was therefore able to describe his returns as 'a farce and an insult to Parliament and the nation'.[44]

The sabbatarians secured no major legislative success, but by collaborating with temperance reformers in campaigns for Sunday closing, they won victories in 1839, 1854, 1876, and 1881, with only minor setbacks in 1855 and 1874; and they secured several substantial debates on the subject in late Victorian parliaments. At the local level, and in particular instances, their successes in restricting Sunday recreation was more complete. The prohibitionists never secured their Permissive Bill, but their efforts, together with those of more moderate temperance reformers, did help to kill off the free licensing movement in the 1860s, and so prepared the way for H. A. Bruce to take up the licensing question in 1871–2; when it came to the actual moment of legislating, however, they actually increased his difficulties. In many areas, temperance influences were powerful at the local level in limiting the attractions publicans could offer. Gladstone in 1880 commented on the moral reformers' overthrow of the free traders in this sphere. 'While in some subjects,' he said, 'we trace in the mind of the country, and in the mind also of Parliament, a regular progress from the first beginnings of a conviction, along clear and definite lines, to the period of their maturity, this is a subject on which the course taken by Parliament—and, possibly, the public opinion of the country—have been attended by a marked irregularity, and even by a singular reversal.'[45]

44 Quotation from *Zoophilist*, 1 July 1884 (supplement), p. 73.
45 Gladstone, 3 Hansard 251, cc. 470–71 (5 March 1880).

The moral reformers' achievement was therefore substantial, and deeply affected nineteenth century social life. But the peculiar nature of the moral reformers' problems ensured that they never evolved the progressively extending government machinery which the social reformers developed. Moral reformers used interventionist language without ever clothing it with administrative reality. Their interventionism often involved nothing more than a legislative declaration in favour of certain moral values, and relied entirely on individual and voluntary effort for enforcement. Linked as they were with the Charity Organization Society, their view of the State was often tinged with an almost self-regarding pursuit of principle, regardless of political considerations. Moral reform organizations were, in fact, closely associated with individualist organizations such as the Vigilance Association for the Defence of Personal Rights, whose platforms were graced by Auberon Herbert, the most libertarian of late Victorians.

The other-worldly concerns of moral reformers often prevented them from even wanting to be effective legislators. They were convinced that, whatever their immediate failures, their efforts would enjoy the approval both of God and of posterity. Like the late nineteenth century American social gospel leaders, they therefore felt able to 'neglect completely the complicated problem of ends and means in a surge of revivalistic confidence', and felt no need to familiarize themselves with contemporary secular thought; 'the more complex currents of economics, sociology and psychology usually passed them by'.[46] This outlook, though accentuated by participation in moral reform movements, clearly originates elsewhere—in a complex of religious attitudes which lies beyond the scope of this paper.

Much the same mentality characterized many Victorian 'social' reformers, who were by no means as single-mindedly 'collectivist' as one might expect. The machinery of State intervention, which is now seen as so important in originating the Welfare State, owed relatively little to them. The late Victorian growth of socialism obscures from us the fact that the collectivist heroes Manning, Ruskin, and Shaftesbury all joined the Charity Organization Society, and that until the end of the nineteenth century the worlds of moral and social reform were not at all distinct. It is easy now to forget that factory legislation was consciously built upon the precedents afforded by legislation against gambling, obscenity, and sabbath-breaking: that Shaftesbury's much-admired interventionism sprang from the same intellectual climate as the Lord's Day Observance Society: that T. H. Green's 'positive' liberalism was

[46] Quotations from H. F. May, *Protestant Churches and Industrial America* (New York, 1949), pp. 233–4. I am most grateful to Professor W. R. Ward, of Durham University, for guiding me to this source.

commonplace among his prohibitionist connections. Prohibitionists saw
sanitary, factory, adulteration, quarantine, and anti-smoke legislation
as precedents for outlawing the drink trade: 'an effectual liquor law . . .,'
wrote Green in 1881, 'is the necessary complement of our factory acts,
our education acts, our public health acts.'[47] Moral and social reform
legislation have been separated here only for analytic purposes, and not
because Victorian legislators themselves recognized any such distinction.
'Social' reforms were then often directed at moral purposes: improved
housing aimed at sexual modesty, public education at sobriety, Poor
Law relief at respectability, and so on. Conversely, 'moral' reforms were
expected to attain what we would now regard as purely social objectives. Only in Gladstone's old age did the two types of reform become
rivals for public attention.

If, then, we draw together again the two worlds which later diverged,
we can more easily see Victorian social reformers as their contemporaries
saw them. We can more readily understand why such courageous and
apparently far-sighted men were often so bitterly opposed in their day,
and why their opponents attracted such a popular following. Lord
Shaftesbury was, in his own words, 'an Evangelical of the Evangelicals',
and believed that 'a man's religion, if it is worth anything, should enter
into every sphere of life and rule his conduct in every relation'. When
listening to Shaftesbury the social reformer, his opponents inevitably
also heard Shaftesbury the moral reformer, and only by reuniting the
two can we re-create the contemporary mood. It is worth making the
effort, for we thereby follow Shaftesbury's own instructions to his
biographer: 'all I ask is, that the story of my life be told in its entirety—
political, social, domestic, philanthropic, and religious.'[48]

Further Reading

Very little has so far been published on Victorian moral reform movements. There is no general survey of them, though Henry Pelling's 'The
Working Class and the Origins of the Welfare State', in his *Popular
Politics and Society in Late Victorian Britain* (London, 1968) makes some
important points. There is no good study of Josephine Butler or of her
movement, but her *Personal Reminiscences of a Great Crusade* (London,
1896) is useful; censorship of pornographic material, and the history of
the Vice Society during the nineteenth-century have never been
studied. There is no good history of the RSPCA, but A. W. Moss,

[47] T. H. Green, 'Liberal Legislation', p. 385. For the prohibitionists, see Samuel
Pope, in *Alliance Weekly News*, 21 March 1857, p. 347; Lawson, 3 Hansard 225, c. 43
(16 June 1875); *Alliance News*, 11 January 1873, p. 4.
[48] Quotations from E. Hodder, *Shaftesbury*, I, pp. ix, vi.

Valiant Crusade (London, 1961) provides an introduction; see also my 'Animals and the State in Nineteenth Century England', *English Historical Review*, 1973, and R. D. French, 'Medical Science and Victorian Society: the Anti-Vivisection Movement' (Oxford unpublished D.Phil. thesis, 1973). I have attempted a general survey of legislation affecting recreation in my 'Religion and Recreation in Nineteenth-Century England', *Past and Present*, December 1967; a good study of the sabbatarian movement is much needed, though G. M. Ellis, 'The Evangelicals and the Sunday Question, 1830–1860: Organised Sabbatarianism as an Aspect of the Evangelical Movement' (Harvard unpublished Ph.D. thesis, 1951), covers some of the ground. There are two useful reference works on the temperance movement—Dawson Burns' *Temperance History* (2 volumes, London, 1889) and P. T. Winskill, *The Temperance Movement and its Workers* (4 Volumes, London, 1892). The legislative aspect up to the 1890s is well studied in Henry Carter's *The English Temperance Movement. A Study in Objectives* (London, 1933), and my *Drink and the Victorians* (London, 1971) provides a general study of the temperance movement up to 1872; but many aspects of the subject have yet to be studied.

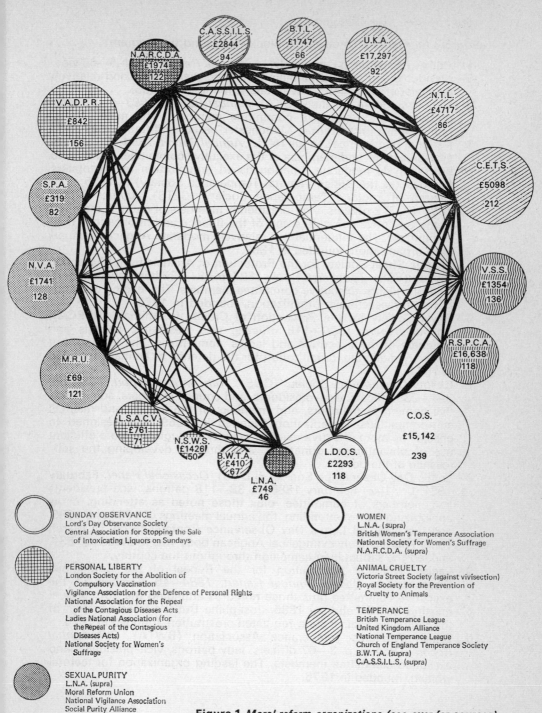

Figure 1 *Moral reform organizations (see over for sources)*

C.A.S.S.I.L.S.
£2844
94

B.T.L.
£1747
66

U.K.A.
£17,297
92

N.A.R.C.D.A.
£1974
122

N.T.L.
£4717
86

V.A.D.P.R.
£842
156

C.E.T.S.
£5098
212

S.P.A.
£319
82

N.V.A.
£1741
128

V.S.S.
£1354
136

R.S.P.C.A.
£16,638
118

M.R.U.
£69
121

L.S.A.C.V.
£761
71

N.S.W.S.
£1426
50

B.W.T.A.
£410
67

L.N.A.
£749
46

L.D.O.S.
£2293
118

C.O.S.
£15,142
239

SUNDAY OBSERVANCE
Lord's Day Observance Society
Central Association for Stopping the Sale
   of Intoxicating Liquors on Sundays

PERSONAL LIBERTY
London Society for the Abolition of
   Compulsory Vaccination
Vigilance Association for the Defence of Personal Rights
National Association for the Repeal
   of the Contagious Diseases Acts
Ladies National Association (for
   the Repeal of the Contagious
   Diseases Acts)
National Society for Women's
   Suffrage

SEXUAL PURITY
L.N.A. (supra)
Moral Reform Union
National Vigilance Association
Social Purity Alliance
N.A.R.C.D.A. (supra)

WOMEN
L.N.A. (supra)
British Women's Temperance Association
National Society for Women's Suffrage
N.A.R.C.D.A. (supra)

ANIMAL CRUELTY
Victoria Street Society (against vivisection)
Royal Society for the Prevention of
   Cruelty to Animals

TEMPERANCE
British Temperance League
United Kingdom Alliance
National Temperance League
Church of England Temperance Society
B.W.T.A. (supra)
C.A.S.S.I.L.S. (supra)

320 *Pressure from Without*

Sources for Figure 1 (proceeding clockwise round the diagram) :

1   British Temperance League (BTL), *Annual Report, 1884–5*—66 vice-presidents and committee members. A northern-based and relatively extremist organization for teetotalers, founded in 1835.
2   United Kingdom Alliance (UKA), *Annual Report, 1883–4*—92 vice-presidents and executive committee members. The major British prohibitionist organization, Manchester-based, and founded in 1853.
3   National Temperance League (NTL), *Annual Report, 1884*—86 officers, vice-presidents and members of the executive committee. A powerful, but relatively moderate, London-based organization for teetotalers, founded (as the British Teetotal Temperance Society) in 1835.
4   Church of England Temperance Society (CETS), *Annual Report, 1884–5*—212 officers, vice-presidents, members of council, members of the executive committee and of the finance and publications sub-committees. The influential but relatively moderate Anglican temperance organization, founded in 1862.
5   Victoria Street Society for the Protection of Animals from Vivisection section (VSS), *Zoophilist*, 1 July 1884, p. 68—136 honorary members, vice-presidents, executive committee members. The leading out-and-out anti-vivisectionist organization, founded in 1875.
6   Royal Society for the Prevention of Cruelty to Animals (RSPCA), *Annual Report, 1883*—118 officers, vice-presidents, patrons and members of the executive and ladies' committees. The leading, but relatively moderate, organization for the defence of animals, founded in 1824.
7   Charity Organization Society (COS), *16th Annual Report, 1884*, pp. 3–4—239 officers, vice-presidents, and council members, administrative committee members, and members of the inquiry and districts sub-committees. Organization founded in 1869, and designed to ensure the more effective relief of poverty through the more efficient use of philanthropic donations, and through developing the self-reliance of the poor.
8   Lord's Day Observance Society (LDOS), *Occasional Paper*, February 1884, pp. 1–2; February 1885, p. 38—118 patrons, vice-presidents and members of committee, plus those noted as attending, or as apologizing for not attending, the annual meetings of 1884 and 1885, and the National Lord's Day Observance Conference on 19 March 1884. This austerely evangelical Anglican body was founded in 1831, and led the sabbatarian campaign throughout the century.
9   Ladies' National Association for the Repeal of the Contagious Diseases Acts (LNA), *Annual Report, 1884*—46 members of the executive committee plus those noted as attending the 15th annual meeting on 19 February 1885. Josephine Butler's female branch of the campaign against state-regulated prostitution, founded in 1870.
10 British Women's Temperance Association (BWTA), *9th Annual Report, 1884–5*, p. 3—67 officers, lady patrons, vice-presidents and executive committee members. The leading organization for teetotal women, founded in 1876.

11 National Society for Women's Suffrage (NSWS), *Annual Report of the Executive Committee, 1884–5*—50 officers and executive committee members. The NSWS was later renamed the National Union of Women's Suffrage Societies, and pursued a constitutional campaign for women's suffrage throughout the suffragette period. It drew together local organizations campaigning for women's suffrage—the first of which had been founded in 1867.

12 London Society for the Abolition of Compulsory Vaccination (LSACV), *6th Annual Report, 1886*, pp. 145 ff.—71 officers, vice-presidents and executive committee members. Founded in 1880, and more militant than the provincially-based National Anti-Compulsory Vaccination League which preceded it.

13 Moral Reform Union (MRU), *4th Annual Report, 1884–6*, pp. 20–21—121 members. Organization founded in 1882 to publish literature and enforce the law against the double standard in morality, and attracting several prominent unitarians.

14 National Vigilance Association (NVA), *Report of the Executive Committee, 1886* (cover)—128 officers and council members. Organization founded in 1885 to oppose the sale of indecent literature, and to protect young girls from corruption.

15 Social Purity Alliance (SPA), *Laws and Operations and Address* (Croydon, 1883)—82 officers and members of the central executive and local branch committees. London-based organization supported by F. W. Newman and Mrs Butler, founded in 1873 to campaign for moral progress.

16 Vigilance Association for the Defence of Personal Rights (VADPR), *13th Annual Report, 1884*, p. 2; *14th Annual Report, 1885*, pp. 13–14—156 officers, subscribers in 1884, and executive committee members. Organization founded in 1871 and designed to defend the individual against bureaucratic encroachments on his freedom—through resisting compulsory vaccination, the C.D. Acts, etc.

17 National Association for the Repeal of the Contagious Diseases Acts (NARCDA), *General Report … 1883 and 1884*, pp. 4 ff.—122 officers, vice-presidents and general committee members. The first, and male-dominated, organization formed to combat the Acts; founded in 1869, and disbanded once victory had been achieved, in 1886.

18 Central Association for Stopping the Sale of Intoxicating Liquors on Sundays (CASSILS), *Sunday Closing Reporter*, 20 March 1884, p. 281; 12 March 1885, pp. 355 ff.—94 noted as attending, or as apologizing for not attending, the Sunday closing meetings referred to there. The leading Sunday closing organization, founded in 1866.

The general secretaries of the British National Temperance League, the UKA, RSPCA and LDOS kindly provided me with the information I needed on their organizations. I am grateful to Paul McHugh, formerly of Oriel College, Oxford, and to A. F. Thompson of Wadham College, Oxford, for suggestions which extended the scope of this diagram.

Interpretation

The circles representing each individual organization correspond very roughly in size to the size of the sample analysed in each case. The figures inside the circle represent the size of the sample, and the annual income of the organization. The latter figure is for the year 1884, or for the financial year which most coincides with 1884, except in the following cases— figures for the LDOS are for 1881, for the RSPCA for 1883, and for the LSACV and NVA for 1886.

The diagram is unavoidably misleading in certain respects. The longer lines obviously make more immediate visual impact than the shorter, though each should carry equal weight. The samples unfortunately differ in size from one organization to another, and it is impossible to ensure that supporters of equivalent importance have been analysed for each organization: for example, it has been necessary to analyse mere subscribers for the VADPR, but for no other body. The basic assumptions behind the diagram, however, seem plausible enough: that shared prominent supporters indicate an affinity between two organizations: and that the same linkage pattern is likely to emerge from analysing prominent supporters as from analysing humbler sympathizers. A nineteenth century reform movement does, after all, set its 'tone' by the names it includes among its vice-presidents and officials, and these are the men who control policy. Besides, for five reasons, the Figure 1 probably underestimates the strength of connections between the organizations:

1 Some organizations (UKA, CASSILS, BTL, NTL, CETS, LDOS) apparently excluded women from prominent posts, whereas others (LNA, BWTA) were exclusively drawn from women. But for this, the strong feminist-temperance connections, for instance, would be clearer.
2 Some organizations (UKA, BTL) were predominantly provincial in character, whereas others (COS, RSPCA, NTL) were predominantly metropolitan. If the samples in each case had been drawn from the whole country, the strength (for example) of COS–temperance links might have been clearer.
3 The CETS and LDOS were Anglican organizations, which minimizes the possibility of links with the predominantly dissenting temperance and purity organizations; yet in both the spheres of temperance and Sunday observance, Anglicans readily co-operated with dissenters.
4 The samples are drawn only from the *activists* in each organization: if sympathizers were included, the links would in many cases be stronger. Sheer lack of time doubtless often prevented an individual prominent in one organization from being anything more than a sympathizer in another.
5 The small discrepancy between the years from which samples are drawn in some cases (see above, for the analysis of sources for the diagram) may have eliminated some links.

Notes on Contributors

DR PATRICIA HOLLIS is a lecturer in nineteenth century English History at the University of East Anglia. She has published *The Pauper Press* (Clarendon, 1970), *Class and Conflict in 19th Century England* (Routledge and Kegan Paul, 1973), and with Brian Harrison the forthcoming *Robert Lowery: Portrait of a Radical* (Collier Macmillan), as well as various articles and reviews.

DR HOWARD TEMPERLEY is senior lecturer in American History at the University of East Anglia; taught previously at the University of Manchester. His publications include 'The British and American Abolitionists Compared', in M. Duberman (ed.), *The Antislavery Vanguard* (Princeton, 1965), and *British Antislavery, 1833–1870* (Longman, 1972).

WILLIAM THOMAS is a student and tutor in modern history at Christ Church, Oxford, and author of various articles on nineteenth century radicalism. He is working on a study of the philosophic radicals.

DR ALEXANDER WILSON is Director of Extra-Mural Studies in Management and Industrial Relations at Manchester University. His publications include *The Chartist Movement in Scotland* (Manchester University Press, 1970), *Advertising and the Community* (MUP, 1968), 'The Chartist Movement in Glasgow', in A. Briggs (ed.), *Chartist Studies* (1958), and 'Chartism' in J. Ward (ed.), *Popular Movements* (1970).

DAVID LARGE is a senior lecturer in history at the University of Bristol; and is the author of articles in *English Historical Review*, *Irish Historical Studies* and other periodicals.

DR DAVID MARTIN is a lecturer in economic history at the University of Sheffield where he is continuing his research on land reform. He is a contributor to Joyce Bellamy and John Saville (eds.), *Dictionary of Labour Biography*.

GEOFFREY B. A. M. FINLAYSON is a lecturer in history in the University of of Glasgow, and visiting professor, 1972–3, at Queens College, City University of New York. He has published *England in the Eighteen Thirties. Decade of Reform* (Edward Arnold, 1969), and several articles. He is currently working on a biography of the Seventh Earl of Shaftesbury, to be published by Eyre Methuen.

DR DEREK FRASER is a senior lecturer in the school of Social Sciences at the University of Bradford. His first book, *The Evolution of the British Welfare State*, was published in 1973, and his *Urban Politics in Victorian England* will appear in 1974. Articles on the press, on the anti-corn law movement, and on reform politics have appeared in several historical journals.

DR DAVID M. THOMPSON is a fellow of Fitzwilliam College, Cambridge, and University Assistant Lecturer in Modern Church History. His publications include *Nonconformity in the Nineteenth Century* (Routledge and Kegan Paul, 1972) and various articles and reviews.

DR RICHARD SHANNON is a reader in English history at the University of East Anglia. He has published *Gladstone and the Bulgarian Agitation, 1876* in 1963, 'John Robert Seeley and the Idea of a National Church', in R. Robson (ed.), *Ideas and Institutions of Victorian England*, 1967, and various articles on New Zealand history and nineteenth century English history. He is now preparing a general survey of British History 1865–1915 for a new series to be published by Granada.

DR OLIVE ANDERSON is reader in history at Westfield College, University of London. She is the author of *A Liberal State at War: English Politics and Economics during the Crimean War* (Macmillan, 1967), and frequent contributor to a wide range of British and American historical journals.

DR BRIAN HARRISON is fellow and tutor in modern history and politics at Corpus Christi College, Oxford. He has published *Drink and the Victorians* (Faber, 1971), and several articles on nineteenth century social and political history.

Index